DIMENSIONS

of

CONSUMER

BEHAVIOR

CONTRIBUTING AUTHORS

MILTON ALEXANDER
Fordham University

JAMES A. BAYTON
Howard University

LESLIE A. BELDO
Vice President, Market Facts, Inc.

PEGGY BOOMER
Special Projects Editor, PRINTERS' INK

FRANCIS S. BOURNE
Columbia University

HARPER W. BOYD, JR.
Northwestern University

STEUART HENDERSON BRITT
Northwestern University

DONALD T. CAMPBELL
Northwestern University

JAMES F. ENGEL
The Ohio State University

ALFRED E. GOLDMAN
*Director of Research Development,
National Analysts, Inc.*

MORRIS J. GOTTLIEB
Arthur D. Little, Inc.

HARRISON L. GRATHWOHL
University of Washington

EDWARD L. GRUBB
Portland State College

EUGENE L. HARTLEY
College of the City of New York

CHRISTEN T. JONASSEN
The Ohio State University

CHARLES W. KING
Purdue University

PHILIP KOTLER
Northwestern University

HERBERT E. KRUGMAN
*Vice President & Director of
Research, Marplan*

PAUL F. LAZARSFELD
Columbia University

WILLIAM LAZER
Michigan State University

SIDNEY J. LEVY
*Director of Psychological Research,
Social Research, Inc.*

PIERRE MATINEAU (Deceased)
Director of Research & Marketing,
CHICAGO TRIBUNE

FREDERICK E. MAY
University of Texas

JAMES U. McNEAL
Texas A&M University

NEAL E. MILLER
*Institute of Human Relations,
Yale University*

WILLIAM A. MINDAK
University of Texas

JOHN J. PAINTER
University of Utah

MONTROSE S. SOMMERS
The University of Toronto

GREGORY P. STONE
University of Minnesota

W. T. TUCKER
University of Texas

CHARLES E. VAN TASSEL
*Manager of Market Research, Rivana
Foods, Inc.*

JAMES M. VICARY
Research Consultant

DAVID E. WALLIN
*Vice President, Hill, Rogers, Mason
& Scott*

RALPH WESTFALL
Northwestern University

WALTER A. WOODS
*Vice President, Nowland and
Company, Inc.*

DIMENSIONS

of

CONSUMER

BEHAVIOR

SECOND EDITION

Edited by

JAMES U. McNEAL

Texas A&M University

APPLETON-CENTURY-CROFTS
EDUCATIONAL DIVISION
MEREDITH CORPORATION

New York

698-1

Library of Congress Card Number: 69-15369

PRINTED IN THE UNITED STATES OF AMERICA

390-62531-0

to
MONIE
and
CATHY

PREFACE

This is the second edition of *Dimensions of Consumer Behavior*. When the first edition was introduced a few years ago it was the first book wholly on the subject of consumer behavior to be widely used by academicians. Since its introduction, it has been utilized in courses in consumer behavior, principles of marketing, selling, advertising, marketing problems, in graduate marketing courses, and in courses in the behavioral sciences. It has also been used in executive development programs. It is hoped that this new addition proves to be as serviceable.

Interest in consumer behavior has expanded greatly. This is evidenced by the increased number of courses on the subject. Further evidence is the mass of printed matter now available on the topic.

However, it is disappointing to report that the output of *basic* material on the subject has not kept up with the interest in it. When the first edition of this book was developed, the future output of basic material on consumer behavior was expected to follow a path similar to that of the theoretical learning curve. This has not been the case. Significant articles have been sparse. Four or five anthologies similar to this one, and a few textbooks, have appeared, but they have contained little new fundamental material about consumer behavior.

Either we have reached a synthesizing period in the study of consumer behavior—although it seems a little early to reach such a point in this new discipline—or we have reached a temporary stalemate and we are preparing to enter a new era of sophistication (The latter is more likely.)

This second edition of *Dimensions of Consumer Behavior* is an attempt to reflect new thought on the subject. Like the first edition, the purpose of this edition is to present fundamental ideas specifically about consumer behavior.

Soundings were sought from users of the first edition to ascertain what changes should be made to improve the book. The consensus was that the papers in the first edition were, for the most part, classics that should remain.

Thus, no readings from the first edition have been deleted. Instead, current materials have been searched, and from them new papers containing basic thought about consumer behavior have been selected and added to this second edition. Consequently, the result is a volume larger than the first edition.

Users of the first edition will recognize that additions have been made to each section of the book. These new materials should broaden one's understanding of consumer behavior and stimulate more thought on the subject.The changes, in total, are not great, but they do attempt to integrate fresh fundamentals with the classics.

The layout of the book has not been changed significantly. Part I, the Introduction, consists of two chapters. Chapter 1 briefly states some of the important reasons for studying consumer behavior. The instructor will want to expand these and introduce more. This chapter also gives a brief picture of consumers' behavior today. Again, this needs to be expanded with such information as can be found in Steuart Britt's book, *The Spenders,* or perhaps, with the instructor's own research and experiences. Lastly, Chapter 1 introduces the student to a simplified framework for viewing consumer behavior. This will afford the instructor an opportunity to (1) set the stage for the rest of the course at the level suitable for his particular students, (2) elaborate on the uses of the behavioral sciences in studying consumer behavior, and (3) determine the behavioral background that generally characterizes his students. The results of the latter task probably will determine, to a great extent, the amount of library work in behavioral books that will be necessary for the students. Chapter 2 of the introduction section is a paper by Kotler that introduces the reader to a number of theoretical viewpoints from which to approach consumer behavior. This paper should provide anchor points for the reader as he moves through the remainder of the book.

With the exception of the final chapter, the remainder of the book consists of previously written articles. These articles were selected out of hundreds for their direct contribution to explaining, researching, and predicting consumer behavior. Vintage and source were not a consideration in their selection; only their content. Each article contains material essentially about consumer behavior; not general statements about human behavior that must be transposed into a framework of consumer behavior.

Part II is a group of articles concerning the consumer behavior of *individuals.* This is why it is termed "Psychological Aspects of the Consumer Role." Each article permits discussion about one or more behavioral constructs relative to individual consumer behavior. For example, "Personality and Product Use," by Tucker and Painter, could conceivably produce several classroom hours of discussion about the elements of personality and their influence on consumer behavior patterns.

The next section of the book, Part III, deals with sociological aspects of consumer behavior. It might be viewed in two parts. Some of the articles deal with interpersonal influences on consumer behavior patterns. They emphasize the fact that one's consumer behavior often is swayed by any of a number of cultural agents, such as parents, group leaders, and reference persons. The remainder of the articles in Part III describe consumer behavior of groups. This approach is termed *market segmentation* from the marketer's point of view. The underlying assumption of market segmentation, and of these articles, is that people with like characteristics often possess similar consumer behavior patterns. Consequently, large numbers of consumers with a common characteristic, such as age or race, are classified as markets. These articles describe the consumer behavior patterns of several of these markets.

At this point in the book the instructor may wish to develop a discussion of market segmentation. The advantages and disadvantages of this marketing concept can be pointed out to the class, as well as the influence that this type of thinking has on marketing effort (the marketing mix). This discussion may also provide an opportunity to compare viewing the consumer as an individual with viewing him as a member of a group. Certainly, it would be an opportune time to mention other bases on which we may practice market segmentation.

The next group of articles, Part IV, deals with the application of *behavioral research techniques* to the examination and prediction of consumer behavior patterns. These articles point out a variety of ways to determine the "whys" of consumer behavior. They also allow an opportunity for an evaluation of the various research techniques suggested. The instructor probably will want to discuss a number of other research procedures at this point. It is also a good time to bring up the small-sample as opposed to the large-sample argument for discussion.

Obviously, research is the key to advancing an understanding of consumer behavior. Therefore, a discussion of research methods should not be limited to the last section only but should also accompany Parts II and III. For example, recall again the Tucker and Painter article in Part II, "Personality and Product Use." When this article is discussed it would be appropriate to ask the students to evaluate the techniques that these two authors employed to produce their results. It would also be a good time to discuss marketers' dependency on the research techniques of behavioral scientists-and the problems involved with their direct application to marketing problems.

The last section of the book, Part V, Conclusions, consists of two chapters. The first, by May, attempts to sum up some substantial findings about consumer behavior. In effect he states that we at least know *this much* about the consumer. The final chapter is a brief evaluation of the progress and changes being made toward a discipline of consumer behavior. It also does some armchair forecasting about future progress in this area. Last, it begs for more serious attention to be devoted to studying consumer behavior in order to provide a firm body of knowledge about the subject.

There is a revised bibliography attached that is divided according to the format of the book. It should allow flexibility in a consumer behavior course and give the reader direction for further study.

It was mentioned earlier that the main purpose of this book was to provide material for courses about consumer behavior. The book also should be viewed as a useful supplement to other marketing courses such as marketing research, promotion, product development, and marketing policy, and to courses in psychology and sociology that study business problems. It is also hoped that businessmen will consider the book useful in enhancing their marketing knowledge.

ACKNOWLEDGMENTS

The contributors to this book and their publishers are the ones to whom I am most grateful. They make such a book possible. I particularly want to acknowledge the American Marketing Association.

Certainly, clerical work is a major aspect of a readings book. The tireless efforts on the first edition by Mrs. Charlotte Wood and Miss Mary Lee Williams are gratefully recognized. Mrs. Clarice Cain and John Lewis assisted immensely on this second edition.

Finally, I wish to give recognition to the valuable influence of two colleagues: Jerome Kernan of the University of Cincinnati; and to Irwin Shapiro, wherever he may be.

J. U. McN.

CONTENTS

IV RESEARCH TECHNIQUES IN CONSUMER BEHAVIOR

I

INTRODUCTION

1

INTRODUCTION

CONSUMER BEHAVIOR – INTRODUCTION

I. WHY STUDY CONSUMER BEHAVIOR

This is a book about consumers and their behavior. Specifically, it is about the behavior of *final* consumers. This distinction should be made since there is also consumption by businessmen (such as wholesalers and retailers), whom we call *intermediate* consumers. They consume such items as typewriters, machinery, and accounting paper in their efforts to produce and market goods and services to final consumers. So, whenever we use the term *consumer,* we will be speaking of final consumers. Also, we will employ the term *product* to include both products and services.

Every person in the world is a consumer, which should alone be substantial reason for studying consumer behavior. As business students, however, we are interested in consumer behavior for other more relevant reasons. Let us review some of these.

Nature of Our Economy

People are living bundles of needs. They need life-giving substances, transportation, and thousands of other items. The manner in which these needs are met by a nation generally describes its economy. Essentially there are two sources of satisfaction for people's needs—governments or the people themselves, or perhaps a combination of both. As for our nation, the United States, it was decided in its beginning that the people would provide for most of their needs. It was decided in fact, with few reservations, that anyone who wished to undertake the provision of any of the various needs could do so (as long as it was in the public interest). Implicit in this type of economy was risk and profit; providing satisfactions obviously involves some risk, and the person who undertakes the risk also merits a reward (profit.) Profit, further, provides an incentive for a person to continue his risk-taking venture. Thus was born the American businessman—a private citizen who provides satisfactions of needs in return for profits. We call this process of providing satisfactions in return for profits, *business*.

Regarding this brief discussion of our economy, one can see that the consumer is half of the business process; that is, business, conceptually, consists of businessmen and consumers, as illustrated in Figure I. Obvi-

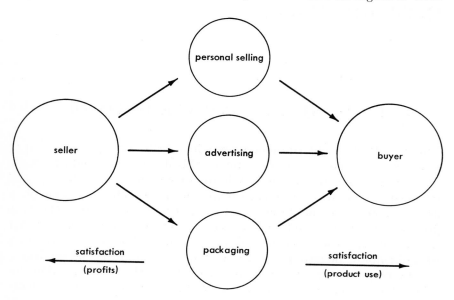

Figure 1.   The business process. This is a simplified model of business indicating that the business process is made up essentially of a seller (businessman) and a buyer (consumer). Within the process the businessman exchanges a product or service for money. The exchange takes place mainly through the media of advertising, personal selling, and packaging, or a combination of these. Satisfaction to the consumer is in terms of product use and ownership; the businessman's satisfaction is profits. Note that the arrows indicate action from seller to buyer. There are two reasons for this: (1) it is the businessman's duty to seek consumers for the satisfactions he produces, and (2) consumers in our economy typically do not initiate the business process.

ously, then, it is just as important for us to study consumer behavior as it is to study business behavior, such as financing, marketing, and production. Ironically, though, the study of consumer behavior generally takes a subordinate position to the study of the businessman.

The Marketing Concept

The term *marketing concept* may be new to you, but its meaning probably is not new for it is the old logic of consumer sovereignty cloaked under a new title. The essence of the marketing concept is that all elements of a business should be geared to the satisfaction of its consumers. The concept is at least as old as Adam Smith but has gained renewed attention during the past decade. Most businesses today will tell you that they are operating under the marketing concept but some are more verbose about it than others.

If a business is organized and operating under the marketing concept, then its marketing strategy should function in the following manner:[1]

1. Define, in as great detail as possible, the characteristics of the market for the product (the people who need the product and who can be served profitably).

2. Direct all the marketing effort, such as advertising and personal selling, in such a manner that it will provide satisfaction to the consumers to be served while obtaining a fair profit for the seller.

Such a marketing strategy is logical. If a businessman, retailer or manufacturer, has a product that a certain group of people desire, then the efforts of the business should be directed to that specific group of potential consumers, rather than to the "average consumer."[2] Actually, in addition to selling and distributing, the marketing concept should also embrace the planning and development of a product. A new product should not be developed unless there is evidence of a need for it. Likewise, a retailer should not stock and introduce a new product unless he is aware of a group of people who have need for it.

Operating under the marketing concept thus requires a thorough understanding of consumer behavior. The first step in marketing strategy set out above assumes that businessmen understand consumer behavior enough in order to investigate and make predictions about it. Step 2 likewise contains the same assumption, for it is improbable that a businessman could design effectively such marketing tools as advertising and packaging without a good knowledge of the buying behavior of the people who will purchase the product.

Product Mortality

In terms of what has been said above we can define a product as a bundle of satisfactions designed to meet certain needs of certain people. Apparently, though, not all products meet the needs for which they were designed. In fact, most of them do not! It has been estimated that between

[1] For a more comprehensive presentation of marketing strategy under the marketing concept see E. Jerome McCarthy, *Basic Marketing, A Managerial Approach* (Homewood, Ill.: Richard D. Irwin, Inc., 1964).

[2] While there is nothing seriously wrong with using the term *average consumer,* we should keep in mind that, in actuality, there is no such thing, that is, there is no pattern of consumer behavior that is generally representative of all consumer behavior.

80 and 95 percent of all products fail. This means that consumers turn their noses up at the majority of the products introduced. Why? Is it because most products are bad products? The answer to this question is definitely *no,* if by the term bad, we mean poor quality, for most manufacturers attempt to make the highest quality product possible for the price asked. Consider the analgesic-antacid called Analzose that Bristol-Myers introduced a few years ago. Its quality and effectiveness were unquestionable. Yet, it failed.

One might ask if a large share of the product failures occur among small inexperienced producers. The answer to this question is also definitely *no.* The Edsel automobile that became a $250 million failure was the product of one of the finest producers and marketers in the automobile industry—Ford Motor Company. And the failure of Philco's ultramodern Predicta television sets in 1959 is another example of product mortality by a leader in its industry.

In all the cases mentioned—Bristol-Myers, Ford, and Philco—a lack of understanding about consumer behavior was obviously a major cause of product failure. And these companies admit it. It is often difficult to judge the true costs of product failures. For example, in addition to actual dollar outlays, there is the danger that the company's image may be damaged among final consumers as well as among dealers. In such a case many extra dollars for promotion may be required to restore the image. Whatever the costs of product failures, they are usually great, and it is possible that a better understanding of people's buying habits would prevent them.

There are surely many other important reasons for studying consumer behavior. Listing a dozen more, however, would only obscure the fundamental fact that *businessmen must understand their customers in order to stay in business.* The maxim is so self-evident that it seems absurd to dwell on it further. So, let us begin our examination of consumer behavior by first placing today's American consumer in perspective.

II. NATURE OF THE CONSUMER

The American consumer today is the richest in the world. His average income is about ten times that of the average consumer in the rest of the world. The average consumer unit has an annual income (after taxes) of around $7,400, and 30 percent of consumer units earn over $10,000 annually. We are truly a nation of "big spenders."

As a result of his wealth the consumer has a great amount of power. In fact, he is often called the king of our economy (while the businessman is his servant). The consumer, in great part, dictates the products made, the channels of distribution for them, and their prices. He demands extensive choices within product categories—and gets them. Witness the wide range of flavors of cake mixes, for example, or the many forms of detergents, such as low-sudsing and high-sudsing, those with or without bleach, and those in granular, cake, and flake forms. The powerful consumer also demands a variety of conveniences in his shopping. For example, he expects some stores to be open evenings and some open all night, he expects curb-service and self-service in some of his shopping and full-service in other, and he often demands the convenience of credit-card shopping and shopping by telephone. And all of these conveniences and many others are offered by a variety of merchants who know that the "secret to success" is meeting the demands of the regal consumer.

There seem to be peculiarities and inconsistencies in consumer behavior that make it difficult to predict and understand. It is almost as though the consumer recognizes that he is king and intends to be as whimsical as possible. Of course, this is not true to any great extent. It just seems that way. Actually, most consumer behavior that appears peculiar is normal human behavior. What makes it seem peculiar is the fallacious assumption that everyone's consumer behavior should be alike, or more specifically, that everyone's consumer behavior should be like our own. If it were possible to prove, we probably would find that this assumption is the cause of a significant number of business failures.

While consumer behavior cannot be described fairly as whimsical or peculiar, it can, indeed, be described as complex and varied. Consider Mrs. Consumer and her behavior towards clothing fashions. At one point in time she desires high necklines and low hemlines. She is a regular Mrs. Modesty, while lower necklines or higher hemline are "bold and brazen." At another point in time her neckline and hemline seem to be racing to meet each other at the middle, and more coverage of the skin is considered "old-maidish" and "out-of-date."

Typically, it is considered logical for buyers to seek as much product for their money as they can get. In fact, this kind of thinking is common among a large group of microeconomists. Yet, examination of a number of purchases might give one the impression that this concept is often violated. For example, there are many products purchased whose packages cost as much as the products, and, in the case of a few, the packages cost three to five times as much as the products. It also is true that people often knowingly pay a great deal more for many standardized products in full-service stores that could be obtained for much less in discount stores. Likewise, it is true that people often knowingly pay more for food goods at drive-in-grocers than they would pay for the same products at supermarkets.

Consider further these examples of the consumer's demand for combination (or balance) in many of his purchases.

1. During the last decade there has been an intense movement of people from "in-town" to "out-of-town." Yet, while living "out-of-town," they demand "in-town" accommodations such as nearby shopping and city transportation.

2. Further, while furnishing the interior of the home with the most modern decor, the exterior often consists of bricks with a used appearance and pre-warped roof shingles.

3. The most popular style of automobile sold is one that combines some of the features of a convertible with those of a sedan—the hard-top convertible. Psychologists say it is a combination of the daring and the conservativeness.

4. A very popular hairdo among women is one called "windblown." It is both neat and messy.

5. Lastly, consider the modern camper who wants to "rough it" but employs such modern conveniences as foam mattresses, propane stoves, canned dinners, and battery-driven shavers. It has been estimated that the cost of a night out for the modern camper may be greater than a night in an elaborate hotel.

III. CONSUMER BEHAVIOR IN PERSPECTIVE

Before beginning our examination of consumer behavior let us develop a frame of reference from which to approach it. Let us, so to speak, put it in its place. In order to do this we first need to make three assumptions.

1. *The human being is constantly active. There is no need for a theory that will explain why he acts. Neither do we need an explanation for why he consumes.* Therefore we will not be concerned with why people consume, but rather with why they consume one way instead of another. Or, better still, we will be concerned with *patterns* of consumer behavior.

2. *Consumers are people. Therefore, it is human behavior with which we are concerned.* This is not to take away from the very fine studies conducted by psychologists with rats, monkeys, and fish, for example, but it is meant to imply that the consumption habits of nonhumans are of little use to us for studying the consumption habits of humans.

3. *Consumer behavior is only one type of human behavior and can be isolated and studied with only small concern for the many other kinds of human behavior.* This approach is no different from that taken by the sociologist to study marital behavior or the industrial psychologist to study occupational behavior.

Accepting these assumptions, let us develop our frame of reference by first modeling human behavior. Then we will "break off" consumer behavior and present a model of it. This procedure will provide us with "pictures" of human behavior in general and consumer behavior in particular as well as illustrate their relationship. It also will help us to remember that while it is permissible to isolate consumer behavior for study purposes, in real life it is only a part of a much greater behavioral complex.

Figure II illustrates a model that represents all human behavior. It consists primarily of four parts:

1. The social setting, (S)
2. Social forces, (F_s)
3. Roles, (R_1 to R_n)
4. Attitudes and knowledge relative to roles, (A_r and K_r).

Let us examine each of these major constituents.

Roles[3]

A *role* is a pattern of behavior actually or expected to be associated with a position in a social setting. It is, for example, the organization of behavior related to a position in a family such as father or child, a position in a business organization such as president or secretary, or even a position in the chronological system of a social unit such as a seven-year-old or a teenager. *Role behavior* is simply those activities of a person performing in his capacity as occupant of some specific position. Usually these activities are similar within a social group, *i.e.*, persons within a given social group normally will behave in a similar manner when performing a certain role. This similarity in role behavior results from similarity in viewpoints among group members and from the expectations that group members have regarding each member's behavior. Differences, however, can be expected in role behavior within a group simply because the activities are performed by individuals. Thus role behavior is not *always* the behavior *expected* of a person when he performs a specific role.

The number of roles which a person may perform is infinite (R_1 to R_n) and varies for each individual. There are those traditional roles such as father, mother, and doctor. There are general roles such as child and

[3] The concept of role is only one of a number of ways of explaining patterns of human behavior. It assumes that all behavior is associated with the various positions that one occupies in a society.

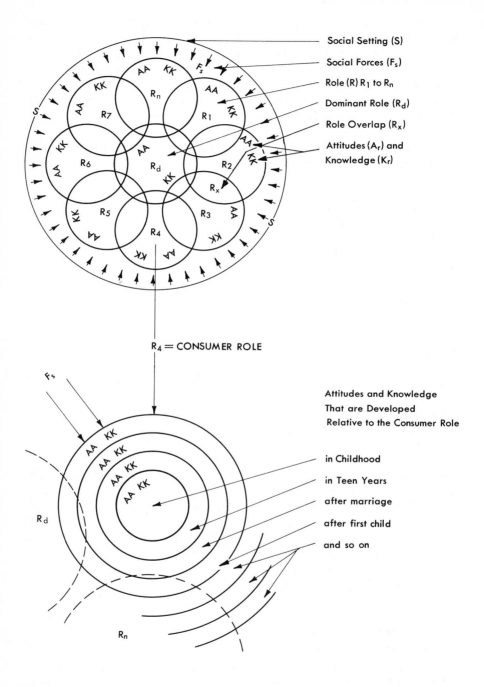

Figure II.   Human behavior and consumer behavior.

10

girl, and there are specific roles such as secretary to Mr. Jones. Generally, at any point in time a person is more characterized by one particular role than by any of the others he performs. This role can be termed the person's dominant role (R_d). The dominant role, having a superordinate relationship to other roles with which a person is associated, often influences the performance of other roles. For instance, the dominant role of the average upper-lower class male is that of worker. His life centers around his job and it, in great part, directs his performance of other roles such as consumer and husband. When studying individual role behavior, knowledge of the dominant role is useful in predicting performance of other roles.

Social Setting

All behavior takes place in a social setting. No man is an island; it is practically impossible for him to behave without having an influence on others or others having an influence on him. Even when a person is alone he usually feels the presence of others. For instance, when a young child is left alone at home he takes few liberties without considering the consequences (the resulting behavior of his parents). Or consider the situation where you are driving alone and there is no other traffic. Before you increase the speed of your auto beyond the speed limit you probably also will calculate the consequences (the resulting behavior of a law enforcement officer). So the social setting (often called the behavioral field) includes all individuals and their artifacts that, at any particular point in time, may influence one's behavior or be influenced by it. The social setting in which a person acts is unique to that individual. In other words, the social setting of every person differs to some extent. Obviously, the social setting of an executive in Peoria differs from the social setting of a rancher in Texas, just as your social setting differs, at least somewhat, from that of your parents or friends. To the extent that people's social settings are similar, we say those individuals are socially related.

The social setting in which one behaves changes with time. At birth and through infancy one's social setting is very small (if we can think of it as having dimensions), rarely including more than parents, other siblings, and the physical surroundings of the home. Beginning around the age of five the social setting expands rapidly until the end of the teen years. From this point on, the expansion increases throughout life at a decreasing rate.[4]

[4] For the mathematically inclined reader, we might say that the relationship between age and size of social setting is a log function.

Social Forces

In a community of 25,000 inhabitants, for example, there are 25,000 individual kinds of behavior, yet a casual observation will indicate some order in the community and similarity among much behavior. This order in behavior derives, in great part, from social forces (F_s). These are shown in Figure II as arrows that have varying degrees of influence on all of our numerous role behaviors. In a societal unit there are rules and regulations, written and unwritten, by which its members must abide if they are to be "accepted" members. In other words, there are certain kinds of behavior *expected* from certain individuals. These expectations (social forces) operate for practically all positions in a society and *there are specific expectations for specific positions.* Said another way, there are role expectations that direct and regulate the behavior of each role.

To the extent that one's behavior in a role conforms to the expectations relative to that role, we say that the behavior is *acceptable.* If one's behavior of a role deviates markedly from that expected, we say his behavior is *unacceptable.* There are, of course, tolerances attached to role expectations to allow for individual differences. Behavior beyond these tolerances, however, is not condoned and is countered by such behavior as ostracism or legal action. Laws are actually role expectations that have been finalized with definite tolerance limits. They describe behavior for a role that is either unacceptable or acceptable and provide for punishment and/or corrections for unacceptable behavior. Consider the role of the marketer, for example. There are both written (law) and unwritten role expectations to guide his behavior. The Robinson–Patman Act is a set of written role expectations that govern a certain part of the marketer's role relative to his selling behavior in interstate commerce. Expecting a businessman to maintain certain store hours and to handle certain merchandise are examples of unwritten role expectations.

It should also be mentioned that the rules and regulations that society sets out for role behavior apply to normal conditions. Unusual circumstances require the role player to use judgment and do what he thinks is right, that is, what he thinks will be judged as acceptable behavior. Such a situation is exemplified when we find ourselves in "awkward positions." They are awkward because there is no clearly defined acceptable behavior for them. Often, in such cases, an individual will seek advice from persons purported to be authority on the subject of acceptable behavior (such as "Dear Abby").

How does one know what behavior is expected of him in a certain role? He *learns* it. He learns it by (1) *observing* others performing the role, (2) actually *participating* in the role, and (3) receiving *training* in that role by cultural agents. Take, for example, the consumer role, since that is the one with which we are most concerned. Youngsters as early as age four, *observe* and *copy* their parents' shopping behavior. And it is often reinforced through practice when the children play "store." Also, in our society, parents encourage their children to *participate* in the consumer role at a very early age by permitting the youngsters to make in-store selections and run errands to a nearby store. Lastly, it is typical of parents to *train* their children to perform such consumer behaviors as counting money, weighing fruits and vegetables, and squeezing bread in order to determine the freshest loaf.

Social forces, or role expectations, do not originate with people in general but with specific people related to specific groups. *Group leaders,* for example, usually set standards (role expectations) for members of a group, whether the group is a bowling league or a neighborhood clique. Often too, influential group members, called *opinion leaders,* establish role expectations. *Fashion leaders,* such as the "ten best dressed women" exemplify standard-setters in regard to dress. *Reference persons,* or heroes, are sources of expectations for many individuals. Presidents, movie stars, and outstanding athletes are reference persons whose behavior becomes expectations for others.

Attitudes and Knowledge

Referring again to Figure II, the reader will note that each role contains an orderly arrangement of attitudes (A_r) and knowledge (K_r). What this implies is that most attitudes and knowledge that one possesses are related and stored according to the various roles one performs. It also means that the longer one participates in a specific role the wider the array of attitudes and knowledge (relative to that role) he possesses.

Just as social forces provide external controls over one's role behaviors, attitudes and knowledge lend direction and magnitude to his behavior from the inside. A great portion of attitudes consists of role expectations that have been learned. They, therefore, also become social forces to other individuals.

The sum total of role-related attitudes and knowledge constitutes one's *personality.* Each person's personality differs because it developed under different societal circumstances (in different social settings). On the other hand, there is a great deal of similarity among the personalities of many people because these individuals were subjected to similar social forces during their development.

The concept of personality presented here may be considered narrow by some psychologists, for they have been guilty of stuffing the personality with many other elements over the past years. There seems to be no reason, however, to clutter it up any more than necessary. Some of the typical constituents of personality that have been omitted are the following:

1. *Motives.*   This is a broad term indicating causes of behavior. Personality, that is, attitudes and knowledge, does indeed give direction and magnitude to behavior, but there are no motives floating around within the personality—only potential motives. The potential motives, of course, are the attitudes and knowledge. The concept of motive is quite useful in speaking of behavior and it will play a major role in this book. But we will not view motives as having substance or as elements of personality.

2. *Habits.*   Some psychologists place habits in the personality. The term *habit,* however, describes behavior, and there is no behavior within the personality. What is located there, though, are some fixed attitudes that cause the organism to respond effortlessly in the same manner to a given stimulus. So, we see no habits floating around in the personality either.

3. *Beliefs.*   There is no good reason to specify beliefs as elements of personality. Beliefs are only well-ingrained attitudes. For convenience, we might view attitudes on a continuum where one end represents permanent attitudes (beliefs) and the other end, weak or unstable attitudes.

4. *Traits.*   Many psychologists describe our personalities in terms of traits. The concept of trait is, in fact, a very useful one in explaining personality content. When we speak of traits, we are describing consistencies in personality, though, and not actual personality elements. Thus when we speak of introversion as a trait, for example, we are referring to an arrangement of attitudes that causes a person to behave in an introverted manner toward some stimulus.

Up to this point we have been speaking of the personality as if it existed in the same sense that one's arm or leg exists. Well, it does. Where is it? Many psychologists will not permit this question, much less answer it. Its answer really is not important to us either. For the sake of eliminating loose ends, however, we will say that the personality is located in the brain and is the storage place of attitudes and knowledge. This answer seems justifiable when defining personality as we have.

Role Overlap

The term *role overlap,* which is symbolized by R_x in Figure II, describes the influence of one role upon another (or others). The role overlap may produce a favorable or unfavorable result depending on whether the attitudes and knowledge related to one of the roles are compatible or incompatible with those of the other. If there is disagreement between overlapping roles we call it *role dissonance*. We describe agreement between roles as *role consonance*. Consider this situation. An individual, in his role of worker, is required to work on Sunday due to an emergency. His role as faith-worshiper, however, forbids him to work on Sunday. This is *role dissonance*. On the other hand, suppose this worker has been having trouble "making ends meet" in his role as family provider (head of household). In this case the opportunity to get overtime work, even on Sunday, would be welcomed. This relationship between the role of worker and the role of household head would be termed *role consonance*.

Summing up our model of human behavior, we may say that behavior within a role (and all behavior occurs within a role) is a function of role-related attitudes and knowledge, role-related social forces, the dominant role, and any number of other roles. Said another way,

$$B_r = f\,[(A_r + K_r),\, F_{sr},\, R_d,\, R_1 \ldots {}_n].$$

For exactness one might also want to include the physical environment within the social setting, such as weather, physical barriers, and so on. If so, then our symbolic relationship above would have a **P** attached to it to represent physical environment.

The Consumer Role

For the past few pages we have been concerning ourselves with a brief treatment of role theory. The purpose was not to make sociologists of us but to place the consumer role in its proper perspective. While the consumer role is only one of perhaps hundreds of roles performed by an individual, it is a very significant one in our affluent society. It is rare that a person can or wishes to escape performing this role. Like other role behavior, consumer role behavior is enacted to satisfy wants or needs, but it probably provides satisfaction for a greater variety of wants and needs than any other role behavior. For example, through this role behavior one can satisfy the biological need for food, the psychological need for beauty, and the sociological need for status.

Figure II illustrates the consumer role (arbitrarily selected as R_4) being separated from the role complex representing all human behavior. This is typical procedure for examining the part of any whole. Although the consumer role is isolated from the behavioral complex, consideration is still given to those factors that directly influence consumer behavior; namely, the social forces related to consuming, the dominant role, any other influential roles, and, of course, consumer role-related attitudes and knowledge.

Notice that the consumer role is illustrated as a group of concentric circles. This is done to point out three important facts:

1. An individual's consumer behavior patterns differ at different points in his life.

2. One's consumer behavior at any point in time is influenced by any past consumer behavior.

3. One's attitudes and knowledge relative to the consumer role at any point in time represent an accumulation of all attitudes and knowledge during the entire time that he has participated in the consumer role.

In our society consumer behavior patterns begin in childhood. So, the nucleus of the consumer role illustrated in Figure II is childhood consumer behavior.[5] Research has shown that consumer behavior patterns change with certain events in one's life. As a result, we have illustrated the consumer role as having significant developments during childhood, during the teens, after marriage, and after children. Actually, we could offer more detail than this, but it should be sufficient to make our three points noted above. By the time a youngster reaches adulthood he possesses a multitude of attitudes and knowledge about the consumer role and its elements. Any one of these variable can cause the individual to behave differently from another person in the consumer role. This fact makes prediction of consumer role behavior difficult. Fortunately, as noted in our earlier discussion, individuals within a certain group, such as an ethnic group or social class, tend to possess similar attitudes and knowledge about the consumer role, and if these are known, predictability of consumer role behavior within a group is enhanced.

A good argument could be developed in favor of the premise that the consumer role is often a dominant role for many individuals. Behavior in this role frequently consumes a relatively large part of many individuals' time, particularly housewives'. Further, the consumer role provides a means by which a person may express himself. Martineau has noted that "everything we buy helps us to convey to others the kind of people we are, helps us to identify ourselves to the world at large."[6] For many individ-

---

[5] There is an age-old argument among behavioral scientists about whether or not a child's behavior influences his adult behavior. We will resolve this conflict, for expediency, by stating that one's adult behavior is influenced by his childhood behavior to the extent that the role that we are speaking of was also performed in childhood. In the case of the consumer role, then, we can say that a child's behavior may, indeed, influence his adult behavior.

[6] Pierre Martineau, *Motivation in Advertising* (New York: McGraw-Hill Book Co., 1957), p. 197.

uals, consumer role behavior is a pastime—something to do—when required tasks such as housework are completed. Paralleling our symbolic representation of human behavior, let us do the same for consumer role behavior. It would look like this (assuming that consumer behavior is R_4),

$$R_4 = f\left[(A_4 + K_4), Fs_{(4)}, R_d, R_i\right],$$

where R_4 = consumer role
A_4 = attitudes relative to the consumer role
K_4 = knowledge relative to the consumer role
$Fs_{(4)}$ = social forces relative to the consumer role
R_d = dominant role
R_i = any other role(s) affecting the consumer role.

The variables presented are in descending order of importance.

In essence then, consumer role behavior is a significant and complex group of activities for most individuals in our society. Its significance is evident from the great amount of time and attention devoted to it by most individuals from childhood to death. Its complexity is evident from the mass of information that has been gathered about it while a serious lack of understanding of it still exists.

IV. HOW TO STUDY CONSUMER BEHAVIOR

Since consumer behavior is only a part (although a significant part) of human behavior, it is obvious, then, that those individuals who theorize about and examine human behavior would possess the most useful tools and approaches for a study of consumer behavior. Those individuals could be broadly classed as sociologists and psychologists, or, with more detail, social psychologists, motivational psychologists, developmental psychologists, clinical psychologists, rural and urban sociologists, cultural sociologists, and social anthropologists, for example. Hoping not to slight anyone, we will employ the two broad terms. It should be noted that we are not forgetting the economist, for his contributions to consumer behavior have been greater than any other discipline. It is assumed, though, that the reader possesses a familiarity with these contributions and will attempt to integrate them with the other behavioral views expressed here. In fact, this constitutes the essence of our recommendation for studying and understanding consumer behavior. Specifically, *the path to understanding consumer behavior lies in the integration of those disciplines devoted to the quest of facts about human behavior.* In other words, rather than approaching consumer behavior from one discipline, such as psychology, we shall employ any useful ideas or information from any discipline.

There is no reason for us to seek or attempt to develop data for "average consumers." As we noted earlier, there is no such thing, no more than there is an average marriage, or an average worker. What we must do is seek out and recognize those factors that influence consumer behavior and develop an understanding of them. This will help us predict consumer behavior when these factors are operating.

For the beginning student of consumer behavior, then, we need to acquaint ourselves first with already existing information on consumer behavior determinants. The major part of this book is devoted to this purpose. Next, we need to know how to use this information to enhance marketing decision-making. Small portions of the book deal with application of data on consumer behavior determinants. Lastly, we need to acquaint ourselves with the tools employed by behavioral specialists in studying consumer behavior. Knowledge of the tools should come automatically as we pursue the prior two objectives. Nevertheless, there is a separate treatment of research tools in the latter part of the book. A final result of this approach to studying consumer behavior should be the ability to generate useful data of our own and to develop new and improved research tools.

2

BEHAVIORAL MODELS
for ANALYZING BUYERS

PHILIP KOTLER

In times past, management could arrive at a fair understanding of its buyers through the daily experience of selling to them. But the growth in the size of firms and markets has removed many decision-makers from direct contact with buyers. Increasingly, decision-makers have had to turn to summary statistics and to behavioral theory, and are spending more money today than ever before to try to understand their buyers.

Who buys? How do they buy? And why? The first two questions relate to relatively overt aspects of buyer behavior, and can be learned about through direct observation and interviewing.

But uncovering *why* people buy is an extremely difficult task. The answer will tend to vary with the investigator's behavioral frame of reference.

The buyer is subject to many influences which trace a complex course through his psyche and lead eventually to overt purchasing responses. This conception of the buying process is illustrated in Figure 1. Various influences and their modes of transmission are shown at the left. At the right are the buyer's responses in choice of product, brand, dealer, quantities, and frequency. In the center stands the buyer and his mysterious psychological processes. The buyer's psyche is a "black box" whose workings can be only partially deduced. The marketing strategist's challenge to the behavioral scientist is to construct a more specific model of the mechanism in the black box.

Reprinted from the *Journal of Marketing*, national quarterly publication of the American Marketing Association, Volume 29 (October, 1965), pp. 37-45.

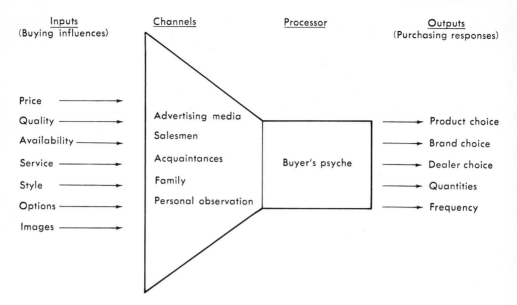

Figure 1.   The buying process conceived as a system of inputs and outputs.

Unfortunately no generally accepted model of the mechanism exists. The human mind, the only entity in nature with deep powers of understanding, still remains the least understood. Scientists can explain planetary motion, genetic determination, and molecular behavior. Yet they have only partial, and often partisan, models of *human* behavior.

Nevertheless, the marketing strategist should recognize the potential interpretative contributions of different partial models for explaining buyer behavior. Depending upon the product, different variables and behavioral mechanisms may assume particular importance. A psychoanalytic behavioral model might throw much light on the factors operating in cigarette demand, while an economic behavioral model might be useful in explaining machine-tool purchasing. Sometimes alternative models may shed light on different demand aspects of the same product.

What are the most useful behavioral models for interpreting the transformation of buying influences into purchasing responses? Five different models of the buyer's "black box" are presented in the present article, along with their respective marketing applications: (1) the Marshallian model, stressing economic motivations; (2) the Pavlovian model, learning; (3) the Freudian model, psychoanalytic motivations; (4) the Veblenian model, social-psychological factors; and (5) the Hobbesian model, organizational factors. These models represent radically different conceptions of the mainsprings of human behavior.

THE MARSHALLIAN ECONOMIC MODEL

Economists were the first professional group to construct a specific theory of buyer behavior. The theory holds that purchasing decisions are the result of largely "rational" and conscious economic calculations. The individual buyer seeks to spend his income on those goods that will deliver the most utility (satisfaction) according to his tastes and relative prices.

The antecedents for this view trace back to the writings of Adam Smith and Jeremy Bentham. Smith set the tone by developing a doctrine of economic growth based on the principle that man is motivated by self-interest in all his actions.[1] Bentham refined this view and saw man as finely calculating and weighing the expected pleasures and pains of every contemplated action.[2]

Bentham's "felicific calculus" was not applied to consumer behavior (as opposed to entrepreneurial behavior) until the late 19th century. Then, the "marginal-utility" theory of value was formulated independently and almost simultaneously by Jevons[3] and Marshall[4] in England, Menger[5] in Austria, and Walras[6] in Switzerland.

Alfred Marshall was the great consolidator of the classical and neo-classical tradition in economics; and his synthesis in the form of demand-supply analysis constitutes the main source of modern micro-economic thought in the English-speaking world. His theoretical work aimed at realism, but his method was to start with simplifying assumptions and to examine the effect of a change in a single variable (say, price) when all other variables were held constant.

He would "reason out" the consequences of the provisional assumptions and in subsequent steps modify his assumptions in the direction of more realism. He employed the "measuring rod of money" as an indicator of the intensity of human psychological desires. Over the years his methods and assumptions have been refined into what is now known as *modern utility theory:* economic man is bent on maximizing his utility, and does this by carefully calculating the "felicific" consequences of any purchase.

---

1 Adam Smith, *An Inquiry into the Nature and Causes of the Wealth of Nations,* 1776 (New York: The Modern Library, 1937).
2 Jeremy Bentham, *An Introduction to the Principles of Morals and Legislation,* 1780 (Oxford, England: Clarendon Press, 1907).
3 William S. Jevons, *The Theory of Political Economy* (New York: The Macmillan Company, 1871).
4 Alfred Marshall, *Principles of Economics,* 1890 (London: The Macmillan Company, 1927).
5 Karl Menger, *Principles of Economics,* 1871 (Glencoe, Illinois: Free Press, 1950).
6 Leon Walras, *Elements of Pure Economics,* 1874 (Homewood, Illinois: Richard D. Irwin, Inc., 1954).

As an example, suppose on a particular evening that John is considering whether to prepare his own dinner or dine out. He estimates that a restaurant meal would cost $2.00 and a home-cooked meal 50 cents. According to the Marshallian model, if John expects less than four times as much satisfaction from the restaurant meal as the home-cooked meal, he will eat at home. The economist typically is not concerned with how these relative preferences are formed by John, or how they may be psychologically modified by new stimuli.

Yet John will not always cook at home. The principle of diminishing marginal utility operates. Within a given time interval—say, a week—the utility of each additional home-cooked meal diminishes. John gets tired of home meals and other products become relatively more attractive.

John's *efficiency* in maximizing his utility depends on the adequacy of his information and his freedom of choice. If he is not perfectly aware of costs, if he misestimates the relative delectability of the two meals, or if he is barred from entering the restaurant, he will not maximize his potential utility. His choice processes are rational, but the results are inefficient.

Marketing Applications of Marshallian Model

Marketers usually have dismissed the Marshallian model as an absurd figment of ivory-tower imagination. Certainly the behavioral essence of the situation is omitted, in viewing man as calculating the marginal utility of a restaurant meal over a home-cooked meal.

Eva Mueller has reported a study where only one-fourth of the consumers in her sample bought with any substantial degree of deliberation.[7] Yet there are a number of ways to view the model.

From one point of view the Marshallian model is tautological and therefore neither true nor false. The model holds that the buyer acts in the light of his best "interest." But this is not very informative.

A second view is that this is a *normative* rather than a *descriptive* model of behavior. The model provides logical norms for buyers who want to be "rational." Although the consumer is not likely to employ economic analysis to decide between a box of Kleenex and Scotties, he may apply economic analysis in deciding whether to buy a new car. Industrial buyers even more clearly would want an economic calculus for making good decisions.

A third view is that economic factors operate to a greater or lesser extent in all markets, and, therefore, must be included in any comprehensive description of buyer behavior.

Furthermore, the model suggests useful behavioral hypotheses such as: (a) The lower the price of the product, the higher the sales. (b) The

[7] Eva Mueller, "A Study of Purchase Decisions," Part 2, *Consumer Behavior, The Dynamics of Consumer Reaction,* edited by Lincoln H. Clark (New York: New York University Press, 1954), pp. 36-87.

lower the price of substitute products, the lower the sales of this product; and the lower the price of complementary products, the higher the sales of this product. (c) The higher the real income, the higher the sales of this product, provided that it is not an "inferior" good. (d) The higher the promotional expenditures, the higher the sales.

The validity of these hypotheses does not rest on whether *all* individuals act as economic calculating machines in making their purchasing decisions. For example, some individuals may buy *less* of a product when its price is reduced. They may think that the quality has gone down, or that ownership has less status value. If a majority of buyers view price reductions negatively, then sales may fall, contrary to the first hypothesis.

But for most goods a price reduction increases the relative value of the goods in many buyers' minds and leads to increased sales. This and the other hypotheses are intended to describe average effects.

The impact of economic factors in actual buying situations is studied through experimental design or statistical analyses of past data. Demand equations have been fitted to a wide variety of products—including beer, refrigerators, and chemical fertilizers.[8] More recently, the impact of economic variables on the fortunes of different brands has been pursued with significant results, particularly in the case of coffee, frozen orange juice, and margarine.[9]

But economic factors alone cannot explain all the variations in sales. The Marshallian model ignores the fundamental question of how product and brand preferences are formed. It represents a useful frame of reference for analyzing only one small corner of the "black box."

THE PAVLOVIAN LEARNING MODEL

The designation of a Pavlovian learning model has its origin in the experiments of the Russian psychologist Pavlov, who rang a bell each time before feeding a dog. Soon he was able to induce the dog to salivate by ringing the bell whether or not food was supplied. Pavlov concluded that learning was largely an associative process and that a large component of behavior was conditioned in this way.

Experimental psychologists have continued this mode of research with rats and other animals, including people. Laboratory experiments

8 See Erwin E. Nemmers, *Managerial Economics* (New York: John Wiley & Sons, Inc., 1962), Part II.

9 See Lester G. Telser, "The Demand for Branded Goods as Estimated from Consumer Panel Data," *Review of Economics and Statistics*, Vol. 44 (August, 1962), pp. 300-324; and William F. Massy and Ronald E. Frank, "Short Term Price and Dealing Effects in Selected Market Segments," *Journal of Marketing Research*, Vol. 2 (May, 1965), pp. 171-185.

have been designed to explore such phenomena as learning, forgetting, and the ability to discriminate. The results have been integrated into a stimulus-response model of human behavior, or as someone has "wisecracked," the substitution of a rat psychology for a rational psychology.

The model has been refined over the years, and today is based on four central concepts—those of *drive, cue, response,* and *reinforcement*.[10]

Drive. Also called needs or motives, drive refers to strong stimuli internal to the individual which impels action. Psychologists draw a distinction between primary physiological drives—such as hunger, thirst, cold, pain, and sex—and learned drives which are derived socially—such as cooperation, fear, and acquisitiveness.

Cue. A drive is very general and impels a particular response only in relation to a particular configuration of cues. Cues are weaker stimuli in the environment and/or in the individual which determine when, where, and how the subject responds. Thus, a coffee advertisement can serve as a cue which stimulates the thirst drive in a housewife. Her response will depend upon this cue and other cues, such as the time of day, the availability of other thirst-quenchers, and the cue's intensity. Often a relative change in a cue's intensity can be more impelling than its absolute level. The housewife may be more motivated by a 2-cents-off sale on a brand of coffee than the fact that this brand's price was low in the first place.

Response

The response is the organism's reaction to the configuration of cues. Yet the same configuration of cues will not necessarily produce the same response in the individual. This depends on the degree to which the experience was rewarding, that is, drive-reducing.

Reinforcement

If the experience is rewarding, a particular response is reinforced; that is, it is strengthened and there is a tendency for it to be repeated when the same configuration of cues appears again. The housewife, for example, will tend to purchase the same brand of coffee each time she goes to her supermarket so long as it is rewarding and the cue configuration does not change. But if a learned response or habit is not reinforced, the strength of the habit diminishes and may be extinguished eventually. Thus, a housewife's preference for a certain coffee may become extinct if she finds the brand out of stock for a number of weeks.

Forgetting, in contrast to extinction, is the tendency for learned associations to weaken, not because of the lack of reinforcement but because of nonuse.

[10] See John Dollard and Neal E. Miller, *Personality and Psychotherapy* (New York: McGraw-Hill Book Company, Inc., 1950), Chapter III.

Cue configurations are constantly changing. The housewife sees a new brand of coffee next to her habitual brand, or notes a special price deal on a rival brand. Experimental psychologists have found that the same learned response will be elicited by similar patterns of cues; that is, learned responses are *generalized*. The housewife shifts to a similar brand when her favorite brand is out of stock. This tendency toward generalization over less similar cue configurations is increased in proportion to the strength of the drive. A housewife may buy an inferior coffee if it is the only brand left and if her drive is sufficiently strong.

A counter-tendency to generalization is *discrimination*. When a housewife tries two similar brands and finds one more rewarding, her ability to discriminate between similar cue configurations improves. Discrimination increases the specificity of the cue-response connection, while generalization decreases the specificity.

Marketing Applications of Pavlovian Model

The modern version of the Pavlovian model makes no claim to provide a complete theory of behavior—indeed, such important phenomena as perception, the subconscious, and interpersonal influence are inadequately treated. Yet the model does offer a substantial number of insights about some aspects of behavior of considerable interest to marketers.[11]

An example would be in the problem of introducing a new brand into a highly competitive market. The company's goal is to extinguish existing brand habits and form new habits among consumers for its brand. But the company must first get customers to try its brand; and it has to decide between using weak and strong cues.

Light introductory advertising is a weak cue compared with distributing free samples. Strong cues, although costing more, may be necessary in markets characterized by strong brand loyalties. For example, Folger went into the coffee market by distributing over a million pounds of free coffee.

To build a brand habit, it helps to provide for an extended period of introductory dealing. Furthermore, sufficient quality must be built into the brand so that the experience is reinforcing. Since buyers are more likely to transfer allegiance to similar brands than dissimilar brands (generalization), the company should also investigate what cues in the leading brands have been most effective. Although outright imitation would not necessarily effect the most transference, the question of providing enough similarity should be considered.

The Pavlovian model also provides guide lines in the area of adver-

[11] The most consistent application of learning-theory concepts to marketing situations is found in John A. Howard, *Marketing Management: Analysis and Planning* (Homewood, Illinois: Richard D. Irwin, Inc., revised edition, 1963).

tising strategy. The American behaviorist, John B. Watson, was a great exponent of repetitive stimuli; in his writings man is viewed as a creature who can be conditioned through repetition and reinforcement to respond in particular ways.[12] The Pavlovian model emphasizes the desirability of repetition in advertising. A single exposure is likely to be a very weak cue, hardly able to penetrate the individual's consciousness sufficiently to excite his drives above the threshold level.

Repetition in advertising has two desirable effects. It "fights" forgetting, the tendency for learned responses to weaken in the absence of practice. It provides reinforcement, because after the purchase the consumer becomes selectively exposed to advertisements of the product.

The model also provides guide lines for copy strategy. To be effective as a cue, an advertisement must arouse strong drives in the person. The strongest product-related drives must be identified. For candy bars, it may be hunger; for safety belts, fear; for hair tonics, sex; for automobiles, status. The advertising practitioner must dip into his cue box—words, colors, pictures—and select that configuration of cues that provides the strongest stimulus to these drives.

THE FREUDIAN PSYCHOANALYTIC MODEL

The Freudian model of man is well known, so profound has been its impact on 20th century thought. It is the latest of a series of philosophical "blows" to which man has been exposed in the last 500 years. Copernicus destroyed the idea that man stood at the center of the universe; Darwin tried to refute the idea that man was a special creation; and Freud attacked the idea that man even reigned over his own psyche.

According to Freud, the child enters the world driven by instinctual needs which he cannot gratify by himself. Very quickly and painfully he realizes his separateness from the rest of the world and yet his dependence on it.

He tries to get others to gratify his needs through a variety of blatant means, including intimidation and supplication. Continual frustration leads him to perfect more subtle mechanisms for gratifying his instincts.

As he grows, his psyche becomes increasingly complex. A part of his psyche—the id—remains the reservoir of his strong drives and urges. Another part—the ego—becomes his conscious planning center for finding outlets for his drives. And a third part—his super-ego—channels his instinctive drives into socially approved outlets to avoid the pain of guilt or shame.

[12] John B. Watson, *Behaviorism* (New York: The People's Institute Publishing Company, 1925).

The guilt or shame which man feels toward some of his urges—especially his sexual urges—causes him to repress them from his consciousness. Through such defense mechanisms a rationalization and sublimation, these urges are denied or become transmuted into socially approved expressions. Yet these urges are never eliminated or under perfect control; and they emerge, sometimes with a vengeance, in dreams, in slips-of-the-tongue, in neurotic and obsessional behavior, or ultimately in mental breakdown where the ego can no longer maintain the delicate balance between the impulsive power of the id and the oppressive power of the super-ego.

The individual's behavior, therefore, is never simple. His motivational wellsprings are not obvious to a casual observer nor deeply understood by the individual himself. If he is asked why he purchased an expensive foreign sports-car, he may reply that he likes its maneuverability and its looks. At a deeper level he may have purchased the car to impress others, or to feel young again. At a still deeper level, he may be purchasing the sports-car to achieve substitute gratification for unsatisfied sexual strivings.

Many refinements and changes in emphasis have occurred in this model since the time of Freud. The instinct concept has been replaced by a more careful delineation of basic drives; the three parts of the psyche are regarded now as theoretical concepts rather than actual entities; and the behavioral perspective has been extended to include cultural as well as biological mechanisms.

Instead of the role of the sexual urge in psychic development—Freud's discussion of oral, anal, and genital stages and possible fixations and traumas—Adler[13] emphasized the urge for power and how its thwarting manifests itself in superiority and inferiority complexes; Horney[14] emphasized cultural mechanisms; and Fromm[15] and Erickson[16] emphasized the role of existential crises in personality development. These philosophical divergencies, rather than debilitating the model, have enriched and extended its interpretative value to a wider range of behavioral phenomena.

Marketing Applications of Freudian Model

Perhaps the most important marketing implication of this model is that buyers are motivated by *symbolic* as well as *economic-functional* product

[13] Alfred Adler, *The Science of Living* (New York: Greenberg, 1929).

[14] Karen Horney, *The Neurotic Personality of Our Time* (New York: W. W. Norton & Co., 1937).

[15] Erich Fromm, *Man For Himself* (New York: Holt, Rinehart & Winston, Inc., 1947).

[16] Erik Erikson, *Childhood and Society* (New York: W. W. Norton & Co., 1949).

concerns. The change of a bar of soap from a square to a round shape may be more important in its sexual than its functional connotations. A cake mix that is advertised as involving practically no labor may alienate housewives because the easy life may evoke a sense of guilt.

Motivational research has produced some interesting and occasionally some bizarre hypotheses about what may be in the buyer's mind regarding certain purchases. Thus, it has been suggested at one time or another that

Many a businessman doesn't fly because of a fear of posthumous guilt—if he crashed, his wife would think of him as stupid for not taking a train.

Men want their cigars to be odoriferous, in order to prove that they (the men) are masculine.

A woman is very serious when she bakes a cake because unconsciously she is going through the symbolic act of giving birth.

A man buys a convertible as a substitute "mistress."

Consumers prefer vegetable shortening because animal fats stimulate a sense of sin.

Men who wear suspenders are reacting to an unresolved castration complex.

There are admitted difficulties of proving these assertions. Two prominent motivational researchers, Ernest Dichter and James Vicary, were employed independently by two separate groups in the prune industry to determine why so many people dislike prunes. Dichter found, among other things, that the prune aroused feelings of old age and insecurity in people, whereas Vicary's main finding was that Americans had an emotional block about prunes' laxative qualities.[17] Which is the more

17 L. Edward Scriven, "Rationality and Irrationality in Motivation Research," in Robert Ferber and Hugh G. Wales, editors, *Motivation and Marketing Behavior* (Homewood Illinois: Richard D. Irwin, Inc., 1958), pp. 69-70.

valid interpretation? Or if they are both operative, which motive is found with greater statistical frequency in the population?

Unfortunately the usual survey techniques—direct observation and interviewing—can be used to establish the representativeness of more superficial characteristics—age and family size, for example—but are not feasible for establishing the frequency of mental states which are presumed to be deeply "buried" within each individual.

Motivational researchers have to employ time-consuming projective techniques in the hope of throwing individual "egos" off guard. When carefully administered and interpreted, techniques such as word association, sentence completion, picture interpretation, and role-playing can provide some insights into the minds of the small group of examined individuals; but a "leap of faith" is sometimes necessary to generalize these findings to the population.

Nevertheless, motivation research can lead to useful insights and provide inspiration to creative men in the advertising and packaging world. Appeals aimed at the buyer's private world of hopes, dreams, and fears can often be as effective in stimulating purchase as more rationally-directed appeals.

THE VEBLENIAN SOCIAL-PSYCHOLOGICAL MODEL

While most economists have been content to interpret buyer behavior in Marshallian terms, Thorstein Veblen struck out in different directions.

Veblen was trained as an orthodox economist, but evolved into a social thinker greatly influenced by the new science of social anthropology. He saw man as primarily a *social animal*—conforming to the general forms and norms of his larger culture and to the more specific standards of the subcultures and face-to-face groupings to which his life is bound. His wants and behavior are largely molded by his present group-memberships and his aspired group-memberships.

Veblen's best-known example of this is in his description of the leisure class.[18] His hypothesis is that much of economic consumption is motivated not by intrinsic needs or satisfaction so much as by prestige-seeking. He emphasized the strong emulative factors operating in the choice of conspicuous goods like clothes, cars, and houses.

Some of his points, however, seem overstated by today's perspective. The leisure class does not serve as everyone's reference group; many persons aspire to the social patterns of the class immediately above it. And important segments of the affluent class practice conspicuous undercon-

[18] Thorstein Veblen, *The Theory of the Leisure Class* (New York: The Macmillan Company, 1899).

sumption rather than overconsumption. There are many people in all classes who are more anxious to "fit in" than to "stand out." As an example, William H. Whyte found that many families avoided buying air conditioners and other appliances before their neighbors did.[19]

Veblen was not the first nor the only investigator to comment on social influences in behavior; but the incisive quality of his observations did much to stimulate further investigations. Another stimulus came from Karl Marx, who held that each man's world-view was determined largely by his relationship to the "means of production."[20] The early field-work in primitive societies by social anthropologists like Boas[21] and Malinowski[22] and the later field-work in urban societies by men like Park[23] and Thomas[24] contributed much to understanding the influence of society and culture. The research of early Gestalt psychologists—men like Wertheimer,[25] Köhler,[26] and Koffka[27]—into the mechanisms of perception led eventually to investigations of small-group influence on perception.

Marketing Applications of Veblenian Model

The various streams of thought crystallized into the modern social sciences of sociology, cultural anthropology, and social psychology. Basic to them is the view that man's attitudes and behavior are influenced by several levels of society—culture, subcultures, social classes, reference groups, and face-to-face groups. The challenge to the marketer is to determine which of these social levels are the most important in influencing the demand for his product.

Culture

The most enduring influences are from culture. Man tends to assimilate his culture's mores and folkways, and to believe in their absolute right-

[19] William H. Whyte, Jr., "The Web of Word of Mouth," *Fortune,* Vol. 50 (November, 1954), pp. 140 ff.

[20] Karl Marx, *The Communist Manifesto,* 1848 (London: Martin Lawrence, Ltd., 1934).

[21] Franz Boas, *The Mind of Primitive Man* (New York: The Macmillan Company, 1922).

[22] Bronislaw Malinowski, *Sex and Repression in Savage Society* (New York: Meridian Books, 1955).

[23] Robert E. Parks, *Human Communities* (Glencoe, Illinois: Free Press, 1952).

[24] William I. Thomas, *The Unadjusted Girl* (Boston: Little, Brown and Company, 1928).

[25] Max Wertheimer, *Productive Thinking* (New York: Harper & Brothers, 1945).

[26] Wolfgang Köhler, *Gestalt Psychology* (New York: Liveright Publishing Co., 1947).

[27] Kurt Koffka, *Principles of Gestalt Psychology* (New York: Harcourt, Brace and Co., 1935).

ness until deviants appear within his culture or until he confronts members of another culture.

Subcultures

A culture tends to lose its homogeneity as its population increases. When people no longer are able to maintain face-to-face relationships with more than a small proportion of other members of a culture, smaller units or subcultures develop, which help to satisfy the individual's needs for more specific identity.

The subcultures are often regional entities, because the people of a region, as a result of more frequent interactions, tend to think and act alike. But subcultures also take the form of religions, nationalities, fraternal orders, and other institutional complexes which provide a broad identification for people who may otherwise be strangers. The subcultures of a person play a large role in his attitude formation and become another important predictor of certain values he is likely to hold.

Social Class

People become differentiated not only horizontally but also vertically through a division of labor. The society becomes stratified socially on the basis of wealth, skill, and power. Sometimes castes develop in which the members are reared for certain roles, or social classes develop in which the members feel empathy with others sharing similar values and economic circumstances.

Because social class involves different attitudinal configurations, it becomes a useful independent variable for segmenting markets and predicting reactions. Significant differences have been found among different social classes with respect to magazine readership, leisure activities, food imagery, fashion interests, and acceptance of innovations. A sampling of attitudinal differences in class is the following:

Members of the *upper-middle* class place an emphasis on professional competence; indulge in expensive status symbols; and more often than not show a taste, real or otherwise, for theater and the arts. They want their children to show high achievement and precocity and develop into physicists, vice-presidents, and judges. This class likes to deal in ideas and symbols.

Members of the *lower-middle* class cherish respectability, savings, a college education, and good housekeeping. They want their children to show self-control and prepare for careers as accountants, lawyers, and engineers.

Members of the *upper-lower* class try to keep up with the times, if not with the Joneses. They stay in older neighborhoods but buy new kitchen appliances. They spend proportionately less than the middle class on major clothing articles, buying a new suit mainly for an important ceremonial occasion. They also spend proportionately less on services, preferring to do their own plumbing and other work around the house. They tend to raise large families and their children generally enter manual occupations. This class also supplies many local businessmen, politicians, sports stars, and labor-union leaders.

Reference Groups

There are groups in which the individual has no membership but with which he identifies and may aspire to—reference groups. Many young boys identify with big-league baseball players or astronauts, and many young girls identify with Hollywood stars. The activities of these popular heroes are carefully watched and frequently imitated. These reference figures become important transmitters of influence, although more along lines of taste and hobby than basic attitudes.

Face-to-Face Groups

Groups that have the most immediate influence on a person's tastes and opinions are face-to-face groups. This includes all the small "societies" with which he comes into frequent contact: his family, close friends, neighbors, fellow workers, fraternal associates, and so forth. His informal group memberships are influenced largely by his occupation, residence, and stage in the life cycle.

The powerful influence of small groups on individual attitudes has been demonstrated in a number of social psychological experiments.[28] There is also evidence that this influence may be growing. David Riesman and his coauthors have pointed to signs which indicate a growing amount of *other-direction,* that is, a tendency for individuals to be increasingly influenced by their peers in the definition of their values rather than by their parents and elders.[29]

[28] See, for example, Solomon E. Asch, "Effects of Group Pressure Upon the Modification & Distortion of Judgments," in Dorwin Cartwright and Alvin Zander, *Group Dynamics* (Evanston, Illinois: Row, Peterson & Co., 1953), pp. 151-162; and Kurt Lewin, "Group Decision and Social Change," in Theodore M. Newcomb and Eugene L. Hartley, editors, *Readings in Social Psychology* (New York: Henry Holt Co., 1952).

[29] David Riesman, Reuel Denny, and Nathan Glazer, *The Lonely Crowd* (New Haven, Connecticut: Yale University Press, 1950).

For the marketer, this means that brand choice may increasingly be influenced by one's peers. For such products as cigarettes and automobiles, the influence of peers is unmistakable.

The role of face-to-face groups has been recognized in recent industry campaigns attempting to change basic product attitudes. For years the milk industry has been trying to overcome the image of milk as a "sissified" drink by portraying its use in social and active situations. The men's-wear industry is trying to increase male interest in clothes by advertisements indicating that business associates judge a man by how well he dresses.

Of all face-to-face groups, the person's family undoubtedly plays the largest and most enduring role in basic attitude formation. From them he acquires a mental set not only toward religion and politics, but also toward thrift, chastity, food, human relations, and so forth. Although he often rebels against parental values in his teens, he often accepts these values eventually. Their formative influence on his eventual attitudes is undeniably great.

Family members differ in the types of product messages they carry to other family members. Most of what parents know about cereals, candy, and toys comes from their children. The wife stimulates family consideration of household appliances, furniture, and vacations. The husband tends to stimulate the fewest purchase ideas, with the exception of the automobile and perhaps the home.

The marketer must be alert to what attitudinal configurations dominate in different types of families, and also to how these change over time. For example, the parent's conception of the child's rights and privileges has undergone a radical shift in the last 30 years. The child has become the center of attention and orientation in a great number of households, leading some writers to label the modern family a "filiarchy." This has important implications not only for how to market to today's family, but also on how to market to tomorrow's family when the indulged child of today becomes the parent.

The Person

Social influences determine much but not all of the behavioral variations in people. Two individuals subject to the same influences are not likely to have identical attitudes, although these attitudes will probably converge at more points than those of two strangers selected at random. Attitudes are really the product of social forces interacting with the individual's unique temperament and abilities.

Furthermore, attitudes do not automatically guarantee certain types of behavior. Attitudes are predispositions felt by buyers before they enter the buying process. The buying process itself is a learning experience and can lead to a change in attitudes.

Alfred Politz noted at one time that women stated a clear preference for G.E. refrigerators over Frigidaire, but that Frigidaire continued to outsell G.E.[30] The answer to this paradox was that preference was only one factor entering into behavior. When the consumer preferring G.E. actually undertook to purchase a new refrigerator, her curiosity led her to examine the other brands. Her perception was sensitized to refrigerator advertisements, sales arguments, and different product features. This led to learning and a change in attitudes.

The Hobbesian Organizational-Factors Model

The foregoing models throw light mainly on the behavior of family buyers.

But what of the large number of people who are organizational buyers? They are engaged in the purchase of goods not for the sake of consumption, but for further production or distribution. Their common denominator is the fact that they (1) are paid to make purchases for others and (2) operate within an organizational environment.

How do organizational buyers make their decisions? There seem to be two competing views. Many marketing writers have emphasized the predominance of rational motives in organizational buying.[31] Organizational buyers are represented as being most impressed by cost, quality, dependability, and service factors. They are portrayed as dedicated servants of the organization, seeking to secure the best terms. This view has led to an emphasis on performance and use characteristics in much industrial advertising.

Other writers have emphasized personal motives in organizational buyer behavior. The purchasing agent's interest to do the best for his company is tempered by his interest to do the best for himself. He may be tempted to choose among salesmen according to the extent they entertain or offer gifts. He may choose a particular vendor because this will ingratiate him with certain company officers. He may shortcut his study of alternative suppliers to make his work day easier.

In truth, the buyer is guided by both personal and group goals; and this is the essential point. The political model of Thomas Hobbes comes closest of any model to suggesting the relationship between the two goals.[32] Hobbes held that man is "instinctively" oriented toward pre-

---

[30] Alfred Politz, "Motivation Research—Opportunity or Dilemma?", in Ferber and Wales, same reference as footnote 17, at pp. 57-58.

[31] See Melvin T. Copeland, *Principles of Merchandising* (New York: McGraw-Hill Book Co., Inc., 1924).

[32] Thomas Hobbes, *Leviathan,* 1651 (London: G. Routledge and Sons, 1887).

serving and enhancing his own well-being. But this would produce a "war of every man against every man." This fear leads men to unite with others in a corporate body. The corporate man tries to steer a careful course between satisfying his own needs and those of the organization.

Marketing Applications of Hobbesian Model

The import of the Hobbesian model is that organizational buyers can be appealed to on both personal and organizational grounds. The buyer has his private aims, and yet he tries to do a satisfactory job for his corporation. He will respond to persuasive salesmen and he will respond to rational product arguments. However, the best "mix" of the two is not a fixed quantity; it varies with the nature of the product, the type of organization, and the relative strength of the two drives in the particular buyer.

Where there is substantial similarity in what suppliers offer in the way of products, price, and service, the purchasing agent has less basis for rational choice. Since he can satisfy his organizational obligations with any one of a number of suppliers, he can be swayed by personal motives. On the other hand, where there are pronounced differences among the competing vendors' products, the purchasing agent is held more accountable for his choice and probably pays more attention to rational factors. Short-run personal gain becomes less motivating than the long-run gain which comes from serving the organization with distinction.

The marketing strategist must appreciate these goal conflicts of the organizational buyer. Behind all the ferment of purchasing agents to develop standards and employ value analysis lies their desire to avoid being thought of as order-clerks, and to develop better skills in reconciling personal and organizational objectives.[33]

SUMMARY

Think back over the five different behavioral models of how the buyer translates buying influences into purchasing responses.

Marshallian man is concerned chiefly with economic cues—prices and income—and makes a fresh utility calculation before each purchase.

[33] For an insightful account, see George Strauss, "Tactics of Lateral Relationship: The Purchasing Agent," *Administrative Science Quarterly*, Vol. 7 (September, 1962), pp. 161-186.

Pavlovian man behaves in a largely habitual rather than thoughtful way; certain configurations of cues will set off the same behavior because of rewarded learning in the past.

Freudian man's choices are influenced strongly by motives and fantasies which take place deep within his private world.

Veblenian man acts in a way which is shaped largely by past and present social groups.

And finally, *Hobbesian* man seeks to reconcile individual gain with organizational gain.

Thus, it turns out that the "black box" of the buyer is not so black after all. Light is thrown in various corners by these models. Yet no one has succeeded in putting all these pieces of truth together into one coherent instrument for behavioral analysis. This, of course, is the goal of behavioral science.

II

PSYCHOLOGICAL ASPECTS
of the CONSUMER ROLE

First and foremost we are *individuals*. We hear talk about losing our individualism, but in a strict sense this is impossible. Each of us behaves a bit differently—individually—including twins. Nothing short of robotism can prevent this.

The tasks of studying and explaining individual differences locate in the broad discipline of psychology. Because the examination of individuality is such a massive job, however, psychology has divided itself into subdisciplines. In fact, there are about as many subdisciplines of psychology as there are constructs of individuality. Some of the more established ones are:

1. Developmental psychology—studies the progressive changes in the individual that take place from conception to death.

2. Educational psychology—studies such topics as learning, intelligence, memory, guidance, and so on, as they apply to educational procedures.

3. Experimental psychology—applies experimental methods (mostly those used in physics and physiology) to the study of mental activities.

4. Genetic psychology—concerns the growth and development of the individual from conception to maturity.

5. Psychiatry (also a branch of medicine)—deals with the diagnosis and treatment of mental disorders.

6. Social psychology—deals with individual behavior, its influence on other persons, and their influence on the individual.

It is essentially from psychology and its subdisciplines that we obtain the means to study and to explain the individual behavior of consumers. Typically, it has been the practice of marketers to borrow concepts and research tools from the various facets of psychology and apply them on a trial-and-error basis to the explanation of individual consumer behavior. Sometimes they have produced good results; often they have not.

This section of the book contains a series of well-written articles that discuss a number of the significant concepts of psychology and their relevance to explaining consumer behavior. The writings are both theoretical and empirical, but all focus on the advancement of consumer behavior knowledge.

The first two articles in this section illustrate the wide range of psychological concepts that are available for examining consumer behavior. In fact, James A. Bayton, in the first article, "Motivation, Cognition, Learning—Basic Factors in Consumer Behavior," warns against what he calls a "one-sided" application of psychological material, and suggests that the person interested in explaining consumer behavior avail himself of other important psychological dimensions. As the title suggests, Bayton believes that in addition to *motivation*, the dimensions of *cognition* and *learning* find important use in a discipline of consumer behavior.

The following article by Walter A. Woods, "Psychological Dimensions of Consumer Decision," parallels Bayton's article and suggests that research in consumer choice should embrace more psychological constructs than just motivation. He indicates that differences in purchase behavior can be explained more fully by the additional constructs of *cognition, habit,* and *learning.* Then, like Bayton, Woods attempts to illustrate the application of these concepts through examples of consumer behavior.

Grubb and Grathwohl follow with a paper that suggests that purchase behavior is related to one's self-concept. A model of this relationship is developed.

The next three presentations essentially involve *learning theory.* The article "Social Sciences and the Art of Advertising," by Neal E. Miller, demonstrates how a learning theory can be employed to explain a great deal of behavior. Using the constructs of *drive, cue,* and *reward,* Miller indicates the value of his behavioral theory to the function of advertising. It obviously has value to other marketing functions.

The next article, by Steuart H. Britt, entitled "How Advertising Can Use Psychology's Rule of Learning," also applies learning theory to advertising. The approach, however, is different from that of Miller's. Britt presents twenty *principles* of learning and briefly notes their usefulness to advertising. They are principles, rather than theory as Miller employs, in the sense that they have been tested by a vast amount of research.

The last writing on learning theory is one by Herbert E. Krugman and Eugene L. Hartley, entitled "The Learning of Tastes." Their material relates learning principles to a topic of vital interest to marketers—*consumer taste.* They present three experiments conducted to discover the underlying principles connected with the learning of tastes, and also provides us with directions for further experimentation in this area. Krugman's and Hartley's work has great value in helping us to understand why individuals may or may not subscribe to new fashions or new models of consumer products.

Following the material on learning theory there are two articles that deal with the subject of *perception* from different points of view. The first, written by Sidney J. Levy and called "Symbols by Which We Buy," is a practical and interesting article that treats perception by dwelling on the objects *perceived,* in this case consumer behavior objects. Levy discusses how such characteristics of the objects as color and shape symbolize various qualities to different individuals.

The second article on perception, "The Influence of Needs and Attitudes on the Perception of Persuasion" by James F. Engel, approaches the subject from the viewpoint of the *perceiver.* The author considers why a stimulus, for example an advertising message, is perceived differently by different individuals or by one individual at different times. He postulates that *needs* and *attitudes* possessed by the individual are, at least in part, responsible for the differences. Engel notes that, presently, little marketing use can be made of this fact due to methodological difficulties, but sets out briefly some current thinking that he feels should lend direction to further research on the subject.

Subsequently, McNeal presents a paper concerning cognitive dissonance theory and its application to consumer behavior. Cognitive dissonance theory is relatively new and proposes a cause of behavior based on cognitive activities.

The remaining two articles in this section discuss and demonstrate the significant influence of *personality* on consumer behavior patterns. In their presentation, "Personality and Produce Use," W. T. Tucker and John J. Painter explain a study that was undertaken to test the hypothesis that personality traits and consumer behavior are related. Their results essentially proved their hypothesis by producing thirteen significant relations.

The other article dealing with personality and its relation to consumer activity is "Segmentation and Personality Types," written by Morris J. Gottlieb. In his article Mr. Gottlieb suggests that it is possible to divide markets according to personality types and illustrates some cases to prove his point. Like Tucker and Painter, this author provides strong evidence of the influence of one's personality on his purchase behavior.

3

MOTIVATION, COGNITION, LEARNING—BASIC FACTORS in CONSUMER BEHAVIOR

JAMES A. BAYTON

MOTIVATION, COGNITION, LEARNING

The analysis of consumer behavior presented here is derived from diverse concepts of several schools of psychology—from psychoanalysis to reinforcement theory.

Human behavior can be grouped into three categories—motivation, cognition, and learning. Motivation refers to the drives, urges, wishes, or desires which initiate the sequence of events known as "behavior." Cognition is the area in which all of the mental phenomena (perception, memory, judging, thinking, etc.) are grouped. Learning refers to those changes in behavior which occur through time relative to external stimulus conditions.

Each broad area is pertinent to particular problems of consumer behavior. All three together are pertinent to a comprehensive understanding of consumer behavior.

Motivation

Human Needs

Behavior is initiated through needs. Some psychologists claim that words such as "motives," "needs," "urges," "wishes," and "drives" should not

Reprinted from the *Journal of Marketing*, national quarterly publication of the American Marketing Association, Volume 22 (January, 1958), pp. 282-289.

be used as synonyms; others are content to use them interchangeably. There is one virtue in the term "drive" in that it carries the connotation of a force pushing the individual into action.

Motivation arises out of tension-systems which create a state of disequilibrium for the individual. This triggers a sequence of psychological events directed toward the selection of a goal which the individual *anticipates* will bring about release from the tensions and the selection of patterns of action which he *anticipates* will bring him to the goal.

One problem in motivation theory is deriving a basic list of the human needs. Psychologists agree that needs fall into two general categories—those arising from tension-systems physiological in nature (biogenic needs such as hunger, thirst, and sex), and those based upon tension-systems existing in the individual's subjective psychological state and in his relations with others (psychogenic needs).

Although there is not much disagreement as to the list of specific biogenic needs, there is considerable difference of opinion as to the list of specific psychogenic needs. However, the various lists of psychogenic needs can be grouped into three broad categories:

1) *Affectional needs*—the needs to form and maintain warm, harmonious, and emotionally satisfying relations with others.

2) *Ego-bolstering needs*—the needs to enhance or promote the personality; to achieve; to gain prestige and recognition; to satisfy the ego through domination of others.

3) *Ego-defensive needs*—the needs to protect the personality; to avoid physical and psychological harm; to avoid ridicule and "loss of face"; to prevent loss of prestige; to avoid or to obtain relief from anxiety.

One pitfall in the analysis of motivation is the assumption that a particular situation involves just one specific need. In most instances the individual is driven by a combination of needs. It seems likely that "love" brings into play a combination of affectional, ego-bolstering, and ego-defensive needs as well as biogenic needs. Within the combination some needs will be relatively strong, others relatively weak. The strongest need within the combination can be called the "prepotent" need. A given consumer product can be defined in terms of the specific need-combination involved and the relative strengths of these needs.

Another pitfall is the assumption that identical behaviors have identical motivational backgrounds. This pitfall is present whether we are thinking of two different individuals or the same individual at two different points in time. John and Harry can be different in the motivational patterns leading to the purchase of their suits. Each could have one motivational pattern influencing such a purchase at age twenty and another at age forty.

Ego-Involvement

One important dimension of motivation is the degree of ego-involvement. The various specific need-patterns are not equal in significance for the individual. Some are superficial in meaning; others represent (for the individual) tremendous challenges to the very essence of existence. There is some evidence that one of the positive correlates of degree of ego-involvement is the amount of cognitive activity (judging, thinking, etc.) involved. This means that consumer goods which tap low degrees of ego-involvement will be purchased with a relatively lower degree of conscious decision-making activity than goods which tap higher degrees of ego-involvement. Such a factor must be considered when decisions are made on advertising and marketing tactics.

At times the ego-involvement factor is a source of conflict between client and researcher. This can occur when research reveals that the product taps a low degree of ego-involvement within consumers. The result is difficult for a client to accept; because *he* is ego-involved and, therefore, cognitively active about his product, consumers must certainly be also. It is hard for such a client to believe that consumers simply do not engage in a great deal of cognitive activity when they make purchases within his product class. One way to ease this particular client-researcher conflict would be for the researcher to point out this implication of the ego-involvement dimension.

"True" and Rationalized Motives

A particular difficulty in the study of motivation is the possibility that there can be a difference between "true" motives and rationalized motives. Individuals sometimes are unaware of the exact nature of drives initiating their behavior patterns. When this occurs, they attempt to account for their behavior through "rationalization" by assigning motivations to their behavior which are acceptable to their personality structures. They may do this with no awareness that they are rationalizing. There can be other instances, however, in which individuals are keenly aware of their motivations, but feel it would be harmful or socially unacceptable to reveal them. When this is the case, they deliberately conceal their motivations.

These possibilities create a problem for the researcher. Must he assume that every behavior pattern is based upon unconscious motivation? If not, what criteria are to be used in deciding whether to be alert to unconscious motivation for this behavior pattern and not that one? What is the relative importance of unconscious motives, if present, and rationalized motives? Should rationalized motives be ignored? After all, rationalized motives have a certain validity for the individual—they are the "real" motives insofar as he is aware of the situation.

The situation is even more complicated than this—what about the dissembler? When the individual actually is dissembling, the researcher must attempt to determine the true motives. But, how shall we determine whether we are faced with a situation where the respondent is rationalizing or dissembling? In a given case, did a projective technique reveal an unconscious motive or the true motive of a dissembler? Conceptually, rationalized motives and dissembled motives are not equal in psychological implication; but it is rare, if ever, that one finds attempts to segregate the two in consumer research directed toward the analysis of motivation. This failure is understandable, to some extent, because of the lack of valid criteria upon which to base the distinction.

COGNITION

Need-Arousal

Motivation, thus, refers to a state of need-arousal—a condition exerting "push" on the individual to engage in those activities which he anticipates will have the highest probability of bringing him gratification of a particular need-pattern. Whether gratification actually will be attained or not is a matter of future events. Central to the psychological activities which now must be considered in the sequence are the complex of "mental" operations and forces known as the cognitive processes. We can view these cognitive processes as being *purposive* in that they serve the individual in his attempts to achieve satisfaction of his needs. These cognitive processes are *regulatory* in that they determine in large measure the direction and particular steps taken in his attempt to attain satisfaction of the initiating needs.

The Ego—Superego Concept

The ego–superego concept is pertinent to a discussion of cognitive activities which have been triggered by needs. Discussions of the ego-superego concept usually come under the heading of motivation as an aspect of personality. It is our feeling that motivation and the consequences of motivation should be kept systematically "clean." In the broadest sense, ego and superego are mental entities in that they involve memory, perceiving, judging, and thinking.

The Ego

The ego is the "executive," determining how the individual shall seek satisfaction of his needs. Through perception, memory, judging, and thinking the ego attempts to integrate the needs, on the one hand, and the conditions of the external world, on the other, in such manner that needs can be satisfied without danger or harm to the individual. Often this means that gratification must be postponed until a situation has developed, or has been encountered, which does not contain harm or danger. The turnpike driver who does not exceed the speed limit because he sees signs saying there are radar checks is under the influence of the ego. So is the driver who sees no cars on a straight stretch and takes the opportunity to drive at excessive speed.

The Superego

The superego involves the ego-ideal and conscience. The ego-ideal represents the positive standards of ethical and moral conduct the individual has developed for himself. Conscience is, in a sense, the "judge," evaluating the ethics and morality of behavior and, through guilt-feelings, administering punishment when these are violated. If a driver obeys the speed limit because he would feel guilty in doing otherwise, he is under the influence of the superego. (The first driver above is under the influence of the ego because he is avoiding a fine, not guilt feelings.)

Specific Examples

Credit is a form of economic behavior based to some extent upon ego-superego considerations. It is generally felt that one cause of consumer-credit expansion has been a shift away from the superego's role in attitudes toward credit. The past ego-ideal was to build savings; debt was immoral—something to feel guilty about, to avoid, to hide. These two superego influences restrained the use of credit. For some cultural reason, credit and debt have shifted away from superego dominance and are now more under the control of the ego—the primary concern now seems to be how much of it can be used without risking financial danger.

The purchasing of specific consumer goods can be considered from the point of view of these two influences. Certain goods (necessities, perhaps) carry little superego influence, and the individual is psychologically free to try to maximize the probability of obtaining satisfaction of his needs while minimizing the probability of encountering harm in so doing. Other goods, however, tap the superego. When a product represents an aspect of the ego-ideal there is a strong positive force to possess it. Conversely, when a product involves violation of the conscience, a strong negative force is generated against its purchase.

Let us assume that, when the need-push asserts itself, a variety of goal-objects come into awareness as potential sources of gratification. In consumer behavior these goal-objects may be different brand names. The fact that a particular set of goal-objects comes into awareness indicates the generic character of this stage in the cognitive process—a class of goal-objects is seen as containing the possible satisfier. What the class of goal-objects and the special goal-objects within the class "promise" in terms of gratification are known as "expectations."

There are, then, two orders of expectation: generic expectancies, and object-expectancies. Suppose the needs were such that the individual "thought" of brands of frozen orange juice. Some of the generic expectations for frozen orange juice are a certain taste, quality, source of vitamin C, protection against colds, and ease of preparation. The particular brands carry expectations specifically associated with one brand as against another. The expectation might be that brand A has a more refreshing taste than brand B.

In many instances, cognitive competition occurs between two or more generic categories before it does between goal-objects within a generic category. Much consumer-behavior research is directed toward the investigation of generic categories—tires, automobiles, appliances, etc. But perhaps not enough attention has been given to the psychological analysis of cognitive competition between generic categories. An example of a problem being studied is the competition between television viewing, movie going, and magazine reading. For a particular producer, cognitive competition within the pertinent generic category is usually of more concern than cognitive competition between his generic category and others. The producer usually wants only an intensive analysis of consumer psychology with respect to the particular generic category of which his product is a member.

Let us now assume that under need-push four alternative goal-objects (brands A, B, C, and D) came into awareness. Why these particular brands and not others? Why are brands E and F absent? An obvious reason for brand E's absence might be that the individual had never been exposed to the fact that brand E exists. He had been exposed to brand F, however. Why is it absent? The problem here is one of memory—a key cognitive process. The producers of brands E and F obviously are faced with different problems.

Two sets of circumstances contain the independent variables that determine whether a given item will be remembered. One is the nature of the experience resulting from actual consumption or utilization of the goal-object. This will be discussed later when we come to the reinforcement theory of learning. The other is the circumstances present on what might be called vicarious exposures to the goal-object—vicarious in that at the time of exposure actual consumption or utilization of the goal-object does not occur. The most obvious example would be an advertisement of the goal-object. Of course, the essential purpose of an advertisement is to expose the individual to the goal-object in such a manner that at some subsequent time it will be remembered readily. The search for the most effective methods of doing this by manipulation of the physical aspects of the advertisement and the appeals used in it is a continuing effort in consumer-behavior research. Finally, for many consumers these two sets of circumstances will be jointly operative. Experiences with the goal-object and subsequent vicarious exposures can coalesce to heighten the memory potential for an item.

Making a Choice

With, say, four brands in awareness, the individual must now make a choice. What psychological factors underlie this choice? The four brands could be in awareness due to the memory factor because they are immediately present in the environment; or some because they are in the environment, and the others because of memory.

The first problem is the extent to which the items are differentiated. The various goal-objects have attributes which permit the individual to differentiate between them. The brand name is one attribute; package another, design still another. These differentiating attributes (from the point of view of the consumer's perceptions) can be called signs or cues. All such signs are not equally important in consumer decisions. Certain of them are depended upon much more than others. For example, in a study of how housewives select fresh oranges, the critical or key signs were thickness of skin, color of skin, firmness of the orange, and presence or absence of "spots" on the skin.

The signs have expectancies associated with them. Package (a sign) can carry the expectancy of quality. Thin-skin oranges carry the expectancy of juice; spots carry the expectancy of poor taste quality and insufficient amount of juice. Often sign-expectancies determined through consumer research are irrelevant or invalid. Signs are irrelevant when they do not represent a critical differentiating attribute of a goal-object. Certain discolorations on oranges have nothing to do with their intrinsic quality. Expectancies are invalid when they refer to qualities that do not in fact exist in association with a particular sign.

The different goal-objects in awareness can be assessed in terms of the extent to which they arouse similar expectancies. This phenomenon of similarity of expectations within a set of different goal-objects is known as generalization. One goal-object (brand A, perhaps), because of its associated expectancies, can be assumed to have maximum appeal within the set of alternative goal-objects. The alternates then can be ordered in terms of how their associated expectancies approximate those of brand A.

brand A	brand A
brand B	

or

	brand B
brand C	brand C

These differences in ordering and psychological distance are referred to as generalization gradients. In the first case, the expectancies associated with brand B are quite similar to those for brand A, but are not quite as powerful in appeal. Brand C has relatively little of this. In the second case, the generalization gradient is of a different form, showing that brand B offers relatively little psychological competition to brand A. (There will also be generalization gradients with respect to cognitive competition between generic categories.) In addition to the individual producer being concerned about the memory potential of his particular brand, he needs to determine the nature of the generalization gradient for his product and the products of his competitors. Mere ordering is not enough—the "psychological distances" between positions must be determined, also, and the factor determining these distances is similarity of expectancy.

The discussion above was concerned with cognitive processes as they relate to mental representation of goal-objects under the instigation of need-arousal. The items brought into awareness, the differentiating sign-expectancies, and the generalization gradient are the central factors in the particular cognitive field aroused under a given "need-push." One important dimension has not yet been mentioned—instrumental acts. These are acts necessary in obtaining the goal-object and the acts involved in consuming or utilizing it. Examples are: "going downtown" to get to a department store, squeezing the orange to get its juice, ease of entry into service stations, and the operations involved in do-it-yourself house painting.

Instrumental acts can have positive or negative value for the individual. One who makes fewer shopping trips to downtown stores because of traffic and parking conditions displays an instrumental act with negative value. Frozen foods are products for which much of the appeal lies in the area of instrumental acts. The development of automatic transmissions and of power-steering in automobiles are examples of product changes concerned with instrumental acts. The point is that concentration upon cognitive reactions to the goal-object, *per se,* could be masking critical aspects of the situation based upon cognitive reactions to the instrumental acts involved in obtaining or utilizing the goal-object.

LEARNING

Goal-Object

Starting with need-arousal, continuing under the influence of cognitive processes, and engaging in the necessary action, the individual arrives at consumption or utilization of a goal-object. Using our consumer-behavior illustration, let us say that the consumer bought brand A and is now in the process of consuming or utilizing it. We have now arrived at one of the most critical aspects of the entire psychological sequence. It is with use of the goal-object that degree of gratification of the initial needs will occur.

Reinforcement

When consumption or utilization of the goal-object leads to gratification of the initiating needs there is "reinforcement." If at some later date the same needs are aroused, the individual will tend to repeat the process of selecting and getting to the same goal-object. If brand A yields a high degree of gratification, then at some subsequent time, when the same needs arise, the consumer will have an increased tendency to select brand A once again. Each succeeding time that brand A brings gratification, further reinforcement occurs, thus further increasing the likelihood that in the future, with the given needs, brand A will be selected.

This type of behavioral change—increasing likelihood that an act will be repeated—is learning; and reinforcement is necessary for learning to take place. Continued reinforcement will influence the cognitive processes. Memory of the goal-object will be increasingly enhanced; particular sign-expectancies will be more and more firmly established; and the generalization gradient will be changed in that the psychological distance on this gradient between brand A and the competing brands will be increased.

Habit

One of the most important consequences of continued reinforcement is the influence this has on the extent to which cognitive processes enter the picture at the times of subsequent need-arousal. With continued reinforcement, the amount of cognitive activity decreases; the individual engages less and less in decision-making mental activities. This can continue until, upon need-arousal, the goal-obtaining activities are practically automatic. At this stage there is a habit.

Note this use of the term "habit." One frequently hears that a person does certain things by *"force* of habit," that habit is an initiator of behavioral sequences. Actually habits are not initiating forces in themselves; habits are repeated response patterns accompanied by a minimum of cognitive activity. There must be some condition of need-arousal before the habit-type response occurs. This has serious implications in the field of consumer behavior. The promotional and marketing problems faced by a competitor of brand A will be of one type if purchase behavior for brand A is habitual, of another if this is not true. If the purchase is largely a habit, there is little cognitive activity available for the competitor to "work on."

Frequency of repeating a response is not a valid criterion for determining whether or not a habit exists. An act repeated once a week can be just as much a habit as one repeated several times a day. The frequency of a response is but an index of the frequency with which the particular need patterns are aroused. Frequency of response also is often used as a measure of the *strength* of a habit. The test of the strength of a habit is the extent to which an individual will persist in an act after it has ceased providing need gratification. The greater this persistence, the stronger was the habit in the first place.

PROBLEM—CONCEPT—RESEARCH

The above views integrate concepts in contemporary psychology which seem necessary for a comprehensive explanation of human behavior, and apply these concepts to the analysis of consumer behavior. Each psychological process touched upon contains areas for further analysis and specification.

Some type of comprehensive theory of human behavior is necessary as a *working tool* to avoid a lack of discipline in attacking problems in consumer behavior. Too frequently a client with a practical problem approaches a researcher with an indication that all that is needed is a certain methodology—depth interviewing, scaling, or projective devices, for example.

The first step should be to take the practical problem and translate it into its pertinent conceptual entities. This phase of the problem raises the question of motivations. Here is a question involving relevance and validity of sign-expectancies. There is a question dealing with a generalization gradient, etc. Once the pertinent conceptual entities have been identified, and only then, we arrive at the stage of hypothesis formulation. Within each conceptual entity, a relationship between independent and dependent variables is established as a hypothesis to be tested.

Often the relation between conceptual entities must be investigated. For example, what is the effect of continuing reinforcement on a specific generalization gradient? Within the same research project, one psychological entity can be a dependent variable at one phase of the research and an independent variable at another. At one time we might be concerned with establishing the factors associated with differential memory of sign-expectancies. At another time we could be concerned with the influence of remembered sign-expectancies upon subsequent purchase-behavior.

Discipline requires that one turn to methodology only when the pertinent conceptual entities have been identified and the relationships between independent and dependent variables have been expressed in the form of hypotheses. Fundamentally this sequence in the analysis of a problem serves to delimit the methodological possibilities. In any event, the methodologies demanded are those which will produce unambiguous tests of each particular hypothesis put forth. Finally, the results must be translated into the terms of the original practical problem.

We have used the term "discipline" in this phase of our discussion. The researcher must discipline himself to follow the above steps. Some find this a difficult thing to do and inevitably their data become ambiguous. They must resort to improvisation in order to make sense of the results *after* the project is completed. A research project is truly a work of art when the conceptual analysis, the determination of the hypotheses, and the methodologies have been developed in such an "air-tight" sequence that practically all that is necessary is to let the facts speak for themselves.

4

PSYCHOLOGICAL DIMENSIONS
of CONSUMER DECISIONS

WALTER A. WOODS

Motivational research has grown at such a great pace because consumer attitudes and behavior are so important in solving marketing and advertising problems. But motivational research as commonly practiced has often been undisciplined and even capricious. Psychological and sociological theories are often ignored. Old dimensions, often inadequate, are not replaced with new dimensions to provide a systematic way of looking at the consumer.

One reason is a common tendency to miss the differences between motivational and psychological research. Today the two terms are often used incorrectly as interchangeable.

As a result of these errors in definition, other psychological points are often understressed. Theories of consumer behavior have tended to ignore important determinants such as habit, cognition, and learning.[1]

CONSUMER DIMENSIONS VERSUS PRODUCT DIMENSIONS

Consider two distinct processes which work to determine that a particular product will be bought or consumed: (1) The process of motivation —someone is hungry and needs food. (2) The process of discrimination— the hunger is satisfied by selecting particular foods, or particular brands of foods.

Reprinted from the *Journal of Marketing*, national quarterly publication of the American Marketing Association, Volume 24 (January, 1960), pp. 15-19.

[1] An attempt to remedy this is represented in James A. Bayton, "Motivation, Cognition, Learning—Basic Factors in Consumer Behavior." *Journal of Marketing*, Vol. 22 (January, 1958), pp. 282-289.

This is oversimplification, of course. To be sure, the factors under-lying eating (food consumption) are motivational. Theoretically, people eat for several reasons: they are hungry, they are bored, it is time to eat, or they require an outlet for some psychological force.

But what a person (or group) eats at a particular time is usually outside the realm of this kind of motivation. Cereal may be eaten at breakfast because (1) cereal is always eaten for breakfast (habit); (2) the cereal box was in view as breakfast was considered (impulse); (3) cereal is "healthy" (motivational); or (4) everyone else was having cereal (social pressure).

As to why cereal was available in the household, there are other possibilities: (1) cereal is always purchased (habit); (2) there was no cereal but mother wanted a change (cognition plus motivation); (3) cereals are inexpensive (cognition); or (4) the young son shopped with her, and he liked the package (impulse).

As to brand selected, there are also several possibilities: (1) the same brand is "automatically" purchased (habit); (2) brand X is considered best (cognition); or (3) brands of "big" manufacturers are preferred (mo-tivation).

Contrast this with the purchase of a car, where there is a basic need for transportation (motivation), and a secondary need for ownership. When we inquire as to make of car, the question, "What car for what purpose?", is raised. New reasons come into play: cost and economy (cog-nition), appearance (impulsivity), prestige (motivation).

Cereals and cars are different. Habitual and rational forces are more at work with cereals, irrational forces with cars. Consumers identify with and get more involved emotionally with automobiles than with cereals. All consumer behavior is motivated, but actual choices made to satisfy motives may depend on other psychological variables. Motivation, per se, is most often a secondary factor in consumer choice, although it underlies all consumer behavior. Two sets of factors determine the choices which are made: personality of the purchaser, and character of the product. There are thus two sets of variables:

1. Consumer variables, the differences among consumers in their habits, cognitive structure, and motives which cause them to behave differently in pur-chase situations.

2. Differences among products in "demand character" which cause consum-ers to become more ego-involved with some products than with others.

CONSUMER VARIABLES

Consumers pass through an organizing and integrating process during which patterns of behavior are established with respect to purchasing and product use. The newly married woman brings certain attitudes to her new home, but she has no set ways of running her new home. Because of the major recurring problems of personal, family, and social growth, she solves her minor problems by establishing routines (a motive common to everyone).[2] Frequently these routines are established without awareness or deliberate intent.

Among the behaviors frequently relegated to routine are menu planning and preparation, and shopping. Once housewives have routinized these activities, they become relatively "closed" to new product introductions and to brand promotion.

But no consumer solves all problems at the same time. For example, the problem of cake baking may persist long after the problem of coffee preparation is solved. Also, problems are not solved once and for all. The problem of storing perishables may be solved by a new refrigerator; but the problem may recur if, for instance, the family grows in size and more space is needed.

Thus, particular buying habits persist because they have solved some household problems, and they continue until changes in circumstances or outlook present new problems. No published studies are known which discuss the extent to which such behavior (habit-determined behavior) exists, but for some product areas about 60 per cent of the market may be habit dominated.

On the other hand, consumer behavior may remain unstable. Brands and products may be freely changed on the basis of rational factors (cognitive behavior) such as price or convenience. One study suggests that cognitive behavior exists in about 20 per cent of the market.[3]

The cognitive-habit dimension does not explain all purchasing behavior. Purchasing decisions may be made on the basis of other forces. Two such types of behavior may be identified: behavior in response to *affective* appeal and behavior in response to *symbolic* appeal.[4] Although these behavior types are often loosely grouped together as "irrational," they do differ.

Response to affective appeals is probably best described as "impulsive" behavior. As used here, it refers to reactions to product qualities which are primarily physical. Included would be such qualities as color, design, flavor, odor. For example, a shopper impulsively purchases candy because of its inherent physical appeal; or a shopper impulsively selects an automobile because of the inherent appeal of its color and design.

[2] As exemplified by the principle, referred to in psychological literature as "The Principle of Least Effort"; see G. K. Zipf, *Human Behavior and the Principle of Least Effort* (Boston: Addison-Wesley Press, 1949).

[3] Ben Gedalecia, "The Communicators: An All-Media Study"; a report made at the 3rd Annual Advertising Research Foundation Conference, November 14, 1957.

[4] The term "cathectic," as used by T. Parsons, E. A. Shils, and others in *Toward a General Theory of Action* (Cambridge: Harvard University Press, 1951), pp. 8-12, appears to include both "affective" and "symbolic" as used here.

Response to symbolic appeals might best be termed "emotional" behavior. As used here, it refers to behavior which is generated by thinking about the meaning of a product purchase rather than the function of the purchase. Thus, the perceived prestige of owning a Cadillac may be more important in bringing about its purchase than is the function which the Cadillac would serve. This is irrational behavior.

This discussion of consumer variables has suggested that particular people tend consistently to behave in particular ways. Although it is unlikely that a given consumer always reacts in one way rather than another, people do react predominantly in one way rather than in other ways. The market for consumer products probably is composed of:

1. *A habit-determined group* of brand loyal consumers, who tend to be satisfied with the last purchased product or brand.

2. *A cognitive group* of consumers, sensitive to rational claims and only conditionally brand loyal.

3. *A price-cognitive group* of consumers, who principally decide on the basis of price or economy comparisons.

4. *An impulse group* of consumers, who buy on the basis of physical appeal and are relatively insensitive to brand name.

5. *A group of "emotional" reactors,* who tend to be responsive to what products symbolize and who are heavily swayed by "images."

6. *A group of new consumers,* not yet stabilized with respect to the psychological dimension of consumer behavior.

This discussion of consumer variables has been concerned with behavior and *not* with attitudes. Behavior and attitudes are not the same. A favorable attitude toward a TV message is not the same thing as in-store purchasing of the product advertised.

PRODUCT VARIABLES

Superimposed across the entire gamut of consumer cognition and motivation is the character of the product itself. Some products have the capacity to get consumers ego-involved to a high degree. That is, consumers identify with the product. Other products have this capacity to a lesser degree. Still other products depend on their sensory appeal, and others on the function they perform.

Thus, the demands of products on the consumer fall into three classes:

A.   Demands of ego-involvement in the external symbols which the product conveys. ("All executives ride in big cars like mine.")

B.   Hedonic demand. ("It's so beautiful, I can't resist it.")

C.   Functional demands. ("Here it is Tuesday again; we may as well have tuna casserole for dinner.")

Although product variables have been studied to a much lesser degree than consumer variables and less is known about them, it is possible to describe rather unambiguous variables of this sort. Group A above can be broken down into four sub-classes of products where ego-involvement is at issue: (1) prestige products; (2) maturity products; (3) status (or membership) products; (4) anxiety products. These four, along with B and C, provide six psychological product classes.

1. Prestige Products

Prestige products are those which themselves become symbols. The product not only *represents* some image or personality attribute, but *becomes* that attribute. For example, ownership of a Cadillac is not only a symbol of success, but is evidence of success. Products which fall into this class include automobiles, homes, clothing, furniture, art objects, newspapers, and magazines.

The function which these products serve is to extend or identify the ego of the consumer in a direction consistent with his self-image, in such a way as to give him individuality.

2. Maturity Products

Maturity products are those which because of social customs are typically withheld from younger people. The initial use of such products symbolizes a state of maturity on the part of the consumer. Intrinsic product merit is not a factor, at least in the beginning stages of use. Products in this category include cigarettes, cosmetics, coffee, beer, and liquor.

3. Status Products

Status products serve the function of imputing class membership to their users. The intrinsic merit of products in this class is an important factor in continued usage. However, consumers tend to select "big-name" brands because they believe such brands impute "success" "substance," "quality," or similar attributes. "Bigness," in turn, is often imputed from familiarity or frequency of exposure of the consumer to the brand. Packaged foods and gasoline are often in this category. While prestige products connote leadership, status products connote membership.

4. Anxiety Products

Anxiety products are those products which are used to alleviate some presumed personal or social *threat*. Products in this category include soaps, dentifrices, "health" foods, perfumes, and razors. This group of products involves ego-defense, whereas the three preceding categories are concerned with ego-enhancement.

5. Hedonic Products (or Product Features)

Hedonic products are those which are highly dependent on their sensory character for their appeal. Moreover, their appeal is immediate and highly situational. This category includes snack items, many types of clothing, pre-sweetened cereals. Visual (style) features of any product fall within this area; automobile design and color are examples.

6. Functional Products

Functional products are those products to which little cultural or social meaning has, as yet, been imputed. Included in this category are the staple food items, fruits, vegetables, and also most building products.

The differences between these product classes have important implications for competitive marketing. Where ego-involvement can be developed, a high degree of interest can be won on the basis of product image. This, in turn, means a high susceptibility to "other-brand" image and a less habit-bound audience. For such products, marketing success hinges heavily on motivational selling.

On the other hand, where involvement is low, loyalty to one's brand must be achieved differently. Product image becomes unimportant, while product identity and familiarity become very important. Once loyalty is established, threat from "other-brand" penetration is considerably less than with "ego-involving" products. Moreover, "other-brand" success will be much more costly for the "other" manufacturer to achieve, since the other brand must get through on the basis of cognitive appeals to a habit-bound, closed-out audience. For this reason, "lead time" becomes a highly important requirement for success of a product whose appeal is primarily functional or hedonic.

INTERRELATIONS OF VARIABLES

It might seem that the above listed person variables and product variables are two views of the same panorama. But this is not the case.

The psychological character which a product has is a true character which has been imputed to it by society as a whole through long periods of time, and is independent of the psychological character (or personality) of particular individuals. For example, no matter whether the consumer be "habit determined," "cognitive," or "impulsive," he will still acknowledge that Cadillacs do convey prestige connotations of some sort, and that cosmetics do represent a means of conveying "maturity."

Yet, while product variables and person variables represent two sets of variables, it is also true that interrelations do exist. The very nature of impulsivity as a personality characteristic leads to greater susceptibility to products with hedonic appeal. Similarly, social needs will lead to association with products with status connotations.

Although interrelations may exist between these two sets of variables, treatment as a duality is necessary in the development of marketing programs. A true differentiation is required in order to distinguish between market (or consumer) segmentation and product description. A study of consumer variables leads to a description of the market in terms of consumer segments and needs. A study of product variables leads to a definition of product concept and product attributes. Both are required in the development of a product philosophy.

5

CONSUMER SELF-CONCEPT, SYMBOLISM and MARKET BEHAVIOR: A THEORETICAL APPROACH

EDWARD L. GRUBB and
HARRISON L. GRATHWOHL

Efforts to understand the totality of consumer behavior have taken researchers into related fields, with some of the most fruitful results in terms of both theory and practice coming from the behavioral sciences. Two conceptual areas within the behavioral sciences which promise to yield meaningful information about consumer behavior are self-theory and symbolism. A substantial amount of work has been done in these areas, primarily by psychologists, but marketing researchers and theorists do not seem to have developed the marketing potential of the available theory and substance.[1] Some products, brands, and stores have long been recognized as having psychic values to certain market segments, but little has been done to fabricate formal theories useful in predicting consumer behavior.

This article is an effort to develop a partial theory of consumer behavior by linking the psychological construct of an individual's self-concept with the symbolic value of goods purchased in the marketplace. The authors briefly examine previous research and lay theoretical footings from which a set of hypotheses and a qualitative model of consumer behavior are promulgated.

Reprinted from the *Journal of Marketing*, national quarterly publication of the American Marketing Association, Volume 31 (October, 1967), pp. 22-27.

[1] George A. Field, John Douglas, and Lawrence X. Tarpey, *Marketing Management: A Behavioral Systems Approach* (Columbus, Ohio: Charles E. Merrill Books, 1966), p. 106.

REVIEW OF RELATED RESEARCH

Personality and Consumer Behavior

A number of researchers have attempted to relate purchases of product types or specific brands to personality traits of the purchasers. These researchers advanced the basic hypothesis that individuals who consume in a certain manner will also manifest certain common personality characteristics, leading to prediction of consumer behavior. Evans conducted empirical investigations to determine if choice of automobile brand reflects the personality of the owner.[2] Applying the Edwards' Personal Preference Schedule, he could find no important personality differences between a limited sample of Chevrolet and Ford owners and, therefore, could not show that psychological testing predicted consumer behavior more accurately than standard marketing research. However, Kuehn submitted the same data to further statistical analysis and concluded that prediction could indeed be based upon two of the measured personality characteristics (dominance and affiliation).[3]

Westfall experimented with automobile owners to determine if the personalities of owners of standard models, of compact models, and of convertible models varied.[4] Using the Thurstone Temperament Schedule as a personality measuring instrument, he found little difference between the owners of compact and standard models, but discovered that convertible owners are more active, vigorous, impulsive, dominant, and social, yet less stable and less reflective than the other two groups of owners.

The results of these and similar studies demonstrate the existence of some relationship between personalities of the consumers and the products they consume.[5] Yet the results indicate as well the limitations of our understanding of this relationship. Because of the limited results produced by these and similar studies, further refinements in the theoretical foundations may be necessary to provide useful insights.

---

[2] Franklin B. Evans, "Psychological and Objective Factors in the Prediction of Brand Choice: Ford vs. Chevrolet," *Journal of Business,* Vol. XXXII (October, 1959), p. 340.

[3] Alfred A. Kuehn, "Demonstration of a Relationship between Psychological Factors and Brand Choice," *Journal of Business,* Vol. XXXVI (April, 1963), p. 237.

[4] Ralph Westfall, "Psychological Factors in Predicting Product Choice," *Journal of Marketing,* Vol. 26 (April, 1962), p. 34.

[5] For a bibliography of similar studies see: *Are There Consumer Types?* (New York: Advertising Research Foundation, 1964), p. 28.

Personality, Product Image, and the Consumption of Goods

A further refinement in the attempt to relate personality and purchases was the advancement of the assumption that consumer buying behavior is determined by the interaction of the buyer's personality and the image of the purchased product. Pierre Martineau, a strong advocate of this position, argued that the product or brand image is a symbol of the buyer's personality.[6] In later work, Walter A. Woods identified various types of consumers and the importance of the symbolic content of the product to the purchase. Woods asserted that where ego-involvement with the product is high, product image is important to the consumer.[7]

Along similar lines, Duesenberry advanced the idea that the act of consumption as symbolic behavior may be more important to the individual than the benefits provided by the functioning of the product purchased.[8] The relationship of product image and personality was further substantiated by a recent study that found a low, but statistically significant, correlation between the masculinity of cigarette smokers and the perceived masculinity of the brand they consumed.[9]

Though meaningful, the early work has not developed the theoretical relationships between the personality of the individual and the product image. To be useful as a guide to marketing decision-making and research, the variables of the buyer's personality and the image of the purchased products need to be organized into a conceptual totality that will allow relevant material to be systemized, classified, and interrelated. Further, the conceptual interrelationship of these variables should be arranged and developed in such a manner that the *why* of the interrelationship is explained. Exposure of all the elements of the theory to critical evaluation should encourage testing of hypotheses, followed by improvement (re-testing of theory) so that more informed judgments can be made relative to the marketing value of the approach.

[6] Pierre Martineau, *Motivation in Advertising* (New York: McGraw-Hill Book Company, 1957).

[7] Walter A. Woods, "Psychological Dimensions of Consumer Decision," *Journal of Marketing*, Vol. 24 (January, 1960), pp. 15-19.

[8] James S. Duesenberry, *Income, Savings, and the Theory of Consumer Behavior* (Cambridge: Harvard University Press, 1949). For a discussion of the theory of consumption, see James S. Duesenberry, "A Theory of Consumption," *Marketing: The Firm's Viewpoint,* Schuyler F. Otteson, William Panschar, and James M. Patterson (editors) (New York: The Macmillan Co., 1964), pp. 125-132.

[9] Paul C. Vitz and Donald Johnston, "Masculinity of Smokers and the Masculinity of Cigarette Images," *Journal of Applied Psychology,* Vol. XLIX (October, 1965), pp. 155-159.

Self-Theory and Consumer Behavior

A more specific means of developing a theoretical approach to consumer behavior is to link the psychological construct of an individual's self-concept with the symbolic value of the goods purchased in the market-place. The concept of the self is more restricted than personality, which facilitates measurement and centers on the critical element of how the individual perceives himself.[10] Further, use of self-theory allows application of the behavioral concept of symbolic interaction; this provides meaning to the association of an individual's buying behavior with his self-concept.

Self-Theory

Self-theory has been the subject of much psychological and sociological theorizing and empirical research with the accompanying development of a rather large body of assumptions and empirical data.[11] The available knowledge strongly supports the role of the self-concept as a partial determinant of human behavior and, therefore, represents a promising area for marketing research.

Current theory and research places emphasis on the concept of the self as an object which is perceived by the individual. The self is what one is aware of, one's attitudes, feelings, perceptions, and evaluations of oneself as an object.[12] The self represents a totality which becomes a principal value around which life revolves, something to be safeguarded and, if possible, to be made still more valuable.[13] An individual's evaluation of himself will greatly influence his behavior, and thus, the more valued the self, the more organized and consistent becomes his behavior.

The Self and the Interaction Process

The self develops not as a personal, individual process, but it evolves

[10] E. Earl Baughman and George Schlager Welsh, *Personality: A Behavioral Science* (Englewood Cliffs: Prentice-Hall, Inc., 1962), p. 339.

[11] See, for example, Ruth Wylie, *The Self-Concept* (Lincoln, Nebraska: The University of Nebraska Press, 1961).

[12] Calvin S. Hall and Gardener Lindsay, *Theories of Personality* (New York: John Wiley and Sons, Inc., 1957), pp. 469-475, or David Krech, Richard S. Crutchfield, and Egerton L. Ballachey, *Individual in Society* (New York: McGraw-Hill Book Company, 1962), pp. 495-496.

[13] Theodore M. Newcomb, *Social Psychology* (New York: The Dryden Press, 1956), p. 319.

through the process of social experience. From the reactions of others, man develops his self-perception. According to Rogers:

A portion of the total perceptual field gradually becomes differentiated as the self . . . as a result of the interaction with the environment, and particularly as a result of evaluational interactions with others, the structure of the self is formed—an organized, fluid, but consistent conceptual pattern of perceptions of characteristics and relationships of the 'I' or the 'me' together with values attached to these concepts.[14]

Since the self-concept grows out of the reactions of parents, peers, teachers, and significant others, self-enhancement will depend upon the reactions of those people. Recognition and reinforcing reactions from these persons will further strengthen the conception the individual has of himself. Thus, the individual will strive to direct his behavior to obtain a positive reaction from his significant references.

Context of the Interaction Process

The interaction process does not take place in a vacuum; the individuals are affected both by the environmental setting and the "personal attire" of each involved individual. Therefore, the individual will strive to control these elements to facilitate proper interpretations of his performance.[15] Items of the environmental setting or the personal attire become the tools or a means of goal accomplishment for individuals in the interaction process.

Goods as Symbols

A more meaningful way of understanding the role of goods as social tools is to regard them as symbols serving as a means of communication between the individual and his significant references. Defined as "things which stand for or express something else," symbols should be thought of as unitary characters composed of signs and their meanings.[16] If a symbol is to convey meaning it must be identified by a group with which the individual is associated whether the group consists of two people or an entire society, and the symbol must communicate similar meaning

14 Hall and Lindsay, same reference as footnote 12, p. 483.
15 Erving Goffman, *The Presentation of Self in Everyday Life* (Garden City, New York: Doubleday and Co., Inc., 1959), p. 22.
16 Lloyd Warner, *The Living and the Dead* (New Haven: Yale University Press, 1959), p. 3.

to all within the group. The nature of goods as symbols has been attested quite adequately by Veblen,[17] Deusenberry,[18] and Benedict.[19]

Symbols and Behavior

If a product is to serve as a symbolic communicative device it must achieve social recognition, and the meaning associated with the product must be clearly established and understood by related segments of society. This process is in reality a classification process where one object is placed in relation to other objects basic to society.

The necessity for any group to develop a common or shared terminology leads to an important consideration; the direction of activity depends upon the particular way that objects are classified.[20]

Classification systems are society's means of organizing and directing their activities in an orderly and sensible manner.

A prime example of symbolic classification and consumer behavior is fashion. If a particular style becomes popular, behavior of a segment of society will be directed toward the purchase and use of items manifesting this style. As the fashion declines in popularity, the group will discontinue purchase of these items and may reject the use of the remaining portion of previous purchases. Thus, an act of classification not only directs action, but also arouses a set of expectations toward the object classified. Individuals purchase the fashion item because of their feelings about what the item will do for them. The *essence* of the object resides not in the object but in the relation between the object and the individuals classifying the object.

Classification and symbolism become means of communication and of directing or influencing behavior. If a common symbol exists for two or more people, then the symbol should bring forth a similar response in each, and therefore members of a group can use the symbol in their behavior pattern. Further, the symbolic social classification of a good allows the consumer to relate himself directly to it, matching his self-concept with the meaning of the good. In this way self-support and self-enhancement can take place through association with goods which have a desirable social meaning and from the favorable reaction of significant references in the social interaction process.

17 Thorstein Veblen, *The Theory of the Leisure Class* (New York: Mentor Books, 1953).

18 Same reference as footnote 8.

19 Ruth Benedict, *Patterns of Culture* (New York: Mentor Books, 1934).

20 Anselm Strauss, *Mirrors and Masks: The Search for Identity* (Glencoe, Illinois: The Free Press of Glencoe, 1959), p. 9.

Goods and Self-Enhancement

The purchase and consumption of goods can be self-enhancing in two ways. First, the self-concept of an individual will be sustained and buoyed if he believes the good he has purchased is recognized publicly and classified in a manner that supports and matches his self-concept. While self-enhancement results from a personal, internal, intra-action process, the effect on the individual is ultimately dependent upon the product's being a publicity-recognized symbol. Because of their recognized meaning, public symbols elicit a reaction from the individual that supports his original self-feelings. Self-enhancement can occur as well in the interaction process. Goods as symbols serve the individual, becoming means to cause desired reactions from other individuals.

These two means of self-enhancement are represented in diagrammatic form in Figure 1.

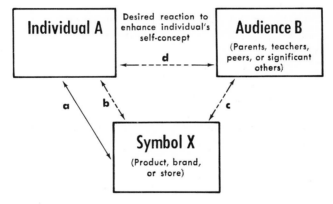

Figure 1.   Relationship of the consumption of goods as symbols to the self-concept.

Individual A purchases and uses symbol X which has intrinsic and extrinsic value as a means of self-enhancement. (Symbol X could include a purchase of a certain product type such as a swimming pool; purchase of a specific brand such as Pontiac GTO; or a purchase from a specific store or distributive outlet.) The intrinsic value is indicated by the double-headed arrow a, while the extrinsic values are indicated by the arrows b, c, and d. By the use of symbol X, an individual is communicating with himself; he is transferring the socially attributed meanings of symbol X to himself. This internal, personal communication process with symbol X becomes a means of enhancing his valued self-concept. An example of this situation is the individual who owns and uses a standard 1300 series Volkswagen. He may perceive himself as being thrifty, economical, and practical; and by using the Volkswagen, which has a strong image of being thrifty, economical, and practical, the individual achieves internal self-enhancement. This private and individual symbolic interpretation is largely dependent on one's understanding of the meaning associated with the product. Though the individual may treat this process in a private manner, he has learned the symbolic meaning from public sources.

By presenting Symbol X to Audience B, which may consist of one or more individuals from parents, peers, teachers, or significant others, the individual is communicating with them. Double-headed arrows b and c indicate that in presenting Symbol X to Audience B, Individual A is attributing meaning to it, and that in interpreting Symbol X, the relevant references in Audience B are also attributing meaning to the symbol. If Symbol X has a commonly-understood meaning between Individual A and the references of Audience B, then the desired communication can take place and the interaction process will develop as desired by A. This means the behavior of the significant references will be the desired reaction to Individual A (as shown by arrow d) and, therefore, self-enhancement will take place.

A Model of Consuming Behavior

The following qualitative model is proposed to clarify the systematic relationship between self-theory and goods as symbols in terms of consumer behavior.

Consumption of Symbols: A Means to Self-Enhancement

1. An individual does have a self-concept of himself.

2. The self-concept is of value to him.

3. Because this self-concept is of value to him, an individual's behavior will be directed toward the furtherance and enhancement of his self-concept.

4. An individual's self-concept is formed through the interaction process with parents, peers, teachers, and significant others.

5. Goods serve as social symbols and, therefore, are communication devices for the individual.

6. The use of these good-symbols communicates meaning to the individual himself and to others, causing an impact on the intra-action and/or the interaction processes and, therefore, an effect on the individual's self-concept.

Prediction of the model:

7. Therefore, the consuming behavior of an individual will be directed toward the furthering and enhancing of his self-concept through the consumption of goods as symbols.

This model becomes the theoretical base for a conceptual means to understand consumer behavior. The self-conception approach to understanding consumer behavior is not all-inclusive but does provide a meaningful conceptual framework for the systematic ordering and comprehension of consumer behavior. Of further importance is that this model, although general, can be an aid to the marketing decision-maker and a guide for future research.

Self-Concept Theory of Behavior and Marketing Research

This theoretical model can and should be used as a guide for further research. As Myers and Reynolds state, "We need to know a good deal more about the matching process and the conditions under which it does and does not occur."[21] Opportunity and need exist for both theoretical and applied research.

Further research is needed in terms of specific consumer decision situations to determine to what extent self-enhancement involves a conformity concept or an ideal self-image concept. For example, are consumers, through their consuming behavior and the interaction process, seeking support for their self-concept as they now perceive themselves, or are they seeking reactions that will promote the attainment of a more ideal self? For the average person, self-concept and self-ideal overlap to a large extent, although in specific circumstances one or the other could be the chief motivator of behavior.[22] This information is of central importance to help management evolve promotional efforts that either support the self-concepts of consumers as they now are *or* as they would like to be.

Useful results will be obtained from well-designed research pertaining to the present and desired symbolic content of products, brands, or

[21] James H. Myers and William H. Reynolds, *Consumer Behavior and Marketing Management* (New York: Houghton Mifflin Co., 1967), p. 204.
[22] Same reference as footnote 10, p. 348.

stores, and how these symbolic meanings can be related to the self-concepts of present and potential users. Success or failure of a product often depends upon the social classification given to the product. Therefore, it is vital that the firm identify those specific products where the symbolic meaning of the product and its relation to the self-concept of the purchaser are active influences in the consumer decision process.

Self-Concept Theory of Behavior and Marketing Management

Firms can and should identify and/or segment their markets in terms of differentiated self-concepts. Recent research has indicated significant differentiated in self-concepts of different consuming groups both for product classes and for different brands.[23] Identification of self-concept segments may be a key element in the determination of marketing strategy and how, where, and to whom the exact tactics should be directed to achieve the desired goals.

Of real importance to the success of a brand of product is the development of a commonly understood symbolic meaning for the product. This means that management of a firm should carefully control the marketing of a product so that the relevant segments of the market properly classify the product and, therefore, behave toward the product in the manner desired by the marketer. Through product design, pricing, promotion, and distribution the firm must communicate to the market the desired clues for consumer interpretation and, therefore, develop the desired symbolic meaning for the brand.

SUMMARY

From a review of the literature of the behavioral sciences, the authors have developed a more complete theory of consumer behavior based upon self-theory and symbolism. This theory can serve as a theoretical foundation for understanding and predicting consumer market behavior, with particular emphasis on its role as the guide for research and decision-making.

The hypothesis presented by the authors stresses the role of the image an individual has of himself as a motivator of human behavior in the marketplace. Because the self-concept is of value and of central importance to the individual, he will direct his behavior to maintain and enhance his self-concept. The self-concept is formed in the interaction

23 Edward L. Grubb, "Consumer Perception of 'Self-Concept' and Its Relationship to Brand Choice of Selected Product Types," unpublished D.B.A. dissertation, University of Washington, 1965, pp. 120-124.

process between the individual and others; therefore, the individual will strive for self-enhancement in the interaction process. Of prime importance is the fact that the interaction process will be affected by the "tools" used by individuals and their significant references. Many of these tools are consumer goods, serving as symbolic communication devices. By carefully using goods as symbols, the individual communicates meaning about himself to his references, which causes a desired response and has an impact on the interaction process, thus reenforcing and enhancing his self-concept.

Enhancement of the self-concept can occur through an intra-action process whereby an individual communicates with himself through the medium of goods-symbols, thus supporting his self-concept. This is an internal process which takes place without specific response from others regarding a particular act. However, intra-action self-enhancement is possible only through group classification systems which bestow symbolic value upon certain goods or "tools."

The model of consuming behavior presented here is still in a theoretical state and, therefore, in need of research to refine and further substantiate its predictive value. Research is needed to determine whether and in what circumstances the motivating force is the presently held self-concept or the ideal self-concept. Basic research also is needed to determine what products have symbolic value and how this meaning is related to the consumers' self-concepts.

The advanced hypothesis is an activist theory having real value as a guide for present marketing decision-making. Marketers should consider segmenting their markets on the basis of consumer self-concepts as well as on demographic factors. Further, they must develop and direct their marketing strategy to meet the needs of these specific self-concept segments. Management would be wise to recognize that the success or failure of a product may depend upon the symbolic meaning established for that product. Significant marketing effort should be employed to ensure that the relevant segments of the market properly classify the product which in turn will tend to bring about desired consumer behavior.

6

SOCIAL SCIENCE and the ART of ADVERTISING

NEAL E. MILLER

What odds would you want to bet your life against a good dinner? I imagine it would have to be a pretty sure thing before you would make that bet.

It is often thought that human behavior is unpredictable. But within a half hour I often bet my life more than a hundred times on the predictability on human behavior. As I drive along the highway at 40 miles an hour, I bet my life that none of the drivers coming the other way at the same rate will suddenly decide to swerve in front of me.

It is a fact that human behavior, following the laws of psychology, is often more predictable than the performance of machines that are governed by the laws of physics and chemistry. In riding on trains I have been held up by broken driving rods, hot boxes, and many other mechanical failures, but never because the engineer decided to stop and pick daisies. When the conditions are right, human behavior is highly predictable. If it were not so, a great civilization like ours would be impossible. Both social science and the art of advertising are founded on the firm conviction that human behavior can be predicted and controlled when the factors governing them are lined up in the right way.

I believe that the relationship of the psychological principles that govern human behavior to the art of advertising is analogous to that of the laws of perspective to the art of painting. In order to be a great painter, one must know the laws of perspective, and most of the great masters had a rather exact knowledge of those laws. But one might have

Condensed from a paper given to the Creative Group Meeting of the 1949 Eastern Annual Conference of the American Association of Advertising Agencies, and reprinted from the *Journal of Marketing*, national quarterly publication of the American Marketing Association, Volume 14 (January, 1950), pp. 580-584.

the best knowledge in the world of the laws of perspective and yet never be able to produce a decent painting. The scientific law is a valuable foundation, but the final results must be produced by a creative artist. Scientific knowledge assists, but can never replace creative talent.

Three of the factors that control human behavior are drives, cues, and rewards. I shall comment on each of these as a social scientist sees them. The first of these factors is drive, or as advertisers call it, appeal. One of the reasons why your behavior is so predictable when you meet a car coming the other direction on the open road is because of the strong drive involved. If for any reason you threaten to hit the other car, this frightens you. The strong drive of fear motivates trying to avoid hitting the other car and resolving to be more careful next time. But when the drive of fear is weakened or a strong competing drive is produced the behavior of the driver becomes much less predictable.

There are two kinds of drives: primary and learned. The primary drives, like hunger, thirst, pain, cold, and fatigue, are innate and common to all men. Their strength, however, is not constant; it varies with the conditions of deprivation. For example, if you hold your breath for more than 60 seconds, you experience a tremendous drive to breathe but normally this drive is important to only a few people, like asthmatics. It is the function of the excellent technology and production of our society to keep most of the primary drives relatively satisfied. Therefore they generally do not exert that tremendous potential power which can be seen in a less efficient society or under the unusual conditions of war, famine, or disaster. Whenever such a drive actually is present in any portion of the population (and pain and fatigue are examples) the advertiser has a sure-fire appeal.

The same conditions of complex social life that tend to keep the primary drives at a relatively low level operate to produce secondary, or learned drives, such as pride, ambition, or the desire for money. They also serve to modify the primary drives, so that hunger becomes the desire for particular kinds of foods.

Since these drives are learned, we will expect them to vary with the conditions of learning. This is indeed the case; they are only as constant as the social conditions that produce them. Anthropologists studying other cultures show us how surprisingly variable these drives can be. In some cultures husbands feel no jealousy when certain other men make love to their wives, and still more incredibly a number of women seem to be able to share the same husband amicably. In certain cultures the son feels it his filial duty to kill his parents as soon as they have outlived their economic usefulness, and the parents seem to want to be killed. Once one gets away from the purely physical, human nature is not constant; it is amazingly subject to change, and advertising has already accomplished some interesting changes in it.

The primary drives vary with the conditions of deprivation; the secondary or learned drives vary with the conditions of learning. Although the most striking differences are between completely different cultures, there are many important differences in various segments of our own American society. Quite rightly advertising has concentrated first on the similarities, or the most universal appeals. But it may be worthwhile to try paying somewhat more attention to the differences. What are the most important differences in the segments of the American public and how are these related to their responsiveness to appeals?

The significant point is that there are important differences, and that almost everyone greatly underestimates their importance. This is because most of the people one chooses to associate with intimately are so much like himself. Almost everyone thinks he understands the total picture fairly well; very few actually do. Perhaps advertising men, having been forced to learn from experience, are less in need of this caution than most other people. Whenever you are dealing with people from the same general social background as your own, you can trust your intuition. Whenever you are dealing with people from a different social background, it will be wise for you to call in the excellent research men that you have in your profession to help you to find out how that particular audience reacts.

Some of the most important variables to watch are: age, sex-typing, social class, and regional and ethnic groups.

Many differences are correlated with age. Thus it sometimes is hard for the younger and older generations to understand each other. Of the many things that could be said, I shall remind you of only one. This is that the young person is more willing to try out new things than the older one; his tastes are more flexible. Perhaps long-range advertising campaigns aimed at overcoming stubborn resistances should bear this in mind. Youth may not have the immediate purchasing power, but it is much easier to mold, will eventually grow up, and often exerts a strong influence on its elders.

Another important variable is sex-typing. As is well known to advertisers, there is a marked difference between what appeals to women and what appeals to men. What might not be noticed without a special study, however, is that the interests of the relatively small group of the well educated upper-middle and upper-class women are much more similar to those of men. The things that appeal to the much larger group of lower-middle and lower-class women are quite different.

To give one example, sexual themes can be handled much more openly and adventurously in stories for men or upper-class women. For the much larger number of women below that class, anything too openly erotic arouses strong conflict and is avoided. On the basis of this difference, I shall venture one tentative suggestion. It is that a perfume advertisement with an openly erotic suggestion like "Midnight Seduction" would not be the best approach to increasing sales in this section of the market. Something might possibly be done, however, by a campaign stressing the themes of house and home, good mother, faithful wife, and loyal husband, with just a dash of strictly conventional moonlight and romance.

Another important variable is social class. Advertisers are used to breaking their audience down into different educational and economic groups. These are somewhat correlated with social class, but class is more important because it describes the kinds of people who associate with each other in intimate cliques. These cliques select people by their social behavior, and mold that behavior. Thus membership in these cliques is more significant than mere money.

There are many important differences between classes. For example, being a good fighter is highly valued in the lower class, while in the middle class it is important to control one's temper and not to fight. One of the most important reasons for lower-class children doing poorly in school is that the appeals the middle-class teacher uses successfully to motivate the children from her own class do not motivate the children from the lower class. They have a quite different set of interests and values. There are differences in dress, religion, recreation, reading habits, and a host of other things. These differences include differences in learned drives, or in other words, appeals. I believe that a creative advertising man could make excellent use of the scientific studies that sociologists and social anthropologists have made of the variable of social class.

My final point about drives is that they summate. For example, the desire for money is the focus of many needs; its possession is the means to many rewards. This is why it is so popular. In fact, money would be such an ideal product to advertise, it's a pity that it needs no campaign to make it popular. Advertisers have made good use of the principle of summation. Thus toothpaste is no longer merely something that cleans teeth; it gives one an attractive smile, helps to make one beautiful, popular, and successful.

The next important factor in controlling human behavior is that of *cue,* or as it is often called, stimulus. One of the reasons that your behavior is so predictable when you meet a car on the open road is because the stimulus situation is relatively clear-cut. The behavior becomes much less predictable when the cues are obscure. Advertisers are already aware of the importance of cues and of attracting attention to them. It is obvious that an advertisement must be seen or a commercial heard in order to be effective. It is towards another aspect of the problem that I would like to direct your attention. The responses aroused by the advertisement or commercial have to be transferred to the store or sales counter before the purchase is made. The two stimulus situations—reading or listening in the home and buying in the store—are quite different. How can the maximum transfer be secured from the advertisement to the sales counter? Everything that we know about learning indicates that more transfer occurs when two situations have more cues in common. Thus the problem confronting the creative worker in advertising is: how can important cues from the buying situation be worked into the advertisement or the commercial? Trademarks, brand names, distinctive cartons, and phrases like "When you see your grocer ask for Ultra Plus" help.

The third factor that I shall discuss is *reward*. This is closely related to drive in that a person must want something before it can serve as a reward. Furthermore, the promise of reward can be used to increase motivation. Because of the close relationship, everything that I have said about drives varying with age, sex, and social class also applies to rewards. I would like to direct your attention to some other aspects of the problem.

The ultimate reward is the satisfaction that the purchaser gets from the use or consumption of the product. Since the situation in which the customer is rewarded by the product may be quite different from the one in which he buys it, there is a gap to be bridged analogous to the one between the advertisement and the purchase. Here again what is needed is a conspicuous cue. Again the cue should be one that is present at the sales counter, but this time it should also be present when the customer is rewarded by consuming or using the product. Since the immediate effects of rewards are much greater than the delayed ones, this distinctive cue should be present at the very moment the customer is being rewarded by using the product, or as near as possible to that moment.

This crucial transfer of the effects of reward from the breakfast table (or other situation in which the product is used) to the sales counter is helped by distinctive features such as pictures on boxes, brand names, trademarks, and devices such as writing the name right on the biscuit so that the customer sees that name immediately before experiencing the delicious taste. How to achieve most effectively this transfer from the rewarding use to the sales counter is a challenge to the creative worker in advertising.

Finally, a word about fear. Fear is a drive just like hunger or thirst. It is important to note that it is *the escape from fear* that rewards and strengthens the responses producing that escape. The escape from fear is a reward, just like the food that gets rid of hunger. The same is true with disgust and other similar drives. If an advertisement attempts to use fear or disgust, the reader has two ways to escape. One is by buying the product that will presumably avoid the danger and reduce the fear. The other is by looking away from the advertisement and putting its fear-provoking message out of mind. If the customer does the second, the fear will only teach him to avoid your product.

Fear is an extremely powerful drive. It is also an extremely malleable one; people can learn new fears quickly. But appeals using fear must feature the means of escape. The social scientist would expect the use of fear as a drive, and escape from fear as a reward, to present special dangers and challenges to the creative workers in advertising.

7

HOW ADVERTISING CAN USE PSYCHOLOGY'S RULES of LEARNING

STEUART HENDERSON BRITT

Most advertising men don't realize it, but their work requires them to use psychological principles of learning. Both advertising men and psychologists want to know more about people's minds.

Every time an advertisement or commercial appears, the objective is to have the reader or viewer *learn* something . . . and *remember* what he learned.

In other words, whether advertising men are aware of it or not, they constantly employ psychological principles. And when psychologists pin down additional facts about learning, they may be making contributions to advertising.

This article presents 20 principles of learning which have been established experimentally by psychologists, and which have practical applications for advertising men. While some of these principles may have been followed by more experienced advertising people, others may be new to them. And all the principles should prove useful to advertising practitioners.

1. Unpleasant things may sometimes be learned as readily as pleasant things, but the most ineffective stimuli are those which arouse little or no emotional response.

The application is that it is better to have rewarding conditions than unpleasant conditions, but either is preferable to learning under neutral

Reprinted from *Printers' Ink,* Volume 252 (September 23, 1955), pp. 74, 77, 80, with permission of *Printers' Ink.*

conditions. The annoying radio or TV commercial works, but not as well as a message which gives the audience a promise of a rewarding experience.

The closer the actual rewarding experience is to the presentation of the message, the more likely it is to be remembered. Thus, the procedure of giving out samples at the point of purchase is a good one, providing the proper advertising message is used at the time.

> 2. The capacities of learners are important in determining what can be learned and how long it will take.

The implication of this principle is that *advertisers should know their audience.* Bright people can grasp a complex message that is over the heads of less bright ones. And they grasp the significance of a simple message in less time.

The ability to learn changes with age. For most people, ability to learn reaches a peak around 16 years of age, then begins to decline steadily. Consequently, an advertiser should know his market and be more patient if he is trying to reach an older audience, or one of lower intelligence.

> 3. Things that are learned and understood tend to be better retained than things learned by rote.

Mere repetition of ads is of no great value unless the message is understood by the people who see and hear it. It must be remembered, however, that extensive drill is still very important in getting facts across. For example LS/MFT *can* be put across, but only by an enormous expenditure of money. Experimental evidence indicates that understanding contributes more to remembering than merely frequent repetition.

> 4. Practice distributed over several periods is more economical in learning than the same amount of practice concentrated into a single period.

In planning a campaign, the prospects should usually be exposed to the advertising over a relatively long period. Brief, concentrated, and temporary high pressure campaigns should be avoided, except in exceptional circumstances, such as making a favorable impression on channels of distribution. Thus, a campaign would probably be more effective if spaced over a period of months rather than concentrated in one week.

> 5. When teaching people to master mechanical skills, it is better to show the performance in the same way that the learner would see it if he were doing the job himself.

For example, in a TV commercial in which a sequence of acts is being demonstrated which you want the viewers to repeat, it may be better to employ "subjective camera angle," that is, place the camera so it is shooting over the demonstrator's shoulder.

In this way the viewers can see the demonstration in the same way they would see it if they were doing it themselves. This is somewhat comparable to writing copy from the "you" attitude.

6. The order of presentation of materials to be learned is very important.

Points presented at the beginning and end of the message are remembered better than those in the middle. Thus, if 4 reasons "why" are given in a series in copy, the 2 most important points should be given first and last.

7. If material to be learned is different, or unique, it will be better remembered.

An outdoor poster may be better recalled if it stands alone than if it is one of a group. If a magazine contained *nothing but* 4-color advertisements, a black-and-white one might get greater attention value than another color one, just because of the uniqueness. Likewise, a TV or radio commercial employing unusual sounds tends to stand out. The "man in the Hathaway shirt" will be long remembered as the first model who wore an eye patch.

8. Showing errors in how to do something can lead to increases in learning.

The effectiveness of a demonstration on television might be increased by showing not only *"what to do"* but *"what not to do."* Thus, to show how not to use a product and also how to use a product may be very useful. In print advertising, Sanforized has done an outstanding job of showing the shrunken garments that are not Sanforized.

9. Learning situations which are rewarded only occasionally can be more efficient than those where constant reward is employed.

For example, it is more efficient to employ deals or premiums over fairly short periods rather than over extended periods. The reason is that short-time deals are looked upon as some sort of bonus, whereas extended deals come to be expected, and consumers feel cheated if they are cut out. There is likely to be more brand switching away from a product after an extended deal than after a temporary one.

10.   It is easier to recognize something than it is to recall it.

The application is obvious. Make the name of your product . . . your package . . . and your sales message easy to recognize. A fine example is the detergent *all* for automatic washing machines. Its distinctive type face stands out in both advertising and packaging.

11.   The rate of forgetting tends to be very rapid immediately after learning.

Accordingly, the *continuing repetition of the advertising message is desirable*. It usually takes a lot of advertising in the early weeks of a campaign to overcome rapid forgetting. In fact, it takes a lot of advertising all the time, since the advertising by competitors helps people to forget your product.

12.   Messages attributed to persons held in high esteem influence change in opinion more than messages from persons not so well-known, but after several weeks both messages seem equally effective.

The implication for advertising is that it is not essential to employ high-priced, well-known talent in testimonials if you are trying to build a long-range favorable climate for your product. The use of less well-known people should also prove effective and less expensive.

13.   Repetition of identical materials is often as effective in getting things remembered as repeating the same story but with variations.

Psychologists term this *identical* vs. *varied* repetition. Using training films, they have failed to find significant differences in learning, after employing a lot of different examples *versus* repeating the same few over again. The implication is that exactly the same advertisements can be run over and over again, with real sales effectiveness each time.

14.   In a learning situation, a moderate fear appeal is more effective than a strong fear appeal.

This means that a fear appeal that is too strong is likely to lead to a rejection of the whole sales message.

To take a far-fetched example, it would be poor strategy for a cigarette manufacturer to claim that he now uses treated tobaccos that prevent cancer. The mere association of cancer with smoking may set up a fear that is so strong as to lead to a rejection of the whole sales message.

15.   Knowledge of results leads to increases in learning.

If you are interested in teaching a given amount of material to people, knowledge of how well they are doing as they are learning leads to greater learning gains. Advertisers should use this principle, by telling the consumer what specific benefits he will get from the product or service advertised.

16.   Learning is aided by active practice rather than passive reception.

This point is of great importance to advertisers. If you can get your audience members to "participate" in your sales message, they are much more likely to remember your brand.

Participation can be accomplished in a number of ways. Get consumers to repeat key phrases, fill in coupons, or even make puns about the brand name. Whatever you do, get the audience to take part in the sales message. Contests with "I like _____ because" tend to put people in a buying mood.

17.   A message is more easily learned and accepted if it does not interfere with earlier habits.

Thus, a sales theme which draws upon prior experiences of the audience will help the learning of the sales message. Recent examples are the new uses of aluminum foil, which show how familiar jobs may be done *better* rather than how familiar jobs may be done *differently*.

18.   The mere repetition of a situation does not necessarily lead to learning. Two things are necessary—"belongingness," and "satisfiers."

Belongingness means that the elements to be learned must seem to belong together, must show some form of relationship or sequence. As an example, it is easier to learn 2, 4, 6, 8, 10, which seem to belong together, than to learn 2, 1, 4, 7, 43, which do not.

Satisfiers are real or symbolic rewards, as distinguished from annoying consequences that may be present in the learning process. In many learning experiments, it has been demonstrated that merely to say the word "right" when the person is making the correct response is a satisfier and helps to speed up the learning process. To say the word "wrong" is an annoyer or "punishment" and is relatively less effective.

Because of the importance of belongingness and of satisfiers, a good deal of advertising could gain in effectiveness if more attention were paid to the organic unity of the total advertising message (belongingness), and also the element of reward or consumer benefits (satisfiers).

> 19. When two ideas are of equal strength but of unequal age, new repetition increases the strength of the earlier idea more than that of the newer idea.

By the same token, if there are two ideas of the same strength but of unequal age, the older idea will not be forgotten as rapidly as the newer idea.

The application to various brands of merchandise is obvious. For instance, if there are two different brands—one older and one newer—which have equal association with a product, and if both brands are given the same amount of advertising, the older brand will probably benefit more from the advertising than the newer brand. Similarly, the older brand will not be forgotten to as great an extent as the newer brand.

> 20. Learning something new can interfere with the remembering of something learned earlier.

Psychologists refer to this as retroactive inhibition. As a hypothetical case, if you study French for an hour and then study Italian for an hour, your ability to recall the French will probably be less than it would have been had you substituted an hour's interval of rest in place of the hour's study of Italian.

There are many applications of the principles of retroactive inhibition to advertising. Suppose that a person has been looking at a one-hour television show, sponsored by just one advertiser. He is much more likely to remember that sponsor and his adertising message than in the situation where there is multiple sponsorship. The later commercial or commercials tend to interfere with the remembrance of the earlier commercial. The more similar the later commercials are to the earlier ones, the greater is the interference. That is why it is poor practice to have similar products advertised on shows which are too close together.

We should not just blindly apply every one of these principles to the field of advertising. However, we can point out certain applications that these principles suggest to the advertising practitioner.

After all, individuals exposed to advertising and people used in learning experiments are much the same kind of people; and all are reacting to materials that someone wants them to learn.

8

THE LEARNING of TASTES

HERBERT E. KRUGMAN and
EUGENE L. HARTLEY

The subject of consumer taste has proved an elusive one for social scientists and businessmen alike. But while the latter energetically pursue the public on a day-to-day basis with ever new baubles and gadgets, the social sciences have for the most part confined their interest to a broad and distant view and only rarely descended to research on the specific processes of taste formation. For students of public opinion the particular process of familiarization has special relevance in view of their concern with the *new,* if not in products then certainly in ideas. Too often in the past, furthermore, explanations for public acceptance or rejection of the new have wandered without restraint between such commonplaces as "Repetition equals reputation," and "Familiarity breeds contempt," *or* "It's the novelty that attracts people," and "It's too new for the public."

All the social sciences have made at least some broad-gauged attempts to come to grips with the problem. Anthropologists like Kroeber and sociologists like Sorokin have made long-term historical analyses of changing styles in dress fashion and art, respectively.[1] Psychologists like Hurlock have studied personality factors in dress.[2] Social historians like

Herbert E. Krugman and Eugene L. Hartley, "The Learning of Tastes." *The Public Opinion Quarterly,* 24 (Winter, 1960), pp. 621-631.

[1] A. L. Kroeber, and J. Richardson, *Three Centuries of Women's Dress Fashions: A Quantitative Analysis* (Berkeley, Calif.: University of California Press, 1940), and P. Sorokin, *Social and Cultural Dynamics,* Vol. I, *Fluctuations in Forms of Art* (New York: American Book, 1941).

[2] E. B. Hurlock, *The Psychology of Dress: An Analysis of Fashion and Its Motive* (New York: Ronald, 1929).

Wector have traced the course of a broad variety of taste and style changes in upper-class American society.[3] A great deal of interest has been focused by sociologists on what is called "mass culture," or "popular culture," and here Rosenberg and White have brought together a wealth of material on the changing contents and functions of this culture.[4] Russell Lynes has written entertainingly about the differences between high-brow, middle-brow, and low-brow culture in America,[5] and Vance Packard has attempted to create a social issue out of the malevolent and omnipotent business forces which he sees as controlling the taste and buying habits of the general public.[6] What has not been dealt with, however, is the close study of the rise and/or fall of specific tastes. In a way, the sudden rise and often equally sudden fall of "fads" and fancies in the marketplace are treated as temporary aberrations not worthy of serious attention—perhaps in part because of the plainly trivial nature of some of the objects involved, for example, beanie caps, hula-hoops, and beards. When perchance a fad or newly popular item becomes generalized into a broad acceptance for some new theme, i.e., when a new "style" or fashion" is born, then it is true there is talk of norms and mores and the social scientists may be interested. The question of how a fad turns into a style or fashion is necessarily unanswered, however, since the antecedent fad and the whole subject of fads have been left unexplored and ununderstood. This applies equally to the new style or fashion which achieves a quiet and unobtrusive acceptance without benefit of an antecedent and much-commented-upon fad.

The subject is important for several reasons. To the small businessman it represents a particularly tragic area of decision making. How often a manufacturer finds a sudden "hit" on his hands and borrows capital to expand plant and equipment, only to find in the midst of trebled production that the will-o'-the-wisp public has lost interest. At the other extreme, we have the manufacturer who is rightly convinced of the worth and potential of his new product, who miscalculates the time it will take for his product to catch on, and who closes his doors financially, unable to wait even in the face of mounting public interest.

For the social sciences, and especially for psychology, the subject is important because it concerns the question of how we *learn to like* objects or ideas. While there is a great deal of research and tested knowledge concerning our ability to learn new skills or solve new problems, we do not confidently know if the principles uncovered in those areas apply

---

[3] D. Wector, *The Saga of American Society* (New York: Scribner, 1937).
[4] B. Rosenberg, and D. M. White, *Mass Culture: The Popular Arts in America* (Glencoe, Ill.: Free Press, 1957).
[5] R. Lynes, *The Tastemakers* (New York: Harper, 1954).
[6] V. O. Packard, *The Hidden Persuaders* (New York: McKay, 1957).

to the learning of likes or dislikes or, if not, what principles do apply.

To the market or consumer researcher, the subject is also unclear. Most tests of consumer likes and dislikes involve one-time exposure procedures, for example, "Madame, how do you feel about this new product X (Like . . . . dislike . . . . or no opinion . . . .)?" No single-exposure procedure can allow for so many of the problems inherent in the learning process. Learning often implies time and repeated trials or exposures. What we like today may seem dull tomorrow. What seems uninteresting on first view may prove somewhat intriguing with a second look, etc. Indeed the market researchers' pre-testing of television and other programs on a single-exposure basis may in part be responsible for the low levels of taste in much of what is presented to the public. If repeated- rather than single-exposure tests were made, it might be demonstrated that the audience could "develop a taste" for something new and different, and the sponsor might thereby be encouraged to forego the luxury of immediate popularity for his show.

When time *is* taken into account, and when it is determined how well an object or idea might wear ("Will it prove popular in the long run? Will it hold up?") we encounter another equally significant part of the subject of consumer taste, the problem of familiarity. At the other extreme from faddism, yet theoretically its blood brother, we find innumerable examples of manufacturers offering beautiful and superior new styles, fabrics, devices or packages to a strange market that seems perversely to prefer going along with the older but more familiar items. The psychologist's interest may be engaged here as he identifies a familiar problem, "resistance to social change." While it is a familiar problem in those terms, however, it may not be so familiar when linked with fads and fancies as one and the same problem. That problem concerns the beginning and the end points of *learning to like*. It is the problem of some new things becoming popular quickly and others slowly, or some dying out quickly and others slowly, of some fads broadening into fashions and some fashions persisting indefinitely. It concerns the question of when novelty is delightful and when familiarity outweighs all other considerations. Put simply and perhaps best, however, it is the question of how we learn to like, and what is the influence of the extent of familiarity on the degree of liking. We would like to know more, therefore, about familiarity and liking, about fads becoming fashions, and about the qualities that enable some individuals to "make" fashions or sense new ones in the making while others dismiss them as "only fads." The subject, it may be noted, involves not only the suddenly successful novelties known as fads but the liking or disliking, popularity or unpopularity, of any and all tastes and styles evoking different kinds and degrees of public comment and reaction.

BACKGROUND

The study of learning, especially in its relation to the phenomenon of memory, is perhaps the oldest of the classic interests of academic psychology. Indeed, it goes well back into the nineteenth century. Since that time the world of education has created enormous pressures and opportunities for psychologists to contribute to better understanding of the learning process in the classroom situation. Out of the vast body of research and literature produced to meet this challenge there developed several major and competing theories of learning, differing in important theoretical respects but similar in the factors or variables considered important to study, and similar also in many of the principles which later emerged as practical guides in the classroom.

The most widely accepted principles can be summarized thus: In learning new skills, repetition or practice is effective; active practice, or recitation, is more effective than passive practice; the learning of the task as a whole is more effective than learning it piece by piece; short practice sessions spread over a longer period of time are more effective than longer practice sessions crammed into a shorter period of time; when practice is continued beyond what is required for successful accomplishment of the task at hand, there is little forgetting of what has been learned even after long periods without practice.

Now the businessman may become interested and ask what implications there are here for how complete his advertisements should be in describing his product, how often and over how long a period his advertisements should be spaced, etc. To some extent practical implications do exist, but as far as we know only in terms of product awareness. We do not know but are now asking what implications there are in terms of product liking and disliking. One difficulty lies in the difference between classroom and marketplace. In the former we have motivated individuals actively coping with difficult problems, whereas in the latter we are much more involved with capturing the attention of a passive audience and creating likes for objects, forms, and ideas which, despite the manufacturers' pride, may be quite trivial in importance or consumer concern. These qualifications do not prevent us, however, from singling out the major factor in learning, *i.e.*, repetition, and putting it in terms of exposure and familiarity, to see where and how it can be linked to the development of likes and dislikes.

Two aspects of repetition and familiarity may be defined. One concerns what is called cognitive, or perceptual, learning, for example, how often do we have to look at an object or hear a theme before we recognize it as "familiar"? The second concerns what is called affective learning, for example, how often do we have to look or hear before we "like"? Both aspects will concern us, and the interrelationship of the two will be our particular focus.

THREE EXPERIMENTS

Familiarity may affect our attitudes toward a wide variety of items from everyday life. A pioneer attempt to study such variety in an experimental setting was made by Maslow.[7] He recruited fifteen students for a ten-day, two-hours-a-day experiment. During each session the students met in the same room and took the same seats. The room had large, bright pictures on the wall and a metronome ticking in the background. The sessions were devoted to looking at a series of paintings by fifteen well-known artists, trying to write down and spell correctly the names of Russian women read to them by the experimenter, copying out of a book those sentences that contained key words provided on a separate list, and marking true-false tests. Throughout the experiment the students wore smocks, used grey rubber bands, large paper clips, yellow blotters, unlined 3 × 5 cards, used copies of books, yellow paper, and pens. Cookies were available for refreshment. These conditions prevailed generally throughout the sessions until the last few, when periodically the students were offered something different, without warning, or asked to make a judgment of personal preference.

The students were offered a chance to change seats, to have the pictures on the wall removed, to have the metronome stopped; they were shown a matched series of paintings by the same fifteen artists and asked which in each matched pair was more beautiful; they were read a similar series of Russian women's names and asked which in each matched pair sounded nicer; they were offered the choice of copying significant parts rather than whole sentences, and of writing original sentences rather than copying; they were offered an easier test-marking system; in addition, they were offered a chance to remove their smocks and to use red rubber bands, small paper clips, orange blotters, lined 3 × 5 cards, new books, blue writing pads, pencils, and a new kind of cookie.

The results showed a general tendency to choose the "familiar," although some students were more likely to do this than others. More important, there was a great difference in what kinds of choice were affected by familiarity and what kinds were not.

Students did not care to change their seats and were no longer aware

[7] A. H. Maslow, "The Influence of Familiarization on Preference," *Journal of Experimental Psychology,* Vol. 21, 1937, pp. 162-180.

enough of the bright pictures on the wall or the metronome ticking in the background to care about these matters one way or another. These items were apparently peripheral to the tasks at hand and, while distracting at first, eventually disappeared into the background. Thus familiarity *neutralized* them to the point where no liking or disliking was involved, but only indifference.

Judgments of paintings and names were clearly affected by familiarity, that is, the more familiar were preferred as more beautiful. In addition, half or more of the students preferred the familiar ways of copying sentences or marking tests even though the new methods offered were easier. It is in these two areas that familiarity seemed to have its most positive effect. These represented, of course, the focus of the students' attention. In the case of paintings and names, however, it was more surely demonstrated that familiarity was responsible for preference of the original series by showing that another group of students, not previously exposed to the original series, split their preferences more evenly between the two.

Students did not, at first, care about removing their smocks, but half of them did so with further encouragement. No preference was shown for rubber bands or blotters of one or another color, or for large or small paper clips. There were some tendencies to prefer the familiar unlined 3 × 5 cards, old books, pens, and original cookies. In one case, that of blue writing pads versus yellow paper, the new item was preferred. However, results might have been different if single sheets of blue paper had been compared with the single sheets of yellow paper.

In all, this study is a challenging demonstration of the potent and yet varied influence of familiarity. Some items were affected greatly, others less, and still others not at all. We would understand more, perhaps, if we knew how repeated exposures affected the responses of those who initially liked a picture or name as opposed to those who initially disliked a picture or name. We would also like to know which kinds of familiarized preference stood up over a long period of time and which disappeared with time.

Most important, we would want to bring more directly into play the concept of the learning process. In Maslow's study he deals with items that are familiar and not familiar, on a cognitive level, rather than with items of a measured degree of more or less familiarity. Thus it would be instructive to know if the influence of repeated exposures upon preference for a picture or name was greater among those students who had learned to remember the pictures more vividly or to spell the names of Russian women more correctly.

A later study of Krugman attempts to control initial familiarity with the items used in the experiment, and also raises the question of generalization, that is, what happens to liking for the general category within which one may have learned for the first time to like a single item.[8] In his study he used "swing" and "classical" music as the categories and individual musical selections as the items. He first measured students' attitudes toward swing and classical music, then selected nine students, three each who were pro-swing, pro-classical, and indifferent to both. The three at each extreme were clearly prejudiced in their attitude and rarely listened to music of the other category.

A second step was to play classical music to the swing fans and to the indifferent students, and to play swing music to the classical fans. For each student the items to be played were selected by playing a number of records until three were found which he neither liked nor disliked. From then on the same selections were played once a week for eight weeks. Degree of liking was rated by the student after every playing.

Results showed a general increase in liking from week to week, typically for at least two of the three selections per student, at least until the sixth week, when some flattening of the general upward trend appeared. At the end of the experiment all the students agreed that they could get to like some selections representing a category of music to which they had previously felt a marked prejudice. Furthermore, when the initial measure of attitudes toward categories of music was repeated, it was found that some had shifted in their attitudes toward the category as well as toward the individual items.

The questions posed by the Maslow study apply to this one as well. What would the results be if one started with items that were initially liked or disliked by the students? Which likes persist and which fade away? Do eight sessions or exposures constitute the same degree of learned familiarity and recognition for one student as they do for another? In addition, what is the difference between those students who learned to like the individual items but maintained their attitude toward the category and those who shifted in their attitude toward the category?

Perhaps the main contribution of this experiment was to suggest that the development of "new" likes of specific items is closely correlated with number of exposures, that the learning involves a gradual but regular process. A secondary contribution was to show that some students generalize from their experience with the new while others do not.

A third and more recent experiment by Hartley takes a closer look at the relationship between familiarity and liking for items and categories, and he does this for different types of categories, in an attempt to discover for what categories generalization from item to category is most

---

[8] H. E. Krugman, "Affective Response to Music as a Function of Familiarity." *Journal of Abnormal and Social Psychology,* Vol. 38, 1943, pp. 338-392.

and least likely.[9] In his study he used "Oriental," "modern," "portrait," "floral," and "landscape" as his categories, and individual paintings as his items.

Hartley had twenty-three students rate each of ten paintings on a five-point scale of familiarity, and then again on a five-point scale of liking. The ten paintings involved two each representing Oriental, modern, portrait, floral, and landscape subjects or styles. These he called the test paintings. A week later and five times during the three weeks thereafter the students were shown five other paintings, one for each of the categories above, and asked to study them carefully for twenty seconds. They then were asked to imagine the paintings and rate them for various aspects of clarity. These were called the familiarization paintings. After the five exposures were over and these exercises in imagery completed, the original test paintings were re-rated for familiarity and liking.

Comparison of the before and after ratings of the test paintings showed a general increase in familiarity for the ten items, but with different degrees of increase by category. Thus increases were greatest for Oriental, floral, modern, and landscape in that (decreasing) order, while portraits showed a decrease in familiarity, that is, exposure to portraits made them seem less familiar. Comparison also showed that there was no general change in liking for the categories but that moderns, especially, and portraits, slightly, were more liked, while florals were less liked.

In order to discover what these differential shifts implied for the relationship between items and categories, the question was raised as to the extent to which the two Orientals, moderns, portraits, florals, and landscapes were seen or treated as members of the same category. This was done by correlating the initial ratings of familiarity and of liking for each of the two paintings in the test series: did the two Orientals get similar or dissimilar ratings on familiarity and on liking?

Keeping the very rough $(N = 2)$ definition of category in mind, it may be reported nevertheless that all correlations on familiarity were significant and positive, and that this was especially true of portraits and florals; on a cognitive level these were all true categories or fell into accepted categories. As for liking, however, the correlations were both negative and positive, and only landscapes and moderns showed significant and positive correlations. In short, there were no prejudices or tendencies to like or dislike the items as a category except for landscapes and moderns. Furthermore, when familiarity and liking were correlated with each other by category, it was found that portraits and florals showed consistent and high negative correlations for the four items involved— the more familiar the more disliked. Orientals showed a consistent positive correlation for the two items involved—the more familiar the more liked.

What, then, are the implications of these initial reactions? First let us summarize the results as follows (with F = familiarity, L = liking, and D = disliking):

Category	Initial test of F as a category	Initial test of L or D as a category	Initial relation of L and D as items	Re-test increase in F of the category	Re-test shifts in L of the category
Oriental	Yes	No	Increased F = L	Most	None
Floral	Especially	No	Increased F = D	Second	Decrease
Modern	Yes	Yes	None	Third	Increase
Landscape	Yes	Yes	None	Fourth	None
Portraits	Especially	No	Increased F = D	Decrease	Increase (slight)

The Oriental paintings were seen as a category but were (predominantly) liked more on an item-by-item than on a category basis. Familiarity with the category increased more than any other, perhaps because the category is strange to Americans, but no increase in liking for the category took place.

Floral paintings were especially seen as a category but were (predominantly) disliked more on an item-by-item than a category basis. Familiarity with the category increased significantly and apparently produced dislike for the category as such.

Modern paintings were seen and liked or disliked as a category without much item-by-item sensitivity. Familiarity with the category increased significantly.

Landscape paintings were also seen and liked or disliked as a category without item-by-item sensitivity. Familiarity with the category increased, but liking for the category did not.

Portraits were especially seen as a category, but were (predominantly) disliked more on an item-by-item than a category basis. Familiarity with the category decreased, i.e. began to be seen as different, and even produced some increase in liking for the category.

One might characterize the Oriental situation as "open"; individual items can be liked, but familiarity with the category still provides room for increase without any shift in liking for the category. Florals, on the other hand, could be characterized as a dead category, where further exposure and familiarity will only broaden the dislike for individual items into a dislike for the category as a whole. Moderns and landscapes are perhaps the most popular categories of those studied here, and further familiarity with the more popular moderns increases their popularity, while further familiarity with landscapes has no further effect on their popularity. Portraits, on the other hand, represent a dead category that apparently can be resurrected or reappreciated.

In general, then, Hartley has shown that familiarity with and study of items (in this case, the exercises in imagery) for the most part increase familiarity with the category. What then happens to liking for the category may depend on what room for further familiarity still exists (as with Orientals), on the relationship between familiarity and liking for individual items (as with florals), on the popularity of the category (as with moderns), or possibly on other factors not involved in the categories used in this study. The case of the portraits suggests that the students learned to see the category differently. It would have been useful therefore to have had a direct measure of how successful or revealing the imagery exercises were. It would seem that something was learned there about portraits which would have been measurably larger than what was learned about other categories.

To sum up the three experiments discussed, it may be said that Maslow demonstrated that familiarity with items created liking for some items but not for others; Krugman demonstrated that when familiarity with items created liking for the items then some combination of familiarity and liking could create liking for the category; Hartley showed that familiarity with items created familiarity with the category, but that this might or might not create liking for the category depending upon a number of different factors.

Taken as a group these three experiments suggest what elements ought to be included in a more ideal experiment or series of experiments:

1. Measures of initial familiarity with, and liking for, items representing categories that are old and new, popular and unpopular, familiar and unfamiliar.

2. Measures of initial familiarity with, and liking for, each category, using more than two items as a basis for measurement, or using a more direct measure.

3. Measures of the individual's ability to learn, and to generalize from learning.

4. Repeated measures of liking for items.

5. Repeated measures of "true" familiarity (*i.e.*, cognitive learning) apart from judgments of "apparent" familiarity.

6. Comparison of results with different degrees of exposure or number of trials (i.e. "assumed" familiarity).

7. Repeated but less frequent measures of familiarity with, and liking for, the category.

8. Comparisons between items that showed more and less change.

9. Comparisons between categories that showed more and less change.

10. Comparisons between people who showed more and less change.

The elements above may be used to conduct research on products, brands, tastes, styles, or ideas. It matters less what is actually studied than the fact that a real gap in our knowledge is represented here, a gap that should be a matter of concern to both the social scientist and the businessman.

9

SYMBOLS by Which WE BUY

SIDNEY J. LEVY

The science and practice of marketing have recently been infused with new life. There are many reasons for this. One of the core reasons is that behavior in the market place has become increasingly elaborated. The great multiplicity of goods, the burgeoning of new products, and their eager fruition in the consumers' homes, have moved our society to a point where practical considerations in the purchase of goods are often not given the central attention that was true in the past. The modern marketplace—exemplified so dramatically in the vast supermarket, whether called food, drug, or furniture store—reminds us daily of the marketing revolution that has come about.

In these new settings, with their astonishing arrays of merchandise, their frozen, prepackaged, precooked foods; their plastic containers; their polyethylene gadgets; and their intellectual appliances that can thoughtfully govern their own behavior—what kind of consumer is conjured into being? It is hardly an economic man—especially since there is a lot of evidence that he does not buy economically; is often vague about the actual price he pays for something; has few standards for judging the quality of what he buys; and often winds up not using it anyway! This is not just a joke. The point I am making is that nowadays when people shop, they buy relatively lavishly. They still talk about price and quality and durability, since these are regarded as sensible traditional values. At the same time, they know that other factors influence them, and they believe these to be legitimate influences. This point is worth some emphasis since there are many who disapprove of the fact that purchases

Reprinted from Lynn H. Stockman (ed.), *Advancing Marketing Efficiency* (Chicago: American Marketing Association, 1959), pp. 409-416.

may be made on grounds they think are insubstantial. The fact that people don't buy their furniture to last 20 years may be deplored as a sign of the lightheadedness of our times; on the other hand, such massive, stoutly made furniture may be dismissed from the home at the behest of other values in comfortable living and changing tastes.

Not only do people not want furniture such as grandmother used to cherish; they also know that practical considerations can hardly determine their choice between Post or Kellogg, between Camels or Luckies, between Buick or Oldsmobile, between Arpège or Chanel. They know that package color and television commercials, newspaper and magazine ads incline them toward one preference or another—and when they can't really tell the difference among competitive brands of the same product, they don't believe that any of them should necessarily go out of business for being unable to distinguish his product.

At the heart of all this is the fact that the consumer is not as functionally oriented as he used to be, if he ever really was. The esthetic preferences that were there have changed somewhat—we no longer go in for stained glass lamps and antimacassars, although the latter were probably more attractive than transparent couch covers; and the diversity of choices that are now possible in the ways people can spend their money makes for a diversity of reasons for the choices. When people talk about the things they buy and why they buy them, they show a variety of logics. They refer to convenience, inadvertence, family pressures, other social pressures, complex economic reasonings, advertising, pretty colors, a wide range of feelings and wishes. They are trying to satisfy many aims and circumstances. The pleasure they gain from buying objects is ever more playful—less the question, do I need this? more the ideas, do I want it? do I like it? Answering these questions takes the definition of goods into new realms—at least new in the sense that they are studied more nowadays. The things people buy are seen to have personal and social meanings in addition to their functions. Modern goods are recognized as psychological things, as symbolic of personal attributes and goals, as symbolic of social patterns and strivings. In this sense, all commercial objects have a symbolic character, and making a purchase involves an assessment—implicit or explicit—of this symbolism, to decide whether or not it fits. Energy (and money) will be given when the symbols are appropriate ones, and denied or given parsimoniously when they are not. What determines their appropriateness?

A symbol is appropriate—and the product will be used and enjoyed when it joins with, meshes with, adds to, reinforces, the way the consumer thinks about himself. In the broadest sense, each person aims to enhance his sense of self, to behave in ways that are consistent with a set of ideas he has about the kind of person he is or wants to be. Prescott Lecky has written an interesting essay on how people behave in consistence with their self-concepts.[1] The variety of goods available permits more ways of living than was ever the case. Because of their symbolic nature, consumer goods can be chosen with less conflict or indecision than would otherwise be the case. Buridan's ass starved to death equidistant between two piles of attractive hay; he wouldn't have had the problem if one pile had been a bit more asinine—let's say—than the other. Our choices are made easier—either more routine, or more impulsive, seemingly—because one object is symbolically more harmonious to our goals, feelings, and self-definitions than is another. The difference may not be a large one, nor a very important one, in the manufacture or advertising of the products; but it may be big enough to dictate a constant direction of preference in the indulgence of one's point of view. There is then more well with the world when the bathroom tissue is pastel blue, the car a large one, the newspaper a tabloid size, the trousers with pleats, and so on. It becomes increasingly fashionable to be a connoisseur or gourmet of *some* kind, to consume with one or another standard of discrimination at work.

Research helps to identify the kinds of symbols utilized in the market, and the intensity with which they operate as determinants of purchases. Because some people don't like the idea that such things as feelings and symbols are influential in situations which they feel should be more purely utilitarian, they dislike research that investigates such ideas and meanings. Sometimes they even blame the research for having caused the phenomena, as though a microscope were responsible for the goodness or badness of the bacteria it examines.

In several years of research into the symbolic nature of products, of brands, of institutions and media of communication, much has been shown of the way consumers are able to gauge subtly and grossly the symbolic language of these objects, and to translate them into meanings for themselves. They understand that darker colors are symbolic of more "respectable" products, that pastel colors mean softness, youthfulness, femininity; that yellows and browns are manly, that red is exciting and provocative. They "know" that science means technical merits and an interest in quality and probably less enjoyment; that theatrical references imply glamour and the suspension of staid criteria. They think that Winston Churchill would be good testimony for cigars, whiskey, and books; and if they are very average consumers they are apt to miss (or ignore) the point of a Springmaid sheet ad altogether.

One of the most basic dimensions of symbolism is gender. Almost all societies make some differential disposition of the sexes, deciding who will do what; which objects will be reserved to men and which to women. They usually find it hard to evade thinking of inanimate things as male or female. Through such personalization, vessels tend to become fem-

[1] Prescott Lecky, *Self-consistency* (New York: Island Press, 1945).

inine—and motherly if they are big enough. Men are challenged by the virgin forest which must be raped of its resources; they fall in love with their ships and cars, giving them women's names. And such places and objects are reserved for men, relatively speaking.

In America there has been complaint that some of this differentiation is fading, that women get more like men, and men shift to meet them, in a movement toward homogeneous togetherness. No doubt hunting and agricultural societies make sharper distinction between what is masculine and what is feminine. Still, products and behaviors tend to be more one or the other, and in minutely graded ways. Probably all cigarette brands could be placed on a continuum of degrees of gender, as one of their complex symbolic patternings. The same is true for musical compositions, and the recorded interpretations of any one of them, of cheeses and the brand versions of each kind.

These sexual definitions may seem absurd at times, and often are of modest influence in one or another choice. But they are at work and form a natural part of, for instance, the housewife's logic (and teaching) as she makes her selections in the food store and serves her family. She sums it up by thinking of what will please her husband's preference, what a growing boy should have, what is just right for a girl's delicate tastes. Since smoothness is generally understood to be more feminine, as foods go, it seems fitting that girls should prefer smooth peanut butter and boys the chunky. While the overlap is great, a cultivated society teaches such a discrimination, and the children, being attentive to their proper sex roles, learn it early. Families work busily at such indoctrination of symbolic appropriateness. One little 6-year-old boy protested in an interview how he had never liked peanut butter, but that his mother and sister had always insisted that he did, and now he loved it. Apparently a violent bias in favor of peanut butter is suitable to little boys, and may be taken as representing something of the rowdy boyishness of childhood, as against more restrained and orderly foods.

Similarly, in a recent study of a pair of cheese advertisements for a certain cheese, one wedge of it was shown in a setting of brown wooden cutting board, dark bread, and a glimpse of a chess game. The cheese wedge was depicted standing erect on its smallest base. Although no people were shown, consumers interpreted the ad as part of a masculine scene, men playing a game, being served a snack. The same cheese was also shown in a setting with lighter colors, a suggestion of a floral bowl, with the wedge lying flat on one of its longer sides. This was interpreted by consumers as a feminine scene, probably with ladies lunching in the vicinity. Each ad worked to convey a symbolic impression of the product, to modify or enhance the beliefs already held about it. Symbols of gender are among the most readily recognized. Most people are usually quite alert to whether something is addressed to them as a man or as a woman.

Similarly, symbols of age are familiar. Teenagers are quite sensitive to communications which imply childishness. Presented with a layout showing a family going on a picnic, their reaction is apt to be, "Kid stuff." They are trying to break away from the family bosom. While they might actually enjoy a family picnic, the scene symbolizes restraint, being unable to get away to be with people their own age. Clothing is quite carefully graded in people's eyes; we normally judge within a few years' span whether some garment is fitted to the age of the wearer. Women are particularly astute (and cruel) in this, but men also observe when a pinstriped suit is too mature for one wearer, or when an outfit is too young for a man who should be acting his age.

Symbols of social participation are among the most dramatic factors in marketing. Most goods say something about the social world of the people who consume them. Debate goes on now whether automobiles are still related to people's social wishes or strivings, because some motivation research brought this rather well-known fact to the fore, and because some advertising has taken rather self-conscious account of it. This hardly changes the fact that cars say prominent things about their owners, and are likely to continue to do so. Like it or not, there are social class groupings formed by the ways people live, the attitudes they have, the acceptance and exclusiveness of their associations. The things they own are partly chosen to attest to their social positions, in one way or another. The possession of mink is hardly a matter of winter warmth alone, as all women know who wear mink with slacks while strolling at a beach resort. The social stature of mink—and its downgrading—leads us to marvel that it is now sold at Sears. But then, Sears has upgraded itself and become more middle class too. Shopping at Sears is symbolic of a certain chic among many middle class people who used to regard it as much more working class. Now they boast that Sears is especially suitable for certain kinds of merchandise, and their candor in saying they shop there is not matter-of-fact but is laughing, as if to point out that it is an amusing quirk in one's social behavior.

Membership in one social class or another tends to affect one's general outlook, modes of communication, concreteness of thinking and understanding.[2] Advertising often says different things to people of different social levels. A perfume ad showing an anthropological mask and swirling colors is likely to be incomprehensible to many working class women, whereas New Yorker readers will at least pretend they grasp the symbolism. On the other hand, working class women will accept a crowded, dark, screaming sale advertisement as meaning urgency and potential interest, while higher status women will ignore it as signaling inferiority. Sometimes, the symbolism becomes confined to a social class

[2] Leonard Schatzman and Anselm Strauss, "Social Class and Modes of Communication," *The American Journal of Sociology,* January, 1955, Vol. LX, No. 4.

subgroup; even some upper middle class people aren't sure what is being said in various modern liquor ads with their groups of sinister men, their red shoes, and handsome males riding sidesaddle. Even while suspecting the symbolic language may be gibberish, they have some undercurrent of anxiety about not being part of the ingroup who use these "nonsense syllables" to tell each other about vodka. Since, as Susanne Langer discusses so well, symbolizing is a natural human function, it is not reserved to such formal categories as gender, age, and social status.[3] Any given complex of acts, gestures, movements, pictures, words, will signify much to the consumer. From commercials and ads, from television shows and editorial materials, the viewer or reader concludes about the meanings being offered. These meanings may correspond to the advertiser's intention—although often they are separate from, in addition to, or even contrary to his aim. A striking instance of such contradictory communication was an advertisement with a headline claiming the product was worth 1¢ more than it cost when compared to its competitors. Housewives interpreted this claim as a sign of cheapness; they needed only to see the 1¢ in the headline to believe it was "one of those penny deals." Merely the idea of talking about 1¢ suggested cheapening, even to those readers who understood literally what was said. The literal aim had been to refer to the greater worth of the product; the symbolic means used were poor.

As consumers, we buy our way through a welter of symbols reflecting taste patterns, and the multitudes of human qualities we want to attach to ourselves. Just to refer to some of these symbolic poles brings images to our minds of "what that's like." The Ivy League cluster of symbols organizes purchases in one direction; being a suburbanite is a broad identification, but it starts one's purchasing ideas moving in certain lines. Name your own suburb, and they leap into rather sharp focus. Neighbors are quite acute judges of the symbolic significance of how money is spent; they are quick to interpret the appropriateness of your spending pattern for the community, the kind of people you are, making reasonable or unreasonable deductions from books, liquor, power mowers, cars, and the gifts your children give at birthday parties.

Some objects we buy symbolize such personal qualities as self-control, others expose our self-indulgence. We reason in these directions about people who drink and smoke or who don't—and such reasoning will play a role in our choices of doing one or the other. A hard mattress is readily justified on pragmatic grounds of health, sound sleep, and the like; but people recognize the austere self-denial at work that will also strengthen the character. Then again, soft drinks may quench thirst, but people know that they are also buying an indulgent moment, a bit of ease, a lowering of adult restraints.

---

[3] Susanne K. Langer, *Philosophy in a New Key* (New York: The New American Library of World Literature, Inc., 1942).

An outstanding dimension of symbolic guidance to consumers is that of conventionality versus self-expression. Some purchases are very conventional—a quart of milk, for instance. Others are conventional, but allow room for individuality—dishes, cups, silverware, let's say. Books become quite personal purchases, by and large. So, no one thinks much if you have milk on your table; (at least, they reason only generally about children)—it's different when you order a glass of milk at a businessmen's lunch. They also expect dishes, but may admire the taste demonstrated by the pattern. They will respect you personally for *Dr. Zhivago* on the coffee table, and perhaps raise an eyebrow at *Lolita*.

A whole treatise could be written on the symbolic dimension of formality-informality. A great many of our decisions to buy take into account the degree of formal or informal implication of the object. Housewives are constantly gauging the place of hot dogs, the gifts they are giving, the tablecloth they plan to use, with an eye to how informal things are or they want them to be. The movement toward informality has been a fundamental one in recent years, governing the emphasis on casualness in clothes, backyard and buffet meals, staying at motels, and bright colors —with some current overtone of reaction to this and seeking of contrast again in the direction of more graciousness in living, a new interest in the elegance of a black car, a wish for homes with dining rooms, and greater individual privacy.

As this indicates, among all the symbols around us, bidding for our buying attention and energy, there are general trends that seem to fit the spirit of the time more aptly. Every so often there comes along a new symbol, one which makes a leap from the past into the present and has power because it captures the spirit of the present and makes other ongoing symbols old-fashioned. The Pepsi-Cola girl was a symbol of this sort. She had precursors, of course, but she distinctly and prominently signified a modern phantasy and established an advertising style, one somewhat removed from the Clabber girl.

I have touched on only a few of the varieties of symbols encountered in the identification of goods in the marketplace, especially as these become part of the individual identities of consumers. The topic is as ramified as our daily lives and behaviors, and everyone handles symbols of these sorts with relatively little strain. Nevertheless, the interactions that go on around the symbols by which we buy are likely to involve the difficulties of all communications, and warrant study. Talking about symbols often involves discussion of much that is obvious or easily apparent —and most of us think we say what we mean. But much marketing and advertising thinking goes on with little actual regard given to the kinds of symbolic meanings that are so intrinsic to consumer viewpoints. Greater attention to these modes of thought will give marketing management and research increased vitality, adding to their own practical and symbolic merits.

10

THE INFLUENCE of NEEDS and ATTITUDES on the PERCEPTION of PERSUASION

JAMES F. ENGEL

My purpose is to review and interpret the literature of psychology and communications pertaining to what is loosely called "selective perception." The topic has been defined to encompass the evidence on the manner in which an individual's needs and attitudes affect his reactions to persuasive communication.

This paper will discuss the nature of selective perception, a summary of the findings of a literature survey, a discussion of the implications of these findings, and a statement of directions for future research.

THE NATURE OF PERCEPTION

An unequivocal definition of perception is sidestepped by most authorities. Generally, the concept refers to the process by which a stimulus and a response are related. The nature of this assumed relationship can best be grasped by a diagram.

An individual is exposed to a stimulus of some sort which he receives through his five senses to taste, touch, smell, sight, and hearing. Something happens in his unseen mental mechanisms, or "black box," to give meaning to these inputs, and this reaction is translated into an output— either overt behavior or some other response. To explain this process an inference is necessary to what happened within the black box, and the literature of psychology abounds with theories of this type.

Reprinted from Stephen A. Greyser (ed.), *Toward Scientific Marketing* (Chicago: American Marketing Association, 1964), pp. 18-29.

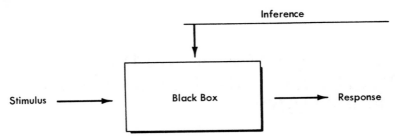

Much of contemporary perception theory is built on the assumption that each stimulus or information input is somehow checked against stored categories of meaning. Many of these categories function quite predictably from individual to individual. For example, a yellow pencil is usually perceived as a yellow pencil because of its distance and angle from the perceiver, its relationship to its surroundings, and common individual experience with pencils among other reasons. Other times, however, the response is unpredictable and appears to depend upon unique individual predispositions such as physical needs, psychological needs, and attitudes. In the latter instance the person is said to perceive selectively.

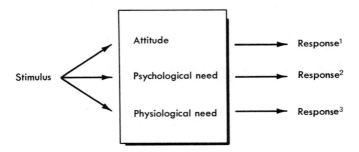

Each of these factors (attitude, psychological need, or physiological need) can become dominant and affect the response, and it is also probable that they somehow work in combination. It will become apparent, however, that little is known about how and why they work in this manner, and this is an important limitation to be elaborated upon later.

SUMMARY OF EVIDENCE

Let us now proceed to a summary of the findings of the review of literature. The discussion will be organized under the three headings used above: (1) physiological influence; (2) psychological influence; and (3) attitudes.

Physiological Influence

The typical experiment designed to isolate the influence of physiological or bodily needs on perception usually encompasses experimental manipulation of need. A typical experimental design may include deprivation of a subject for a period of time followed by momentary exposure to some kind of ambiguous stimuli which will permit responses consistent with a state of need. In one important study, for instance, Atkinson and McClelland deprived a group of subjects of food for varying periods of time up to 24 hours.[1] Some subjects were led to believe they viewed the projection of slides on a screen, but nothing appeared. Even in the absence of real stimuli, subjects replied that they saw food objects, and this tendency increased reliably as hours of food deprivation increased.

Numerous other experimenters have found similar results, leading Jenkin to conclude that properly designed stimulus objects will induce selective perception in keeping with a state of bodily need.[2]

Psychological Influence

Literally hundreds of experimental reports in the literature affirm that psychological needs and personal values can affect perception. For example, Bruner and Goodman determined in their now classic 1947 study that children from low socio-economic backgrounds tend to overestimate the size of coins when adjusting a patch of light to correspond with various types.[3] Similar tendencies were not exhibited by wealthy children. Supposedly, then, the variable of social class mirrors a need for money which is reflected in perceptual reactions. Other experimenters have found conflicting results, but most authorities feel that the evidence favors the interpretation that value and need, working through perceptual mechanisms, are determinants of size judgments.

Another important series of experiments has been undertaken to

[1] D. C. McClelland and J. W. Atkinson, "The Projective Expression of Needs: 1. The Effect of Different Intensities of the Hunger Drive on Perception," *Journal of Psychology,* 25 (1949), pp. 205-22.

[2] Noel Jenkin, "Affective Processes in Perception," *Psychological Bulletin,* 54 (1957), pp. 100-127.

[3] J. S. Bruner and Cecile C. Goodman, "Value and Need as Organizing Factors in Perception," *Journal of Abnormal and Social Psychology,* 42 (1947), pp. 33-44.

assess the role of personal values on thresholds for value-related words. The common hypothesis seems to be that individuals are sensitive to words reflecting values which are important to them, and hence the perceptual threshold or reaction time will be lower for these words. Early studies verified this hypothesis but neglected to control for the possibility that individuals will be more familiar with value-related words and should be expected to react quickly for this reason alone. Later studies have determined that value appears to influence reactions only on words which are infrequent in usage. Perhaps it is acceptable to conclude that the selective influence of values on perception appears to have been demonstrated, but ambiguities of evidence still remain due to methodological difficulties.

Other published studies indicate that there appears to be little doubt that psychological influences in perception are pervasive. The value and size judgment experiments are mentioned here primarily to point up a problem in interpreting the psychological literature. Note that word familiarity, if uncontrolled, will itself dictate findings consistent with the hypothesis in the value studies. Therefore, artifacts of the research design can be responsible for results, and the variables under analysis are obscured. The history of psychological experimentation shows a tortuous process in arriving at generalizations which withstand methodological criticism. Perhaps the best conclusion to draw is the fallacy of accepting any study at face value without awareness of its predecessors and its followers. This precaution has sometimes been violated by those who would have us believe that the behavioral sciences are some sort of salvation for marketing theory and practice. All too frequently, this is far from being true.

Before leaving this series of studies, let us raise the question as to whether or not individuals can unconsciously screen stimuli and distort their response. The evidence on this issue is complicated, and a controversy was generated by the finding that GSR (skin response) shows elevation upon exposure to unacceptable stimuli such as swear words. The presumption is that GSR reflects unconscious reaction.

Critics have since claimed that the common definition of threshold (the division point between perception and non-perception) which relies on current reactions 50 per cent of the time does not rule out conscious perception below the threshold. It is claimed that some information is gathered from the stimulus even though an incorrect verbal response is given, and there is supporting evidence for this point of view. Once again methodological difficulties have introduced uncertainty, so the most that can be claimed is that unconscious perceptual screening has neither been proved nor disproved convincingly. Perhaps it is sufficient to state that advertisers have enough problems without worrying about unconscious perceptual activity until more convincing evidence is available.

The Influence of Attitudes

No specific attention has thus far been directed toward studies documenting the role of motivational influences on reactions to persuasion. The primary reason is that experiments conducted for this purpose largely focus on attitudes.

It appears on the basis of an extensive volume of evidence that three generalizations are warranted. All other things being equal:

1. Persuasion which contradicts or otherwise is inconsistent with the predispositions of those for whom it is intended is likely to provoke a reaction of selective exposure whereby non-acceptable messages are avoided.

2. Once exposed to the message, the individual may perceive and interpret it in a manner consistent with his predispositions toward that topic, and appeals which deviate substantially from these predispositions are likely to be distorted or otherwise interpreted in a manner not intended.

3. Recipients of persuasive communication messages will tend selectively to recall appeals in a manner consistent with existing predispositions toward the topic. Unacceptable appeals are likely to be forgotten.

The data relative to these generalizations are extensive, and they warrant careful study by all involved in advertising or selling. It does appear, as Bauer points out, that a communication tends to trigger a response representing substantially what the individual was likely to do in any event.[4]

IMPLICATIONS OF FINDINGS

A full appreciation of the implications of the evidence on motivational influences in perception, of course, requires a more extensive appreciation of methodological problems and the chain of evidence which has been generated over time on each topic. By necessity, these points have been referred to here only briefly.

In general, it seems safe to state that motivational factors such as needs, values, and attitudes can and do influence perception. Probably

[4] Raymond A. Bauer, "The Communicator and the Audience," *Journal of Conflict Resolution,* 2 (1958), pp. 67-77.

it goes without saying that this evidence should put to an end all beliefs that consumers can be appealed to in any manner without knowledge of their psychological makeup. A market can be segmented along any of these variables, so a real service has been performed by the psychologist in isolating factors which *can induce* selective reactions to persuasion.

Do we now know enough, however, to state clearly what is likely to happen when, say, a consumer is exposed to an advertisement? Can we predict his reaction and thereby provide a firm basis for decision making? The answer unfortunately must be "no" at this time. Perhaps one could state that it may be rewarding to attempt to assess reactions to promotional appeals when subjects are experimentally placed under states of need deprivation, for example, or when distinct attitudinal differences exist. Laboratory experimentation along these lines may give an insight into the manner in which motivational states direct responses to an appeal, but such efforts can only be tentative and perhaps speculative. Prediction of response, our ultimate objective, still remains for the future.

It is important that we see the reasons for this somewhat negative conclusion. In exposing our consumer to the advertisement, what is the stimulus? Is it the product feature, the use of color, or what? Then, what is his response? He might purchase the product, show an elevated skin response, react with a look of boredom, or perhaps give no visible response. The point is that the stimulus used and the resulting response must be specified with great precision, and this strikes at the heart of many methodological criticisms appearing in the psychological literature such as those referred to earlier. The evidence by and large must remain tentative for predictive purposes until greater precision is attained in research methodology. Broadbent puts it this way:

The classical type of perception experiment is eminently suitable for fields in which all subjects behave similarly, in which the subjects possess an accurate vocabulary for describing their experience and in which a fairly brief experience is followed by an interval in which it may be described. But these are severe limitations, particularly the last: the closer we come to the problems of everyday life, the harder it is to stay within them.[5]

Perhaps even more important is the question of why his response or lack of response occurred. No unifying theory of perceptual processes has yet emerged. Perception has been conceived as covering a practically limitless list of variables such as needs, wishes, and rationalizations. We appear to have gone too far and have included nearly everything under this concept, thereby obscuring the mechanisms involved. In other words, it is necessary to attempt to uncover more specifically *what the individual*

---

[5] D. E. Broadbent, *Perception and Communication* (New York: Pergamon Press, 1958), pp. 7-8.

does with information received from the environment before the evidence will attain much predictive usefulness. New insights may then be derived into the relationship between inputs and outputs.

To sum up, a large and valuable step has thus far been taken—the isolation of key motivational influences in perception. Hurdles yet remain, however, before these findings attain real practical significance.

DIRECTIONS FOR FUTURE RESEARCH

A revolution is now underway in thinking and experimentation on perception, and there are two key incidents to report: (1) experimentation on higher mental processes and (2) dissonance theory.

Experimentation on Higher Mental Processes

Broadbent and others are exploring some exciting new frontiers. Primary attention is being directed to the mechanisms which seem to influence perception. Broadbent in particular departs somewhat from stimulus-response methods and considers the translation of perceptual input into output in view of a whole group of possible stimuli.[6] He clearly distinguishes between the arrival of this information to one's senses and the uses made of the information by the individual. Starting with the assumption that perception is a neural rather than a sensory process, he has postulated the existence of limits on capacity and has isolated important principles which seem to explain why some information is accepted and other information is discarded. Evidence thus far appears to support the existence of a filtering mechanism between the sensory receptors and central mental mechanisms as well as immediate and long-term memory centers, both of which perform very different functions.

Chomsky and others at MIT are pursuing a much broader line of inquiry. They are attempting to develop a theory of the mind which will explain perceptual behavior and other mental processes such as learning. Computer simulation models are being utilized as analogies with little or no reliance on stimulus-response models.

Inquiries of this type are tentative at the moment, but the writer is optimistic that a meaningful theory of perception is not far in the future. This work bears close watching by marketing men, because it may contain some of the missing keys to successful prediction of promotional response.

[6] *Ibid.*

Dissonance Theory

A second promising development, the theory of cognitive dissonance, seems to offer some rich insights into the role of attitudes in reactions to persuasion. Cognitive dissonance refers to a state of anxiety arising from non-fitting cognitions (that is, knowledges, opinions or beliefs) regarding some topic or event. The heavy smoker may very well experience dissonance when he hears claims that smoking may cause cancer. Attempts will no doubt be made to remove this conflict by stopping smoking, by seeking out new evidence to downgrade the claimed relationship between smoking and cancer, or by avoiding exposure to new information causing dissonance.

The evidence on cognitive dissonance to date is tentative, largely because three criteria must be met before dissonance can be demonstrated: (1) the individual must be committed to a point of view; (2) the undertaking of dissonance-causing action must be done as a result of free will (volition), because to offer a reward, for example, may induce behavior to receive the reward without any voluntary commitment to dissonance-causing action; and (3) the issue or behavior must be of some importance to the individual or dissonance will not arise. Nonetheless, the implications of dissonance are worth exploring, because a potentially useful basis is provided upon which to explore the perception of persuasive messages.

Reconstruction of Selective Processes

Hovland has pointed out that attitude change can be produced in the laboratory when subjects have no particular point of view on a topic and when issues often assume little importance.[7] Yet he notes that studies conducted in the field usually involve deep-seated issues such as racial prejudice and political preferences. When this is true, selective exposure, perception, and retention usually result. Notice that the three criteria of dissonance studies appear to be met: (1) commitment to a point of view; (2) opportunity for exposure to contradictory information under volition; and (3) issue importance. The upshot seems to be that individuals can avoid dissonance caused by contradictory information through selective exposure, selective perception, and selective retention.

It thus appears even more definite that the possibility of selective exposure, perception, and retention of promotional messages cannot be dismissed, especially if the target of these efforts is committed to another

---

[7] C. I. Hovland, "Reconciling Conflicting Results Derived from Experimental and Survey Studies of Attitude Change," *American Psychologist*, 14 (1959), pp. 8-17.

product through brand loyalty. If this commitment is present, it seems reasonable to expect that a kind of defense mechanism will be activated through dissonance processes to screen out unwanted promotion and to screen in messages which reinforce preferences.

The difficulty of creating dissonance through advertising also raises the question of the relative efficacy of voluntary versus involuntary exposure. Can involuntary exposure, for example, through television advertisements, arouse dissonance and possibly motivate the viewer to undertake purchasing action? The answer can be yes under most circumstances *only* if the viewer watches the advertisements and voluntarily considers contradictory information, but it is doubtful that true volition accompanies the viewing of many commercials. No doubt selective exposure would occur if the individual had the means readily available. The fallacy of assuming that advertising exposure infers favorable advertising results becomes abundantly obvious. Dissonance theory may thus present a useful perspective to discover the psychological nature of voluntary and involuntary exposure.

The discussion thus far assumes the existence of brand preferences. Evidence seems to indicate that consumers regularly develop smoothly working routines for purposes of buying efficiency and embrace certain brands for this purpose. Continued satisfied use of a product or of several brands which offer comparable satisfactions only reinforces this loyalty and renders the consumer a progressively less accessible promotional target. Furthermore, this situation is likely to become accentuated as the consumer is faced with more new products and more competing advertising messages. A point is simply reached where continued exposure can become overwhelming. This prediction does not paint a pretty picture for the advertiser of tomorrow, but it may be a fatal mistake to assume otherwise.

Seeking Consonant Information

A series of studies in the dissonance literature tentatively supports the hypothesis that a person experiencing dissonance will seek out information to restore a neutral state. It no doubt is fairly common to expect that advertising functions at times to reach dissonant consumers. Perhaps the consumer has experienced negative results with a product or service and finds his commitment badly shaken. Such a situation presents an ideal promotional opportunity; the full informational and persuasive powers of advertising would be exerted. The problem, of course, is that such an opportunity represents only individual incidents that are almost impossible to isolate and capitalize upon in a mass market.

Also notice the possible role of advertising to confirm brand loyalty in existing consumers. The writer has explored the implications of advertising to new owners of automobiles, as have others. While the evidence is contradictory, it may be that new purchasers of many products look to advertisements for reassurance following purchase. Additional investigation into this topic is clearly warranted.

The Role of "Forcing Methods"

Let us turn to quite a different aspect of dissonance theory. Several studies demonstrate the possibility that attitude change can follow commitment to dissonant behavior under conditions of volition. The implications of this finding are intriguing. Quite an assortment of promotional gimmicks is available, such as price offers and premiums, to induce a consumer to try a given product or service. Often such direct action or forcing methods are used on the assumption that trial of a product may weaken or destroy preference for a competing brand. It is more probable, however, that nothing will result, because the consumer was not induced to try the product under true volition. As several studies have demonstrated, she may reason that the offer is too great to pass up for one purchase while existing preferences remain unshaken. Additional research is needed to verify or refute this hypothesis.

Summary

The role of brand loyalty seems to be a central one in the selective perception of advertising. It is recommended that advertisers seriously consider continuing analysis of the strength of brand preferences both of existing consumers and of those buying competing products. Attitude scaling devices and other methodology is available for this purpose. A good indication should thus be provided of the chances of holding one's present market and of making inroads into a competitor's market share. If existing consumers are found to lack commitment to the product, in all probability they are vulnerable to competitive efforts. It is then essential to analyze all phases of the marketing mix with an eye toward remedial efforts.

Additional evidence obviously is required if these suggestions are to have much practical significance. First, it must be determined whether or not brand loyalty represents psychological commitment or merely is an habitual response generated by inertia. Also, it is not known if dissonance resistance arising from commitment can vary from product to product, although one would expect the commitment to a convenience good to be less psychologically secure than to a major purchase item. Furthermore, dissonance has not been examined over time. What will happen, for example, under the cross-fire of competitive advertising over a period of months? Finally, selective exposure, perception, and retention may represent boredom with advertising and not dissonance. These possibilities might be investigated profitably by directing research toward those who were not exposed or who did not react favorably to promotion.

CONCLUSIONS

A full appreciation of this complex subject necessitates a thoughtful analysis of the evidence in my forthcoming longer report. Nevertheless, it should be apparent that a number of key variables which can influence reactions to persuasion have been documented in the psychological literature. No doubt there will always be skeptics saying that most of these variables have been known for years to marketing practitioners and that explorations in the behavioral sciences should be abandoned in favor of the "mainstream of marketing" as it has long been known. There, of course, is one fundamental truth in such a statement: it is totally unwarranted to deny that a valid body of knowledge called marketing exists and to propose that existing literature be abandoned, as some have done recently. On the other hand, long embraced notions must be subjected to experimentation and analysis to assess their validity if progress is to be made. *To the extent that the psychologist has clarified experimentally the variables underlying promotional response, existing marketing knowledge has been expanded and enriched.*

Again it must be stated that for various reasons little predictive use can *now* be made of the findings on perception of promotional messages. I am optimistic that inquiry into higher mental processes ultimately will yield a general theory relating many of the variables discussed in this paper. For now, however, dissonance theory provides one useful meeting ground for psychologists and marketing men in that it represents a welcome step, albeit a small and tentative one, past the listing of variables stage. If nothing else, a heretofore non-existent perspective is provided upon which to base well-oriented research into the promotional task.

It should be clear that psychology has not provided definitive solutions to overcoming selective perception of persuasion, and much is yet to be learned. It is high time that we cease making sweeping and unsupported statements about the great untapped reservoir of knowledge in the behavioral sciences, because such claims usually dissolve upon careful analysis. Critical and knowledgeable analysis of the psychological literature will continue to be rewarding, but improvement in methods and theory is not the psychologist's task alone. As useful developments are reported, it is our role to interpret and apply them whenever there is the smallest hint of managerial significance. With this effort a body of valid experimental evidence should result which moves beyond our present knowledge of perceptual processes. The net result cannot help but be a gain in the efficiency of promotional efforts.

11

COGNITIVE DISSONANCE and CONSUMER BEHAVIOR

JAMES U. McNEAL

Why do consumers often read advertisements of a product more *after* they have purchased the product? Why does preference for a product often increase *after* a product has been purchased? The answer to these questions may lie in a relatively new body of thought called *cognitive dissonance theory.*

Cognitive dissonance theory, developed mainly by Leon Festinger,[1] is a theory of human behavior and is concerned with such matters as attitude change, motivation, and perception. The essentials of cognitive dissonance theory are as follows:

1. A person perceiving inconsistent bits of information about himself or his environment will experience psychological tension, called cognitive dissonance.

2. Having experienced psychological tension, or dissonance, the individual will react in such a way as to remove or reduce the tension.

3. The amount of dissonance experienced by an individual from inconsistent cognitions is a function of the importance of the cognitions.

4. Cognitive dissonance (tension) can be reduced or eliminated by bringing harmony to the dissonant information, reducing the importance of the cognitions, or by some behavior that removes the dissonant information.

[1] Leon Festinger, *A Theory of Cognitive Dissonance,* Evanston, Illinois: Row, Peterson, 1957.

Festinger sums it up in this manner:[2]

This theory centers around the idea that if a person knows various things that are not psychologically consistent with one another, he will, in a variety of ways, try to make them more consistent.

A person can change his opinion; he can change his behavior, thereby changing the information he has about it; he can even distort his perception and his information about the world around him.

Consider an example. Suppose an individual, while attending a movie, decides that he would like some popcorn and a coke. Unfortunately, he does not have enough money to buy both. He evaluates the alternatives and decides on the popcorn. Having purchased the popcorn and returned to the movie, he begins to think of the thirst-satisfying qualities of the coke. Cognitive dissonance arises. He knows he bought the popcorn but he is also aware of the thirst-quenching qualities he could have had by buying a coke. His unrest even distracts him from the movie. What can he do to remove this unrest? He may bring harmony into his thinking by telling himself, for example, that cokes are bad for his teeth. In other words, he can rationalize away the dissonance. Or he might simply go to the water fountain when he becomes thirsty and thus reduce the importance that the coke had for him. In either case, cognitive consistency results and the tension state is removed or reduced.

An important point here is that the cognitive dissonant state was a motivating force. For example, it caused the individual to leave the movie momentarily to get a drink of water. Standard theories of motivation would have explained this action by saying that the thirst motive was operative or that the person was driven by thirst.

To understand cognitive dissonance as a motivating state, it is necessary to have a clearer conception of the conditions that produce it. The simplest definition of dissonance can, perhaps, be given in terms of a person's expectations. In the course of our lives we have all accumulated a large number of expectations about what things go together and what things do not. When such an expectation is not fulfilled, dissonance occurs.[3]

One point becomes clear about cognitive dissonance theory. Man prefers cognitive consistency—a sort of psychological homeostasis—and will take actions to maintain it.

[2] Leon Festinger, "Cognitive Dissonance," *Scientific American*, 207 (October, 1962), p. 93.

[3] *Ibid.*, p. 94.

Now, let us consider an actual example. Ehrlich and others[4] undertook an experiment to test the predictive value of cognitive dissonance. They surmised:

> The purchase of a new automobile, for example, is usually a rather important decision for a person. Considerable dissonance should exist for a new car owner immediately after he has bought his car; all "good" features of the make he considered, but did not buy, and "bad" features of the one he bought are now dissonant with his ownership of the car. He should attempt to reduce the dissonance. In this instance of post-decision dissonance, sources of information in support of the decision are readily available. Since automobile advertising contains material favoring the particular car advertised, reading advertisements of his own make is one way a new car owner can get information supporting his choice and thereby reduce his dissonance.[5]

The investigators thus hypothesized that "new car owners will read advertisements of their own car more often than those of (a) cars which they considered but did not buy, and (b) other cars not involved in the choice."[6]

An experimental survey of new car owners and old car owners examined ad readership habits, and this hypothesis was confirmed: "It was found that new car owners read advertisements of their own car more often than those of cars they considered but did not buy and other cars not involved in the choice."[7]

It is apparent that these new car owners were seeking reassurance regarding their rather expensive purchases. In effect they were looking for ads that said, "You made the right buy." This particular research effort also indicated that the degree of attention devoted to ads of new cars was not common among all car owners. The rate was high for new car owners; low for owners of older cars.

Even though one piece of research such as this cannot be conclusive, it certainly has implications for advertisers of autos and, perhaps, of many other products. That is, that advertisers should design some of their ads for recent buyers as well as potential buyers. Brown observed that this, in fact, is often done.[8] He noted, for example, that "90 percent of the people who recently purchased a Ford read Ford advertisements."[9] Consequently, some of Ford's advertising is aimed at Ford owners.

4 Danuta Ehrlich, Isaiah Guttman, Peter Schönbach, and Judson Mills, "Post Decision Exposure to Relevant Information," *Journal of Abnormal and Social Psychology*, 54 (January, 1957), pp. 98-102.

5 *Ibid.*, pp. 98-99.

6 *Ibid.*, p. 99.

7 *Ibid.*, p. 102.

8 As quoted in James F. Engel, "Are Automobile Purchases Dissonant Consumers," *Journal of Marketing*, 27 (April, 1963), pp. 55-58. (As noted by the title, this particular paper questions if cognitive dissonance is the reason for post-purchase ad readership.)

9 *Ibid.*, p. 56.

There are other questions regarding cognitive dissonance among consumers. How widespread is it? How frequently does it occur?

It is an observable fact that within many product categories there is an array of products where each product is only slightly different from the others. If it is not possible to buy one multi-purpose product for all suggested uses, then some dissonance may occur. For example, among detergents there are those that whiten, brighten, remove stains and "ring around the collar," and those that are gentle, provide bacterial defense, and add pleasant aromas. If a housewife buys only one or two brands she suspects she is not getting the benefit offered by some of the other brands. Whether or not such a small purchase is important enough to cause cognitive dissonance is questionable. But price is not necessarily what makes a purchase decision important. So, indeed, a purchase of detergent may result in cognitive dissonance.

The concept of private branding may produce dissonance. A housewife discovered that a supermarket's private brand of mouthwash was the same as a leading national brand. The private brand cost 30 percent less. Thinking that the national brand was preferred by her family, she continued to buy it even though she knew it was uneconomical. These two cognitions produced dissonance. That is, on the one hand, she thought her family wanted to buy the well-known brand. On the other hand, she knew she was expected to be economical in her shopping. The dissonance was reduced after a discussion with her husband and with a neighboring housewife. Both told her that the sensible thing to do was to buy the private brand. These additional bits of information reduced the dissonance.

Another interesting question regarding post-purchase cognitive dissonance is, "Can advertising *create* as well as remove dissonance?" This appears not only to be possible but probable. For instance, consider an advertisement for a deodorant bath soap. In effect, the message says that people who are not using this deodorant bath soap are offending those with whom they socialize. The impact on a nonuser of this deodorant soap may be cognitive dissonance. There are two pieces of information here that are inconsistent. One, the nonuser knows that he uses a soap that does not contain a deodorant, and that he thus may be offending associates. He also knows that if he uses a deodorant soap he would not offend friends. Today, smelling good is important. To remove the dissonance the logical thing to do is to buy the deodorant soap. At least, the advertiser hopes that this will be the result. However, the nonuser might remove this dissonance by simply realizing that, although he does not use a deodorant soap, he does use a deodorant. Thus, he brings harmony to a dissonant situation.

Salesmanship, like advertising, may also create cognitive dissonance. For example, a salesman may tell a potential customer, "You mean that

you do not use a widget? Mrs. Jones has used one for years!" Immediately, this customer learns two inconsistent pieces of information. One,
she does not use a widget. Two, Mrs. Jones, who is highly esteemed, does.
Result—cognitive dissonance. To remove it, the customer can purchase
the widget, or, perhaps, rationalize her way out of the situation.

SUMMARY

Cognitive dissonance theory appears to be a commonsense way of explaining some consumer behavior. It relies on the apparent fact that people
desire cognitive constancy. The theory also suggests some marketing
strategy. The validity of the theory and its implications for marketing
show promise, but much more study of both is needed.

12

PERSONALITY and PRODUCT USE

W. T. TUCKER and JOHN J. PAINTER

Perhaps no subject in marketing has received greater attention in the past few years than the relationship between personality and purchasing behavior. All of the furor over motivation research is clearly predicated on the premise that such a relationship exists, although some reporters seem to assume that all persons are, at base, alike. Yet even here, the factors referred to as common to all are most often those which personality studies have shown to be variables rather than constants. For instance, the importance of fear of the father image, which is reputed to militate against the use of banking services, must be conceived of as varying with some personality characteristic such as ego strength or emotional maturity if it is not to influence all persons in a highly similar way.

Talk about the importance of personality as a marketing variable has become common at advertising clubs and at marketing association meetings. The recent book by Pierre Martineau (1957) contains a chapter entitled "An Automobile for Every Personality." Charles Cannell (Ferber & Wales, 1958) says: "It may be that the determination of airplane travel has something to do with basic personality characteristics such as personal feelings of security or insecurity" (p. 10). And Ernest Dichter (Ferber & Wales) says confidently: "What we are searching for are psychological and personality elements which may have a dynamic effect on consumers' attitudes toward a product" (p. 26). Newman (1957) views personality as one of the major factors determining marketing behavior.

In the light of such points of view it may seem surprising that few efforts have been made to demonstrate that personality characteristics actually do influence product use. But the dearth of evidence on this

Reprinted from *Journal of Applied Psychology*, Volume 45 (October, 1961), pp. 325-329.

point can be explained in part by supposition. First, the concept of personality itself has not been very clearly formulated. Second, the instruments available for the ready classification of personality types are few and generally suspect. Third, most self-respecting psychologists are apparently convinced that marketing behavior, pervasive as it may be, is of interest for commercial purposes only. Fourth, marketers probably have little understanding of the need for experimental evidence of their assumptions.

Yet it would seem that there is much to be learned about both personality and a large segment of human behavior by such studies. Scott's (1957) study of motion picture preferences is perhaps of less interest to the movie producer than it is to the individual who wants a clearer understanding of the personality factors isolated by the Minnesota Multiphasic Index. That these factors are less than completely clear is indicated by Scott's inability to provide a rationale for all of the significant correlations. And Eysenck's (Eysenck, Tarrant, Woolf, & England, 1960) recent findings that rigidity and extraversion relate to the number of cigarets smoked by an individual may be as important to the understanding of those characteristics as they are as a possible explanation of lung cancer in heavy smokers.

The present study was undertaken to test the hypothesis that marketing behavior is related to personality traits. At the same time, it was expected that the location of significant relationships would throw additional light on the meaning of personality characteristics studied.

METHOD

The Gordon Personal Profile was administered to 133 students of marketing along with a so-called Sales and Marketing Personality Index which included questions on the use of headache remedies, cigarets, chewing gum, deodorants, mouthwash, and other items commonly purchased by college students. Blind questions were interspersed to give the index the appearance of a personality or interest test. Results were then compared to determine the difference in personality trait scores for groups that professed to different rates of product use or interest. That the subjects accepted the index was indicated by the large number of students who asked after completing the forms if they could find out whether they would make good salesmen, advertisers, etc.

Subjects

The subjects were all students of the first course in marketing at the University of Texas. The great majority were juniors; a few were in the last semester of their sophomore year, and others were in the beginning of their senior year. Since the Gordon Personal Profile has different norms for male and female students, and, since the frequency of use of a number of products was clearly related to sex, the 31 responses by females are not included in this report. Also, one subject was eliminated because he failed to fill out the Gordon Personal Profile completely. While this group of subjects can hardly be characterized as representative of even such a limited universe as college juniors, for purposes of this study their only necessary characteristic was that of providing a diverse group of scores on the Gordon Personal Profile and reasonable diversity in response to questions about products.

Test Materials

The Gordon Personal Profile was selected as the personality test to use since it measures four characteristics which seem intuitively meaningful as components of the "normal" personality and since it is based on college student norms. The profile rates persons on the variables of ascendency, responsibility, emotional stability, and sociability.

The form used to determine use of products or other marketing characteristics included nine questions relevant to the experiments and seven blind questions. Most of the experimental questions referred to frequency of use of a particular product, as in the following:

How frequently do you experience a headache that requires a headache remedy (aspirin, Bufferin, Anacin, etc.)?

a. Never
b. Once or twice a year
c. About once a month
d. More often than once a month, but less than once a week
e. Once a week or more

Questions of this sort were asked about the use of headache remedies, vitamins, chewing gum, tobacco, mouthwash, alcoholic beverages, and deodorants. Two other questions related to the readiness with which the individual accepted new styles or fashions and preference in automobiles.

Blind questions were rather similar to those asked on interest tests:

Which of the following positions in an organization would you prefer to hold?

a. Secretary–Treasurer
b. Program chairman

c. President

d. Membership chairman

e. Ordinary member, no office

The list of 16 questions was pretested in order to insure their clearness and to make sure that multiple choice answers would elicit a reasonable spread of response. As a result of this pretesting, multiple choice answers were altered to fit the normal variations in frequency of use of various products. For instance, the most frequent use of headache remedies indicated by answers was "once a week or more," while the most frequent use of deodorants was described as "more than once a day," since the pretest demonstrated these to be common frequencies for heavy users.

Procedure

Subjects filled out both forms at a single sitting of about 20 minutes, answering the Gordon Personal Profile first and the Sales and Marketing Personality Index second. While subjects were asked to fill in their sex, age, marital status, and year in school on the Gordon Personal Profile, names were not taken in order to encourage the greatest frankness in response. Each pair of tests handed out was numbered in advance.

Instructions to Subjects

Students in each class tested were given the following instructions:

As you all know, one of the difficult problems in business is the determination of an individual's interests, or what kind of job he can do best. Attempts to solve such problems have led to the development of a number of written tests—some of which take an hour or more to complete. You have in front of you two rather new tests that try to accomplish this for certain marketing jobs in just a few minutes. We know that one of these is moderately successful. We are interested in whether scores on the other are different or much the same. Do these tests really measure the same things?

To determine this, we need your help. We are not interested in your score as an individual but in the relationship of your score on one test with your score on the other.

For that reason, we do not want your name on the paper; we merely want you to answer the questions honestly and conscientiously. Instructions for each test appear at the top of the test.

First, make sure the red number on each of your tests is the same. Then fill in your age, sex, marital status, and year in school on Test #1, the Gordon Personal Profile. Then read the instructions on that test and answer the questions. When you are finished, go directly to the second test, read the instructions, then answer the questions.

You will find that on both tests there are some questions where none of the answers seem just right for you. Just pick the one that seems closest and do not worry about exact wording. Remember to read the test instructions carefully, since you have to answer each test in a somewhat different way.

Analytic Method

Results were analyzed by comparing the difference in mean scores on one personality characteristic for groups with different product use patterns.

Table 1 shows the mean scores on responsibility for groups which answered the mouthwash question in each of the possible ways.

TABLE 1

MEAN RESPONSIBILITY SCORES FOR GROUPS WITH DIFFERENT
PATTERNS OF USE OF MOUTHWASH

Response	Mean Score	Number of Cases
Never use mouthwash	7.26	31
Quite infrequently	5.00	40
Once or twice a week	4.50	16
Once a day	3.90	10
More than once a day	6.50	4

While responsibility seems to be inversely related to frequency of use of mouthwash, despite relatively high scores for the four persons who use mouthwash more than once a day, the number of cases in some of the cells is too small for analysis of variance to show a significant relationship. For this reason, the last four groups were combined and compared using the *t* test with those who reported never using mouthwash. The resulting *t* of 2.12 is significant at the .05 level. The *F* test for homogeneity of variance was not significant.

This same method of analysis was used for each of the products on each of the personality characteristics, with the point for division into two groups being determined on the basis of scores and the number of subjects remaining in each of the groups.

It is entirely proper to question whether five-point scales of the sort used here should be dichotomized *after* observing the means of each of the categories. Such dichotomization obviously makes it possible to maximize the number of "significant" relationships. Where possible, it should therefore be avoided and some independent method should be used for dichotomization.

Since there is no apparent rationale for predicting relationships between personality characteristics and product use, it seems foolhardy to develop a purely arbitrary dichotomization method in the present case. Such a method could easily minimize relationships if it were only extremes of product use that related to personality measures and the cutting point closest to the median were arbitrarily used, for instance. It happens that dichotomizing the data shown in Table 1 by combining the top two categories and the bottom three does not lead to a significant *t*. The resulting quandary is more philosophical than statistical. It seems to the authors that refusing to locate the cutting point that leads to statistically significant differences is the more serious error when dealing with the kind of problem discussed here.

RESULTS AND DISCUSSION

A total of 36 comparisons (9 product categories × 4 personality characteristics) included 13 significant relationships. As might be expected, some products were associated with no personality trait; others were associated with one or more; and one product, vitamins, was associated with all four of the personality traits.

Table 2 shows those relationships indicating the significance level. In addition it shows correlation ratios in parentheses to indicate the approximate strength of the relationships.

The results clearly indicate that there is a relationship between product use and personality traits. This relationship apparently may include both frequency of use of a particular product and preference among different brands of a single product, since preference in automobiles is significantly related to scores on responsibility. At the same time, some products are used frequently or infrequently without relationship to any of the personality traits tested. Each personality trait seems to bear a relationship to the use of some products, each of the four traits scored by the Gordon Personal Profile relating to the use of at least two of the products considered in the present experiment.

TABLE 2

SIGNIFICANT PERSONALITY TRAITS IN THE USE OR PREFERENCE
FOR SOME CONSUMER PRODUCTS

	Ascendency	Responsi- bility	Emotional stability	Sociability
Headache remedies	—.05	—	—.05	—
	(.464) c		(.320) c	
Acceptance of new fashions	.01	—	—	.01
	(.331) c			(.566) c
Vitamins	—.05	—.01	—.01	—.05
	(.332) c	(.297) c	(.091) c	(.272) c
Cigarettes	—	—	—	—
Mouthwash	—	—.05	—	—
		(.224) c		
Alcoholic drinks	—	—.01	—	—
		(.362) c		
Deodorants	—	—	—	—
Automobiles[a]	—	.01	—	—
		(.281) c		
Chewing gum[b]	—	.05	.01	—
		(.295) c	(.331) c	

Note.—In all cases except for the last two products, the sign indicates the nature of the relationship. High ascendency is related to infrequent use of headache remedies, for instance, but with rapid acceptance of new fashions.

[a] Subjects who preferred the more popular makes of car such as Buick, Dodge, Mercury, Ford, Chevrolet, and Plymouth rated higher on the responsibility scale than those who stated a preference for such sports cars as the Corvette or Thunderbird.

[b] While there is no significant difference in personality trait scores and the amount of gum chewed, those who chew gum *only when offered it by someone else,* are significantly lower than others in responsibility and emotional stability.

[c] Correlations ratios.

It should be pointed out, however, that the relationships located between product use and personality are not particularly strong, certainly less strong than popular marketing concepts of the day suggest.

An obvious corollary to the conclusion that personality traits and product use are related is that the Gordon Personal Profile does isolate personality traits related to behavioral differences. Further, an examination of the pattern of significant relationships shown in Table 2 is persuasive that the four traits, ascendency, responsibility, emotional stability, and sociability have considerable independence. The manual for the test indicates that the intercorrelations are generally low except for those between ascendency and sociability (.43) and between emotional stability and responsibility (.46). Those correlations were considerably higher in the present experiment as shown in Table 3. The remaining

TABLE 3

INTERCORRELATIONS AMONG PERSONALITY TRAITS

Traits	Ascend-ency	Respon-sibility	Emotional stability
Responsibility	.058		
Emotional Stability	.035	.695	
Sociability	.708	.035	.086

correlations are quite low. It must be concluded that the Gordon Personal Profile does not measure four independent characteristics but two independent sets of related characteristics. However, it seems that one of a set of related characteristics can still prove to have enough relative independence to be conceptually valuable.

Most of the significant relationships between product use and character traits located are intuitively acceptable. One would expect that high ascendency and high sociability would be related to the rapid acceptance of new fashions, especially since ascendency is described largely as social leadership. On the other hand there seems to be no particular reason for expecting all personality characteristics to be associated with the frequency of use of vitamins, unless one conceives that personality traits are most likely to affect behavior that society neither rewards nor punishes.

The results cast some possible light on the nature of responsibility as a character trait. It is related to avoidance of vitamins and mouthwash, preference for popular cars and moderate drinking or abstinence. Since these are all modal characteristics of the group being tested, a reasonably strong case might be made for the fact that responsibility is closely related to the acceptance of group norms.

A comparison of the present results with those of Eysenck (1960) suggests that sociability on the Gordon Personal Profile is considerably different from extroversion, with which is might seem related. Eysenck's results showed a strong, significant correlation between extroversion and heavy cigarette smoking, while the present experiment did not even hint at such a relationship between sociability and heavy smoking. It is possible that the difference in age (Eysenck's subjects were considerably older) or difference in nationality (Eysenck's subjects were British) might explain this apparent contradiction.

SUMMARY

The answers to the Gordon Personal Profile and a disguised product use questionnaire by 101 college of business students demonstrate that personality traits are often related to product use. Thirteen of a possible 36 such relations were significant at the .05 level or above.

A corollary conclusion is that the Gordon Personal Profile distinguishes personality traits related to behavioral differences, although the four traits are not "independent."

REFERENCES

EYSENCK, H. J., TARRANT, MOLLIE, WOOLF, MYRA, & ENGLAND, L. Smoking and personality. *Brit. med. J.*, 1960, 5184, 1456-1460.

FERBER, R., & WALES, H. *Motivation and marketing behavior.* Homewood, Ill.: Irwin, 1958.

MARTINEAU, P. *Motivation in advertising.* New York: McGraw-Hill, 1957.

NEWMAN, J. W. *Motivation research and marketing management.* Boston: Harvard Univer. Press, 1957.

SCOTT, E. M. Personality and movie preference. *Psychol. Rep.*, 1957, 3, 17-18.

13

SEGMENTATION by PERSONALITY TYPES

MORRIS J. GOTTLIEB

Every practitioner of marketing research has at one time or another been approached by a sales or advertising executive with a problem stated in terms such as these—"Look," the executive will say, "it's really quite simple. All I want to do is to talk to the people who are buying my product and ask them why they buy it. Then, I want to get the people who are not buying it and ask them why they're *not* buying it."

Really, this is a very reasonable request. It has only three false premises:

1. That it's really quite simple. It practically never is.

2. That you can find out why by asking.

3. That it would necessarily be helpful to know why.

Nevertheless, the request generally stems from a genuine need to know and it is the market researcher's job to find out enough of why people do or do not buy one product rather than another or one brand rather than another to help management do a better marketing job.

One of the modest but important trends in modern marketing research has been to transform these "why" questions into "who" questions. The general idea is that if you know in sufficiently meaningful

Reprinted from Lynn H. Stockman (ed.), *Advancing Marketing Efficiency* (Chicago: American Marketing Association, 1959), pp. 148-158.

terms *who* is and *who* is not buying the product or who is and who is not a *potential* customer you really know why as well.

I'd really like to be able to say that I am going to expound the strategy of market segmentation by personality types, but it will be helpful to think of this segmentation as a research strategy rather than a marketing strategy. Hopefully, it will yield results which would suggest market segmentation strategies.

Rather than attempting to outline a general technique, I shall restrict myself to illustrating some cases where this concept seemed to be useful and discuss some of the limitations as well as the possibilities of this approach.

The first product is a proprietary medicine. It is an antacid and analgesic or pain killer which is sold mainly through drug stores and does not require a prescription. Let's call it Brominex. There are many directly competitive products in the proprietary field. However, the product class boundaries tend to become rather vague—extending from home remedies such as bicarbonate of soda or even water or orange juice on the one hand to analgesics such as aspirin on the other. In addition, many products in this category are prescribed by doctors.

For the purposes of this discussion, the product class was defined as proprietary products which are primarily combinations of antacids and analgesics. The bulk of this market is divided among seven or eight well-known products.

Our hope is that if we can find out how users of antacid-analgesics differ from non-users or how frequent users differ from infrequent users we can learn enough to help us locate the potential Brominex user and to reach him successfully.

At first thought it might seem a very simple matter to define the market for this type of product as simply the people who have upset stomachs and headaches. But it might be of use to know whether any particular type of person tends to have these symptoms. A little introspection will probably convince you of the difficulty of trying to pin down these symptoms. There is actually a considerable element of discretion in judging at what point you have an upset stomach or a headache bad enough to make you use an analgesic.

One person will choose to put up with any amount of pain or discomfort rather than take anything. Another will take something at the slightest suggestion of anything wrong, or as a preventive measure. Another will choose to see a doctor who may prescribe something else.

It is precisely in this kind of situation that the "who" question is interesting. By understanding the differences between users and non-users—or between frequent and infrequent users of a completely discretionary product we can understand more precisely what needs the product class is satisfying and hopefully how the marketing of our product can be effectively geared to this need.

Now, most of the trick in getting useful answers to the "who" question is to ask it the right way. The more thought given to outlining the various dimensions along which to compare users and non-users the more useful the answers will be.

It is generally stated that at this stage of an investigation depth interviewing is of the most use. However, the older I get, the more it is brought home to me that depth interviewing is at best a supplement to and not a substitute for deep thinking.

The only method is to learn the subject thoroughly, to observe carefully with an open mind, to listen to the experts in the field—whether there are any real experts or not. Past experience will suggest many possibilities. Finally, it helps to be insightful, incisive, and wise.

In the Brominex problem, we started by getting some medical counsel. Doctors told us that middle-aged men are the most frequent sufferers from this kind of condition.

One could further anticipate that frequent users of such products would be common among the lower income groups and with a lower educational level because of cultural and economic factors. In any event, one always tries segmenting the market by age, sex, and income whenever there is an adequate sample and in this case there was one.

This analysis showed that age and sex were dominant factors in use, and that use tends to be greater at the lower educational levels in each of the age and sex groups. However, since use is not *completely* universal in the higher usage groups nor completely absent in the lower usage groups, one feels that *other* factors must be operating as well.

It seems a fairly sound principle to examine any factors which reflect group or other cultural influences before turning to an examination of individual characteristics distinguishing users and non-users.

One might suspect that geographic factors would influence usage. However, while usage *is* higher in the South—among white as well as non-white—it turns out upon analysis that this is almost entirely a reflection of income and education. Similarly, greater usage among non-white in the North also reflects income and educational factors. In fact, since education is an important factor in use, one would expect any cultural factors—such as differing ethnic origin—to be cancelled out by education, and in fact this seems to be the case.

Now, one form of education that bears directly on use of this kind of product is based on contact with doctors. One would suspect that people who have more contact with doctors tend to use these products less, since doctors tend to focus on the cause of these symptoms and would be inclined to counsel changes in diet or some form of medical treatment, rather than on the use of proprietary products. However, this study showed that exposure to doctors had no effect on usage for two different reasons:

1. Since there was no accurate way of determining who had the symptoms more frequently, the two factors—existence of symptoms leading to increased usage, and exposure to doctors presumably leading to decreased usage—tended to be confounded and to cancel each other out.

2. Examination of some medical histories showed that doctors rarely discussed the use of this type of product with their patients, so that it would be quite possible that while the doctors might have counseled the patient against the use of such products had the subject come up, the subject rarely came up.

At this point it would seem natural to consider some of the social pressures that might be operating to influence usage of this type of product. However, the social class position information was found to add relatively little to education data.

Now, the use of this type of product is generally a pretty personal affair, so that one suspects that there is a great deal of room for individual personality variables to affect the use of antacid-analgesics.

Given one's cultural background and susceptibility to the relevant symptoms, one suspects that attitudes towards one's own health would affect the decision to use a proprietary medicine. It is significant that use tends to be higher among hypochondriacs—or at least among people who show a greater than average concern with their health. Thus, in the accompanying chart, people who expect a great deal of illness tend to use antacid-analgesics more frequently.

This chart is about men. Note that for every age group and for each educational level, usage is greater among people with a *poor* opinion of their health than among those with a good opinion of their health— with only one exception.

USAGE RELATED TO HEALTH ATTITUDES

| Age | Average annual dosage | | | | | |
| | 35 or under | | 36–50 | | Over 50 | |
Health attitude	Poor	Good	Poor	Good	Poor	Good
Low educational level	4.1	3.9	14.2	12.2	13.5	5.8
High educational level	3.2	3.4	15.7	10.8	11.5	4.9

The questions I'd like to answer here are:

1. How do you decide which attitude or temperament variables to examine?

2. Of what earthly use is the information?

Answer the first question by saying—deep thinking. But the fact is that while this finding of the relation between hypochondria and ant-acid-analgesic usage seems just what you'd expect after you see it, it was called to our attention rather dramatically by some depth interviews which were really intensive case histories. In some 20 case histories it was obvious that the more frequent users were all marked hypochondriacs and the non-users were people who were aggressive in their assertions that they enjoyed perfect health.

Back in the early days of marketing research—three or four years ago—there would have been many people in the marketing research business who would have been content to take the results of these 20 interviews and form conclusions. But enough of us feel the need for a sample large enough to permit an analysis of the relation between different factors.

The answer to the second question is that to be effective, the advertising message must take into account the health attitudes of the potential user. One would expect to communicate one way with a person who hated to admit that he was ill and was only seeking relief for a well localized symptom, and another way with a person who complained about various vague aches and pains and was possibly seeking to allay non-specific anxieties.

Another personality variable which appears to differentiate users of this product is what one might call "compulsiveness." This is measured by the extent of agreement or disagreement with such statements as:

I like to set up a schedule for my activities and then stick to it

I never seem to be able to throw things away

Most people don't keep themselves as clean as they should

I make decisions only after a great deal of thought

The following chart shows the effect of compulsiveness—as measured by agreement with the first of these statements on antacid-analgesic usage.

Usage Related to Compulsiveness

Age	Average annual dosage					
	35 or under		36–50		Over 50	
	Com-pulsive	Non com-pulsive	Com-pulsive	Non com-pulsive	Com-pulsive	Non com-pulsive
Low education	6.5	4.2	14.5	9.9	9.2	10.0
High education	3.5	2.8	13.9	12.9	8.2	4.5

The significance of this factor is illustrated by the fact that our client had been having considerable success with an advertising campaign based on a principal theme which was in itself ineffective. However, the advertising presented Brominex in the context of a routine or schedule or regimen. It seemed to be this element of imposed orderly routine which was appealing to the compulsive tendencies of the users of this product class. Incidentally, establishing this conjecture required a secondary analysis to show that compulsives were more attracted by the advertisement in question than non-compulsives.

Still another area which was relevant in the examination of this product class was the attitude toward discipline and punishment. Some people tend to be punitive or puritanical, others permissive. People who tend to be more self-punitive rather than hedonistic in their outlook might want a medicine that gives relief to taste bad in order to do them good. The analysis of this factor is interesting because it illustrates an ever present pitfall in considerations of this sort. Our first conclusion was that *punitiveness* is positively associated with usage. Here, punitiveness is measured by agreement with such statements as:

People learn a great deal from suffering

Discipline is the single most important factor in building children's character

However, it can be seen from the following chart that if one shows the appropriate regard for the basic variables of age and education, the opposite is the case. Within any age-education cell, punitive people use less than non-punitive ones. What misled us at the outset was the compound effect that:

1. Lower education groups tend to have more punitive attitudes

2. Lower education groups tend to use more antacid-analgesics

The fallacious conclusion that antacid-analgesic users tend to have more punitive attitudes was avoided by observing that *within* a given age-education stratum, usage is *negatively* rather than positively associated with punitiveness. In other words, it is *not* necessary or desirable that the product should taste bad.

USAGE RELATED TO PUNITIVENESS

Age	35 or under		Average annual dosage 36 to 50		Over 50	
	Punitive	Non-punitive	Punitive	Non-punitive	Punitive	Non-punitive
Low education	6.4	4.5	12.7	17.7	7.4	9.1
High education	3.1	3.9	13.6	15.5	4.7	5.1

Now let's try to make the transition from research strategy to marketing strategy. On the basis of these findings one would expect the most successful product in this class to be a lower class product which made extensive claims,[1] advertised regular use, and tasted good. Actually the *single* dominant product in the field was one used widely by the higher status groups, which advertised very specific use and made fewer broad claims than other products. It was a product which had higher approval by doctors and hospitals than most others. It didn't taste particularly good but was in the process of correcting this defect; it was not our client's product.

[1] It would have to cure many things to satisfy the hypochondriac.

The reason for the unexpected success of this leading product was simple. Instead of competing with other products for the most profitable segments of the antacid-analgesic market, that contrary product had captured the less prominent—but still highly significant minority segments—where it had no competitor.

Incidentally this was a pleasant by-product of the study. Our client had been developing a different type of analgesic beamed toward this segment. The study confirmed his hunch that there was room for a competitive product here.

So, answering the *why* question with a *who* question had these positive results:

1. It pointed to an important segment which offered potential for a new product which our client was developing to supplement his present major product.

2. It enabled him to direct the advertising for his present major product more effectively since he knew whom he was speaking to.

Now let's examine some of the limitations and difficulties of this approach of segmentation by personality types.

It is interesting that the difference in usage between the various personality groups is not very large. Thus, it is not as large as the difference between age or sex groups or between social class groups.

This phenomenon occurs rather frequently. One might think that it was a function of scales or tests to characterize these groups. It is true that where one is dealing with a scalable characteristic and where it is possible to pick out the extremes, the differences between these extremes are a little larger, but even then the differences are small.

It is probably not possible to address oneself to a clearly delineated compulsive group. *What one should do is to address himself to the compulsive in all of us.*

Social and personality variables operate in a kind of residual area left by the product considerations. The residual nature of these variables becomes even more pronounced for large ticket items where product or price considerations are more important.

For conspicuous consumption items, social class considerations are likely to outweigh personality factors. To illustrate this another product generally consumed in public has implications of social status. This is a liquor product somewhat like a liqueur or cordial but used more widely than products of that type are generally. Let's call it *Bayou Rum*.

Since this is a drink that would often be served in company, it is not surprising that it has a very definite social position. A broad cut at the subject by such variables as income and education shows that usage is greater *towards* but not *at* the upper end of the scale.

This impression is reinforced by our looking at the relation between

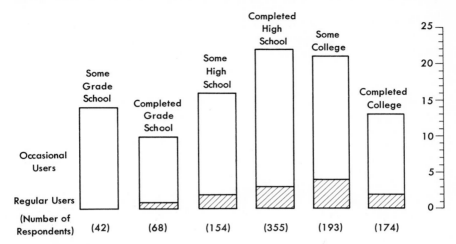

BAYOU RUM USAGE BY EDUCATION

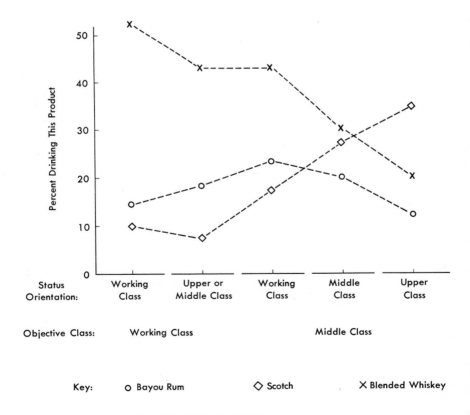

Key: o Bayou Rum   ◇ Scotch   X Blended Whiskey

BAYOU RUM USAGE BY SOCIAL CLASS
Segmentation by Personality Types

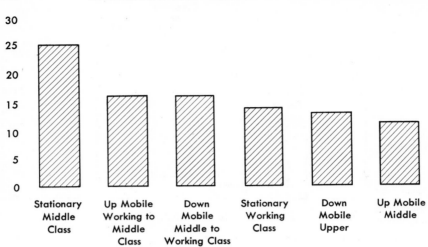

BAYOU RUM USAGE

objective social class as measured by occupation and status orientation as measured by the person's assignment of himself to a social class.

Here it is clear that our product is really a middle class drink.

The social position is spelled out even more clearly by relating usage to social mobility. Its use is by far the greatest among stable members of the middle class.

How does one know whether he should be looking at social characteristics, as personality or temperament traits? What traits are likely to be important? How deep should one go into motivations?

A passage from a recent very interesting book on Motivational Research by Harry Henry puts the matter interestingly. It says, "This sort of case-history makes fascinating reading, for a time. But sooner or later the profit-conscious businessman is bound to ask himself what guidance this gives him for the formulation of manufacturing, marketing, or advertising policies. And it is for this reason that . . . constructive and useful Motivation Research is concerned only with getting *sufficiently* below the surface to do the necessary job."

I don't think that anyone can disagree with this statement any more than anyone can use it for practical guidance. It is patently uneconomical to get more information or more depth than one needs. But I don't know of anyone who can be certain that he has enough information unless he has too much—at least in the sense of being able to select and reject, or who can be sure he's thought enough about something until he's thought too much.

Many of us in the marketing research profession pride ourselves on the desire to focus research on a specific marketing decision. True, this makes for efficient research. But I wonder if there isn't failure to understand all aspects of a problem. In fact, it is only when the researcher knows much more about a situation that he can profitably communicate an airtight case to management.

Finally, no matter how skillfully such an analysis has been conducted, the road to a marketing strategy is still tortuous. What starts out as a good idea based on sound research may lead to a poor strategy.

As we get more sophisticated in developing research which produces ideas leading to marketing strategies, we will have to start tackling seriously the tremendously difficult problem of testing these strategies—of measuring advertising and marketing success and relating it to the specific components of the strategies developed.

III

SOCIOLOGICAL ASPECTS OF CONSUMER BEHAVIOR

In spite of the individuality possessed by everyone, all persons are members of one or more groups. It is for this reason that some behavioral scientists state that all behavior is *social* in nature. What they mean is that no matter how isolated one seems to be, his behavior is still influenced by others. Even the youngster who sneaks away to his "secret hideout" cannot ignore the influence of his parents and, perhaps, other people.

As a group member, each person possesses some behavioral patterns that are similar to those of other members of the group. If he is a member of ten groups, and this would probably be a small number, then he will display some behavioral patterns that are like those of the members of each of the ten groups. Thus a man will behave somewhat like other people with whom he works, other members of his family, social class, ethnic group, and community. It is because of this fact that we often expect the consumer behavior patterns of members of a group to be alike. In such a case, we call the group a *market*.

The study of groups and the interaction of their members is essentially the task of sociology. Like the discipline of psychology, sociology consists of many sub-disciplines. Usually the sub-disciplines have developed to study the behavior of specific groups. For instance, the fields of urban, rural, and industrial sociology study the behavior of their respective groups. There is also a sub-discipline termed sociometry that is concerned with the measurement of social phenomena. Many of the areas of sociology have made direct and indirect contributions to the study of the consumer role. Most of the consumer behavior information in this section has been derived through the use of sociological concepts.

The reader may note that this section contains more readings than the previous section. This was intentional since marketers have more interest in group (market) behavior than individual behavior.

The first article takes the form of an introduction to sociology and its significance to marketing. In the article, "Contributions of Sociology to Marketing," Christen T. Jonassen demonstrates that sociological findings on the subjects of population, collective behavior, stratification, motivation, research designs, measurement, and human ecology, have application to marketing's search for consumer behavior data.

The next four articles deal mainly with the influence of social forces and social agents on consumer behavior patterns. The first of these, "Who Are the Marketing Leaders?" by Paul Lazarsfeld, explains the effect of *opinion leaders* on various consumer activities. Lazarsfeld also sets out a number of characteristics for identifying the opinion leaders in a group.

A presentation similar to Lazarsfeld's is one by Charles W. King entitled, "Fashion Adoption: A Rebuttal to the 'Trickle Down' Theory." King first attempts to refute the traditional "trickle down" theory which states essentially that the acceptance of fashion flows from upper to lower socio-economic classes. Then he presents empirical evidence for a new approach to understanding fashion adoption which is built around the influence of a social agent whom he calls an *innovator*.

The next writing, "Life Style Concepts and Marketing," by William Lazar, views *marketing* as a major institution that influences the *life styles* of our society as well as international life styles. The author offers some interesting examples of marketing's impact on our patterns of behavior, particularly consumer behavior, and notes that too often we are not cognizant of its influence.

The last article concerning the influence of social agents on consumer behavior is, "Group Influence in Marketing and Public Relations" by Francis S. Bourne. In this article Bourne points out that *reference groups* influence the operation levels and behavior patterns of individuals. Then he proceeds to show that buying decisions can also be affected by reference groups.

The reader will recall that in Part II it was suggested that marketers might group consumers according to psychological characteristics. This practice, termed *market segmentation,* is employed more often with sociological factors as demonstrated in the remaining eight articles of this section. First, there is an article by Gregory Stone entitled, "City Shoppers and Urban Identification: Observations on the Social Psychology of City Life," that views *city dwellers* as a group and reports on their consumer behavior. Stone succeeds in dividing city shoppers into four categories: personalizing, economic, ethical, and apathetic shoppers.

The following article, "Social Class and Spending Behavior" by Pierre Martineau is an outstanding report on the consumer behavior patterns of *social classes*. In this article Martineau shows how such consumer behavior as selection of stores, saving, and spending vary among social classes. The next two articles describe two very broad groups of consumers; namely, *males* and *females*. The article on the male market, entitled, "Male Market: Big, Rich, Tough," appeared in *Printers' Ink*. It provides a great amount of data on the consumer behavior patterns of adult males and also notes the procedure that some marketers are using to serve this market. The article on female consumers, "Survey Shows How American Women Buy," is also a product of *Printers' Ink*. It discusses a survey of the female market and concludes that the American woman represents the nation's richest market.

The three articles that follow report on the consumer behavior patterns of *age* groups. The first, "An Exploratory Study of the Consumer Behavior of Children" by James U. McNeal, sheds light on how consumer behavior patterns begin. McNeal reports a study on the buying activities of *children* from ages five to ten.

The second of these three articles describes *teen-age* consumers. The article, "Do Ad Men Understand Teen-agers?", is written by the *Printers' Ink* staff and terms the teen-ager a "many-sided buyer" who not only has a great amount of money to spend but also influences a significant portion of parental expenditures.

The third article, "A Marketing Profile of the Senior Citizen Group" by David E. Wallin, recognizes what is essentially a new market consisting of adults *over 65* years of age. Wallin describes this group of consumers in terms of such factors as size, location, amount of expenditures, and buying habits, and then suggests ways of marketing to them effectively.

Finally there follows two papers on the consumer behavior of ethnic groups. The first paper by Alexander reports some empirical material on Italian, Jewish, Puerto Rican, and Negro consumers. The other paper by Van Tassel is devoted strictly to an understanding of the Negro consumer.

14

CONTRIBUTIONS of SOCIOLOGY to MARKETING

CHRISTEN T. JONASSEN

A sociologist is a social scientist who undertakes to isolate, define, and describe human behavior in groups and social settings. He seeks to formulate valid laws and generalizations about human nature, social interaction, social organization, and culture.

Anyone who engages in such activities, seeks such ends, and who in the eyes of other sociologists contributes to these functions is practicing sociology. Therefore, a *sociological contribution* to marketing is anything done by a recognized sociologist that leads to a better understanding of the nature, functions, and processes of marketing.

In what areas and in what ways have sociologists developed materials significant for marketing? And what impact has this knowledge had on marketing, and through what channels has this impact been transmitted? This article gives some of the answers.

NATURE OF MARKETING

We have come a long way from the mechanistic, self-regulating approach of the *laissez-faire* economic theorists. They viewed the market in terms of an equilibrium of forces and general, universalistic, immutable, physical-like laws. The classical economist saw the consumer as an "economic man," a creature who exercised free individual choice in a market

Reprinted from the *Journal of Marketing*, national quarterly publication of the American Marketing Association, Volume 24 (October, 1959), pp. 29-35.

which seemed to operate in a cultural and social vacuum. This view looked on individual wants and desires as motivating forces, and on individuals as the acting agents.

Sociological influences are most apparent in the modern institutional approach, which sees economic processes as part of an organic whole of the total society. This approach means that marketing activities are not looked on as the individualistic acts of atomistic man, but rather as *functions* operating through various marketing structures which are part of the total social organization.

It views marketing processes as the *activities* of groups of people: buyers, sellers, and marketing functionaries, who are motivated by group pressures as well as individual predilections. It recognizes the influence of culture, custom, heritage, and mores in determining the final outcome.

Its emphasis throughout is not on the individual, but on the *group* . . . not on mechanistic, self-regulating, universalistic forces, but on particularistic *social* and cultural forces . . . not on "rational economic" man, but on men as members of *social* groups susceptible to irrationality and sentiment, as well as social values and pressures generated within such groups. Duddy and Revzan, for example, say that "what the producer is finally confronted with is the forecasting of human behavior," and that "in our modern dynamic society the individual, whether consciously or unconsciously, more often acts as a member of a group."[1]

Such terms as "institution," "group," "society," "mass," "culture," "structure," and "structure-function," are found in the institutional approach. These are terms constantly in use by sociologists, and they have had considerable influence on people in other disciplines. Fundamental changes in viewpoint about the nature of man and his marketing behavior have been due largely to the impact of sociological thought and research on economics, psychology, and marketing.

SOCIOLOGICAL CONTRIBUTIONS

Population Studies

The statement, "Markets are people with money to spend—and the desire to spend it"[2] points to two additional areas of sociological contribution: *population studies and consumer motivation.*

[1] Edward A. Duddy and David A. Revzan, *Marketing* (New York: McGraw-Hill Book Co., Inc., 1953), pp. 124 and 125.

[2] Duddy and Revzan, same reference, p. 8.

For a long time population studies have been a branch of sociology. In most universities the subject is taught in the department of sociology, and sociological journals contain numerous articles on this subject. Precise knowledge of population factors enables the marketing man to determine how many and what kinds of people there are and where they are. This enables him to predict future populations and thus gives him lead time which helps to adjust the distribution system to future requirements. This is an obvious necessity for a scientific approach to marketing.

Thompson and Whelpton,[3] Hauser, Ogburn, Margaret Hagood, Hawley, Kingsley Davis, Paul Hatt, Kiser, Duncan, Bogue, and Schmid are a few of the sociologists who have made contributions to our knowledge and understanding of populations, processes, and problems. Their publications in this area are so numerous that each would require a bibliography too long to cite here.

Consumer Motivation

In some of the early marketing texts motivation is discussed in terms of the now-discarded instinct theories, emphasizing the individual and largely ignoring the group. But marketing men today are aware that men do not possess "instincts," and that if they have such desires or motives they are the products of group life. This evolution of thought owes much to sociological influences. Knowledge significant for understanding motivation has emerged from sociological research on class, voluntary association, leisure-time activities, and attitude measurement.

Numerous studies of social class—such as those of the Lynds,[4] Davis,[5] Dollard,[6] Hollingshead,[7] Warner,[8] and Kahl[9]—have focused attention on the implications of class and status, and have described differential motivational patterns and styles of life in different classes. Understand-

3 Warren S. Thompson and P. K. Whelpton, *Population Trends in the United States* (New York: McGraw-Hill Book Co., Inc., 1933); Warren S. Thompson, *Population Problems* (New York: McGraw-Hill Book Co., Inc., 1953).

4 Robert S. Lynd and Helen M. Lynd, *Middletown* (New York: Harcourt, Brace & Co., Inc., 1929); *Middletown in Transition* (New York: Harcourt, Brace & Co., Inc., 1937).

5 Allison Davis, Burleigh Gardner, and Mary Gardner, *Deep South* (Chicago: University of Chicago Press, 1941).

6 John Dollard, *Caste and Class in a Southern Town* (New Haven: Yale University Press, 1954).

7 August B. Hollingshead, *Elmstown's Youth* (New York: John Wiley and Sons, Inc., 1949).

8 Lloyd Warner and Paul S. Lunt, *The Social Life of a Modern Community* (New Haven: Yale University Press, 1941).

9 Joseph A. Kahl, *The American Class Structure* (New York: Rinehart and Co., Inc., 1953).

ing of motivation is also aided by findings from research on participation in voluntary association such as that of Kamarovsky,[10] and by studies of leisure and recreation such as the one made by Alfred Clarke.[11]

Men like Bogardus[12] and many of the sociologists discussed below in the section on measurement and scaling were among the first to devise valid and reliable instruments and scales for the measurement of attitudes. Sociologists also have been a healthy counterbalance to the more extreme claims of Freudians and some of their anthropological followers. Rigorous research like that of Sewell, Mussen, and Harris[13] has shown that there is little evidence for many of the theoretical pronouncements regarding the effects of early child-rearing on the personality.

Human Ecology

Another area where sociologists have made a considerable contribution is in human ecology which analyzes the processes involved in the spatial and temporal adaptation and distribution of human beings and their institutions. Those aspects of marketing which can most directly profit from a knowledge of ecology are: transportation and storage, and the whole area concerned with market-area structures.

In all approaches to marketing, the *area* is an important variable and factor. Sociologists have been concerned with spatial systems for over forty years—in 1915 Galpin[14] brought out *The Social Anatomy of an Agricultural Community*, and in 1916 Robert E. Park[15] published his article "The City" in the *American Journal of Sociology*. Galpin's pioneering study introduced a technique of marketing research which has been widely used since, with certain modifications.

Since then the contributions of sociologists to the description, delineation, and analysis of the dynamics of spatial and temporal systems has been continuous and constitutes a vast amount of research too great to analyze here. There should be mentioned, however, the contributions

[10] Mirra Kamarovsky, "The Voluntary Association of Urban Dwellers," *American Sociological Review,* Vol. 11 (December, 1946), pp. 686-699.

[11] Alfred C. Clarke, "The Use of Leisure and Its Relation to Levels of Occupational Prestige," *American Sociological Review,* Vol. 21 (June, 1956), pp. 301-307.

[12] Emory S. Bogardus, "Measuring Social Distance," *Journal of Applied Sociology,* Vol. 9 (March-April, 1925), pp. 299-308.

[13] William H. Sewell, Paul H. Mussen, and Chester W. Harris, "Relationships Among Child Training Practices," *American Sociological Review,* Vol. 20 (April, 1955), pp. 137-148.

[14] C. J. Galpin, *The Social Anatomy of an Agricultural Community* (Madison: Agricultural Experiment Station of the University of Wisconsin, May, 1951), Research Bulletin 34.

[15] Robert E. Park, "The City," *American Journal of Sociology,* Vol. 20 (March, 1916), pp. 577-612.

of Odum and Moore,[16] Mukerjee,[17] and Mangus[18] to the study of regional systems; of R. D. McKenzie,[19] Hawley,[20] and Bogue[21] to the analysis of metropolitan community systems; of Park, Burgess, and McKenzie,[22] Schmid,[23] Firey,[24] Wirth,[25] Duncan and Reiss,[26] and Quinn[27] to the analysis of urban systems; and of Galpin,[28] Kolb and Polson,[29] and Brunner[30] to investigation of rural systems.

Most marketing people are familiar with Reilly's[31] law, and equations of retail gravitation. Those interested in the mathematical-model approach to spatial systems would be rewarded by a study of Stouffer's[32] theory of intervening opportunities, of Zipf's[33] equations and hypothesis on intercity movement of persons, and of Dodd's[34] equations describing message diffusion.

[16] Howard W. Odum and Harry E. Moore, *American Regionalism* (New York: Henry Holt and Company, 1938).

[17] Radhakamal Mukerjee, "Social Ecology of River Valley," *Sociology and Social Research*, Vol. 12 (March, 1928), pp. 341-347.

[18] A. R. Mangus, *Rural Regions of the United States* (Washington, D.C.: U. S. Government Printing Office, 1940).

[19] Roderick D. McKenzie, *The Metropolitan Community* (New York: McGraw-Hill Book Company, Inc., 1933).

[20] Amos H. Hawley, "An Ecological Study of Urban Service Institutions," *American Sociological Review*, Vol. 6 (October, 1941), pp. 629-639; also *Human Ecology* (New York: The Ronald Press Company, 1950).

[21] Don J. Bogue, *The Structure of the Metropolitan Community: A Study of Dominance and Subdominance* (Ann Arbor: Horace H. Rackham School of Graduate Studies, University of Michigan, 1949); see also the numerous population studies by the same author published by the Scripps Foundation, Miami University, Oxford, Ohio.

[22] R. E. Park, E. W. Burgess, and R. D. McKenzie, *The City* (Chicago: University of Chicago Press, 1925); E. W. Burgess, "The Growth of the City: An Introduction to a Research Project," *Publications of the American Sociological Society*, Vol. 18 (1924), pp. 85-97.

[23] Calvin F. Schmid, *Social Saga of Two Cities* (Minneapolis: Minneapolis Council of Social Agencies, 1937); *Social Trends in Seattle* (Seattle: University of Washington Press, 1944).

[24] Walter Firey, *Land Use in Central Boston* (Cambridge: Harvard University Press, 1947).

[25] Louis Wirth, *The Ghetto* (Chicago: The University of Chicago Press, 1928); "Urbanism as a Way of Life," *American Journal of Sociology*, Vol. 44 (July, 1938), pp. 1-24.

[26] Otis Dudley Duncan and Albert J. Reiss, Jr., *Social Characteristics of Urban and Rural Communities, 1950* (New York: John Wiley and Sons, Inc., 1956).

[27] James A. Quinn, *Human Ecology* (New York: Prentice-Hall, Inc., 1950).

[28] Galpin, same reference as footnote 14.

[29] J. H. Kolb and R. A. Polson, *Trends in Town-Country Relations,* Research Bulletin 117, Agricultural Experiment Station, University of Wisconsin (September, 1933).

[30] Edmund de S. Brunner, "Village Growth and Decline, 1930-1940," *Rural Sociology,* Vol. 9 (June, 1944), pp. 103-115; "Village Growth 1940-1950," *Rural Sociology,* Vol. 16 (June, 1951), pp. 111-118.

[31] William J. Reilly, *The Law of Retail Gravitation* (New York: W. J. Reilly, Inc., 1931).

[32] Samuel A. Stouffer, "Intervening Opportunities: A Theory Relating Mobility and Distance," *American Sociological Review,* Vol. 5 (December, 1940), pp. 845-867.

[33] George Kingsley Zipf, "The Pl. P2/D Hypothesis: On the Intercity Movement of Persons," *American Sociological Review,* Vol. 11 (December, 1946), pp. 677-686.

[34] Stuart Carter Dodd, "Diffusion Is Predictable: Testing Probability Models for Laws of Interaction," *American Sociological Review,* Vol. 20 (August, 1955), pp. 392-401.

Collective Behavior

The realization of distribution specialists that they are dealing with interacting groups, masses, and publics, and the fact that our nation and the world are developing more characteristics of the mass society make the area which sociologists call "collective behavior" ever more important and relevant for marketing. The contributions of sociologists to this area of human behavior have been fairly continuous since Durkheim's[35] early work. Another pioneer in this area was LeBon.[36] Recent contributors are Albig,[37] LaPiere,[38] Lazarsfeld,[39] Merton,[40] Raper,[41] Lee,[42] and Blumer.[43] *An Experiment in Mass Communication* by Otto Larsen and Melvin L. DeFleur[44] contributes to the understanding of the phenomena indicated by the title.

Measurement and Scaling

Another contribution to marketing research made by sociologists is in methodology, measurement, scaling, and prediction. Chapin,[45] Sletto,[46] Bogardus,[47] and Guttman[48] have made basic contributions to scale con-

[35] Émile Durkheim, *Les Formes élémentaires de la vie religieuse, le système totémique en Australie* (Paris: F. Alcan, 1912). Translated by Joseph Ward Swain, *The Elementary Forms of Religious Life: A Study of Religious Sociology* (London: George Allen and Unwin, Ltd., 1915; also Glencoe, Ill.: The Free Press, 1947).

[36] Gustave LeBon, *The Crowd* (London: Unwin, 1899).

[37] William Albig, *Public Opinion* (New York: McGraw-Hill Book Co., Inc., 1939).

[38] Richard T. LaPiere, *Collective Behavior* (New York: McGraw-Hill Book Co., Inc., 1938).

[39] Paul F. Lazarsfeld, Bernard Berelson, and Hazel Gaudet, *The People's Choice* (New York: Duell, Sloan and Pearce, 1944).

[40] Robert K. Merton, *Mass Persuasions: The Social Psychology of a War Bond Drive* (New York: Harper and Brothers, 1946).

[41] Arthur F. Raper, *The Tragedy of Lynching* (Chapel Hill: University of North Carolina Press, 1933).

[42] Alfred McClung Lee, *The Daily Newspaper in America* (New York: Macmillan, 1937).

[43] Herbert Blumer, "Collective Behavior," Part IV of *An Outline of the Principles of Sociology*, Robert E. Park, Editor (New York: Barnes and Noble, 1939).

[44] Otto Larsen and Melvin L. DeFleur, *An Experiment in Mass Communication* (New York: Harper and Brothers, 1958).

[45] Stuart F. Chapin, "Preliminary Standardization of a Social Insight Scale," *American Sociological Review*, Vol. 7 (April, 1942), pp. 214-224.

[46] Raymond F. Sletto and E. A. Rundquist, *Personality and the Depression* (Minneapolis: University of Minnesota Press, 1936); Sletto, *Construction of Personality Scales by the Criterion of Internal Consistency* (Hanover: The Sociological Press, 1937).

[47] Bogardus, same reference as footnote 12.

[48] Louis Guttman, "A Basis for Scaling Qualitative Data," *American Sociological Review*, Vol. 9 (April, 1944), pp. 139-150.

struction; Burgess,[49] Hornell Hart,[50] Monachesi,[51] and Stuckert[52] to the science of prediction; Chapin[53] and McCormick[54] to the development of models and research design; Parten[55] to sampling; Sletto[56] to the use of control groups in social research; Bowers[57] to methods of studying paths of diffusion in the use of new products; Galpin[58] and Schmid[59] to techniques for mapping quantitative social data; Lazarsfeld[60] and Stouffer[61] to the use of quantitative methods in the study of many areas of human behavior; and Moreno[62] and Lundberg[63] to sociometry.

IMPACT OF SOCIOLOGISTS ON MARKETING

How much impact, if any, have sociological contributions had on marketing? This is difficult to determine. But inferences may be drawn from marketing literature, from an examination of activities of sociologists in the marketing field, and from a look at the structures and proc-

[49] E. W. Burgess, "Factors Determining Success or Failure on Parole," in A. A. Bruce, E. W. Burgess, and A. T. Harno, *The Workings of the Indeterminate Sentence Law and the Parole System in Illinois* (Springfield: The State of Illinois, 1928).

[50] Hornell Hart, "Predicting Parole Success," *Journal of the American Institute of Criminal Law and Criminology*, Vol. 14 (Nov., 1923), pp. 405-413.

[51] Elio D. Monachesi, *Prediction Factors in Probation* (Hanover: The Sociological Press, 1932).

[52] Robert Paton Stuckert, *A Configurational Approach to Social Prediction*, unpublished Ph.D. Dissertation, The Ohio State University, 1956; "A Configurational Approach to Prediction," *Sociometry*, Vol. 21 (September, 1958), pp. 225-237.

[53] S. F. Chapin, *Experimental Designs in Sociological Research* (New York: Harper and Brothers, 1947); *Design of Social Experiments* (New York: Harper and Brothers, 2nd ed., 1956).

[54] Thomas C. McCormick, *Elementary Social Statistics* (New York: McGraw-Hill Book Co., Inc., 1941); Thomas C. McCormick and Roy G. Francis, *Methods of Research in the Behavioral Sciences* (New York: Harper and Brothers, 1958).

[55] Mildred B. Parten, "Leadership Among Preschool Children," *Journal of Abnormal and Social Psychology*, Vol. 27 (January-March, 1933), pp. 430-440; *Surveys, Polls and Samples* (New York: Harper and Brothers, 1950).

[56] Raymond F. Sletto, "Sibling Position and Juvenile Delinquency," *American Journal of Sociology*, Vol. 34 (March, 1934), pp. 657-669.

[57] Raymond B. Bowers, "The Direction of Intra-Societal Diffusion," *American Sociological Review*, Vol. 2 (December, 1937), pp. 826-836.

[58] Galpin, same reference as footnote 14.

[59] Schmid, same reference as footnote 23; also *Handbook of Graphic Presentation* (New York: The Ronald Press Co., 1954).

[60] Paul F. Lazarsfeld, *et al.*, *Mathematical Thinking in the Social Sciences* (Glencoe, Ill.: The Free Press, 1954).

[61] Samuel A. Stouffer, *et al.*, *The American Soldier: Adjustment During Army Life*, Vol. 1 (Princeton: Princeton University Press, 1949).

[62] J. L. Moreno, *Who Shall Survive?* (Washington, D.C.: Nervous and Mental Disease Publishing Co., 1934).

[63] George A. Lundberg and Mary Steele, "Social Attraction Patterns in a Village," *Sociometry*, Vol. 1 (April, 1938), pp. 375-419.

esses through which sociological knowledge diffuses into the marketing area.

Publications

Normally one should expect academic channels and textbooks to be an important means of diffusion, but they appear not to be in this instance. Writers of marketing textbooks, while showing evidence of some of the substance of sociology, rarely mention sociology or sociologists. It would require considerable research to determine definitively what emphasis if any is given to sociology in undergraduate courses; but if textbooks are a guide it would seem to be rather negligible. On the graduate level, however, there seems to be more attention given to this subject matter; *The Shopping Center versus Downtown*,[64] for example, is being used in graduate marketing training programs of some universities.

In marketing and business publications, on the other hand, evidence of sociological influence is more evident. Bartels, for example, in an article in the *Journal of Marketing* in 1951 considers certain aspects of sociology, economics, and some other disciplines, to be part of the area of marketing.[65] *Business Week* of March 29, 1958, reporting on a marketing conference, featured the remarks of sociologist David Riesman.[66] *The Shopping Center versus Downtown* mentioned above has been reviewed extensively by marketing and business publications. *Consumer Behavior*,[67] published in 1955, has an article by Nelson N. Foote on "The Autonomy of the Consumer," and another by Frederick L. Strodtback on "Recent Developments in Attitude Research." An article entitled "A Commercial Application of Guttman Attitude Scaling Techniques"[68] appeared in the *Journal of Marketing* in 1957.

Climate of Ideas

Much sociological influence on marketing, of course, is exerted indirectly through the medium of the general culture and climate of ideas. An- as psychology and economics, which in turn produces similar reactions in marketing. other means is through the effect of sociology on other disciplines such

[64] Christen T. Jonassen, *The Shopping Center versus Downtown: A Motivation Research on Shopping Habits and Attitudes in Three Cities* (Columbus: The Ohio State University Bureau of Business Research, 1955); also published as *Shopper Attitudes,* Special Report 11-A (Washington, D.C.: Highway Research Board, National Research Council, 1955).

[65] Robert Bartels, "Can Marketing Be a Science?" *The Journal of Marketing,* Vol. 15 (January, 1951), pp. 319-328, at p. 323.

[66] "The Riddle of Consumer Behavior," *Business Week* (March 29, 1958), p. 95.

[67] Committee for Research on Consumer Attitudes and Behavior, *Consumer Behavior,* Lincoln H. Clark, editor (New York: New York University Press, 1955).

[68] Elizabeth A. Richards, "A Commercial Application of Guttman Attitude Scaling Techniques," *Journal of Marketing,* Vol. 22 (October, 1957), pp. 166-173.

Sociological contributions to the general evolution of thought about the nature and dynamics of man as a consumer and of the market as a social institution and structure have already been discussed. But much sociological material reaches marketing men second hand, very late, and sometimes in garbled fashion.

Participation of Sociologists in Marketing

Another path of diffusion of sociological knowledge is through direct participation of sociologists in the marketing process as researchers, consultants, and participants in marketing seminars and conventions. The participation of David Riesman in the *Life* sponsored regional roundtable in Chicago has already been mentioned. Packard would have us believe that there may be sociologists behind the so-called "hidden persuaders," and states that Likert and Stouffer participated in a public-relations conference at Columbia University.[69] Some sociologists are now found in marketing-research organizations and on the staffs of advertising agencies.

Evidence of direct and indirect influence of sociologists is furnished by the results of some recent marketing research. For example, one of the most ambitious pieces of marketing research of recent years, the *Life Study of Consumer Expenditures*,[70] conducted by Alfred Politz Research, Inc., offers much internal evidence of sociological influence in research design, sampling, questionnaire construction, and selection of essential categories of analysis. The "wave" technique of intermittent interviewing of the same households, for example, is very similar to the technique developed by Lazarsfeld in his study of voting behavior.

The study is not of individuals, but of groups, families, and households living in the United States. These families and households are studied by socioeconomic status; education of head of family; stage of "life cycle"; age of household head; and by regions, urban, rural, and different-sized communities.

One category which appears in the *Life* research that is not common in previous marketing studies is "Household's Stage in the Life Cycle." The study credits the development of this concept to the Survey Research Center of the University of Michigan;[71] but the concept of stages in family life cycle has been common coin in sociology for a long time. In their *Systematic Source Book in Rural Sociology*,[72] Sorokin, Zimmerman, and Galpin discussed four stages of family life cycle as

69 Vance Packard, *The Hidden Persuaders* (New York: David McKay Co., 1957), pp. 220, 221.

70 Time, Inc., *Life Study of Consumer Expenditures*, 1957, Vol. 1.

71 Same reference, p. 13.

72 Pitirim Sorokin, Carl C. Zimmerman, and C. J. Galpin, *Systematic Source Book in Rural Sociology* (Minneapolis: University of Minnesota Press, 1931), Vol. 2, p. 31.

early as 1931; and E. L. Kirkpatrick in 1934 wrote an article entitled "The Life Cycle of the Farm Family in Relation to Its Standard of Living."[73] The concept appears in a book of Waller's[74] in 1938; and it is the organizing theme of Duvall's *Family Development*.[75] Thus, what appeared originally as a concept in sociological literature appears about a generation later in a marketing study as an important category in terms of which data are gathered and analyzed.

Similarly, the use of such categories as "metropolitan" and "nonmetropolitan" owes much to McKenzie, whose writings on the metropolitan region appeared as early as 1924 and 1926, and whose *The Metropolitan Community* was published in 1933.[76] Bogue's *The Structure of the Metropolitan Community* appeared in 1949;[77] and this research monograph as well as the earlier work of McKenzie, Hawley, and other sociologists probably contributed heavily to the decision of the U.S. Bureau of the Census to order its data in terms of Standard Metropolitan Areas.

In Conclusion

Lack of space has made it necessary to omit names of other sociologists and also some relevant work of the sociologists who are mentioned. Many sociologists have made significant contributions to marketing by their impact on the general climate of ideas concerning the nature of man and society and the relations of economic institutions to society. They have also carried out important studies on population, communication, collective behavior, motivation, stratification, methodology, research design, measurement, prediction, human ecology, and the family. Sociological knowledge and methods have diffused into marketing through marketing publications, through participation of sociologists as consultants and researchers, and to a lesser extent through academic channels.

The participants in the *Life* marketing conferences mentioned earlier stressed the necessity of developing basic theories and facts to explain buying behavior. The present article has pointed to some aspects of sociological activity and to some materials that might aid in the solution of this problem.

[73] El L. Kirkpatrick, *et al.*, "The Life Cycle of the Farm Family in Relation to its Standard of Living," Research Bulletin No. 121 (Madison, Wisconsin: Agricultural Experiment Station, University of Wisconsin, 1934).

[74] Willard Waller, *The Family: A Dynamic Interpretation* (New York: The Cordon Co., 1938).

[75] Evelyn Millis Duvall, *Family Development* (New York: J. B. Lippincott Co., 1957).

[76] McKenzie, same reference as footnote 19.

[77] Bogue, same reference as footnote 21.

15

WHO ARE the MARKETING LEADERS?

PAUL F. LAZARSFELD

According to Paul Lazarsfeld, the key to economic and efficient marketing lies in locating and reaching the opinion leaders who through personal contact with small groups, notably family, friends and neighbors,
influence the purchasing decisions of the majority of consumers. A number of studies conducted by other experts reinforce this theory.

William H. Whyte, Jr., in his study of air conditioner ownership
in a Philadelphia community, records a very high degree of interpersonal influence in the purchase of the units. In addition, his study shows
that the direction of the flow of interpersonal influence is directly correlated with social contact, namely the friendship patterns of the housewives and children of the community.

In other words, Whyte discovered that sheer location of a house
can play a major role in opinion leadership. He contends that marketing influence tends to flow up and down streets and across narrow alleys
—where there is the greatest chance for casual everyday contact, rather
than across the street—where there is apt to be less casual neighboring
among the people who live on the two sides.

The importance of opinion leadership and social contact is even
more clear in a recent Columbia study of the pattern of adoption of a
new ethical drug by a group of doctors.

Opinion leaders were located by having the doctors name the three
colleagues whom they see most often socially, the three with whom they
most often discuss their cases and the three of whom they usually go for
professional information and advice.

Significantly, the study found that the doctors' willingness to try the drug is directly related to their degree of social integration or gregariousness. On the average, the doctors named by many of their colleagues started using the drug earlier than those who were mentioned by few or none of their associates.

The study also charts the acceptance pattern of the drug, thus how buying influence spread through four different groups of doctors: first, of course, the socially integrated "innovators" who took the lead, but whose action did not immediately result in a rush to follow suit; the drug was adopted next by the "influentials"; their action was followed shortly by the largest group, the "followers"; finally, the remaining small groups, the "diehards," who are the least socially integrated of all, adopted the drug.

Thus, from these studies it's clear that there exist certain specific marketing leaders who exert significant influence on the purchasing decisions of their fellow consumers. What practical value does the theory of marketing leadership have for advertisers?

For one thing, it suggests that a radical reappraisal of advertising strategies may be in order. The mere knowledge that most consumers take their purchasing leads from a smaller select group seems to indicate a more specialized selling approach.

Second, the studies indicate the grave importance of aggressive advertising and selling in the initial stages of a campaign, particularly in the case of new products. For example, in his studies Whyte finds that in close-knit communities the earliest buyers of appliances (who are comparable to the "innovators" in the drug study) are generally subject to "raised eyebrows." However, once the proportion of appliance ownership has spread sufficiently to include the marketing leaders, the biggest group of consumers—the followers—jump on the bandwagon and tend to "punish" those who lag behind.

Thirdly, an awareness of the existence of marketing leaders could be an invaluable weapon in the planning of ad copy and the buying of media. Once the advertiser knows who the marketing leaders are, he can direct his advertising to this select group that will eventually, through its influence, establish the buying pattern of his total market.

Who, then, is this marketing leader? Locating him is probably the toughest problem of all. In the first place, since his "leadership" is of the casual, everyday face-to-face variety, it is usually so invisible and inconspicuous that it would actually be more accurate to call it "guidance." It's the very unobtrusiveness of his leadership or guidance that makes the marketing leader exceedingly difficult to pin down.

Lazarsfeld has one suggestion for locating marketing leaders on a local level. Since opinion leadership of any sort is directly related to social integration or gregariousness, marketing leaders in specific communities could be pinpointed through the membership rolls of organized groups such as clubs, civic associations or the PTA.

According to Lazarsfeld, this technique could be a boon for advertisers who work through local dealers and for those who distribute trial samples of products or use direct mail.

On a broader or national level, locating marketing leaders is not quite so simple. Lazarsfeld goes about it by isolating the specific characteristics that seem to distinguish opinion leaders from non-leaders. As benchmarks he uses three factors: position on the social and economic ladder, position in the life-cycle, the degree of social integration or gregariousness.

In studying the relationship of marketing leadership to status Lazarsfeld finds, contrary to traditional sociological thinking, that influence does not emanate from the highest status group and trickle down to the lower levels.

Instead, in what he terms a "horizontal pattern" of influence, each status group has its own corps of leaders who generally influence only the members of their own group.

In the relatively rare instances when marketing influence does exist among people of different status groups, says Lazarsfeld, this influence is just as likely to emanate from the low status group and move upward as it is to start from the top and flow down the status ladder. Again contrary to popular opinion, Lazarsfeld finds that the highest status group does not account for a great preponderance of opinion leaders. As his study of 800 women in Decatur, Ill., shows, marketing leaders are found in almost equal numbers on all status levels (see chart A).

Lazarsfeld concludes that if women consumers in the highest status group do seem a little more likely to emerge as marketing leaders than women of the lowest group it is because of two things: their ability to afford more household help leaves them more time for socializing; the sheer prestige of their high status position might make them appear more highly qualified as marketing leaders (although, according to Lazarsfeld, there is absolutely no evidence that they are actually any more skilled in marketing than any other women).

Lazarsfeld says there are two sound reasons for the tendency to status-bound, horizontal marketing leadership. Obviously, women of like status have similar budgetary problems and limitations. Therefore, it seems only natural that they should look to members of their own group for marketing advice.

Second, Lazarsfeld maintains that today's stores and shopping centers tend to cater somewhat to women of one particular status group. Therefore, in the course of shopping, when immediate marketing advice is needed, the women on hand to provide it are likely to be of similar status.

In short, with marketing leaders existing on all three status levels, it's obvious that a single advertising campaign is not the most effective way to reach the total market. Clearly, advertisers must use separate and appropriate approaches to appeal to the marketing leaders on each of the three levels, who in turn influence the marketing decisions on the other members of their group.

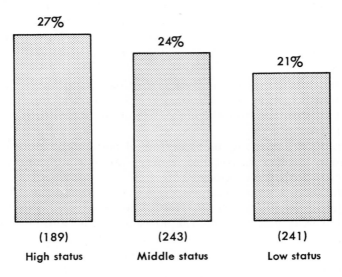

Chart A.   Marketing leaders are found in almost equal numbers on all three status levels. *Note:* Numbers in parentheses under each bar represent the total number of cases on which the percentage of opinion leadership is based. Thus 27% of the 189 high status women in our sample are marketing leaders. This procedure is used in all subsequent charts.

The second criterion that Lazarsfeld uses to determine the characteristics of opinion leaders is position in the life-cycle (age, marital status, number of children and their ages). He works on the premise that holding a particular position in the life-cycle naturally inclines a person to some special interests rather than others. It is these interests, he says, that characterize her as either a leader or a follower.

Although position on the status ladder seems to have little relevance to marketing leadership, position in the life-cycle is a different story. Lazarsfeld's studies find that among women one particular group —large family wives (two or more children)—emerge strongly as marketing leaders. In fact, according to the Decatur study, large family wives are almost twice as likely to be marketing leaders as women of any other life-cycle type (see chart B).

This concentration of marketing leaders among the large family wives clearly indicates this: the most important factor in marketing leadership is the intensive, everyday "experiencing" of marketing problems, characteristic of a woman with a large or growing family.

Interestingly, Lazarsfeld's studies indicate that the matron (over 45 years of age) with all her years of experience in managing households, is no more likely to emerge as a marketing leader than unmarried girls or

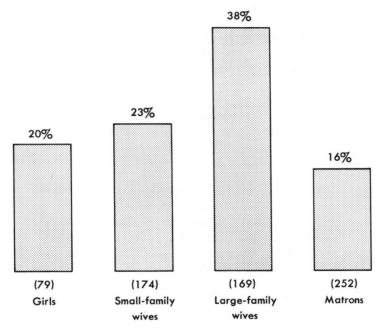

Chart B.   The large family wives are the marketing leaders.

small family wives (one or no children). In other words, "experiencing" is far more vital to marketing leadership than "experience—the symbol of the matron and her years."

The fact that the greatest concentration of marketing leaders is found among large family wives raises two important questions:

Do large family wives influence the marketing decisions of the majority of all women?

Or is their marketing leadership of the horizontal variety, and confined to other large family wives?

Lazarsfeld concedes that a good case can be made for both wives.

On the first score, he says it's possible that large-family wives are much more concerned with marketing problems than are women in other positions in the life-cycle.

They are the women who seek advice most. Therefore, out of necessity they generate the greatest number of marketing leaders to provide this advice.

On the other hand, it's just as possible that marketing activities are about the same among all women. This would mean that advice-seeking is distributed about evenly throughout the population.

If such is the case, then the concentration of marketing leaders among large family wives can mean only one thing: women of all life-cycle types turn to the large family wives for marketing advice.

Unfortunately, there are no studies directly corroborating either of the two alternatives. Lazarsfeld approaches the problem by analyzing the ages of both people involved in specific advice-giving marketing situations.

Using this method he finds that large family wives are the prime marketing advisors for women of all other life-cycle types as well as their fellow large family wives. His conclusions are based on the following research findings:

About half of advice-seeking women consult other women of about their own age.

Of the 50% who seek advice from women either younger or older than they, the greatest number seem to turn to women in the 25-44 age group. In other words, both the younger and older women seek market leadership from the group classified as "wives."

When these "wives" themselves seek advice outside their own life-cycle group, they tend to consult older women somewhat more than younger ones.

Furthermore, younger women are far more inclined to consult their seniors on marketing problems than are older women apt to seek advice from their juniors.

William Whyte also notes a high degree of interpersonal advice-giving among young white-collar consumers. He attributes it to two factors: today's young consumers face many more marketing decisions regarding purchasing than did any of their counterparts in the past. Sometime, they have far less contact with tradition than did their parents and grandparents. Therefore, they depend upon the opinions of their contemporaries to guide them in the "delicate job of keeping in tune with the life style of the moment."

In addition, Whyte's studies find that the more similar the houses in the neighborhood or block, the more important the minor differences become to the people living there. That's why, according to Whyte, marginal purchases are the key ones.

Clearly, then, with marketing leadership concentrated in young consumers, particularly large family wives, advertisers would do well, advises Paul Lazarsfeld, to make their biggest pitch to the young (under 45) housewife with two or more children.

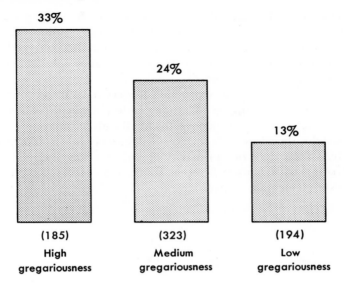

33%

24%

13%

(185)
High
gregariousness

(323)
Medium
gregariousness

(194)
Low
gregariousness

Chart C.   The more gregarious women are more likely to be marketing leaders.

Of the three factors used to locate the opinion leader, Lazarsfeld finds the greatest correlation between market leadership and gregariousness. From the findings of his Decatur study he concludes that the greater the extent of a woman's social contacts, the greater are her chances of emerging as a marketing leader (see chart C).

The correlation between gregariousness and marketing leadership holds true for each life-cycle type. However, says he, among the large family wives, even the least gregarious women have a better chance of becoming marketing leaders than the most gregarious members of the other life-cycle groups.

It's Lazarsfeld opinion that the combined factors of life-cycle and gregarious "tell the marketing leadership story." He points out that the slightly higher incidence of marketing leaders among high status women is merely a result of their greater opportunity for social contact. In fact, according to the findings of the Decatur study, a highly gregarious low status woman is four times as likely to be a marketing leader than a non-gregarious woman of high status.

Obviously, the marketing leaders get the information they disseminate from somewhere. Do they get it from other opinion leaders or from sources such as mass media?

Lazarsfeld says that "ideas often flow from air media and print media to the opinion leaders and from them to the less active sections of the population" in what he calls a "two-step flow of influence."

In writing of Lazarsfeld's studies, University of Georgia assistant marketing professor Robert C. Brooks says that opinion leaders are sought out because of their knowledge acquired through media exposure. He also believes that because the leaders are sought out, they feel an obligation to keep informed.

Yet despite the fact that marketing leaders have more contact with media than consumers in general, studies indicate that their own buying decisions are not especially influenced by media advertising.

Lazarsfeld theorizes that marketing leaders, much like the non-leaders, base their decisions primarily on information obtained through personal contact—perhaps with other marketing leaders, and use media only as a supplementary device.

16

FASHION ADOPTION: a REBUTTAL to the "TRICKLE DOWN" THEORY

CHARLES W. KING

The oscillations and vagaries of fashions in women's apparel have been the topic of social critics for centuries. A sizable body of literature has developed in fashion based on over three hundred years of conceptual commentary and anecdotal evidence. Collectively, these contributions have become the core of modern day "fashion theory."

What is known as fashion theory, however, is more an amorphous network of concepts than an integrated paradigm predictive of modern fashion behavior. *The loose conceptual framework is organized around a basic model of the fashion adoption process—the "trickle down" theory of fashion adoption. The theory unfortunately lacks contemporary validation in empirical research.* Virtually none of the proponents of the "trickle down" process have tested the details of the model. Historically, specific anecdotal evidence supporting the traditional notion has been limited. Even in the era of the consumer survey, published studies of fashion behavior are scarce.

In this project, fashion adoption has been attacked as a specific type of innovative behavior within the broader contexts of social change and product innovation. Contemporary innovation research and methodology have been applied in the fashion adoption context. Specifically, the project has involved an exploratory consumer survey of the consumer change agents—the innovator (the early season buyer) and the influential (the opinion leader) in the fashion adoption process within the product category of women's millinery. The central theme of the re-

Reprinted from Stephen A. Greyser (ed.), *Toward Scientific Marketing* (Chicago: American Marketing Association, 1964), pp. 108-125.

search is that the traditional fashion adoption process model—the "trickle down" theory—does not reflect contemporary fashion behavior.

THE "TRICKLE DOWN" THEORY

What is the "trickle down" theory? The flavor of the theory can be most fully appreciated by quoting directly from its supporters. Though the theory has been implied by many early economists such as Rae,[1] Foley,[2] and Veblen,[3] one of the first detailed presentations was made by Simmel,[4] a sociologist:

Social forms, apparel, aesthetic judgment, the whole style of human expression are constantly transformed by fashion, in such a way, however, that fashion—in all these things affects only the upper classes. Just as soon as the lower classes begin to copy their style, thereby crossing the line of demarcation the upper classes have drawn and destroying the uniformity of their coherence, the upper classes turn away from this style and adopt a new one, which in its turn differentiates them from the masses; and thus the game goes merrily on. Naturally, the lower classes look and strive toward the upper, and they encounter least resistance in those fields which are subject to the whims of fashion; for it is here that mere external imitation is most readily applied. The same process is at work as between the different sets within the upper classes, although it is not always visible here. . . .

Barber in more recent research on social stratification has emphasized the "trickle down" process in women's clothes,[5] and Robinson[6] argues essentially the same vertical flow notion, modifying it slightly to include horizontal movement within particular social strata:

. . . any given group (or cluster of groups forming a class) will tend to take its cues from those contiguous with it. Horizontally fashions will spread outward from central loci; and vertically—the more important consideration—any given group will tend to adopt as its mentor not the highest distinguishable group, but, rather, those immediately above it. In consequence of the vertical contiguity of class groupings, new fashions tend to filter down by stages through the levels of affluence. The process of discarding any fashion will be a mere

[1] John Rae, *The Sociological Theory of Capital* (London: Macmillan Company, 1834), Chapter 13, and Appendix I.

[2] Caroline R. Foley, "Fashion," *Economic Journal*, Vol. 3, 1893, p. 458.

[3] Thorstein Veblen, *The Theory of the Leisure Class* (New York: Macmillan, 1912).

[4] Georg Simmel, "Fashion," *American Journal of Sociology*, Vol. 62, May, 1957, pp. 541-558. (Reprinted from the International Quarterly, Vol. X, October, 1904, pp. 130-155.)

[5] Bernard Barber, *Social Stratification* (New York: Harcourt, Brace and Company, 1957), p. 150.

[6] Dwight E. Robinson, "The Economics of Fashion Demand," *The Quarterly Journal of Economics*, 75:3, 1961, p. 376.

reflex of its proliferation. For an object of fashion to lose its meaning for the topmost class, it is only necessary for it to be taken up by the secondmost and so on down the line.

In essence, then, *the vertical flow hypothesis simply states that the upper socio-economic classes adopt fashions first in the time dimension as symbols of distinction and exclusiveness.* In the course of inter-intra class competition, the lower classes, each and in turn, emulate and follow the upper class leaders. At a certain level of adoption by the lower levels the syndrome of styles becomes vulgarized and is discarded by the upper class in favor of a new set of fashion symbols. The "trickle" is again activated and the process repeats itself.

For the sophisticated marketer and social scientist, this discussion of the vertical flow hypothesis may have added little in terms of substantive knowledge. The purpose of the detailed quotations from these theorists has been to highlight the similarity of the fashion adoption process model among different writers over time (Simmel wrote in 1904, Robinson in 1961). Despite a changing social and business environment, the conceptualizations have remained essentially static in theme and detail for at least sixty years.

A REBUTTAL TO "TRICKLE DOWN"

The basic question is, *does the "trickle down" theory accurately describe the contemporary fashion adoption process?* The traditional notion is vulnerable. The historical evidence quoted by the early theorists strongly indicates the vertical flow process may have been functional in earlier periods in different types of class structures. The modern social environment, mass communications, and the fashion industry's manufacturing and merchandising strategies, however, almost impede any systematic vertical flow process.

Changing Social Environment

During the past 30 years in the United States, social and economic "leveling influences" have changed the entire profile of the consumer market. The once obviously structured class system has changed; class lines are clearly drawn only at extreme points on the social class continuum. As a result of the leveling influences, a much broader slice of the population can afford to be in fashion. The traditional value of material and craftsmanship in labeling social position still exists. But quality apparel is now within the reach of more people. The population's affluence reverberates through other facets of the theory also.

Impact of Mass Media

Mass communication media rapidly accelerate the spread of fashion awareness and influence mass market endorsement. The traditional upper class fashion leader directing the lower levels is largely short-circuited in the communication process. Within hours after the exclusive Paris and American designers' showings, the season's styles have been passed to the mass audiences via newspaper and television. The mass media "fashion seminars" also reflect the short-cutting of upper class influence in a direct sense. The woman's fashion page universally geared to "middle majority," the "woman's problems" columns, the fashion journals, and the broadcast media's fashion programs provide detailed "what to wear" and "how to wear it" instruction aimed directly at the mass market buyer. The traditional process of vertical personal transmission is again challenged.

Fashion Industry Manufacturing and Merchandising

Fashion industry manufacturing and merchandising methods actually impede any vertical flow process of fashion adoption.

Adoption and the Fashion Season

Fashion adoption is a process of social contagion by which a new style or product is adopted by the consumer after commercial introduction by the designer or manufacturer. Though gradual long term secular trends in apparel fashions have been documented,[7] the actual consumer adoption decision is made within the time dimension of a season. Though historically, the fashion seasons have roughly paralleled climatic seasons, in recent years fashion merchandisers have tended to accelerate the transitions from season to season. In women's apparel, the season is typically three to six months in length.

As a merchandising strategy, designers and manufacturers strive to differentiate products between comparable seasons over time. Though classic styles and silhouettes may carry over, new styles are introduced

7 For example, see A. L. Kroeber, "Order in Changes in Fashion" (1919), *The Nature of Culture* (Chicago: University of Chicago Press, 1952), pp. 332-337; Jane Richardson and A. L. Kroeber, "Three Centuries of Women's Dress Fashions: A Quantitative Analysis," *Anthropological Records* (October, 1940), pp. 111-153; Agnes Brooks Young, *Recurring Cycles of Fashion, 1760-1937* (New York: Harper and Brothers, 1937).

and colors and fabrics changed. Therefore, the adoption of a new fashion entails a shift within the population from the styles appropriate at a given time the previous year to the new style offerings. Individuals make the adoption decisions at different speeds and at different times. The aggregate fashion cycle for a style is an expression of this continuum of adoption.

The Effect of Adoption within the Season

The net impact of operating within the time dimension of a season is to compress the adoption process into a blur. The rapidity of adoption dictated by the fashion season directly challenges the operationality of the "trickle down" process.

The lag time for vertical flow of fashion adoption at the consumer level is almost non-existent. From creation to mass market introduction, there may be virtually no opportunity for vertical flow. Paris fashions pose a good example. Many of the Paris designers are concentrating almost exclusively on "originals" for the mass fashion industry. In 1957, an estimated 30 per cent of Paris *haute couture* volume was accounted for by manufacturers and retail syndicate and store buyers.[8] In these cases, there is little upper class style endorsement supporting mass market adoption. In 1960, for further support, the August showings in Paris that were purchased or leased by American concerns were flown to the United States on the same plane on August 23. On September 5, New York fashion houses introduced the fall collection of copied Paris originals to the fashion press. Following five days of manufacturing and merchandise preparation, Macy's, Gimbels, and other leading New York department stores introduced the "popular priced" fall fashions to the consumers.[9] Again, where was the vertical flow process and upper class initiation and lower class emulation?

Product Design and Consumer Choice

In the area of product design, the consumer moves from one extreme of virtually no choice in fashion selection to the other extreme of wide freedom of choice. The fashion industry defines basic colors, fabrics, and silhouettes for all price lines for a given season months before the season actually gets underway at the retail level. Once the basic dimensions of a season's fashions are set, a multiplicity of contemporary and classic styles are introduced. These decisions are certainly the result of a vast

[8] "Yield from High Fashion Is Low: Paris Haute," *Business Week* (February 16, 1957), pp. 68-70.

[9] "Bringing Paris Fashions Down to the Mass Market," *Business Week* (August 20, 1960), pp. 72-77.

distillation of fashion design experience, success, and failure. These product decisions are rarely the result of empirical research beyond review of last season's trends.

Theoretically, the consumer can select from a wide range of current and classic designs and still be entirely "in fashion" regardless of the particular selection she makes. The consumer has comparative freedom across styles to satisfy personal tastes and physical features with little social penalty.

Product Differentiation

Product differences between price lines are almost exclusively quality based rather than design based. The same basic silhouettes, materials and imitations, and colors are featured in each broad price range. The higher priced lines tend to be merely of higher quality in material and craftsmanship. Styling may be more versatile and creative in the higher priced lines because of the wider profit margins. The obvious differences, however, are difficult to recognize once the economy lines are excluded.

Fashion Retailing—Simultaneous Introduction Across Price Levels

The time factor in retail merchandising impedes much vertical flow except on a very rapid basis. In fact, modern retailing almost guarantees simultaneous adoption of the same basic styles across status levels. The volume fashion manufacturing and retailing industry operates essentially in the same way and on the same basic seasonal schedules in the higher priced and in the lower priced categories. The season's styles at each price level tend to be introduced at approximately the same time. In millinery, departments introduce new season items at essentially the same time in the seasons. Stores at all price levels tend to follow basically the same fashion calendar in fashion promotion.

Why Continued Support of the Theory

Given these contradictions of the vertical flow process, how does the notion marshal support from sophisticated fashion theorists?

Vertical Flow within the Fashion Industry

The confusion is, in part, a product of using the fashion industry as a source of information.[10] Defining the broad fashion innovation process

10 Robinson, for example, relied heavily on fashion industry interviews. No formal consumer research was reported.

as the entire range of activities from conceptualization of a new style through detailed design to market introduction, a vertical flow definitely operates *within* the industry. The character of that process is entirely different from the consumer reaction outlined by Simmel and others.

The three elements of the innovation process—manufacturers, trade channel buyers, and consumers—represent a great filtering system. The three elements or sub-systems operate as interdependent yet independent evaluation and adoption centers. The manufacturers select a finite number of styles to feature from an almost infinite array of possibilities. The trade channel buyers then select a sampling of styles for ultimate sales from the universe of lines offered by all manufacturers. The consumers then adopt a sampling of these selections and endorse them as accepted fashions.

Within the industry subsets, a vertical flow exists also. The exclusive and famous designers are watched closely and emulated by lesser designers. Major manufacturers are studied and copied by smaller and less expert competitors. Design piracy is a well established competitive strategy.

Little Factual Consumer Information

In describing the consumer fashion adoption process, industry spokesmen are surprisingly uninformed.[11] An enigmatic "fashionable woman" guides many fashion managers. Others refer to the all pervasive importance of celebrity endorsement in influencing fashion trends. Some recognize the mass market influence but understand little of its complexity.

Some "Trickle" May Exist

In modest defense of the vertical flow supporters, it must be granted that some upper class influence undoubtedly exists. The question really is: *does it dictate market behavior as predicted by the theory?* In one segment of the market, a narrowly defined vertical flow can be recognized. The small, chic, and very wealthy upper class indirectly influences styles through the private designer. The social elite nurture the private designers through their patronage. More importantly, the private designers test new styles with this group and adapt successful trends for mass market showings. The garment manufacturers' and retail buyers' offerings, then, are partially distillations of upper class taste. Therefore, an indirect and hazy "vertical flow" process might be considered at work.

[11] Based on approximately 30 interviews with major millinery manufacturers, retail syndicate and retail buyers, and leading fashion journalists and researchers.

This type of function, however, falls far short of the all pervasive social status emulation outlined by Simmel, Barber, Robinson, and others. To use this evidence in defense of the traditional vertical flow theory may be theoretically appropriate but pragmatically irrelevant.

If this limited interpretation of the "trickle down" process is to be applied then there is no current fashion adoption theory. The great adoption function occurs within the mass market. This limited interpretation gives no explanation of mass market adoption. What goes on there? This is the crucial question to fashion management and social scientists.

RESEARCH DESIGN

The research described here has involved an exploratory consumer survey of the key figures in fashion adoption, the innovator (the early buyer) and the influential (the opinion leader). The context has been confined to the product category of women's millinery and the geographical area of Metropolitan Boston. The field research was conducted immediately following the close of the Fall (1962) millinery season.

The millinery buying context has proven particularly suitable to fashion adoption research. Millinery is recognized as a highly fashion oriented item of women's apparel. Fashion change occurs semi-annually and is an accepted social phenomenon. Involvement in millinery adoption is high and almost all women can discuss the adoption process with some expertise.

The cornerstone of the project involved inclusion of the time of adoption as the critical variable in the research design. Respondents were qualified on a continuum of adoption based on their Fall buying behavior. The objective was to segment the adoption continuum into independent parts as accurately as possible within the financial constraints. Time of adoption was defined as the month of first purchase of a hat during the Fall season. The adoption decision was not defined as adoption of any specific style but merely purchase in time since the consumer can "adopt" from a wide range of styles *within the season's merchandise* and be "in style" regardless of the specific selection. The "early" and "late" buyers were operationally defined:

1. "early" buyers—late August or September purchasers representing the first 35% of the Fall season's buyers.
2. "late" buyers—October through mid-January purchasers representing the latter 65% of the season's buyers.

The field research involved two phases: a brief telephone interview, and a one hour personal interview with selected respondents.

Based on the Metropolitan Boston Telephone Directory, a random cluster sampling procedure was used to select 1,934 adult women, who were classified into the adopter categories. Of these, 303 respondents in the early and late buyer categories were selected and personally interviewed to probe their general fashion and hat adoption processes in detail, including coverage of an extensive array of demographic, psychological, social, and mass communication, and personal influence variables.

REJECTIONS OF THE "TRICKLE DOWN" THEORY

The empirical data support rejection of the "trickle down" theory of fashion adoption in this product context. Two broad questions central to the theory have been analyzed:

1. Are the early buyers, in fact, the high status "elite esotery" depicted by the vertical flow notion?
2. Are the early buyers more influential than late buyers in dictating fashion adoption?

The traditional theory implies a form of personal influence in which the high status, early buyers directly influence the lower status, later adopters in the interpersonal network of information transmission.

Socioeconomic Status of the Adopter Categories

The socioeconomic status of the respondents was measured on three levels: total annual family income, husband's occupational status, and self designated or perceived social class position. The three measures are obviously highly intercorrelated but each taps a somewhat different dimension of social status. The three measures produced essentially identical results.

The basic conclusion to be drawn from the analysis of social status was that early buyers were consistently higher status than late buyers *but* the early buyers were not "upper class." Specifically:

In terms of annual family income, 59% of the early buyers had income under $9000 per year; 19% had income of less than $6000.

In terms of husband's occupational status, 62% of the early buyers were "middle class" or lower; 33% were "lower middle class" or lower.

In terms of respondent's perceived class position, despite the expected clustering of reports in the "middle class," 16% of the early buyers located themselves in "lower middle" or "lower class" social positions.

Is this group of early buyers the "elite esotery" the traditional theorists have labeled as the fashion innovators initiating the "trickle down" process?

Personal Influence and the Adopter Categories

Even if the early buyers were assumed to meet the status requirements for the "elite esotery," the second question of personal influence in fashion adoption must be answered. Admittedly, the early buyer does levy some visual influence through displaying the season's fashions early in the season. In turn, because of the reliance of retailers on early season sales as a guide to later season inventory purchases, the early buyer exercises influence over retail inventories. The issue here, however, centers on the early buyer's role as a personal influence in the interpersonal network of information transmission.

As a first step in the analysis, "influentials" were identified in two contexts: general fashion and hat buying. In the general fashion context an influential was anyone who had "been asked her advice" or "offered any suggestions" on fashions recently or felt she was "more likely" to be asked than any of her friends. The hat influentials were those respondents who felt they were "more likely" to be asked their advice about hats than their friends. This approach to identifying influential opinion leaders has frequently been used in other contexts.[12]

Reliance on personal interactions in information receiving and transmitting is high, particularly in the general fashion context. Approximately 73% and 25% of the respondents relied on personal interactions in the general fashion and hat buying contexts respectively. The lower incidence of interaction in hat buying is largely a result of narrowing the reporting context from broad fashion to the specific product category of women's millinery.

Given the role of personal influence and the identification of influentials, three dimensions were explored in measuring the dynamics of influence exercised by early versus late buyers:

1. The frequency of interaction by the influentials within adopter groups.
2. The number of influentials within the adopter group.
3. The status compatibility between the receiver and the influential in the reported interactions.

Frequency of interactions

There were no significant patterned differences in the frequency of reported interactions by influentials in the early versus late adopter groups as indicated in Table 1. It should be noted that only the interactions from the general fashion context are reported in Tables 1 and 4. Too

---

12 See Elihu Katz and Paul F. Lazarsfeld, *Personal Influence* (Glencoe, Ill.: The Free Press, 1955); and Everett M. Rogers and David G. Cartano, "Methods of Measuring Opinion Leadership," *Public Opinion Quarterly*, 26:3 (Fall, 1962), p. 435.

few interactions were fully reported in the hat context to justify detailed presentation. The general pattern reflected by the data in the two contexts, however, were essentially identical.

TABLE I

COMPARISON OF EARLY VS. LATE BUYERS BY INFLUENCE INTERACTION
FREQUENCY GENERAL FASHION CONTEXT

	Early buyer	Late buyer
Number of interactions per influential	1.06*	1.10
Base number of influentials	66	86

* *I.e.*, early buyer influentials reported 1.06 interactions per influential.

The Influentials within the Adopter Groups

Recognizing the importance of the level of influence, the analysis has concentrated on the influentials within the adopter groups. Though the early buyers have been found to be well distributed across the class structure rather than "upper class," supporters of the "trickle down" theory could argue that the influence in the early buyer group was concentrated in the upper income sector. If this were the case, greater credence might be given the "trickle down" concept.

To attack this hypothesis, the adopter groups were divided into high, medium, and low income subsets. To eliminate the impact of the slightly larger number of higher income respondents in the early group, the percentage of respondents qualifying as influentials *within each income subset* was calculated. As presented in Table 2, in both the general fashion and hat buying contexts, influence was not concentrated in the early buyer, high income subset.

TABLE 2

COMPARISON OF EARLY AND LATE BUYERS BY INCIDENCE OF INFLUENCE
WITHIN INCOME SUBSETS GENERAL FASHION AND HAT
BUYING CONTEXTS

Family income	General fashion context		Hat buying context	
	Early buyer	Late buyer	Early buyer	Late buyer
Under $6000	50%*	41%	4%	13%**
$6000 to $8999	50%	51%	17%	10%
$9000 or more	51%	62%	10%	21%

Note: Percentages do not add to 100%.

* *I.e.*, 50% of the early buyers reporting "under $6000" income qualified as influentials in the general fashion context.
** *I.e.*, 13% of the late buyers reporting "under $6000" income qualified as influentials in the hat buying context.

In the general fashion context, the early buyers within each income subset had essentially identical probabilities of being influentials. In the hat buying context the early buyer, middle income respondents had a somewhat higher probability of qualifying as influentials. Nor were the early buyer, high income respondents more influential than their late buyer, high income counterparts. In fact the late buyer, high income subset had more per capita influence in both contexts than any other subset—further refutation of the "trickle down" theory.

A logical question would be: *are early buyers in total more influential than late buyers?* The basic data presented in Table 3 indicate

TABLE 3

COMPARISON OF EARLY AND LATE BUYERS BY INCIDENCE OF INFLUENCE
GENERAL FASHION AND HAT BUYING CONTEXTS

Respondents qualified as:	General fashion context		Hat buying context	
	Early buyer	Late buyer	Early buyer	Late buyer
Receiver	23%	23%	14%	16%
Influential	49*	51	11**	14
Uninvolved	28	26	75	70
TOTAL	100%	100%	100%	100%
BASE	135	168	135	168

* *I.e.,* 49% of the early buyer group qualified as influentials in the general fashion context.
** *I.e.,* 11% of the early buyer group qualified as influentials in the hat buying context.

that in both the general fashion and hat buying contexts, the percentage of respondents qualifying as influentials *within* the early buyer and the late buyer groups was essentially identical. Though the general incidence of influence was lower in the hat context, the relationship of the adopter categories remained the same. Clearly in contradiction to the traditional theory, the early buyers were no more likely to be influentials than late buyers.

A critical blow to the traditional "trickle down" notion is provided when the early and late buyer groups are weighted according to their relative importance in the Fall hat buying market. By definition, the early buyer group (August and September buyers) represented 35% of the total buyers, and the late buyers represented 65% of the market. Therefore, since the two adopter groups had essentially identical levels of influence *within* the categories, weighting for market importance indicated there were *86 per cent more late buyer influentials compared with early buyer influentials* in the total Fall season hat buying population. *In direct contradiction to the "trickle down" theory, the total impact of influence by late buyers was markedly greater than that of early buyers.*

Status Compatibility in Reported Interactions

The third question to be answered centers around the interpersonal interaction itself. Who talks to whom? The traditional notion would predict that influentials influence those lower in social status and receivers receive from those higher in social status than themselves. In the personal interview, each time an interaction was reported, a series of questions was asked concerning the referent with whom the respondent had talked. The referent's husband's occupation was defined and compared with the respondent's husband's occupation as the basis for the status compatibility measure.

Analysis of non-family interactions is presented in Table 4. Though

TABLE 4

COMPARISON OF EARLY AND LATE BUYERS' NON-FAMILY INTERACTIONS BY
SOCIAL STATUS COMPATIBILITY GENERAL FASHION CONTEXT

Referent compared to respondent	Receiving interactions [a]		Influencing interactions [a]	
	Early buyer	Late buyer	Early buyer	Late buyer
Referent of higher social status	16%*	11%	13%**	—
Referent of same social status	80	82	74	86%
Referent of lower social status	4	7	13	14
TOTAL	100%	100%	100%	100%
BASE NUMBERS OF INTER-ACTIONS	25	27	23	35

[a] "Receiving" interactions were those where the respondent primarily received information; in "influencing" interactions the respondent *gave* advice.

* *I.e.,* in 16% of the "receiving" interactions, the referent had a higher social status than the respondent in the early buyer group.

** *I.e.,* in 13% of the "influencing" interactions, the referent had a higher social status than the respondent in the early buyer group.

some "trickle" might be read into the data, the basic conclusion is that the vast majority of receiving and influencing interactions by both early and late buyer were *between individuals of the same social status.* Personal transmission of fashion information moves primarily horizontally rather than vertically in the class hierarchy.

A NEW APPROACH TO FASHION ADOPTION

The critique and rejection of the "trickle down" theory have set the scene for a counter theory—*a "mass market" or "trickle across" scheme of fashion adoption.* The purpose of this discussion is not to present a highly structured or detailed paradigm in the tradition of the deductive method. Rather, the objective is to draw the data presented earlier into a broad conceptual scheme descriptive of modern adoption behavior. The scheme represents only a loose framework of notions but is a first step toward a more definitive model of the adoption process.

In essence, the "mass market" or "trickle across" theory of fashion adoption centers around four broad arguments:

1. Within the fashion season, the social culture and the fashion industry's manufacturing and merchandising strategies almost guarantee adoption by consumers across socio-economic groups simultaneously in the time dimension.

2. Consumers theoretically have the freedom to select from a wide range of contemporary and classic styles in the season's inventory to satisfy the dictates of their physical features and personal tastes.

3. The innovators and influentials play key roles in directing fashion adoption and represent discrete market segments within social strata.

4. The transmission of information and personal influence "trickles across" or flows primarily horizontally within social strata rather than vertically across strata.

The basic contribution of this scheme is to refocus on the horizontal versus the vertical flow and on the major consumer change agents—the innovator and the influential—in the adoption process. Though some vertical flow undoubtedly exists, it does not represent the dominant movement in adoption. Given simultaneous adoption across socioeconomic strata and freedom of choice among consumers, the innovators and the influentials tend to direct fashion adoption within social strata.

In general, the functions of the innovator and the influential appear to differ. The innovator is the earliest visual communicator of the season's styles for the mass of fashion consumers. The influential appears to define and endorse appropriate standards. Both the innovator and the influential are performing advisory functions but the nature of the advice and the respective power are different. For example, in a particular social network, the influential may define the dress appropriate for the bridge party, cocktail party, etc. The innovator, in turn, may present the current offerings consistent with these broad standards. The separate roles of the innovator and the influential are graphically supported by the concentration of the influentials in the late buyer sector of the total Fall millinery market.

Within this framework, the horizontal flow concept is fundamental. When the new fashions are introduced, the innovators and influentials play out their roles within social strata. Given initial introduction across social strata, adoption processes are operative simultaneously within different strata. An abundance of anecdotal evidence exists illustrating products and fashions that have received wide acceptance within some social strata, but have not been successful at other levels.

The new conceptual approach has important implications for fashion management. Though the fashion industry typically segments the market on price dimensions, merchandisers deal in aggregate terms within specific price ranges. To be sure, fashion merchandisers often "sense" style and color trends with uncanny accuracy and intuitively segment markets in this manner. More precise segmentation, however, is rare.

The "mass market" model suggests a form of "functional" segmentation. The innovators and the influentials are identified as discrete market segments within social strata. These groups represent prime sales targets themselves. More importantly, however, they represent the key links to the volume fashion market. Obviously, the fashion manufacturer and merchandiser should cultivate these market segments and utilize them in expediting the fashion flow.

SUMMARY

The central theme of this research has been that the traditional fashion adoption process model—the "trickle down" theory—does not reflect contemporary fashion behavior. Based on a consumer survey of adoption in women's millinery, the empirical data indicated that the innovators or early buyers in the fashion season were not an "elite esotery" of upper class consumers. Nor were the early buyers the dominant personal influentials in the adoption process. In contrast, the fashion influentials were concentrated in the late buyer group. Based on the anecdotal and empirical evidence, the "mass market" or "trickle across" scheme has been presented. The major contribution of this approach is the emphasis on the horizontal flow of adoption within strata and the roles of the innovators and the influentials in the process.

While the scheme is based on research in the product category of millinery, the conclusions have relevance for the entire area of fashion adoption. The specific identity and profile of the innovators and the influentials may vary with fashion products. The *adoption process* outlined in this paper, however, seems applicable across fashion products. Utilization of the scheme by fashion merchandisers is contingent upon identification of the innovator and influential market segments within specific contexts. The scheme does represent a general analytical approach to the mysteries of fashion adoption more descriptive of modern adoption behavior than the traditional "trickle down" theory.

17

LIFE-STYLE CONCEPTS and MARKETING

WILLIAM LAZER

A general concept, referred to vaguely as "life style," is being used by behavioral scientists, especially sociologists. The precise nature and scope of the concept is not clear. However, in interviews about life style, several behavioral scientists revealed that they understood its general meaning and its significance for research purposes. They were also willing to discuss relevant life-style research projects and to recommend a body of literature that reflected a life-style orientation. They did not, however, define the concept specifically, and none of the recommended literature contained a definition.

THE LIFE STYLE CONCEPT

What is life style?

Life style is a systems concept. It refers to the distinctive or characteristic mode of living, in its aggregative and broadest sense, of a whole society or segment thereof. It is concerned with those unique ingredients or qualities which describe the style of life of some culture or group, and distinguish it from others. It embodies the patterns that develop and emerge from the dynamics of living in a society.

Life style, therefore, is the result of such forces as culture, values, resources, symbols, license, and sanction. From one perspective, the ag-

Reprinted from Stephen A. Greyser (ed.), *Toward Scientific Marketing* (Chicago: American Marketing Association, 1964), pp. 130-139.

gregate of consumer purchases, and the manner in which they are consumed, reflect a society's life style.

Following this definition it is logical to speak of the American life style, our family life styles, consumer life styles, the life style of various social strata, and the life style of specific groups in different stages of the life cycle.

In marketing we have been particularly interested in consumer life styles in terms of the way people individualize, and identify themselves as members of various groups, and the resulting patterns of living. For example, we have gathered and analyzed data on consumer incomes, age groups, and expenditure patterns for decades. The goal is not one of assembling statistics for the sake of statistical information. Rather it is one of translating statistical findings about consumers into models of consumer life styles that will permit us to understand and predict various dimensions of consumer behavior, particularly purchase behavior.

A life-style hierarchy may be charted consisting of:

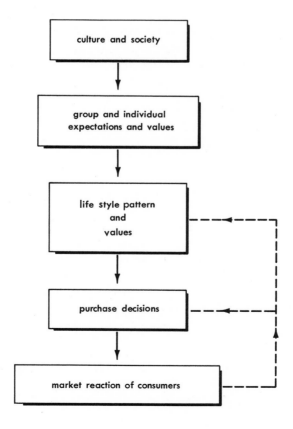

Life style, therefore, is a major behavioral concept for understanding, explaining, and predicting consumer and business behavior. It is a more generalized concept than existing concepts of consumer behavior that have been advanced in marketing. Such topics as mobility, leisure, social class, life cycle, status, conformity, mass, and the family as a consuming unit are all part of the life-style fabric. As a result, life-style studies could foster the unification of findings and theories related to consumer behavior. In fact, life-style is a point of interdisciplinary convergence among marketing and such subject-matter areas as sociology, social and cultural anthropology, psychology, demography, and social psychology.

Economists and marketing people seem to have a different perspective on the value of life style concepts and findings. In most economic studies the life style of a society is usually assumed or ignored. It is part of the "state of the art" and "other things being equal," statements. (One striking exception is Veblen who developed such concepts as vicarious consumption and vicarious leisure.)

By contrast, in marketing, *life-style factors are viewed as among the most important forces influencing and shaping economic activity.* They are the very focus of a major part of marketing. Foote, for instance, has suggested that in essence marketers are becoming taste counselors.[1] If this is the case, marketing and life style are surely intertwined.

Since ours is a materialistic, acquisitive, thing-minded, abundant economy, marketing becomes one of the cores for understanding life styles. Therefore, marketing is in a position to make a significant contribution to a number of life-style oriented disciplines. Moreover, since our life style is being emulated in other parts of the world, such as Europe, Japan and Latin America, a better understanding of our life style may also enhance economic development theory.

MARKETING AND THE LIFE STYLE OF ABUNDANCE

When we think of abundance, we usually perceive of the physical capabilities and potentialities of a society. Abundance, however, is also a result of the culture itself since it stems partly from physical factors and partly from cultural forces. In large measure, our economic abundance results from certain institutions in our society which affect our pattern of living.

---

[1] Nelson Foote, "The Anatomy of the Consumer," in Lincoln H. Clark, ed. *Consumer Behavior, The Dynamics of Consumer Reaction,* New York University Press, pp. 21-24.

Potter maintains that advertising is the institution identified with abundance, particularly American abundance.[2] However, the institution that is brought into being by abundance without previous emphasis or existence in the same form, is the institution of marketing. It is marketing expressed not only in advertising forms, but in such forms as the emphasis upon consumption in our society, marketing research, marketing planning, the marketing concept, new approaches to product development, credit, the management of innovation, the utilization of effective merchandising techniques, and the cultivation of mass markets: that is the institution of abundance.

Ours is a business-dominated society. Hence, business influences our life styles as profoundly as any other force. One of the unique characteristics of American business, however, is the distinctive approach it adopts to marketing. Marketing has reached its most mature form and has had its greatest impact on life styles in the American economy.

Other cultures have made significant contributions to business thought and practice in such areas as business law, ethics, accounting, finance, production systems, and organization theory. By contrast, marketing progress to date is uniquely attributable to the American life style, and it is being studied and emulated in other parts of the world. Such institutions and techniques as self-service, supermarkets, discount houses, marketing research, credit plans, and packaging are spreading part of the American life style in many parts of the world.

In a life-style sense, marketing is an institution of social control. It is an institution of social control in the same sense the school and the home are. It exerts an extensive influence on our life style which I maintain is for the betterment of our social and economic life. Moreover, since marketing is responsible to a very large extent for our standard of living it is impossible to understand our culture fully, and hence our life style, without some comprehension of marketing.

The impact of marketing on our patterns of living, particularly advertising, has not been ignored. Advertising has been criticized pointedly. Toynbee, for example, writes that if it were demonstrated to be true "that personal consumption stimulated by advertising is essential for growth and full employment in an economy of abundance . . . it would also demonstrate to my mind that an economy of abundance is a spiritually unhealthy way of life, and that the sooner we reform it the better . . . The moral that I draw is that a way of life based on personal consumption, stimulated by advertising needs changing."[3] These are strong indictments of unfavorable marketing influences on our life

---

[2] David M. Potter, *People of Plenty* (Chicago: The University of Chicago Press, 1954), p. 167.

[3] "Toynbee vs. Bernbach: Is Advertising Morally Defensible?" *Yale Daily News,* Special Issue, 1963, p. 2.

style and are reinforced by the writings of such people as Warne, Galbraith, and Schlesinger.

When abundance prevails, however, the limitations and constraints upon business and other parts of our life style shift." Potter writes: "The most critical point in the functioning of society shifts from production to consumption . . . the culture must be reoriented to convert the producer's into a consumer's culture . . . and the society must be adjusted to a new set of drives and values of which consumption is paramount."[4] This becomes the challenge of marketing in altering life styles in an abundant economy. *Marketing becomes an instrument for changing production-oriented value into consumption-oriented norms.*

Marketing and Values

Our basic value system determines the nature and significance of various social institutions. These fundamental values, moreover, are not merely the result of the whims of marketers. It is true that we live in a sensate culture, one which stresses sensory enjoyment, materialism and utilitarianism.[5] Consumers desire and can own those items and symbols that are associated with status, achievement, and accomplishment. Material values have become important. Marketing responds to, and reinforces, such values in our abundant culture, and in so doing appeals to the senses and emphasizes materialism.

The life-style question still to be answered, however, is one concerning the relative desirability of our life style with such emphasis as contrasted with other life styles. Great materialistic stress and accomplishment is not inherently sinful and bad. Moral values are not vitiated as many critics seem to think by substantial material acquisitions. In reality the improvement of material situations can lead to a greater recognition of intrinsic values, the lifting of general tastes, the enhancement of a moral climate and the direction of more attention to the appreciation of art and esthetics.

This I would suggest is occurring today. It has also been the pattern of the past. In history great artistic and cultural advancements were at least accompanied, if not shaped, by periods of flourishing trade and commerce.

The next marketing frontier may well be an inner one—the market of the mind and the personal development of consumers.[6] Marketing in

---

4 Potter, *op. cit.,* p. 173.

5 See Pitirim A. Sorokin, *The Crisis of Our Age* (New York: E. P. Dutton & Co., Inc., 1946), especially Chapter III.

6 For a discussion of this point see William Lazer & Eugene J. Kelley Editorial Postscript in William Lazer & Eugene J. Kelley, *Managerial Marketing: Perspectives & Viewpoints* (Richard D. Irwin, Inc., Rev. Ed., 1963), p. 683.

the future may be geared to filling the needs of this inner frontier. One of its roles may be that of encouraging increasing expenditures by consumers, of both dollars and time, to develop themselves intellectually, socially, and morally. This has already been accomplished to a limited degree: witness the increasing demand for classical records, good books, the attendance at symphony concerts, the purchase of good oil paintings through mail order catalogues, and the support for the arts in general. Social critics, while prone to point out the undesirable impact of marketing on our life styles, have neglected to indicate the progress and contributions that have been made.

LIFE STYLE AND CONSUMER EXPECTATIONS

Part of the American life style may be referred to as the American Dream. A big difference exists between the American Dream with its expectations and the dreams and expectations of other countries. The gap, however, is narrowing.

The American Dream as a life style concept includes a belief in equality of opportunity to obtain a good standard of living, to acquire status and success in a community through individual initiative, determination, sacrifice and skill. It involves the contradictory concepts of equality for all and the rank and status orderings that result in the social ladders so characteristic of the functioning of our complex society. It requires the maintenance of an open society with opportunity for upward economic and social movement and the availability of education which is a root for social achievement, occupational advancement, and higher incomes on a widespread basis. These aspects of the Dream are reflected in our life style.

In general, American consumers, especially younger consumers, in living out the Dream exude optimism for the future. They feel sure that tomorrow will be better than today. American consumers believe that they can continue to expand their consumption and increase their relative amount of pleasure rather than merely limit desires. They feel sure they can continue increasing the area of purchasing power under their control.

One result of this optimistic outlook is that American consumers see virtue not so much in curbing desires, but rather in realizing oneself by acquiring the necessary goods and symbols. This optimistic life style has a historical root, for as Kraus has pointed out, unlike the European who only hoped that tomorrow would be no worse than today, Americans felt cheated if tomorrow were not better than today.[7] This orienta-

[7] See Michael Kraus, "The United States to 1865" (Ann Arbor, Mich.: The University of Michigan Press, 1959).

tion is supported and reflected in such marketing concepts and techniques as programmed innovation and product development, installment credit, advertising, sales promotion and merchandising activities.

Life Style and Change

In our life style we do not accept institutions, techniques, and products as permanent. Our society contains a rich tradition of expecting and anticipating change. This anticipation results from a conscious belief that changes are normal, useful, helpful, and good. We seem to accept what appears to be good today and anticipate that it will be superseded by items that are superior tomorrow. The rather trite expression "innovate or perish" has rich meaning for businesses trying to meet the demands of our pattern of life.

Such an attitude is one of the foundations of aggressive marketing. Girod has written that in our culture, "Innovation, change, mobility, and movement are permanent traits," and that, "In stressing the need for innovation, Americans are fighting for the maintenance of this aspect of their way of life for permanency of the one thing to which they are attached."[8]

By contrast, some other cultures which are more restrictive in their anticipations do not expect, hope for, or plan for any great change in their environment. They strive to maintain the status quo. In these cultures which are resolute against the suggestion of new ideas, new products, and new processes, marketing tends to play but a minor role.

To date, technological changes have had the greatest effect on our life styles. Changing methods of marketing are, however, very significant. Consider the effect on our life style, and the life style of other cultures of supermarkets, self-service, discount houses, shopping centers, automatic vending machines, credit plans, new products, packages, and new communications techniques. Such process and service innovations will have an even greater effect in the future.

CONSUMERS, CONSUMPTION, AND LIFE STYLE

In the scheme of our life style, because of a previous production orientation, the relative significance of consumers and consumption as economic determinants has been under-emphasized. The importance of maintaining physical production is, of course, widely recognized. Only limited reference, however, is made to the corresponding necessity of maintain-

[8] Roger Girod, "Comment on Consumer Reaction to Innovation," in Lincoln H. Clark, ed. *Consumer Behavior, Research on Consumer Reactions* (New York: Harper & Brothers, 1958), p. 10.

ing consumption. *The critical nature of consumption in an abundant economy demands that consumption should not be considered as a happenstance activity.* We must establish the necessary conditions for consumption to proceed on an adequate and orderly basis.

Until recently, even the relative significance of consumer investment in our economy was greatly under-emphasized. Business investment, which is certainly a most significant factor in influencing business conditions, received almost all the attention. Katona points out, however, that "growth and expansion of the American economy are dependent on consumer investment as well as business investment . . . business investment and consumer investment are equally important forces which either stimulate or retard the economy."[9]

What must also be recognized is the important fact that consumer investments are not merely the function of increased income. They stem from and reflect life styles.

A distorted picture has been presented of consumers and the purchase and consumption process. Consumers have been portrayed in much of the non-marketing literature as emotional, irrational, uninformed beings, manipulated at will through marketing devices. It is held that conformity, followership, waste, ostentation, and meaningless style changes have been foisted upon consumers by marketers. Rokeach points out, however, that marketers have been using the wrong psychological theory. He emphasizes that the theory that consumers are irrational creatures who must be appealed to only on an emotional level is outmoded. Modern psychological theories view man as "not only a rationalizing creature but also a rational creature—curious, exploratory and receptive to new ideas."[10]

Competition as Part of Our Life Style

Essentially, competition is directly related to and can be defined only in terms of the culture and nature of the environment that surrounds it. Competition has its fullest meaning in the marketing environment of the consumeristic economy rather than in a controlled, planned, or cooperative environment such as exists in many other countries.

In thinking about competition, however, we tend to be retrospective, and do not relate it to current life styles. In interpreting laws and in our economic analysis we often cling to past or previous models of competition and competitive situations. For example, we often conceptualize competition in terms of an emerging industrial society rather

[9] George Katona, *Michigan Business Review* (June, 1961), p. 17.
[10] *New York Times* (November 7, 1963), p. 60, "Advertising: A Wrong Psychological Limb?"

than a maturing industrial society, in terms of price competition neglecting convenience and service competition, in terms of an economy of scarcity with relatively low consumer purchasing power rather than an economy of abundance with widespread discretionary purchasing power, in terms of manufacturers and distributors controlling and dominating the market place rather than an economy governed (or at least influenced to a large extent) by customer sovereignty, and in terms of intra-industry competition rather than inter-industry competition.

In particular, there is a misplaced emphasis, stemming from past economic models, on *price* as the key competitive weapon. This does not mean that price competition is no longer important in our mode of living. Certainly it is. It does mean, however, that ours is a competitive situation in which *price obscurity* and not price clarity seems to be the rule and in which other variables including convenience and service are very important.[11]

We seem to take competition for granted as one of the inherent aspects of our life style. J. M. Clark points out, however, that "there can be no certainty that competition will remain vigorous in American business," and that "the necessary conditions are a fascinating subject for speculation." The necessary and sufficient condition for the existence of keen, vigorous competition, however, is clear. *It is aggressive marketing.* Changes in price, advertising, products, and channels of distribution tend to keep things stirred up and prevent competition from lapsing into routine passivity.[12]

CONCLUSION

To a large extent our marketing technology sets us apart from other cultures. It is a motivating force behind our competitive system and characterizes our life style. Marketing in the future must be recognized as a major institution in our way of life as well as a force that can contribute greatly to the influence of international life styles.

Yet analysts of our culture and life styles have virtually ignored marketing. It is often regarded as but a minor type of activity which is not important enough to be investigated. It has been neglected by psychologists, sociologists, social and cultural anthropologists, economists, and historians. It is treated as though it were a side issue in our economic activity, when in essence, it is one of the core or focal points.

Marketing is one of the longstanding institutions in our society. Its

11 See Eugene J. Kelley, "The Importance of Convenience in Consumer Purchasing," *Journal of Marketing* (July 1958).

12 J. M. Clark, "Competition: Static Models and Dynamic Aspects," *American Economic Review*, Vol. 45, No. 2 (May 1955), p. 462.

impact reverberates throughout our culture. It has shaped our life styles and has affected every one of us significantly. The inextricable intertwinement of marketing and our life style was emphasized by a theologian who wrote, "The saintly cannot be separated from the market place for it is in the market place that man's future is being decided; they must be schooled in the arts of the market place as in the discipline of saintliness itself."[13]

[13] Louis Finkelstein in Conference On The American Character, *Bulletin, Center For The Study of Democratic Institutions* (October 1961), p. 6.

18

GROUP INFLUENCE in MARKETING and PUBLIC RELATIONS

FRANCIS S. BOURNE

THE CONCEPT OF REFERENCE-GROUP INFLUENCE

Basically, the concept [of reference-group] is a very simple one, and it has been recognized both by social scientists and, on a common-sense basis, by practical men for as long as people have been concerned with human behaviour.

On the common-sense level, the concept says in effect that man's behaviour is influenced in different ways and in varying degrees by other people. Comparing one's own success with that of others is a frequent source of satisfaction or disappointment. Similarly, before making a decision one often considers what such and such a person of such and such a group (whose opinion one has *some* reason to follow) would do in these circumstances, or what they would think of one for making a certain decision rather than another. Put in these ways, of course, reference-group influence represents an unanalysed truism which has long been recognized. The problem to which social scientists have been addressing themselves intensively only for the last two decades, however, concerns the refinement of this common-sense notion to the end that it might be effectively applied to concrete situations.

The real problems are those of determining which kinds of groups are likely to be referred to by which kinds of individuals under which kinds of circumstances in the process of making which decisions, and of

Reprinted from Rensis Likert and Samuel P. Hayes, Jr. (eds.), *Some Application of Behavioral Research* (Paris: UNESCO, 1957), pp. 208-210, 211-212, and 217-224.

measuring the extent of this reference-group influence. Towards this end, empirical researches have been conducted in recent years which have at least made a start in the process of refining the reference-group concept.

Reference-group theory, as it has developed, has become broad enough to cover a wide range of social phenomena, both with respect to the relation of the individual to the group and with respect to the type of influence exerted upon the individual by the group in question.

Reference groups against which an individual evaluates his own status and behaviour may be of several kinds:

1. They may be membership groups to which a person actually belongs and may involve either: (a) Small face-to-face groups in which actual association is the rule, such as families or organizations, whether business, social, religious, or political, or (b) groups in which actual membership is held but in which personal association is absent. (For example, membership in a political party, none of whose meetings are personally attended.) These groups may be of the same kinds as the former but differ only in the lack of face-to-face association with other members.

2. They may be groups or categories to which a person automatically belongs by virtue of age, sex, education, marital status and so on. This sort of reference-group relationship involves the concept of role. For example, before taking a certain action an individual might consider whether this action would be regarded as appropriate in his role as a man or husband or educated person or older person or a combination of all these roles. What is involved here is an individual's perception of what society—either in general or that part of it with which he has any contact—expects people of his age, sex, education or marital status to do in given circumstances.

3. They may be anticipatory rather than actual membership groups. Thus a person who aspires to membership in a group to which he does *not* belong may be more likely to refer to it or compare himself with its standards when making a decision than he is to refer to the standards of the group in which he actually belongs but would like to leave. This involves the concept of upward mobility. When such upward mobiliy is sought in the social or business world, it is ordinarily accompanied by a sensitivity to the attitudes of those in the groups to which one aspires, whether it involves the attitudes of country-club members in the eyes of the aspiring non-member or the attitudes of management in the eyes of the ambitious wage-earner or junior executive.

4. They may be negative, dissociative reference-groups. These constitute the opposite side of the coin from the anticipatory membership groups. Thus an individual sometimes avoids a certain action because it is associated with a group (to which the individual may or may not in fact belong) from which he would like to dissociate himself.

Reference-groups influence behaviour in two main ways. First, they influence *aspiration levels,* and thus play a part in producing satisfaction or frustration. If the other members of one's reference-group (for example, the neighbours) are wealthier, more famous, better gardeners, etc., one may be dissatisfied with one's own achievements and may strive to do as well as the others.

Secondly, reference-groups influence *kinds* of behaviour. They establish approved patterns of using one's wealth, of wearing one's fame, of designing one's garden. They also lay down taboos, and may have the power to apply actual sanctions (for example, exclusion from the group). They thus produce *conformity* as well as *contentment* (or discontent).

These two kinds of influence have, however, a good deal in common. Both imply certain perceptions on the part of the individual, who attributes to the reference-group characteristics it may or may not actually have. Both involve psychological rewards and punishment.

THE PRACTICAL VALUE OF THE REFERENCE-GROUP CONCEPT IN MARKETING AND PUBLIC RELATIONS

In applying the reference-group concept to practical problems in marketing and public relations, three basic questions arise:

Reference-group relevance. How do you determine whether and to what extent reference-group influence is operating in a given situation? The reference-group is, after all, only one of many influences in decision-making, varying greatly in prominence from situation to situation.

Reference-group identification. How do you identify the particular reference-group or groups, or individuals, who are most relevant in influencing decisions under given circumstances? This is perhaps the most difficult question to answer in many cases, particularly where multiple reference-groups are involved.

Reference-group identification and effective communication. Once having identified the nature of the group-influence operating in a given situation, how do you then most effectively *communicate* with the groups or individuals you desire to influence?

This, of course, is the crux of the matter, since the answers to the first two questions are of value only to the extent that they can be translated into more pertinent and effective communication, designed to influence purchasing behaviour or the attitudes of various publics towards a firm or industry.

Experimental evidence is now available which sheds light on each of these three questions. From this evidence, and from the general advancement in the methodology of social research in recent years, there have emerged some very tentative generalizations. These can be applied only with the most careful attention to the special circumstances operating in individual instances, and serve more as guides to fruitful ways of examining problems as they arise than as simple answers to problems.

Marketing and Reference-Group Relevance

As already suggested, the reference-group constitutes only one of the many influences in buying-decisions, and this influence varies from product to product. How then does one determine whether reference-group influence is likely to be a factor in buying-behaviour in connexion with a given product or brand? Research has been conducted on the various factors that influence buying-behaviour with reference to several products, and out of this have emerged some general ideas about how reference-group influences may enter into purchasing.

Buying may be a completely individualistic activity or very much socially conditioned. Consumers are often influenced by what others buy, especially those persons with whom they compare themselves or use as reference-groups.

The conspicuousness of a product is perhaps the most general attribute bearing on its susceptibility to reference-group influence. There are two aspects to conspicuousness in this particular context that help to determine reference-group influence. First, the article must be conspicuous in the most obvious sense that it can be seen and identified by others. Secondly, it must be conspicuous in the sense of standing out and being noticed. In other words, no matter how visible a product is, if virtually everyone owns it, it is not conspicuous in the second sense of the word. This leads to a further distinction: reference-groups may influence either (a) the purchase of a product, or (b) the choice of a particular brand or type, or (c) both.

The possible susceptibility of various product and brand-buying to reference-group influence is suggested in Figure 1.

According to this classification, a particular item might be susceptible to reference-group influence in its purchase in three different ways, corresponding to three of the four cells in the above figure. Reference group influence may operate with respect to brand or type but not with respect to product (Brand + Product —) as in the upper left cell, or it may operate both with respect to brand and product (Brand + Product +) as in the upper right cell, or it may operate with respect to product but not brand (Brand — Product +) as in the lower right cell.

Only the "minus-minus" items of the kind illustrated (Brand — Product —) in the lower left cell are not likely to involve any significant reference-group influence in their purchase *at the present time*.

What are some of the characteristics that place an item in a given category, and what significance do such placements have for marketing and advertising policy?

"Product Plus, Brand Plus" Items

Cars are a case in which both the product and the brand are socially conspicuous. Whether or not a person buys a car, and also what particular brand he buys, is likely to be influenced by what others do. This

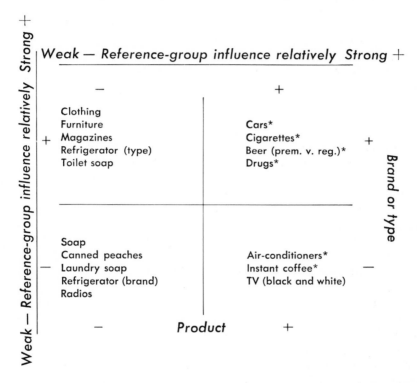

Figure 1.   Products and brands of consumer-goods may be classified by extent to which reference groups influence their purchase.[1]

[1] The classification of all products marked with an asterisk (*) is based on actual experimental evidence. Other products in this table are classified speculatively on the basis of generalizations derived from the sum of research in this area and confirmed by the judgment of seminar participants.

Source. Bureau of Applied Social Research, Columbia University (Glock, unpublished).

also holds true for cigarettes and drugs (decisions made by M.D.'s as to what to prescribe) and for beer with respect to type (premium versus regular) as opposed to brand. Cigarettes and drugs, however, qualify as "plus-plus" items in a manner different from cars.

For example, while the car belongs to a class of products where brand differentiation is based at least substantially on real differences in attributes, the cigarette belongs to a class of product in which it is hard to differentiate one brand from another by attributes; hence attributes are ascribed largely through reference-group appeal built up by advertising. Popular images of the kinds of people who smoke various brands have been created at great cost, and in some cases additional images are being created to broaden a particular brand's market. In the case of drugs, it was found that the reference-group influencing *whether* the product was used was different from that influencing the particular *brand* selected. Reference-group influence was found to be prominent in determining whether or not beer was purchased at all, and also in determining whether regular or premium beer was selected. It did not appear strongly to influence choice of a particular brand.

"Product Plus, Brand Minus" Items

Instant coffee is one of the best examples of this class of item. Whether it is served in a household depends in considerable part on whether the housewife, in view of her own reference-groups and the image she has of their attitudes toward this product, considers it appropriate to serve it. The brand itself, in this instance, is not conspicuous or socially important and is a matter largely for individual choice. In the case of air-conditioners, it was found that little prestige is attached to the particular brand used, and reference-group influence related largely to the idea of purchasing the product itself. Analysis in one city revealed that the purchase of this often "visible from the outside" product was concentrated in small areas. Clusters of conditioners were frequently located in certain rows and blocks. In many cases, clusters did not even cross streets. Immediate neighbours apparently served as a powerfully influential reference-group in the purchase of these appliances. In this general class may also be found the black and white TV set, with its antenna often visible from outside the house. As the saturation point in black and white TV set ownership rapidly approaches, however, the influence of reference-groups may soon become unimportant, and the product can then be put in the "brand minus, product minus" quadrant, beside refrigerators. Colour TV may remain in the "brand plus, product minus" quadrant, with type (colour) rather than brand *per se* as the element strongly related to reference-groups.

"Product Minus, Brand Plus" Items

This group is essentially made up of products that all people or at least a very high proportion of people use, although differing as to type or brand.

Perhaps the leading example in this field is clothing. There could hardly be a more socially visible product than this, but the fact that everyone in our society wears clothing takes the *product* out of the area of reference-group influence. The *type* of clothing purchased is, however, very heavily influenced by reference-groups, with each sub-culture in the population (teenagers, zoot-suiters, Ivy League Collegians, Western Collegians, workers, bankers, advertising men, etc.) setting its own standards and often prescribing, within fairly narrow limits, what those who feel related to these groups can wear. Similarly, though not quite as dramatically, articles like furniture, magazines, refrigerators and toilet soap are seen in almost all homes, causing their purchase in general to fall outside the orbit of reference-group influence. The visibility of these items, however, coupled with the wide variety of styles and types among them, makes the selection of particular kinds highly susceptible to reference-group influence.

"Product Minus, Brand Minus" Items.

Purchasing behaviour in this class of items is governed by product attributes rather than by the nature of the presumed users. In this group, neither the products nor the brands tend to be socially conspicuous. This is not to say that personal influence cannot operate with respect to purchasing the kind of items included in this group. As with all products, some people tend to exert personal influence and others tend to be influenced by individual persons. Reference-groups as such, however, exert relatively little influence on buying behaviour in this class of items, examples of which are salt, canned peaches, laundry soap and radios. It is apparent that placement in this category is not *necessarily* inherent in the product itself and hence is not a static placement. Items can move in and out of this category.

While it is true that items which are essentially socially inconspicuous, like salt and laundry soap, are natural candidates for this category, it is not entirely impossible that, through large-scale advertising and other promotional efforts, images of the kind of people who use certain brands of salt or laundry soap could be built up so as to bring reference-group influence into play on such items, much as in the case of cigarettes. The task would be more difficult, however, since the cigarette is already socially visible. On the other hand, items such as radios and refrigerators, which are conspicuously visible and whose purchase was once subject to considerable reference-group influence, have now slipped into this category through near-saturation in ownership.

IMPLICATIONS OF STRONG AND WEAK REFERENCE-GROUP INFLUENCE FOR ADVERTISING AND MARKETING

It should be stressed again that this scheme of analysis is introduced to show how reference-group influence might enter into purchasing behaviour in certain cases. It cannot be regarded as generally applicable to marketing problems on all levels. There is still a need to know more precisely where many different products or brands fit into this scheme. Attempts to fit products and brands into the preceding classification suggest that research needs to be done in order to obtain more relevant information about each product.

Assuming, however, that a product or brand has been correctly placed with respect to the part played by reference-groups in influencing its purchase, how can this help in marketing the product in question?

1. Where neither product nor brand appear to be associated strongly with reference-group influence, advertising should emphasize the product's attributes, intrinsic qualities, price, and advantages over competing products.

2. Where reference-group influence is operative, the advertiser should stress the kinds of people who buy the product, reinforcing and broadening where possible the existing stereotypes of users. The strategy of the advertiser should involve learning what the stereotypes are and what specific reference-groups enter into the picture, so that appeals can be "tailored" to each main group reached by the different media employed.

Although it is important to see that the "right" kind of people use a product, a crucial problem is to make sure that the popular image of the product's users is as broad as possible without alienating any important part of the product's present or potential market in the process. Mistakes have been made in creating or reinforcing a stereotype of consumers which was too small and exclusive for a mass-produced item; this strategy excluded a significant portion of the potential market. On the other hand, some attempts to appeal to new groups through advertising in mass media have resulted in the loss of existing groups of purchasers whose previous (favourable) image of the product-user was adversely affected. A possible strategy for increasing the base of the market for a product by enlarging the image of its users is to use separate advertising media through which a new group can be reached without reducing the product's appeal to the original group of users. Another method might be to appeal to a new group through co-operative advertising by a number of companies producing the product, possibly through a trade association. This would minimize the risk to an individual producer who, trying to

reach a new group of users through his own advertising (women as opposed to men or wealthy as opposed to average people, for example),
might antagonize people who had a strong need to identify with the
original image of the product's kind of user.

Product Attributes versus Reference-Group Influence

A technique which could serve to assess the relative influence of reference-groups, as compared with product attributes, on the purchase of a
given product was employed in research on a food product which will be
referred to as product "X".

A cross-section of "X" users was asked several questions relating to
particular attributes of "X", such as whether it was more harmful or ben-
eficial to one's health, whether or not it was considered fattening, whether
it was considered extravagant or economical, whether or not it tasted
good, and so on. These same people were also asked a reference-group-
oriented question about "X", to determine whether or not "X" was popular with most of their friends. It was found that there was usually more
"X" eating among people who reacted negatively to the attributes of "X"
but admitted to its popularity among most of their friends, than among
those who reacted positively to the attributes of "X" but indicated that
it was not popular with their friends.

These relationships are shown in Table I below. In this table the
scores in parentheses are those of people whose replies showed both attribute influence and reference-group influence exerting pressure in the
same direction.

Special attention should be directed toward the other scores. These
represent situations in which people are under cross-pressures. For each
of the four attributes considered, the reference-group influence is stronger
than the attribute influence, in the use of "X". This is brought out by
the arrows, which point toward the cross-pressure situations where the
reference-group influence is negative. In all these, consumption frequency
is less than where attribute influence alone is negative. Or, put another
way, positive perception of reference-group behaviour with respect to the
food product ("X" is very popular) coupled with negative perception of
its actual attribute ("X" does more harm than good, is fattening, etc.)
leads to more consumption than negative perception of reference-group
behaviour ("X" not very popular) coupled with positive perception of
actual attribute value ("X" does more good than harm, not fattening,
economical).

As can be seen from the comparisons indicated by the arrows, reference-group influence is markedly stronger than attribute influence for
three of the four attributes. Only for "taste" does the attribute influence

come close to competing with reference-group influence in determining consumption of "X".

TABLE 1

RELATION BETWEEN REFERENCE-GROUP AND ATTRIBUTE INFLUENCE
IN USE OF FOOD PRODUCT "X"

	Index of frequency of eating "X" [1]	
	+ Reference-group —	
	With most of respondent's friends "X" is:	
Product attribute	Very popular	Not very popular
Effect of "X" on health		
+ More good than harm . .	(.41)	—.10
— More harm than good . .	.08	(—.51)
+ Do not avoid fattening food and/or feel "X" is not really or a little fattening . . .	(.30)	—.21
— Try to avoid fattening food and feel "X" is really or a little fattening	.14	(—.29)
Economic value judgment		
+ Fairly economical	(.29)	—.20
— Sort of an extravagance . .	.11	(—.33)
Taste judgement		
+ Tastes good	(.42)	.05
— No reference to good taste [2]	.09	(—.38)

[1] All scores in the above table constitute an index of the frequency of "X" eating among respondents falling into the given cell. The scoring procedure used was: frequent "X" users—score $+1$; medium "X" users—score 0; occasional "X" users—score —1.

The final score is derived by subtracting the number of occasional "X" users in a given cell from the number of frequent users and dividing the remainder by the total number of respondents in the cell. For example, the index score .41 was obtained as follows: 329 respondents felt that a moderate amount of "X" does more good than harm AND report that "X" is very popular with most of their friends. Of these 329 respondents 178 are frequent "X" users, 97 are medium "X" users and 43 are occasional "X" users.

The score: $178 - 43 = 135$ The *Index* value: $135/329 = +.41$

[2] "Tastes good" represents the selection of this phrase from a word list of various attributes that might be applied to "X". "No reference to good taste" refers to those respondents who did not select "Tastes good" from the word list.

Source. Bureau of Applied Social Research, Columbia University.

One implication of this finding would be that advertising by the "X" industry might stress the *social* aspects of the product, and the extent to which it is enjoyed by many groups of people like the audience being appealed to, rather than basing its advertising on the *actual attributes* of the product.

In a study of a beverage, it was found that, of those who drank the beverage in question, 95 per cent claimed that their friends also drank it, while of those who did not drink this beverage 85 per cent also claimed that their friends did *not* drink it.

Some products, then, must be sold to whole social groups rather than primarily to individuals.

19

CITY SHOPPERS and URBAN IDENTIFICATION: OBSERVATIONS on the SOCIAL PSYCHOLOGY of CITY LIFE [1]

GREGORY P. STONE

A growing body of evidence seems to be signifying a change in the focus of urban sociology away from the study of urbanism as a *way* of life toward the study of urbanism as a way of *life*. Until recently the view of urbanism as the polar antithesis of the personal, familistic, sacred, and consensual life of the isolated tradition-bound community has imbued most sociological investigations of the city.[2] Recent research suggests theoretical possibilities for explaining how, in the impersonal and anonymous milieu of the city, the individual can establish the requisite social identification for distinguishing himself as a person. Many studies imply

Reprinted from *The American Journal of Sociology*, 60 (July, 1954), pp. 36-45, by permission of the University of Chicago Press. Copyright 1954 by The University of Chicago.

1 The author wishes to express his gratitude to his wife, Margaret, who assisted in the field work, provided helpful criticisms, and otherwise assisted; also to his colleague, William H. Form, for a critical reading. Some of the observations made here appear in greater detail in Gregory P. Stone, "Sociological Aspects of Consumer Purchasing in a Northwest Side Chicago Community" (unpublished Master's thesis, University of Chicago, 1952).

2 In Durkheim, Maine, and Tönnies the "polarities" proposed are not so antithetical as they have sometimes been construed. It seems quite clear that Tönnies, especially, did not propose *Gemeinschaft* and *Gesellschaft* merely as antithetical categories but also as elements of an antinomy such that any tendency toward one form of social relationship evokes countertendencies (see Ferdinand Tönnies, *Fundamental Concepts of Sociology*, trans. and supplemented by Charles P. Loomis [New York: American Book Co., 1940], esp. pp. 221-22).

the hypothesis that typical social relationships characterized by primacy ("or at least quasi-primacy"),[3] in Cooley's sense, have arisen to provide such a matrix of identifications.[4] These observations are the more theoretically strategic because most refer to contexts where life is supposedly impersonal and anonymous.

This article is an attempt to supplement such findings with data on shopping. Few treatises on the sociology of the city fail to designate the market place as the epitome of those "impersonal," "segmentalized," "secondary," "categoric," and "rational" contacts said to characterize human relations in the city. Yet the study reported here points to the possibility that some urbanites, as a consequence of the relationships they establish with the personnel of retail stores, manage to form identifications which bind them to the larger community.

PROCEDURE

Some time ago the writer was engaged by a private research agency to study popular reactions to the establishment of a large chain department store in an outlying business district on Chicago's Northwest Side. One of the techniques was a schedule administered to 150 adult female residents[5] of the area surrounding the business district. Their responses to

---

[3] They are not primary in the sense of encompassing the lives and aspirations of the participants or secondary in being antithetical to the primary group. Schmalenbach has proposed *Bund* as a category to fill the conceptual lacuna. However, it is not the purpose of this article to make a conceptual contribution, and the gap has been filled by a loose interpretation of the concept "primary group" (see Herman Schmalenbach, "Die Soziologische Kategorie des Bundes," *Die Dioskuren: Jahrbuch für Geisteswissenschaften,* I [1922], 35-105).

[4] Early observations relevant to this hypothesis may be found in Schmalenbach, *ibid.;* more recently, in Harry C. Harmsworth, "Primary Group Relationships in Modern Society," *Sociology and Social Research,* XXXI (March-April, 1947), 291-96; and in Robert E. L. Faris, "Development of the Small Group Research Movement," in Muzafer Sherif and M. O. Wilson (eds.), *Group Relations at the Crossroads* (New York: Harper & Bros., 1953), pp. 155-84. Empirical studies bearing on the hypothesis include William F. Whyte, *Street Corner Society* (Chicago: University of Chicago Press, 1943); Morris Janowitz, *The Community Press in an Urban Setting* (Glencoe, Ill.: Free Press, 1952); and "The Imagery of the Urban Community Press," in Paul K. Hatt and Albert J. Reiss, Jr. (eds.), *Reader in Urban Sociology* (Glencoe, Ill.: Free Press, 1951), pp. 532-41; Erwin O. Smigel, "Unemployed Veterans in New York City" (unpublished doctoral dissertation, New York University, 1948), pp. 134-39. An extensive bibliography on the study of primary groups is available in Edward A. Shils, "The Study of the Primary Group," in Daniel Lerner and Harold. D. Lasswell (eds.), *The Policy Sciences* (Stanford University: Stanford University Press, 1951), pp. 44-70.

[5] Because marital status was a variable which might have distorted the findings of the study, 26 single, widowed, or divorced subjects were eliminated from the original 150 informants. Housewives were originally selected as informants because they do most of the buying, but it seems that this situation is changing.

certain questions indicated disparate definitions of shopping situations and markedly different orientations to stores in general. The latter were implicit in the criteria by which the housewives said they evaluated stores in the area and in the expectations they had of store personnel as they encountered them in shopping. Particularly striking, in contrast to customary sociological notions, was their recurrent statement that market relationships were often personal.

This suggested a typology of shopping orientations as a basis for a more intensive analysis of the anomalies. The procedure for its construction and application consisted of four steps: (1) a fourfold classification of the *responses* to one particularly discerning question, called here the "filter" question; (2) a similar classification of *informants* as consumer types on the basis of demonstrated consistencies between their responses to the filter question and a number of other questions termed "indicator" questions; (3) a schematization of the consumer types as *empirical models;* and (4) the construction of *social profiles* based on the patterns of social characteristics associated with the consumer types. These procedures revealed further anomalies which are analyzed in the concluding section of the article.

ORIENTATIONS TO SHOPPING

Responses to the question, "Why would you rather do business with local independent merchants (or large chain stores, depending on a prior choice)?" persistently revealed markedly different orientations to different kinds of stores as well as diverse definitions of shopping. Because of the discriminating power of the question, it was used as a "filtering" device for achieving a preliminary classification of the consumers on the basis of their orientation to shopping.[6]

Replies to the filter question were grouped into five empirical categories of criteria housewives used to evaluate stores: (1) economic, (2) personalizing, (3) ethical, (4) apathetic, and (5) a residual category of unique or indeterminate criteria. As may be seen, some statements did not fall precisely into single categories. When a response included multiple orientations, it was coded for each category.

---

6 Merton distinguishes orientation from role: "The social orientation differs from the social role. Role refers to the manner in which the rights and duties inherent in a social position are put into practice; orientation . . . refers to the theme underlying the complex of social roles performed by an individual. It is the (tacit or explicit) theme which finds expression in each of the complex or social roles in which the individual is implicated" (Robert K. Merton, "Patterns of Influence," in Paul F. Lazarsfeld and Frank Stanton [eds.], *Communications Research 1948-1949* [New York: Harper & Bros., 1949], p. 187).

The Economic Category

Remarks coded in this category clearly indicated that the informant re-garded shopping as primarily buying, her behavior being unambiguously directed to the purchase of goods. The criteria applied to the evaluation of stores included: an appraisal of the store's merchandise in terms of price, quality, and variety; a favorable evaluation of store practices that maximize the efficient distribution of goods; conversely, an unfavorable evaluation of practices and relationships with personnel which impede the quick efficient sale of merchandise; and a favorable rating of condi-tions which maximized independence of customer choice. The following four responses are typical of this category:

I prefer large department stores. They give you better service. Their prices are more reasonable. . . . There's a wider selection of goods.

I prefer big chains. They have cheaper stuff. It's too expensive in small stores. Then, too, I like the idea of helping yourself. Nobody talks you into any-thing. You can buy what you please.

I suppose I should help the smaller stores, but I can do best at the chains. Local merchants are too nosey—too personal—and their prices are higher. The prices in chains are good, and you get self-service in chains.

I like to shop in local independently owned stores. You can get better grade materials and better service there. If anything goes wrong with the material, you always have a chance to go back and make a complaint. They'll make it good for you. They have more time. You're more familiar with that kind of store and can find what you want in a hurry. Some of them allow you stamps on their budget plan, and that saves you a lot of money.

The Personalizing Category

In this category were placed responses defining shopping as fundamen-tally and positively interpersonal. Such informants expressed a tendency to personalize and individualize the customer role in the store and rated stores in terms of closeness of relationships between the customer and personnel. Consequently, "purely" economic criteria, such as price, qual-ity, selection of merchandise, and highly rationalized retailing techniques were of lesser importance. These four remarks exemplify the category:

I prefer local merchants. They're friendlier and not quite so big. . . . Al-though prices are higher in small stores, when you trade with local merchants you have a better chance to be a good customer. They get to know you. People in smaller stores greet you cordially when you come in. They get to know you, and make an effort to please you.

I'd rather trade at my own store than a public store. That's why I prefer local merchants. They're more personal. They get to know your name. They take more interest in you as a human being.

Local merchants give you better service. They get so they know you. The chains are impersonal. They don't try so hard to please you. The customer doesn't mean anything to the clerk in the big chain stores, because it's not his business.

I shop at independents if they have the merchandise. They usually know you by name and try to please you. In the big store no one knows you. . . . Maybe it's because I feel at home in the smaller store. When you're in them, you feel more wanted. You feel lost in a big store.

The Ethical Category

Responses in this category signified that the informants feel a moral obligation to patronize specific types of stores. They perceive shopping in the light of a larger set of values rather than of specific values and more immediately relevant norms. Store patronage was appraised in anticipation of such moral consequences. The following excerpts express it:

It would be better if they were all neighborhood stores. The chains put people out of work because the people have to wait on themselves. But that's what happens in a machine age. They set up everything like a factory. If there's another depression, the chains will put people out of work, because they are set up on a self-help system. So, if you let the chains run the little business out, they will be wrecking their own chances for jobs, if times get too bad.

I prefer the local independents. I think that the chain store is taking too much business away from the little fellow.

I prefer local merchants if they have the variety and a large selection of goods. You know, they're making a living and you want to help them out. The chain stores are making a living too—a damned good one!

You have to give the independent merchant a chance to earn his bread and butter. The chain stores grab it all. The big chain store has no heart or soul.

The Apathetic Category

Included in this category are responses showing that the informant was not interested in shopping and did not discriminate kinds of stores. They emphasize the minimizing of effort in purchasing. Illustrations are:

I don't know. I guess there's not much difference.

Local merchants are O.K. It depends on where you happen to be. Whichever store is the closest is O.K. with me.

It depends on which is the closest.

Chain stores. You can get everything there in one trip. There's nothing particular to like about either kind of store.

Questions on the consumer's image of a good clerk and good store manager, unpleasant and pleasant shopping experiences, and price, quality, and service satisfactions were used as "indicators" to test the consistency with which the orientations elicited by the filter question were maintained. Responses to these questions lent themselves, with some exceptions,[7] to a classification like that set forth above.

After replies to the filter and indicator questions were coded as described, the interviews were again examined, and the coding of answers tabulated for each interview. Informants were placed in exclusive categories when the tabulation of the relevant coded responses demonstrated consistent orientations to the shopping situation. The essential criterion of consistency in this case was met by the requirement that the *majority* of coded "indicator" responses must coincide with *a* coded "filter" response.

A TYPOLOGY OF CONSUMERS

The final classification of housewives yielded four consumer types: (1) economic, (2) personalizing, (3) ethical, and (4) apathetic. Brief sketches of these types were constructed to summarize the characteristics of each as expressed in clustering and interrelated responses to the "filter" and "indicator" questions. These sketches are *empirical models* of the types; they are not designed as concepts for the formulation of propositions to be directly incorporated into a theoretical system.

The empirical models of the consumer types are presented here with the caveat that probably no single consumer was adequately described by any of the models. The models represent composites of actual consumers and their characteristic role orientations.[8]

---

[7] E.g., the questions directed toward the informant's satisfaction with price, quality, and service in stores forced her thinking into an "economic" frame of reference. Thus, these more structured questions were used as indicators only when "economic" and "apathetic" orientations had been signified in response to the "filter" question.

[8] Nevertheless, a *post hoc* attempt to "verify" the typology met with some success. Specifically, a number of items dealing with shopping behavior but not included in the construction of the typology were significantly associated with variations in consumer type in logically compatible directions: number of shopping trips to the downtown central shopping district ($p < .02$; $T = .18$), patronage of women's department stores and specialty shops for women's clothing ($p < .05$; $T = .16$), acquaintance with salesclerks ($p < .01$; $T = .21$), chain store versus independent store patronage ($p < .001$; $T = .35$).

The Economic Consumer

Here was the closest approximation to the "economic man" of the classical economist. This type of shopper expressed a sense of responsibility for her household purchasing duties: she was extremely sensitive to price, quality, and assortment of merchandise, all of which entered into the calculus of her behavior on the market. She was interested in shopping. Clerical personnel and the store were, for her, merely the instruments of her purchase of goods. Thus, efficiency or inefficiency of sales personnel, as well as the relative commensurateness of prices, quality, or the selection of merchandise, were decisive in leaving her with a pleasant or unpleasant impression of the store. The quality she demanded of a "good" clerk was efficiency.

The Personalizing Consumer

This type of consumer shopped "where they know my name." It was important that she shop at her store rather than "public" stores.[9] Strong personal attachments were formed with store personnel, and this personal relationship, often approaching intimacy, was crucial to her patronage of a store. She was highly sensitized to her experiences on the market; obviously they were an important part of her life. It followed that she was responsive to both pleasant and unpleasant experiences in stores. Her conception of a "good" clerk was one who treated her in a personal, relatively intimate manner.

TABLE 1

Distribution of Consumer Types

Type of Consumer	Number	Per Cent
Economic	41	33
Personalizing	35	28
Ethical	22	18
Apathetic	21	17
Indeterminate	5	4
Total	124	100

9 The personal pronouns "I," "me," and "my" found their way frequently into the interviews, one indication of the extent to which they built up strong identifications with the stores they patronized. Therefore, the relationships with store personnel are referred to later as "primary" or "quasi-primary," for the store has become incorporated into the social self of the consumer. As Cooley put it, "The social self is simply any idea, or system of ideas, drawn from the communicative life, that the mind cherishes as its own." Hence the store may be seen as a part of the social self of the personalizing type of consumer (see Charles Horton Cooley, *Human Nature and the Social Order* [New York: Charles Scribner's Sons, 1902], p. 147).

The Ethical Consumer

This type of shopper shopped where she "ought" to. She was willing to sacrifice lower prices or a wider selection of goods "to help the little guy out" or because "the chain store has no heart or soul." Consequently, strong attachments were sometimes formed with personnel and store owners or with "stores" in the abstract. These mediated the impressions she had of stores, left pleasant impressions in her memory, and forced unpleasant impressions out. Since store personnel did not enter in primarily as instrumentalities but rather with reference to other, more ultimate ends, she had no clear conception of a "good" clerk.

The Apathetic Consumer

This type of consumer shopped because she "had" to. Shopping for her was an onerous task. She shopped "to get it over with." Ideally, the criterion of convenient location was crucial to her selection of a store, as opposed to price, quality of goods, relationships with store personnel, or ethics. She was not interested in shopping and minimized her expenditure of effort in purchasing goods. Experiences in stores were not sufficiently important to leave any lasting impression on her. She knew few of the personnel and had no notion of a "good" clerk.

The distribution of these types in the sample is shown in Table 1.

SOCIAL PROFILES OF THE CONSUMER TYPES

As found in writings on urbanism and the mass society, a city—an area characterized by the absence of many traditional controls, a predominance of segmented depersonalized relationships, and the proliferation of alternative activities—is a place where the consumption of goods is presumably structured as either a highly rational and rationalized activity, the relationship between the consumer and the sales clerk being instrumental, with minimal emotional involvement on the part of either; or an onerous task performed reluctantly by consumers eager to complete their transaction as easily and quickly as possible. Lynd's observations have emphasized the latter consequence, while Simmel has treated both consequences.[10]

---

[10] Robert S. Lynd, "The People as Consumers," in the *Report of the President's Research Committee on Social Trends: Recent Social Trends* (New York: McGraw-Hill Book Co., 1933), p. 242; George Simmel, *The Sociology of Georg Simmel,* trans. with an introduction by Kurt H. Wolff (Glencoe, Ill.: Free Press, 1950), pp. 414-17.

Certainly one cannot deduce from the conventional propositions of urban sociology that buyer-seller relationships would take on quasi-primary characteristics. The ethical type of shopper isolated in this study also presents a paradox. Neither type—the personalizing consumer nor the ethical consumer—fits into the perspective of conventional urban social psychology.[11]

The most obvious and, in the light of conventional urban sociology, the most plausible hypothesis explaining the personalization of market relationships in the city as well as the "moralization" of such relationships is that these processes merely manifest a carry-over of rural or "small-town" shopping habits to the metropolitan market place.[12] We would expect, then, that personalizing and ethical consumers are predominantly housewives who learned to shop in nonurban environments. But the data offered no support for this hypothesis, in so far as the types of consumers studied were not significantly differentiated by place of birth.[13] As a matter of fact, the majority of consumers classified in each type were native-born Chicagoans. Although the types were significantly associated with parental place of birth, this was because ethical consumers—presumably not to be thought of as a characteristically urban type—included proportionately and significantly more *third-generation* Chicagoans than any other type. These data suggest that the orientations to shopping typical of both ethical and personalizing consumers did not originate in an atmosphere foreign to metropolitan life but precisely in the context of the metropolitan milieu.

On the basis of this general hypothesis, relationships between specific social and economic variables and variations in consumer type were subjected to statistical tests of significance. Significant associations were found for number of children, membership in voluntary associations, and social class.[14]

11 Cf. Tönnies' statement: "In the *Gesellschaft,* as contrasted with the *Gemeinschaft,* we find no actions that can be derived from an *a priori* and necessarily existing unity; no actions, therefore, which manifest the will and the spirit of the unity even if performed by the individual; no actions, which, insofar as they are performed by the individual, take place on behalf of those united with them" (*op. cit.,* p. 74). Yet, in the metropolis, we find the consumer who patronizes a particular store with the best interest of the owner in mind—the ethical consumer and the consumer who enters the market place with the "will" to build a unity out of her relationship with the seller—the personalizing consumer.

12 "To a greater or lesser degree, therefore, our social life bears the imprint of an earlier folk society. . . . The population of the city itself is in large measure recruited from the countryside, where a mode of life reminiscent of the earlier form of existence persists" (Louis Wirth, "Urbanism as a Way of Life," *American Journal of Sociology,* XLIV [July, 1938], p. 3).

13 The chi-square test was used as a measure of the significance of all associations reported here, and, where necessary, T has been used to determine the degree of association. A probability of .05 or less was used as an acceptable indication that the association between two variables could not be attributed to chance variations.

14 Social class was determined from the application of the "Index of Status Characteristics" described in W. Lloyd Warner, Marchia Meeker, and Kenneth Eels, *Social*

Explanations of the above relationships always required taking into account the participation of the consumer in the larger social life of her community and suggested that personal involvements in various phases of the social structure of the Northwest Side also played a part in determining her role orientation in the market. On the assumption that variations in personal involvement could be measured by objective and subjective indexes of community identification, further associations were subjected to statistical tests of significance. The results disclosed significant association between variations in consumer type and locus of last place of residence, residence of friends, and the consumer's desire to remain in or leave the Northwest Side.[15]

A qualitative analysis of the above associations suggested that each consumer type was characterized by a distinctive patterning of social position and community identification. To spell out with statistical precision the entire complex of variables identifying each type and assess their relative weights was, at best extremely difficult and rendered unfeasible by the small number of cases and the consequent impossibility of holding variables constant. To circumvent these difficulties, a "social profile" was drawn up for each type of shopper, none of which was intended directly to represent the empirical data. Rather they represent *some* social conditions which the clustering of relationships point to as *probably* shaping orientations.

The Economic Consumer

Youth, aspiration, and economic disadvantage, when they described lower-middle class housewives, set the stage for the formulation of an economic orientation to shopping. The physical requirements of the economic role were exacting and could best be performed by the young. Economic consumers were socially mobile and seldom loath to instrumentalize the customer-clerk relationship as the orientation required.

Class in America (Chicago: Science Research Associates, 1949). Other results not accepted as statistically significant included associations with age ($p < .20$); officerships in associations ($p < .95$); religious denomination ($p < .70$); occupational status of head of consumer's household ($p < .20$); education of consumer ($p < .20$); education of head of consumer's household ($p < .10$); and ethnic status ($p < .20$).

[15] Except for homeownership, all the other indexes used—length of residence in current dwelling place, length of residence in the Northwest Side, age moved into the community, and subjective evaluation of the residential area—were associated at more than the .05 level but less than the .10 level. This clustering of community identification indexes adumbrates the principal point of this article elaborated in the final section. In the Northwest Side, homeownership was structured in such a way that it had to be rejected as a valid index of community identification. Specifically, there were negative associations with education, length of residence, residence of friends, and previous residence; and positive associations with age when the informant moved into the area. Probably that variable reflected the postwar housing shortage more than anything else.

Many were just passing through the Northwest Side on their way to more highly esteemed residences farther out on the metropolitan periphery. Their mobility aspirations, however, were seriously qualified by the presence of children who demanded care and cost money at a period in their married life when funds were already low and by subordinate ethnic status in the local area. These qualifications demanded the exercise of caution on the market and the adoption of an economic definition of shopping. Unattached to the local area and free of encumbering allegiances, the economic consumer was able to participate in the market in a detached, interested, and alert manner.

The Personalizing Consumer

Without access to either formal or informal channels of social participation, because of her lower social status, her very few or very many children, and the fact that she had spent the early years of her married life outside the local area, this type of consumer established quasi-primary relationships with the personnel of local independent retail institutions. In a sense, her selection of local independent merchants coerced her into a personalizing orientation to shopping. For, given her status equality with store personnel and the fact that she was a newcomer, the adoption of a different definition of shopping could have eventuated only in disharmony and friction which would have been difficult to absorb without other available primary relationships to take up the shock. Even so, this coercion was hardly disadvantageous to such a consumer. The quasi-primary relationships she was forced to develop on the market compensated for her larger social losses, for, although she had recently moved into the area leaving most of her old friends behind, she attached positive value to living in the Northwest Side and expressed no desire to leave it.[16]

The Ethical Consumer

Relatively high social status, long residence in the Northwest Side, and an unfavorable response to the "social deterioration" accompanying the rapid business growth of the area were prime requisites for the development of an ethical orientation to the market. The "ethic" is an alignment with the symbols of small business against the big business that menaced the housewives' way of life. Patronage of local independent merchants more concretely realized the alliance. In addition, it maintained social distance between the higher-status customer and the lower-status clerk in a shopping situation where social distance was difficult to maintain but,

---

16 The social characteristics of the personalizing consumer resemble those of the "substitute gratification" readers of the urban community press reported in Morris Janowitz, "The Imagery of the Urban Community Press," *op. cit.*, p. 540.

at the same time, necessary to protect the established status of the customer in the larger community.

The Apathetic Consumer

Characteristically, apathetic consumers sought to minimize effort in shopping, and this characterized the older women. Either downward mobility or a lack of success in attempts at upward mobility [17] constricted the aspirations of apathetic consumers and confined them to local neighborhood life. Long residence in the Northwest Side begun at an early age, and a strong positive local identification promoted strong bonds with others in the community. The market, in any case, was too far beyond the horizon of experience of the typical apathetic consumer to warrant much attention or interest.

The four profiles described above permit some speculation about the temporal allocation of shopping orientations. Apparently, economic and personalizing orientations were more often adopted by housewives who had recently moved into the area, and ethical and apathetic orientations by those who had lived in the area for relatively long periods of time. Aspiration, marginality, and success are perhaps the crucial intervening variables. This suggests the hypotheses: (1) the higher the level of aspiration among newcomers to a residential area, the greater the likelihood that they will adopt economic orientations to shopping; (2) the lower the level of aspiration and the greater the marginality of newcomers, the greater the likelihood that they will adopt personalizing orientations; (3) the greater the success long-time residents of a residential area have enjoyed, the greater the likelihood that they will adopt ethical orientations to shopping; and (4), conversely, the less the success, the greater the likelihood of consumer apathy among long-time residents.

What remains to be discussed and explained is the place of the personalizing role orientation in resolving the disparity between the apparent subjective indications of positive identification with the Northwest

[17] A greater proportion of the husbands of apathetic shoppers had completed their secondary-school education or gone on to college than in any other consumer type. Yet, the husbands of the majority of apathetic consumers belonged to lower social strata. When the social class of the 57 informants whose husbands had either completed high school or attended college was examined, the results showed that 23.8 per cent of the 21 apathetic consumers were included in the higher educational group and could be placed in the upper-middle or lower-middle social classes, while 33.7 per cent had been recruited from the upper-lower social class. In contrast, 38.1 per cent of the remaining 98 informants were included in both the higher educational group and the middle social classes, while 11.1 per cent had completed their secondary education or attended college and were, at the same time, members of the lower status levels. The significance of these relationships was established by the application of the chi-square test; thus a significant proportion of the husbands of apathetic consumers had been educated "above" their social status.

Side offered by personalizing consumers and the fact that objective indexes of community identification did not point to the likelihood that they would develop a sense of community belonging. Objectively, personalized consumers were not integrated with the Northwest Side; subjectively, they were.

URBAN SOLIDARITY AND THE PERSONALIZATION OF MARKET RELATIONSHIPS

Despite the fact that certain objective conditions for a community identification were absent among many personalizing consumers,[18] a clear majority of the informants concerned expressed no desire to leave the community and, at the same time, evaluated it favorably. In short, without objective basis, personalizing consumers seemed typically to have identified themselves with the Northwest Side.

A hypothesis was advanced to explain the discrepancy: *Among the 119 housewives subjective identification of some with the area in which they lived was a latent function[19] of their personalization of market relations.* These consumers usually implied that strong social bonds tied them to the personnel of the stores they patronized. In the absence of other neighborhood ties, such a bond was apparently strong enough to provide the basis for the consumer's attachment. It follows that, if personalizing consumers, *in contrast to the other types,* identified themselves subjectively with the locality when objective indexes of local community identification did not suggest that likelihood, the hypothesis stated above could not be rejected.

To test the hypothesis, all informants who had indicated subjective identification with the community either by expressing a preference for continued residence there or by evaluating the community in positive terms were singled out for analysis. In addition, four objective indexes of local community identification were controlled: (1) length of residence in the Northwest Side; (2) age of the informant when she moved to the Northwest Side; (3) location of last place of residence; and (4) location of most of her friends. Those members of the selected group of "subjectively identified" informants who had lived in the Northwest Side six years or less, moved into the area at twenty-nine years of age or more and into

18 Many had lived a short period of time in their current residences and in the community at large; a majority said that most of their friends lived outside the Northwest Side, and most had moved into the area at a relatively late age.

19 *"Functions* are those observed consequences [of social acts] which make for the adaptation or adjustment of a given system . . . *latent functions* being those which are neither intended nor recognized [by the social actor or actors]" (Robert K. Merton, *Social Theory and Social Structure* [Glencoe, Ill.: Free Press, 1949], pp. 50-51).

their present residences from outside the Northwest Side, and said that most of their friends lived outside the community, were interpreted as having formed subjective identifications with the Northwest Side with *no apparent basis*. Informants characterized by three of the above criteria were said to have formed subjective attachments with *little apparent basis*. Those to whom two of the criteria applied were regarded as having become identified with *some apparent basis*. Finally, informants for whom only one criterion applied were interpreted as having formed a sense of community belonging with *apparent basis*. If personalizing consumers in the selected group of subjectively identified informants were found to have established community identifications without or with little apparent basis more often than the other consumer types, the hypothesis, it is contended, could not be eliminated.[20] Tables 2 and 3 summarize the results of the test.

TABLE 2

BASIS FOR THE IDENTIFICATION OF CONSUMERS PREFERRING TO LIVE
IN CHICAGO'S NORTHWEST SIDE

Objective basis for community iden- tification	Type of consumers				
	Eco- nomic	Person- alizing	Ethical	Apa- thetic	Total
No apparent basis	2	4	—	—	6
Little apparent basis	3	6	—	2	11
Some apparent basis	4	5	6	5	20
Apparent basis	3	2	2	4	11
Total	12	17	8	11	48

TABLE 3

BASIS FOR THE IDENTIFICATION OF CONSUMERS FAVORABLY DISPOSED
TO CHICAGO'S NORTHWEST SIDE

Objective basis for community iden- tification	Type of consumers				
	Eco- nomic	Person- alizing	Ethical	Apa- thetic	Total
No apparent basis	2	3	—	—	5
Little apparent basis	3	6	—	2	11
Some apparent basis	2	5	7	4	18
Apparent basis	2	2	2	4	11
Total	10	16	9	10	45

[20] The data placed severe limitations upon the achievement of any more satisfactory test, largely owing to the fact that the entire range of findings reported here was unanticipated at the inception of the research. For a discussion of the adequacy of the criteria used and the test itself *see* Stone, *op. cit.*, pp. 124-28.

Collapsing the first and second rows of Tables 2 and 3 and comparing the personalizing consumers with the other types taken as a whole permitted the application of the chi-square test of significance to the ensuing fourfold distributions. The results allow the conclusion that a *significantly larger proportion of personalizing consumers had established subjective identifications with the Northwest Side without or with little apparent basis than had consumers of the other three types taken together.*[21] Consequently, the hypothesis was retained.

The hypothesis has important implications for urban social psychology. That field has perhaps been concerned too long with the disintegrative effects or the dysfunctions of urbanism. Urban sociologists have documented with an admirable meticulousness the difficulties accompanying urban living and the obstacles in the path of achieving moral consensus in the metropolis. But they have failed to explain the obvious fact that people in goodly numbers do manage to live and survive in urban environments and that, among many of them, there is a patent sense of identification with the metropolis.

Durkheim observed long ago that the family was being replaced by occupational groupings as the seat of moral consensus in the organically solidary society.[22] However, it may be more sagacious not to single out any one nexus of human relations and attribute to it the function of generating consensus in the mass society. Instead, one might observe that life in the metropolis is largely routinized and that relationships bearing many of the qualities that Cooley spoke of as primary in nature may be established in any area of life where communication is frequent and regular. Such relationships can have the function of integrating the person with the larger society in which he lives.

[21] The level of significance and degree of association for the two distributions are ($p < .02$; $T = .36$) and ($p < .05$; $T = .32$) respectively—a relatively high degree of significance and association for such a small number of cases.

[22] Émile Durkheim, *The Division of Labor in Society*, trans. George Simpson (Glencoe, Ill.: Free Press, 1947), Preface to the Second Edition, pp. 1-31.

20

SOCIAL CLASSES and SPENDING BEHAVIOR

PIERRE MARTINEAU

All societies place emphasis on some one structure which gives form to the total society and integrates all the other structures such as the family, the clique, voluntary association, caste, age, and sex groupings into a social unity.

Social stratification means any system of ranked statuses by which all the members of a society are placed in some kind of a superordinate and subordinate hierarchy. While money and occupation are important in the ranking process, there are many more factors, and these two alone do not establish social position. The concept of social class was designed to include this process of ranking people in superior and inferior social position by any and all factors.

CLASS SYSTEM

It has been argued that there cannot be a class system existent in America when most individuals do not have the slightest idea of its formal structure. Yet in actuality every individual senses that he is more at home with and more acceptable to certain groups than to others. In a study of department stores and shopping behavior, it was found that the Lower-Status woman is completely aware that, if she goes into High-Status department stores, the clerks and other customers in the store will punish her in various subtle ways.

Reprinted from the *Journal of Marketing*, national quarterly publication of the American Marketing Association, Volume 23 (October, 1958), pp. 121-130.

"The clerks treat you like a crumb," one woman expressed it. After trying vainly to be waited on, another woman bitterly complained that she was loftily told, "We thought you were a clerk."

The woman who is socially mobile gives considerable thought to the external symbols of status, and she frequently tests her status by shopping in department stores which she thinks are commensurate with her changing position. She knows that, if she does not dress correctly, if she does not behave in a certain manner to the clerks, if she is awkward about the proper cues, then the other customers and the clerks will make it very clear that she does not belong.

In another study, very different attitudes in the purchase of furniture and appliances involving this matter of status were found. Middle-class people had no hesitancy in buying refrigerators and other appliances in discount houses and bargain stores because they felt that they could not "go wrong" with the nationally advertised names. But taste in furniture is much more elusive and subtle because the brand names are not known; and, therefore, one's taste is on trial. Rather than commit a glaring error in taste which would exhibit an ignorance of the correct status symbols, the same individual who buys appliances in a discount house generally retreats to a status store for buying furniture. She needs the support of the store's taste.

In a very real sense, everyone of us in his consumption patterns and style of life shows an awareness that there is some kind of superiority-inferiority system operating, and that we must observe the symbolic patterns of our own class.

Lloyd Warner and Paul Lunt have described a six-class system: the Upper-Upper, or old families; Lower-Upper, or the newly arrived; Upper-Middle, mostly the professionals and successful businessmen; Lower-Middle, or the white collar salaried class; Upper-Lower, or the wage earner, skilled worker group; and Lower-Lower, or the unskilled labor group.[1] For practical purposes, in order to determine the individual's class position, Warner and his associates worked out a rating index, not based on amount of income but rather on type of income, type of occupation, house type, and place of residence.

Although the Warner thesis has been widely used in sociology, it has not generally been employed in marketing. As a matter of fact, some critics in the social sciences have held that, since Warner's thesis rested essentially on studies of smaller cities in the 10,000-25,000 class, this same system might not exist in the more complex metropolitan centers, or might not be unravelled by the same techniques. Furthermore, many marketers did not see the application of this dimension to the individ-

[1] W. Lloyd Warner and Paul Lunt, *The Social Life of a Modern Community* (New Haven: Yale University Press, 1950). Also, W. Lloyd Warner, Marchia Meeker, and Kenneth Eells, *Social Class in America* (Chicago: Science Research Associates, 1949).

ual's economic behavior, since the studies of Warner and his associates had mostly been concerned with the differences in the broad patterns of living, the moral codes, etc.

SOCIAL CLASS IN CHICAGO

Under Warner's guidance, the *Chicago Tribune* has undertaken several extensive studies exploring social class in a metropolitan city, and its manifestations specifically in family buying patterns. The problem was to determine if such a social-class system did exist in metropolitan Chicago, if the dimensions and the relationships were at all similar to the smaller cities which were studied before the far-reaching social changes of the past fifteen years. The studies were undertaken to see if there were any class significances in the individual family's spending-saving patterns, retail store loyalties, and his expressions of taste in typical areas such as automobiles, apparel, furniture, and house types.

It seems that many an economist overlooks the possibility of any psychological differences between individuals resulting from different class membership. It is assumed that a rich man is simply a poor man with more money and that, given the same income, the poor man would behave exactly like the rich man. The *Chicago Tribune* studies crystallize a wealth of evidence from other sources that this is just not so, and that the Lower-Status person is profoundly different in his mode of thinking and his way of handling the world from the Middle-Class individual. Where he buys and what he buys will differ not only by economics but in symbolic value.

It should be understood, of course, that there are no hard and fast lines between the classes. Implicit in the notion of social class in America is the possibility of movement from one class to another. The "office-boy-to-president" saga is a cherished part of the American dream. Bobo Rockefeller illustrates the female counterpart: from coal miner's daughter to socialite. As a corollary of the explorations in class, the study also tried to be definitive about the phenomenon of social mobility—the movement from one class to another.

There are numerous studies of vertical mobility from the level of sociological analysis, mostly by comparing the individual's occupational status to that of his father. There are also studies at the level of psychological analysis. This study attempted to combine the two levels, to observe the individual's progress and also to understand something of the dynamics of the mobile person as compared to the stable individual. The attempt was to look both backward and forward: tracing such factors as occupation, place of residence, and religion back to parents and grandparents, and then where the family expected to be in the next five or ten years, what were the educational plans for each son, each daughter, a discussion of future goals.

Because this article is confined primarily to social class, this section may be concluded by saying that the studies show a very clear relationship between spend-saving aspirations and the factors of mobility-stability.

FRAMEWORK OF STUDY

Following are Warner's hypotheses and assumptions for the study:

I.   Assumptions about symbols and values and about saving of money and accumulation of objects

Our society is acquisitive and pecuniary. On the one hand, the values and beliefs of Americans are pulled toward the pole of the accumulation of money by increasing the amount of money income and reducing its outgo. On the other hand, American values emphasize the accumulation of objects and products of technology for display and consumption. The self-regard and self-esteem of a person and his family, as well as the public esteem and respect of a valued social world around the accumulator, are increased or not by such symbols of accumulation and consumption.

The two sets of values, the accumulation of product symbols and the accumulation (saving) of money, may be, and usually are, in opposition.

General working hypotheses stemming from these assumptions were: (1) People are distributed along a range according to the two-value components, running from proportionately high savings, through mixed categories, to proportionately high accumulation of objects. (2) These value variations conform to social and personality factors present in all Americans.

II.   Assumptions about product symbols, savers, and accumulations

American society is also characterized by social change, particularly technological change that moves in the direction of greater and greater production of more kinds and more numerous objects for consumption and accumulation.

Hypothesis: New varieties of objects will be most readily accepted by the accumulators, and most often opposed by the savers.

III.   Assumptions about the social values of accumulators and savers

American society is characterized by basic cultural differences, one of them being social status. Social class levels are occupied by people, some of whom are upward mobile by intent and fact. Others are non-mobile, by intent and fact. The values which dictate judgments about actions, such as the kinds of objects which are consumed and accumulated, will vary by class level and the presence or absence of vertical mobility.

IV. Assumptions about the personal values of accumulators and savers

The personality components are distributed through the class levels and through the mobility types. By relating the social and personality components, it is possible to state a series of hypotheses about accumulators and savers as they are related to the object world around them, particularly to objects which are new and old to the culture, those which are imposing or not and those which are predominantly for display or for consumption.

At the direct, practical level, all of these theoretical questions can be summarized by one basic question: What kinds of things are people likely to buy and not buy if they are in given class positions and if they are or are not socially mobile? In other words, what is the effect on purchasing behavior of being in a particular social class, and being mobile or non-mobile?

If this is the crucial question, theoretically grounded, then a whole series of hypotheses can be laid out concerning values about money and values about buying various kinds of objects for consumption and for display. Some of these are:

1. *There will be a relationship between values held by a particular subject and the extent to which particular products exemplify those values.*

2. *There is a differential hierarchy of things for which it is worth spending money.*

3. *Veblen's theory that conspicuous expenditure is largely applied to the Upper Class is erroneous. It runs all the way through our social system.*

From these statements certain other hypotheses follow:

4. *At different class levels, symbols of mobility will differ.*

There is a differential hierarchy of things on which it is worth spending money. Class and mobility will be two of the dimensions that will differentiate—also personality and cultural background.

5. *The place in the home where these symbols will be displayed will shift at different class levels.*

The underlying assumption here is that there is a hierarchy of importance in the rooms of the house. This hierarchy varies with social class, mobility, age, ethnicity. The studies also revealed clear-cut patterns of taste for lamps, furnishings, house types, etc.

6. *The non-mobile people tend to rationalize purchases in terms of cost or economy.*

In other words, non-mobile people tend to be oriented more toward the pole of the accumulation of money. Purchases, then, are rationalized in terms of the savings involved.

The basic thesis of all the hypotheses on mobility is this: Whereas the stable individual would emphasize saving and security, the behavior of the mobile individual is characterized by spending for various symbols of upward movement. All of the evidence turned up indicates that this difference in values does exist, and furthermore that notable differences in personality dynamics are involved. For instance, the analysis of how families would make investments shows that stable people overwhelmingly prefer insurance, the symbol of security. By contrast, the mobile people at all levels prefer stocks, which are risk-taking. In Warner's words, the mobile individual acts as if he were free, white, and twenty-one, completely able to handle the world, and perfectly willing to gamble on himself as a sure bet to succeed.

CLASS PLACEMENT

Returning to the factor of social class, in this study class placement was based on a multi-state probability area sample of metropolitan Chicago, involving 3,880 households. It was found that the matter of placement could not be done by the relatively simple scoring sufficient for the smaller cities. To secure house typings, it was necessary to provide the field investigators with photographs covering a wide range of dwelling types, all the way from exclusive apartments to rooms over stores. Because of the very complexity of metropolitan life, occupations provided the biggest problem. To solve this operational problem, it was necessary to construct an exhaustive list of occupational types involving degree of responsibility and training required by each. The data finally used to calculate the Index of Status Characteristics (ISC) were:

> (weighted by 5)
>   Occupation (from 1 to 7 broad categories)
> (weighted by 4)
>   Sources of income (from 1 to 7 types)
> (weighted by 3)
>   Housing type (from 1 to 7 types)

The sum of the individual's weighted scores was used to predict his social class level as follows:[2]

[2] Dr. Bevode McCall helped to solve the ISC scoring problem for Metropolitan Chicago.

ISC Scores	Predicted social class placement
12-21	Upper Class
22-37	Upper-Middle Class
38-51	Lower-Middle Class
52-66	Upper-Lower Class
67-84	Lower-Lower Class

The study very clearly shows that there is a social-class system operative in a metropolitan area which can be delineated. Furthermore, class membership is an important determinant of the individual's economic behavior, even more so than in the smaller city. The one department store in the smaller city may satisfy almost everyone, whereas in the metropolitan city the stores become sharply differentiated.

This is the social-class structure of Metropolitan Chicago, typifying the transformation of the formerly agrarian Midwestern cites from Pittsburgh to Kansas City into a series of big milltowns:

Upper and Upper-Middle	8.1%
Lower-Middle	28.4%
Upper-Lower	44.0%
Lower-Lower	19.5%

While the Old Families and the Newly Arrived are still recognizable as types, they constitute less than 1 per cent of the population. A similar study in Kansas City turned up so few that they could not be counted at all. On the other hand, we see the emergence of a seventh class, the Upper-Lower "Stars" or Light-Blue Collar Workers. They are the spokesmen of the Upper-Lower Class groups—high income individuals, who have the income for more ostentatious living than the average factory worker but who lack the personal skills or desire for high status by social mobility.

NINE APPLIANCE TYPES—FOUR-YEAR PERIOD

By Income

Over $7,000	36.2%
4,000-6,999	46.0%
Under 4,000	17.8%

By Social Class

Upper and Upper-Middle	16.6%
Lower-Middle	29.2%
Upper-Lower	45.7%
Lower-Lower	8.5%

There is certainly a rough correlation between income and social class. But social class is a much richer dimension of meaning. There are so many facets of behavior which are explicable only on a basis of social class dynamics. For instance, this analysis of the purchase of household appliances in Chicago over a four-year period shows a very different picture by income and by class:

Income analysis shows that the lowest income group represents an understandably smaller market, but nevertheless a market. Social-class analysis highlights a fundamental difference in attitudes toward the home between the two lower classes. The Upper-Lower Class man sees his home as his castle, his anchor to the world, and he loads it down with hardware—solid heavy appliances—as his symbols of security. The Lower-Lower Class individual is far less interested in his castle, and is more likely to spend his income for flashy clothes or an automobile. He is less property-minded, and he has less feeling about buying and maintaining a home.

Several *Tribune* studies have explored the way of life and the buying behavior of many new suburbs and communities. All of them quickly become stratified along social-class and mobility dimensions, and, therefore, differ tremendously among themselves. *Fortune* has reported on Park Forest, Illinois, a middle-class suburb of 30,000 and only ten years old. It is characterized by high degrees of both upward and geographical mobility. The people are overwhelmingly those who had moved from other parts of the United States, who had few local roots, and who consequently wanted to integrate themselves in friendship groups. But this was not typical of the new Lower-Status suburbs where the women did relatively little fraternizing. It was not typical of the new Upper-Middle Class mobile suburbs where the people were preoccupied with status symbols, not in submerging themselves in the group.

One new community had crystallized as being for Higher-Status Negroes. This was a resettlement project with relatively high rents for Negroes. Eighty-five per cent of them had come from the South where social class was compressed. But, as soon as they came to Chicago, the class system opened up and they were anxious to establish a social distance between themselves and other Negroes. Almost all of them said they enjoyed the "peace and quiet" of their neighborhood, which was their way of insisting that they were not like the "noisy" lower-class Negroes. They deliberately avoided the stores patronized by other Negroes.

CHOICE OF STORE

All of these studies reveal the close relation between choice of store, patterns of spending, and class membership. In the probability sample delineating social class, such questions were asked in the total metropolitan area as:

"If you were shopping for a good dress, at which store would you be most likely to find what you wanted?"
"For an everyday dress?"
"For living room furniture?"
"At which store do you buy most of your groceries?"

To assume that all persons would wish to shop at the glamorous High-Status stores is utterly wrong. People are very realistic in the way they match their values and expectations with the status of the store. The woman shopper has a considerable range of ideas about department stores; but these generally become organized on a scale ranking from very High-Social Status to the Lowest-Status and prestige. The social status of the department store becomes the primary basis for its definition by the shopper. This is also true of men's and women's apparel stores, and furniture stores, on the basis of customer profiles. The shopper is not going to take a chance feeling out of place by going to a store where she might not fit.

No matter what economics are involved, she asks herself who are the other customers in the store, what sort of treatment can she expect at the hands of the clerks, will the merchandise be the best of everything, or lower priced and hence lower quality? Stores are described as being for the rich, for the average ordinary people, or for those who have to stretch their pennies.

The most important function of retail advertising today, when prices and quality have become so standard, is to permit the shopper to make social-class identification. This she can do from the tone and physical character of the advertising. Of course, there is also the factor of psychological identification. Two people in the same social class may want different stores. One may prefer a conservative store, one may want the most advanced styling. But neither will go to stores where they do not "fit," in a social-class sense.

In contrast to the independent food retailer, who obviously adapts to the status of the neighborhood, the chain grocers generally invade many income areas with their stores. Nevertheless, customers profiles show that each chain acquires a status definition. The two largest grocery chains in the Chicago area are A. & P. and Jewel; yet they draw very different customer bodies. A. & P. is strong with the mass market, whereas Jewel has its strength among the Middle Class.

While the national brand can and often does cut across classes, one can think of many product types and services which do have social class labels. The Upper-Middle Class person rarely travels by motor coach because none of his associates do so, even though there is certainly nothing wrong with this mode of transportation. On the other hand, even with low air-coach fares, one does not see many factory workers or day laborers on vacation around airports. Such sales successes as vodka and tonic water, and men's deodorants and foreign sports cars, were accomplished without benefit of much buying from this part of the market.

COMMUNICATION SKILLS

There is also a relation between class and communication abilities which has significance for marketing. The kind of super-sophisticated and clever advertising which appears in the *New Yorker* and *Esquire* is almost meaningless to Lower-Status people. They cannot comprehend the subtle humor; they are baffled by the bizarre art. They have a different symbol system, a very different approach to humor. In no sense does this imply that they lack intelligence or wit. Rather their communication skills have just been pressed into a different mold.

Here again, style of advertising helps the individual to make class identification. Most of the really big local television success stories in Chicago have been achieved by personalities who radiate to the mass that this is where they belong. These self-made businessmen who do the announcing for their own shows communicate wonderfully well with the mass audience. While many listeners switch off their lengthy and personal commercials, these same mannerisms tell the Lower-Status individual that here is someone just like himself, who understands him.

Social Research, Inc., has frequently discussed the class problem in marketing by dividing the population into Upper-Middle or quality market; the middle majority which combines both the Lower-Middle and Upper-Lower; and then the Lower-Lower. The distinction should be drawn between the Middle Classes and the Lower-Status groups. In several dozen of these store profiles, there is scarcely an instance where a store has appeal to the Lower-Middle and Upper-Lower classes with anything like the same strength.

It would be better to make the break between the Middle Class, representing one-third of the population and the Lower-Status or Working-Class or Wage-Earner group, representing two-thirds of metropolitan Chicago. This permits some psychological distinctions to be drawn between the Middle-Class individual and the individual who is not a part of the Middle-Class system of values. Even though this is the dominant American value system, even though Middle-Class Americans have been taught by their parents that it is the only value system, this Lower-Status individual does not necessarily subscribe to it.

WHO SAVES, WHO SPENDS?

Another important set of behavioral distinctions related to social class position was revealed in the "save-spend aspiration" study. The question was asked: "Suppose your income was doubled for the next ten years, what would you do with the increased income?" This is a fantasy question taken out of the realm of any pressing economic situation to reflect aspirations about money. The coding broke down the answers to this question into five general categories: (1) the mode of saving, (2) the purpose of saving, (3) spending which would consolidate past gains, meet present defensive needs, prepare for future self-advancement, (4) spending which is "self-indulgent-centered," (5) spending which is "house-centered."

Here are some of our findings:[3] The higher the individual's class position, the more likely is he to express some saving aspirations. Conversely, the lower his class position, the more likely is he to mention spending only. Moreover the higher the status, the more likely is the individual to specify *how* he will save his money, which is indicative of the more elaborate financial learning required of higher status.

Proceeding from the more general categories (such as saving versus spending only) to more specific categories (such as non-investment versus investment saving and the even more specific stock versus real estate investment, etc.) an increasingly sharper class differentiation is found. It is primarily *non-investment* saving which appeals to the Lower-Status person. Investment saving, on the other hand, appeals above all to the Upper-Status person.

Investors almost always specify how they will invest. And here in mode of investment are examples of the most sharply class-differentiated preferences. Intangible forms of investment like stock and insurance are very clearly distinguished as Upper-Status investments. Nearly four times as many Upper-Middles select insurance as would be expected by chance, whereas only one-fifth of the Lower-Lowers select it as would be expected by chance. By contrast, Lower-Status people have far greater preference for tangible investments, specifically ownership of real estate, a farm, or a business.

To sum up, Middle-Class people usually have a place in their aspirations for some form of saving. This saving is most often in the form of investment, where there is a risk, long-term involvement, and the possibility of higher return. Saving, investment saving, and intangible investment saving—successively each of these become for them increasingly symbols of their higher status.

[3] The saving-spending aspiration analysis was carried out by Roger Coup, graduate student at the University of Chicago.

The aspirations of the Lower-Status person are just as often for spending as they are for saving. This saving is usually a non-investment saving where there is almost no risk, funds can be quickly converted to spendable cash, and returns are small. When the Lower-Status person does invest his savings, he will be specific about the mode of investment, and is very likely to prefer something tangible and concrete—something he can point at and readily display.

Turning from mode of saving to purpose of saving, very significant class relationships are likewise evident. Consider the verbalization of saving purpose. Lower-Status people typically explain why one should save— why the very act of saving is important. On the other hand, Middle-Class people do not, as if saving is an end-in-itself, the merits of which are obvious and need not be justified.

Spending is the other side of the coin. Analysis of what people say they will spend for shows similar class-related desires. All classes mention concrete, material artifacts such as a new car, some new appliance. But the Lower-Status people stop here. Their accumulations are artifact-centered, whereas Middle-Class spending-mentions are experience-centered. This is spending where one is left typically with only a memory. It would include hobbies, recreation, self-education and travel. The wish to travel, and particularly foreign travel, is almost totally a Middle-Class aspiration.

Even in their fantasies, people are governed by class membership. In his daydreaming and wishful thinking, the Lower-Status individual will aspire in different patterns from the Middle-Class individual.

PSYCHOLOGICAL DIFFERENCES

This spending-saving analysis has very obvious psychological implications to differentiate between the classes. Saving itself generally suggests foresightedness, the ability to perceive long-term needs and goals. Noninvestment saving has the characteristics of little risk-taking and of ready conversion, at no loss, into immediate expenditures—the money can be drawn out of the account whenever the bank is open. Investment spending, on the other hand, has the characteristics of risk-taking (a gamble for greater returns) and of delayed conversion, with possible loss, to expenditures on immediate needs.

Here are some psychological contrasts between two different social groups:

Middle-Class

1. Pointed to the future
2. His viewpoint embraces a long expanse of time

3. More urban identification
4. Stresses rationality
5. Has a well-structured sense of the universe
6. Horizons vastly extended or not limited
7. Greater sense of choice-making
8. Self-confident, willing to take risks
9. Immaterial and abstract in his thinking
10. Sees himself tied to national happenings

Lower-Status

1. Pointed to the present and past
2. Lives and thinks in a short expanse of time
3. More rural in identification
4. Non-rational essentially
5. Vague and unclear structuring of the world
6. Horizons sharply defined and limited
7. Limited sense of choice-making
8. Very much concerned with security and insecurity
9. Concrete and perceptive in his thinking
10. World revolves around his family and body

CONCLUSIONS

The essential purpose of this article was to develop three basic premises which are highly significant for marketing:

I. *There is a social-class system operative in metropolitan markets, which can be isolated and described.*

II. *It is important to realize that there are far-reaching psychological differences between the various classes.* They do not handle the world in the same fashion. They tend not to think in the same way. As one tries to communicate with the Lower-Status group, it is imperative to sense that their goals and mental processes differ from the Middle-Class group.

III. *Consumption patterns operate as prestige symbols to define class membership, which is a more significant determinant of economic behavior than mere income.* Each major department store, furniture store, and chain-grocery store has a different "pulling power" on different status groups. The usual customers of a store gradually direct the store's merchandising policies into a pattern which works. The interaction between store policy and consumer acceptance results in the elimination of certain customer groups and the attraction of others, with a resulting equilibration around a reasonably stable core of specific customer groups who think of the store as appropriate for them.

Income has always been the marketer's handiest index to family consumption standards. But it is a far from accurate index. For instance, the bulk of the population in a metropolitan market today will fall in the middle-income ranges. This will comprise not only the traditional white collar worker, but the unionized craftsman and the semi-skilled worker with their tremendous income gains of the past decade. Income-wise, they may be in the same category. But their buying behavior, their tastes, their spending-saving aspirations can be poles apart. Social-class position and mobility-stability dimensions will reflect in much greater depth each individual's style of life.

21

MALE MARKET: BIG, RICH, but TOUGH

PEGGY BOOMER

Commuters on the New Haven Railroad's 8:17 out of Norwalk, Conn., were startled out of their matutinal somnolence by an unexpected sight last month. Through aisles usually peopled with sleepy Madison Avenue executives and Wall Street brokers, and among them the more mundane figure of a shiny serge-clad conductor, paraded half-a-dozen male models togged out in natty walking shorts, knee socks and windbreakers.

It was, crowed its perpetrators, Phillips-Van Heusen Corp., railroading's first live male fashion show in 132 years of passenger service.

Not quite so earthshaking statistically, perhaps, but more significant to marketing men was this: The show was another example of the increasingly aggressive efforts of advertisers to reach an elusive but important quarry: the male customer. Companies in many areas are taking a new look at this once-scorned figure, obscured of late by a welter of data showing that he had completely abandoned all claim to his former position as purchasing-decision maker—not only for the family, but even for his own brand of socks.

Renewed efforts to tap this rich but complex market are not only galvanizing advertisers in traditional male-product areas into new action, they are subtly affecting ad appeals for a broad variety of items, and ringing changes in media selection.

Reprinted from *Printers' Ink,* Volume 280 (July 20, 1962), pp. 21-25, with permission of *Printers' Ink.*

I. SIZE AND SCOPE

Statistically, the male market today is a big one. There are some 55-million men 20 and over, with a 13.7 per cent growth projected by 1970, for a total of over 61-million. It's significant that this growth will be an uneven one by age groups (see chart). The fastest-growing (20-to-34-year) group will

	1960	1970 per cent gain
Total men over 20	61,447,000 / 54,021,000	13.7
Young adults, 20–34 College, career, beginnings, marriages, family formation, youthful leisure activities	21,087,000 / 16,900,000	24.8
Early middle years, 35–49 Job advancements, social life, growing children, hobbies and recreation, family, home improvement	17,387,000 / 17,263,000	0.7
Later middle years, 50–64 Job achievement, security, convenience, luxury, travel, preparation for retirement	14,330,000 / 12,370,000	16.2
Retirement years, 65 and up Retirement living, travel, health, grandchildren, reduced income, declining purchases	8,643,000 / 7,531,000	14.8

How the male market will grow—and change. Projections for 13.7 per cent growth of the male population during the sixties also show considerable variation in the increases by age group. Biggest gains will come in the 20–34-year-old young adult group, while the early middle years will show almost no growth at all. Marketing men will be planning product and ad strategies which reflect these trends.

expand by almost 25 per cent in the coming decade. These young adults, with their relatively high discretionary income (particularly bachelors), and pressing needs in all areas for the young husband and father, are already a prime target for alert companies marketing male products like apparel, cigars; and the trend should accelerate.

Equally important, from a negative viewpoint, will be the static number of men in the affluent early-middle years (from 35 to 49), where growing families, rising incomes and job expectations today prompt so much buying, not only of big-ticket necessities, but also of discretionary and status items.

The male consumer accounts for tremendous sums of money spent, on products strictly for his own use or for whose purchase he is largely responsible. These range from some $10.5-billion spent annually on men's clothing and footwear to $165-million laid out for cigars. He's also the prime ad target for most categories in the booming $2-billion sports-equipment industry, and accounts for almost the total yearly expenditure of some $450-million for shaving preparations and equipment.

Equally important is the fact that the U.S. male is raising his voice again in family buying decisions. Many researchers feel that there has been a reversal in the trend that saw women making more and more of the family purchasing choices. This has been quickly reflected in that barometer most sensitive to U. S. culture, the automobile. The swing back toward bigger cars and the promotion of sporty features like bucket seats, even in family sedans, reflects resurgence of the male in the decision-making role.

There is increasing evidence, too, that men are getting more involved in purchases once exclusively female. A recent survey by Coordinated Marketing in 2,000 outlets belonging to 19 supermarket chains showed that 25 per cent of all transactions involved men. Gold Bond Trading Stamps claims that 85 per cent of men have now become "active" savers, and points to a steady increase of male merchandise in its catalogues and redemption centers. Men today are also key figures in a number of newly popular pastimes like backyard barbecuing and winesmanship, which even now are becoming more important as living standards rise, leisure time increases and the flight to the suburb continues.

From a marketing viewpoint, one of the most important characteristics of today's male market is its greatly increased sophistication. This is chiefly due to the fact that, along with rising disposable income and a growing similarity between white- and blue-collar take-home, the country has seen a sharp rise in educational levels. There are two-and-one-half times as many high-school graduates today as there were 20 years ago.

A second important characteristic is the increasing segmentation of the male market into very specific groups (the young urban bachelor, the rural sportsman, etc.), which often can be reached only through specially tailored products, ad appeals, media programs.

II. NEW MARKETING MOXIE

Interestingly, many of the product areas most heavily dependent on the male user and/or purchaser have also been the slowest to revamp conservative product concepts, outdated distribution and merchandising practices. This is all changing now.

A vivid illustration is men's apparel, which recently has undergone a marketing revolution. Until a few years ago the men's-wear industry sold one type of clothing, made few and gradual style changes, and distributed its wares almost exclusively through department or men's specialty stores.

But apparel companies, sensitive to the increasing fragmentation of the market, both in terms of changing tastes and introducing new materials like wash-and-wear, beset by discounter competition and nudged by quickened male interest in fashion, have had to re-evaluate marketing strategies. One interesting affirmation of the growth of male fashion-consciousness has been the success of the first consumer magazine devoted entirely to male fashion. A one-time trade magazine, *Gentlemen's Quarterly* now boasts a circulation of 60,000, only 13 per cent of which represents trade subscriptions. It has also racked up impressive advertising gains— 70.4 per cent increase in revenue between 1958-1961 and 72 new advertisers added in the past year.

Among the first firms to revamp its approach to meet conditions in the segmented market was Phillips-Van Heusen, which five years ago went aggressively after the Ivy League young executive prospect with a line entirely new, from look to labels—the 417 collection. More recently it zeroed in on the fast-growing, faddier youth market with its Van-Go line. One measure of the technique's success: In 1957 the firm was able to get 25 stores to install special 417 shops, by last year 2,000 retailers gave them space.

The result: In this clothing category, which now represents 25 per cent of industry volume and could reach 50 per cent by 1970, Phillips-Van Heusen is, according to marketing vice-president Stanley Gillette, "far and away the largest brand," and the company, which will spend $2-million advertising all its products through spring 1963, will double ad outlays for the 417 line. Here's the key to success in the fast-moving market, according to Gillette: "You must adapt your complete marketing technique to each market, right down to designing special ads for individual media." (Phillips-Van Heusen runs in *Playboy* a completely different series of small-space ads from those running in *Esquire*.)

Another male-product category that has recently gotten a marketing move-on is cigars. The industry now confidently expects that its more vigorous marketing efforts will push 1962 sales over seven-billion units, after a slight drop last year, and a decade that saw slow sales increases fail to keep pace with population changes. Research, new products, packaging and merchandising innovations, bigger promotion outlays (up from $6-million in 1954 to $30-million in 1962), even sprightlier ads, are aimed at broadening the base of cigar sales (only 20 per cent of adult males smoke cigars) and lowering the distinctly "mature" (40-plus) median age of the cigar smoker.

Biggest recent product development has been the introduction of new, smaller, slimmer cigars. They're a direct invitation to the younger man and an effort to shed an unattractive stodgy image that has helped hold down wider acceptance of cigars. Another innovation: current flurry of plastic-tip entries, also aimed at the younger or occasional smoker. Packaging of cigars into five-packs is broadening distribution in self-service outlets.

Typical of the frantic activity in the field are the marketing moves by Dutch Masters division of Consolidated Cigar Corp., which leads the pack with more than one-sixth of total industry dollar sales. In 1961 and 1962 the brand had, among other things: introduced two new, slimmer shapes, the El Dorado and the Dart; repackaged its entire line of eight cigars, utilizing color coding for each shape—a merchandising device that has paid off in other fields; introduced special gift overwraps for Father's Day, Christmas; named young, creative Papert, Koenig, Lois its agency; and gone heavily into TV (latest move here is sponsorship of an upcoming Sid Caesar series of half-hour shows for fall, in which Caesar himself is doing a special series of slapstick-comedy commercials).

III. NEW ATTITUDES NEEDED

In many industries aiming at the male, the problem has been one of adopting entirely new attitudes toward marketing. This is true for key segments of the big ($2.37-billion estimated in 1962) sporting-goods industry. Wares, ranging from boats and baseball goods to firearms and fishing supplies, have been aimed largely at the male. The conservatism that characterizes masculine attitudes toward certain sports is especially true, for example, of the hunter. Avowed effort in the past by companies making guns and hunting supplies to satisfy this conservatism led to antiquated marketing attitudes and practices. Result: The $254.3-billion industry, which was once the dominant category among sporting goods, has lost ground steadily in terms of its share, now ranks third, behind pleasure boats and photographic equipment.

But there's evidence here, too, that attitudes are changing. Said William Kelty Jr., marketing v.-p. of Olin Industries' Winchester-Western division, "Basic problem for our field was the realization that we were not in the guns and ammunition industry—we were in the recreation industry, and in competition for the leisure-sports-equipment dollar against everything from trampolines to tennis racquets; and as a result, we have now begun to adapt the merchandising, sales and ad techniques already in use in other industries."

Winchester-Western has, for example, embarked on a marketing program that effectively combines the traditional with the new, both to sell guns and ammunition and at the same time attempting to broaden the total base of the market. With its lively agency, Doyle Dane Bernbach, recent ads employ big pictures, evocative copy to promote new products like the 59, a lighter rifle with a Fiberglas barrel, new shells with plastic collars, touted as first "real improvement in 40 years."

Last year, as one approach to broadening the base of potential gun buyers, Winchester tested a novel approach to a long-time problem for the industry: the fact that many men would like to know more about guns but don't know how to find out—or are too embarrassed to ask. The company encouraged dealers to establish and promote Winchester Gun Advisory Centers, with accessories ranging from a specially designed hunting plaid used in point-of-purchase displays to mats for local ads. Some 85 per cent of the dealers who tried it, surveyed as to results, said the program helped increase sales an average of 25 per cent.

IV. PRODUCT EXCITEMENT

There is considerable evidence that one of the most effective ways for advertisers to draw a bead on the male market is through genuine new-product excitement—*i.e.*, new products based on thorough research. Two recent and apparently successful attempts along this line were Bulova's introduction of its Accutron men's electronic timepiece and last month's announcement by American Safety Razor of a new stainless-steel adjustable razor. Both entries, embodying genuinely new and exciting concepts, were preceded by extensive research into male needs and wants, research later used to shape effective promotion appeals.

For Bulova, long a leader in medium-priced men's watches, the Accutron (priced at $175 to $2,500) represented a determined bid for leadership in the higher-priced men's field. Its name, styling and promotion were guided by research conducted among 1,178 male watch wearers and—in deference to the fact that almost 60 per cent of all men's watches are given as gifts by women—388 women. Accuracy, reliability and appearance, in that order, emerged as male criteria for a quality watch, while women gave appearance first consideration. Introductory ads stressed all three—in the male order.

Next, radical, conservative and moderate designs were tested, with women opting for radical styling by a slight margin while men preferred a conservative watch with few cases changes. The name was one of nine possibilities originally tested and narrowed down to three—the other two: Satellite, Sonac. Said Alexander D. Goodman, Bulova's market research director: "Accutron conveyed several impressions (accuracy, electronics, scientific achievement, space age and newness) that our studies indicated would be well-received by men particularly and by women to a somewhat less degree." Results? According to Bulova president Harry B. Henshel, commenting on steady sales increases since the introduction, "We have no doubt Accutron will soon rank among the top six or seven fine watches for men on the domestic market."

The PAL razor embodied new concepts, too: the use of stainless steel, first lifetime guarantee for a razor—and quite possibly, for any product in the price category—and its boldly modern design by topflight industrial designer Henry Dreyfuss, whose previous commissions have ranged from farm equipment to the Princess phone.

In marketing the razor, ASR has its eye on a far more lucrative area—the fast-growing injector-blade, which by its very nature assures a high degree of brand loyalty between razor and blade. By this move, third-ranking ASR (behind Gillette, Schick), which has been moving forward aggressively since its acquisition by Philip Morris two years ago, hopes to boost sales for its PAL injector blade.

A crucial factor in the development of the product: intensive and continuing research with shaving panels, into men's likes and dislikes in shaving equipment in general and the new razor in particular. According to ASR marketing vice-president Jay Solomon, the company plans to spend some $5-million in a seven-month introductory push, "definitely aimed at males—we think we'll get the women, too, that way." One plus: The product will be able to ride on Philip Morris' extensive network-TV sponsorship, including such male-oriented buys as pro football. Agency is Benton & Bowles.

Perhaps the most dramatic example of the ability of genuine product excitement and truly masculine appeals to generate sales comes from the boating field. The big (an estimated $610.9-million in 1962, according to the National Sporting Goods Assn.) and booming (up 8.1 per cent since last year) industry beams most of its promotion at men as decision-makers, attempts only indirectly to reassure women by stressing safety, comfort.

An interesting sidelight on the boat as one of the few remaining strongholds of male authority is cast by a recent Dichter survey of cars leaving a large boating area. Only two per cent of those leaving with boat trailers were driven by women—as against the normal ratio of women drivers, which closely parallels the 50-50 division of licenses between the sexes.

An exciting product, and an equally exciting male-directed promotion, underlie boating's newest success story—that of the Bertram division (Miami) of Nautec Corp. Started two years ago with little more than an idea for a radical new design for a quality powerboat, the fledgling firm did $300,000 worth of business its first four months, $3½-million its first full fiscal year, just ended. It's now building a new plant to turn out $10-million of Bertrams annually.

The radical Fiberglas design, brain child of yacht broker and racing enthusiast Dick Bertram, now president of the division, practically launched itself when the first model won the big Miami-Nassau race in 1960—a feat the boat has repeated every year since. But Bertram also credits the effectiveness of a somewhat iconoclastic ad approach. In sharp contrast to the prevailing trend in boat promotion, which relies heavily on a big, beautiful picture, and short text, Bertram's black-and-white double-page ads, relieved only by tiny, technical drawings or small pictures, consist mainly of tightly packed technical copy, liberally sprinkled with terms like "longitudinal lift strakes." Recent Starch reports show the ads beat all other black-and-white boat ads even on "read most."

Bertram, who claims Claude Hopkins as his copy mentor, is convinced that men who are in the market for a specific big-ticket item like power boats "want to know all the facts." Dramatic proof of the effectiveness of the approach came after the company made a brief experiment with the big-picture "prestige"-type ad. It produced between 70 and 90 inquiries a month. When the long-copy ads were resumed, inquiries rose to over 400 a month.

V. AD APPEALS

What other types of advertising appeal to men? Says Dichter's Irving Gilman, "Since the American male is more mature than he was a decade ago, and has more social courage, he can be reached by degrees of sophistication and humor in advertising which would have been impossible ten years ago." However, in product areas like cars, once the exclusive prerogative of the man and now a joint purchase, Gilman sees a need for ad appeals that can overcome the "resentment, resignation, even apathy which makes a man non-catalytic about the purchase." "Triggering him to buy" may even require simulation of special appeals, efforts to recapture feelings of excitement, adventure, masculinity. One approach definitely not recommended is "togetherness," which to most men subconsciously represents downgrading of masculine prestige.

Another authority turning thumbs down on that theme is Johanna T. Rock, manager of readership research at Marplan. Says she: "We often find that the most memorable advertisements (those that include any people at all) picture, or at least feature, only one person—man or woman." Men, although they do tend to give more attention to pictures of men than they do to pictures of women, still seem much more inclined to look at women than women are to look at men—in ads at least. Men are less inclined to notice human-interest pictures and/or hearth-and-home scenes than cars and boats.

Starch's Dr. Morgan Neu stresses the importance of the relevance of illustration in advertising to men, the need for "functional, realistic art that gets men to read the message." This is especially vital since, he points out, women tend to *read* ads more than men.

Some interesting insights into what *not* to do in trying to reach the young male via ads are implicit in Playboy's philosophy of not accepting any ads that might offend the magazine's young urban male reader by suggesting that he has physical, mental, or social shortcomings. Thus the magazine turns down ads ranging from weight-control products and hair pieces to home-study or self-improvement courses. "We assume," says Playboy ad director Howard Lederer, "that our reader has completed his education and reached that point in his career where he needs no help."

Even greater segmentation of the male market, and more sophisticated approaches to it, will be the hallmarks of the future in the field. Advertisers will step up their efforts to pinpoint more precisely the male prospects whom they want to reach. This should prove a boon to those media delivering male audiences. Specialized magazines in the field are already showing growing strength. The first six months of 1962 saw total magazine ad volume rise 1.4 per cent, with the men's category up 3.5, outdoor, sports up 8.5 per cent.

Powerful tools like linear programming and computers will help make optimum media buys for male products, and, according to one top agency media director, may require complete reorientation in media-marketing thinking. This man pointed out that since women tend to read and view more than men, it is now difficult for a mass men's item like a razor blade to buy a 70-to-80 per cent male audience.

Fears that the computer will hurt specialized media, he feels, are completely groundless. In fact, if those media will provide better demographic and other research on their audiences—and there are moves being made in this direction right now—the effect of the computer should be the reverse.

Incidentally this points up one lack that must be remedied before the male market can be properly exploited. There is a crying need for more and better research—research into what and how men buy, their influence on brand selection in different product areas.

The continuing search by traditionally conservative men's products for livelier approaches—which landed accounts like Ambassador Scotch at Hockaday, Winchester at Doyle Dane Bernbach, Ronrico at Papert,

Koenig, Lois—will push more of these accounts to creative and smaller ad agencies.

Advertising directed at men, while hewing to the time-tested appeals like sports-celebrity endorsements and nostalgic themes, will continue to get wittier and more sophisticated, try high-fashion approaches. Success with men of off-beat high-fashion campaigns like the Hockaday "clean white sock" series for Adler socks will undoubtedly prompt more of the type.

Products now concentrating on women will press harder for sales to men, with new appeals, new male lines. One example of this is the recent ad strategy switch by Schenley, for its Dubonnet aperitif, formerly aimed at women. Now shedding any sissy image, current TV commercials plug it as a lunchtime drink for the "heads-up businessman"—presumably instead of his customary two midday martinis.

One area with tremendous growth opportunities, and where some big firms are still only gingerly dipping in a marketing toe: men's toiletries. It's already worth $549-million a year, and could grow faster than current rate.

What it all adds up to is this: For alert companies, willing to research men's needs, design genuinely exciting new products with truly masculine appeals, and market them imaginatively, the men's market offers big rewards.

22

SURVEY SHOWS HOW AMERICAN WOMEN BUY

PRINTERS' INK

"Woman's at best a contradiction still," that famous male jest of Alexander Pope, takes on a different perspective as the result of a new survey released today (October 2). The survey, "The American Woman," offers a new tool for deciphering some of the enigma of woman—an enigma that may be a constant source of whimsey to poets but a serious problem and goal to marketing.

The American woman, after all, represents the richest of all possible markets. Yet how can she be effectively sold when, as a market, the American woman is a virtual unknown?

Considering the progress of research, marketing's ignorance about women has been appalling to many an observer's mind. Men are classified by their jobs, their education, their hobbies, and on and on down an endless list. Women? They are classified as women, generally as female appendages in a dominant male's home. Some of the best refinements consider only this tripartite breakdown: housewife, career girl, afternoon club joiner.

Statisticians list households according to the husband's occupation, never by the wife's, if she works. They are grouped by the "head of the household's" education, as if the man does in fact rule. They are classed according to the man's social and economic progress, never according to the development of the wife.

But women certainly must be something more than cohabital accessories in the consumption chain.

Reprinted from *Printers' Ink*, Volume 269 (October 2, 1959), pp. 25-27 and 30, with permission of *Printers' Ink*.

How much money do women control by themselves? How much influence do they exert on the household purchases financed by their husbands? What do they buy for their personal use? How much do they spend? Do these buying patterns change by geographic region, by income, by age, by education, by employment status?

These are questions that have had to go largely unanswered. But now marketing research is beginning to fill in some of the voids.

I. THE RICHEST MARKET

Of one fact marketing people can be certain: Women outnumber men in the United States now and they will continue that numerical domination for at least the next 20 years. According to the lowest Bureau of Census projections, there will be 89,171,000 females over 14 years of age by 1980. Males over 14-years-old will number only 84,187,000 by that time.

As this numerical domination continues, it will be accompanied by fiscal domination which, in fact, exists now. Women now control 65 per cent of the nation's savings accounts, and a like amount of the nation's privately held securities and bonds. And women, who outlive their men by more than six years, are increasing their wealth as the principal beneficiaries of estates, insurance and social security.

Women, of course, are not sitting back to await widowhood to add to their capital accumulation. Almost 23,000,000 women are now at work. They hold down one-third of the nation's jobs and they hold nearly one out of five of the union membership cards.

Almost 30,000 women hold elective and appointive municipal offices, more than 24,000 are in the armed forces, almost a million are in business management.

The majority of these working women are not "career girls" in the glib sense of the word. By the last official count, 53.8 per cent of all working women also are wives living with their husbands. Single women account for 24.4 per cent of the female work force, and women who are separated, divorced or widowed account for 21.9 per cent.

Almost one out of three married women living with their husbands are represented in this female work force. Non-white wives are more likely to work than white married women (42 per cent vs. 29 per cent) but even the wives of men with substantial incomes are joining the labor force. At work now are 15 per cent of all women whose husbands make an annual salary of $10,000 or more. As could be expected, the percentage of working wives increases as the husband's salary decreases. The top percentage (42.3) is scored by the wives of men earning less than $1,000 a year.

These working wives, in most cases, raise their households to a better than average standard of living. The median income of working women is $2,210 a year. The median household income among families with working wives is $6,141. Almost two out of three families with working wives have an annual household income of $5,000 or more. Less than one half of families without working wives can boast that income level.

Women in the U. S. have total earnings of close to $45-billion a year. About half of that is spent on their homes. About one quarter is spent on themselves.

II. A WOMAN'S INFLUENCE

Obviously, then, the American woman is more than a mere appendage in the chain of consumption. She is a powerful economic force in her own right, with the money she alone controls and the money she alone earns.

What American male could be so egotistical as to believe that the woman's influence stops at the point of her own personal pay? There can be no doubt that the woman exerts a tremendous influence on her husband's spending, if he is allowed to do any spending at all.

The degree of influence, however, still remains one of the great unknowns, an unknown that will have to be answered if marketing is to direct its ad effectively.

According to the Department of Commerce, the American people devoted about $290.6-billion to personal expenditures last year. They spent about $78.3-billion on food and beverages, $37.1-billion on shelter, $26-billion on vacation and travel. One survey said that women overwhelmingly decide how each dollar is spent. But there are other surveys that tend to show that the man rules his home.

Sociologists, for example, like to think of the lower-class male as a man who asserts his dominance. He is supposed to be a husband who insists on making all the decisions himself. The upper-clas male, on the other hand, is pictured as a more solicitous husband who seriously considers his wife's advice. How rigid can this relationship be at the lower level when the woman is the one who is footing many of the bills?

Then, too, consider this piece of evidence. A recent survey conducted for a synthetic textile firm showed that most men consider it the wife's responsibility to keep the male well dressed. Especially among the lower classes, it is the wife who buys her husband's clothing and tells him what suit and shirt and tie to wear. Is this asserted domination? Or is it a replay of the old saw: "I handle the major problems and my wife takes care of the small ones; fortunately, we haven't had any big problems yet."

Assuming this female domination does exist, does it necessarily mean that advertising should try to influence women as family bosses rather than as mere females in a man's world? Should advertising attempt to bypass the male and campaign directly to the women? Or, should it talk as if the campaign were directed at men, and at women only secondarily, with the sly aside that "We realize women make the eventual choice but we don't want to let on that we know."

Assuming this female domination does exist, do women want to be continually reminded about it? Men certainly do not. Perhaps, as some psychologists believe, it might be better to advertise as if wives were submissive beings who "well, maybe, have just a little bit of say."

If an answer is to be found to this perplexing problem, certainly research will have to devise a more detailed list of classifications than housewife, career girl or afternoon club joiner. The desire of a wife to assert her dominance probably will not parallel a husband's income, a husband's education, a husband's economic and social progress. Any meaningful statistical tabulations will have to include classifications based on the wife's background as well.

III. HER OWN CONSUMPTION

It may seem understandable that little is known about the woman's influence on a household's wide range of consumption. So little is known about how people buy and why. Even less is known about the way they can be induced to buy.

To some marketing analysts, however, it seems incomprehensible that so little has been known about what a woman buys for herself—not necessarily why, but simply what she purchases for her own use, how often and how much she pays for it.

A major step in filling this void was made today with the publication of "The American Woman," a detailed compilation of female buying habits prepared by the research department of Street & Smith Publications, now a division of Condé Nast.

The study, supervised by research director Ralph J. Sharp, probed the purchasing patterns of women across the land, not just the women who read specific publications. It detailed what women own, what they have recently bought, how much they paid for it and what they intend to buy. There is information on 33 articles of clothing, 16 items of cosmetics, home sewing, life insurance, travel, automobiles, beverages, movie attendance, smoking and silverware.

The information is computable by the total U. S. population, regional patterns, city size, community type, family income, employment status, the wife's personal income and her educational status.

According to Sharp, the study, which is based on 5,452 mail returns from women 15 years of age and older, points out immediately one striking accomplishment of the apparel industry. Other industries may work to achieve planned obsolescence. The apparel industry already has accomplished it to a high degree. Consistently, women have all intentions of buying less clothing in the year ahead than they had purchased in the previous 12 months. They would seem to be satisfied with their clothes —satisfied, that is, until the fashion industry comes out with a new style which makes them scurry to the store to keep their wardrobes up with the times.

IV. NEW BUYING PATTERNS

Statisticians who insist on grouping women according to the social-economic condition of their husbands or heads of household will find ample argument against this practice in the section of the survey on apparel.

Working women own more clothing, buy more clothing and pay more for clothing than women who are not employed. Then, too, women with some college education outdress women with no college education by an even more substantial margin.

Working women, for example, own 8.1 daytime dresses. Unemployed women own 7.1. Women with some college own 8.2 dresses. Women with no college own 7.0. While the employed woman spends an average of $13.43 for a dress, the non-employed woman pays $11.36. Women with some college pay $15.92; women with no college pay $10.73.

Interestingly, there are certain geographic patterns in the ownership of dresses. Women in the south own considerably more daytime dresses (8.3) than women in the north central region (7.0). Women living in cities under 25,000 population own 7.7 daytime dresses, while women in cities of 500,000 or more own only 7.0.

Younger women, as might be expected, generally are more clothes-conscious than women past 35. They usually own more of all but the most expensive items—with one notable exception, hosiery. Younger women are not as rigid in their use of stockings as are some of the older women, particularly those over 55. And younger women also are not arbitrarily bound to wear a hat, the way some older women apparently feel.

All these considerations of age and employment and the like are not stated to imply that total household income is not an important determinant in predicting the amount of clothing that a woman will own. As the household income increases, so, too, does the amount and price of the clothing a woman will buy.

The point is this: Household income may be important, it may even be the most important consideration. But other factors also exert considerable influence.

These other factors come into dramatic play in the use of cosmetics. The heaviest lipstick users (every day) are not the most affluent women. The $7,000-$10,000 household income category scores highest. Women with household incomes over $10,000 and those under $3,000 score at the bottom of the list.

The leading everyday lipstick user is under 25 years of age, employed, and has attended some college. She lives in the west, in a community of more than 500,000 persons.

V. WINE AND WOMEN

The liquor industry piqued considerable interest last year when it decided that the time had come to allow women in whiskey ads. Are women principal consumers of intoxicants, such as beer, wine and whiskey? The survey shed some revealing light.

About 43 per cent of the women under study admit to serving beer in the home, 31 per cent to serving wine, and 36 per cent to whiskey. The pattern of consumption, however, is influenced by many factors, not the least of which is income. About two-thirds of all families with incomes over $10,000 serve beer, wine or whiskey, or all three. Among families with an income of less than $3,000, only one out of five admits to serving beer, one out of seven admits to serving wine, and only one out of eight admits to serving whiskey.

For all three beverages, the woman who serves intoxicants in her home is likely to be employed, to have attended some college, to be 25 to 35 years of age and live in a city of more than 500,000 population. But, above all, she most probably does not live in the south. While 57 per cent of the northeastern women admit to serving whiskey, only 17.9 per cent from the south make the claim.

The woman who smokes is also probably not from the south. Across the nation, about 28 per cent of the women admit to smoking an average of 15 cigarettes a day. In the northeast, 37 per cent of the women say they smoke. In the south the score is 21.5 per cent. The smoking percentages increase with the size of the city, family income, employment and education. By age group, the heaviest smokers are women 25 to 35 years of age. They consume an average of almost 16 cigarettes a day.

VI. WHY THESE NUMBERS?

Street & Smith's Sharp, in releasing the survey today, declared "service to the advertising industry" prompted the extensive report. Explained the research director:

"For years advertisers and agencies have searched for material on the buying habits of the American woman. Media have tried to supply this information by surveying their own audiences. But these, of course, in no way represent a picture of the habits of the total women of America."

The Street & Smith report is non-competitive in every respect. It provides the base, however, for what could be highly competitive campaigns once executives in all media have checked their audiences against the now-established national norms.

Media, nevertheless, are hardly the principal gainers from a survey such as this. All advertising must benefit from the knowledge now at hand. Here is nationally reliable information about what a woman buys for herself, what economic and social factors influence her possessions, how much she has bought recently, how much she paid for it, and what she intends to buy in the near future.

There is more. The Street & Smith survey amply demonstrates as nonsense the assumption that households can be classed merely according to the male's social and economic situation.

Could some significant female characteristics, which are never grouped together under male classifications, perhaps offer clues to non-women's products—to the purchase and consumption of such household durables as washing machines or such household non-durables as breakfast drinks?

Could we have some hints to the future purchasers of small cars? A cross-tabulation of the survey data might show, for example, that working women use their family automobiles mostly for week-end shopping, vacations and Sunday driving—when the demand is for a vehicle with large passenger and cargo space.

Then, again, in a silverware ad, should a woman be shown smoking? A cross-tabulation might show that women who are non-smokers are the principal owners of sterling flatware. Clothing purchases might be compared with travel, movie attendance compared with home sewing, liquor consumption with insurance ownership.

The new survey answers many questions about women's buying behavior. As well, it raises many more questions—and points the way toward the answers. The possibilities offer rich insights for improving the effectiveness of advertising and marketing.

23

AN EXPLORATORY STUDY of the
CONSUMER BEHAVIOR of CHILDREN

JAMES U. McNEAL

The tremendous interest that marketers have in consumer behavior is attested to by the volumes of material that have been written about the subject. This concern should be expected since the consumer is the other half of the business process—and still the most misunderstood half.

The search for knowledge about consumer behavior has been accelerated since the postwar years due to profit squeezes in many industries and the recognition of the marketing concept in most. The introduction of research tools borrowed from the behavioral scientists has permitted rapid advancement in this undertaking.

Success in consumer behavior research has not been all that marketers hoped for. For various reasons, businessmen have not had much cooperation from behavioral scientists. Results have been varied and little attempt has been made to integrate them. In many cases, too, results have not been made public for competitive reasons. Certainly few gains have been made toward a unified body of knowledge about consumer behavior.

Most of the consumer behavior research has been centered on the adult population since it possesses most of the buying power. From a business point of view, this may seem logical; but in terms of ever achieving an organization of thought about consumer behavior, it is not logical, for it overlooks the fundamental notion that to understand something one must usually start at its beginning. Consumer role behavior does not blossom suddenly with the advent of adulthood; it, like many other significant behaviors, is a product of learning that begins with childhood

Adapted from *Children as Consumers,* Austin: The University of Texas Bureau of Business Research, 1964.

and develops throughout the life cycle. If business practitioners and academicians are ever to develop a basic knowledge of consumer behavior, therefore, it also seems useful to study it from a developmental point of view.

I. THE STUDY

Purpose

As an attempt to gain insight into the beginning of consumer behavior patterns, an exploratory study was initiated. Its purpose was to explore the cognitive and attitudinal patterns of behavior characteristic of the child as those patterns are related to age-graded samples of children's entrance into the consumer role.

The study was expected to generate a number of hypotheses regarding consumer behavior patterns in childhood. From the eventual testing of these hypotheses a great deal of information was hoped for that, when joined together, would form the foundation for a system of knowledge about consumer behavior.

The first major task after setting the objectives and boundaries of the study was to ascertain those indicants, the investigation of which would achieve sufficiently the goals of the study. After all of the indicants were identified, they were stated in the form of questions that were to be answered by the investigation. These preliminary questions then were transformed into a set of questions suitable to the understanding of young respondents and pretested. A final list of the preliminary questions is set out below.

1. Does the child really want to enter the role of a consumer? Why?
2. Does the child seek emancipation from parental control in the consumer role?
3. How does the child view the acquisition process?
    A. As a satisfier of immediate personal needs?
    B. As necessary to his welfare?
4. Does he find the buying act stimulating regardless of what he buys, or are there varying feelings depending on whether the purchases are for him or his parents?
5. Does he want to share the consumer role of his parents?
    A. Does he view this as a training ground?
    B. Is a shopping trip with the parents different (more pleasing or less pleasing) than going by himself?
    C. Does he want his opinion asked about parental purchases?
6. What opinions does he have about the goods that his parents purchase for him?

7. Is he aware of the varying social value of some goods?
8. What material goods are most significant to him?
9. What would he buy if there were no limitations? Why?
10. Does he concern himself with the purchases of others?
11. How do his peers influence his behavior in the consumer role?
12. Where does he enjoy shopping most? Why?
13. Is he aware of business ownership and the motivation for it?
14. Does he know where goods in a store originate?
15. Is he aware of the functions performed in a typical store?
16. Does he have any general opinions of businessmen?
17. How does he view the relationship between himself and businesses?
18. Is he aware of advertisements?
    A. What are his feelings about them?
    B. Do they influence his consumer behavior?

Method

The method consisted of interviewing each child privately for approximately 25 minutes. Specifically, the procedure was as follows: The child was taken from his classroom to a private interviewing room by the investigator. An informal conversation was begun in order to establish rapport after which the child was asked his name, age, grade, and father's occupation. The child was then told that the investigator was interested in talking to boys and girls about their shopping behavior. The interviewer then followed this comment with the first question from the Guide to Interviewer. During the interview the child was asked specific questions and was given situations in which he was to place himself and then talk about his behavior in each situation. An example of giving the child a situation to discuss is, "Tell me about the last time you went shopping with your mother." In either case, question or situation, the child was permitted and encouraged to elaborate, that is, to talk freely about the subject. Answers were recorded and situational behaviors were categorized on the Guide to Interviewer. In addition, by seeking free-flowing responses, it was possible to elicit and record additional comments that might not have manifested themselves in a more formal question-and-answer session.

This technique is quite similar to that employed by Piaget in his exploratory studies of children.[1] Piaget stated, "The advantages of this method seem to us to be that it makes evident what observation left to itself can only surmise."[2] He termed the method "the clinical method" and employed it basically as a way of producing hypotheses which later

[1] See, for example, Jean Piaget, *The Language and Thought of the Child.* Cleveland: The World Publishing Company, 1955, and Jean Piaget, *The Moral Judgment of the Child.* London: Kegan, Paul, Trench, Trubner and Co., Ltd., 1932.
[2] *The Moral Judgment of the Child, Ibid.,* p. viii.

could be subjected to scientific tests. This, also, was what this study attempted to do.

Guide to Interviewer

It was necessary to select some research technique that most efficiently would elicit answers to the questions that prompted the study. After consideration of a number of techniques, it was decided to employ the guided interview method. The Guide to Interviewer was developed. It was tested and changed considerably in a pilot study. The result was a list of twenty questions some of which contained several parts and a number of codings for anticipated answers accompanying each question.

The Guide to Interviewer was very serviceable in that it allowed paper-and-pencil recording of significant data while the respondent spoke. It permitted the recording of a list of answers by simply making check marks beside a word or statement. For example, one question asked, "When you go to the store by yourself, what do you generally buy?" The child may have responded with five or six items in a matter of a few seconds. Because eleven answers had been anticipated as a result of the pilot study, it was rarely necessary to write out more than two items. Most were simply recorded with a check mark.

This recording system is even more useful with an open-end discussion question such as, "Tell me about the last time you went to the store with your mother." This question typically elicited a two- or three-minute recitation. Since certain portions of answers had been anticipated it was possible to record much of the content with check marks in the various blanks.

Due to the economy of time offered by this tool, it was rarely necessary for the respondent to wait while the interviewer recorded the answers. This permitted the interview to move rapidly while keeping the respondent's attention on the subject. Even more important, this feature permitted the interviewer ample time to record additional comments in the margin of the Guide. These comments, although not direct answers to the questions, were categorized and gave the investigator more insight into the child's feelings, lent more meaning to his answers, and actually broadened the results of the study.

Subjects

Sixty non-minority children were selected from age groups five, seven, and nine.[3] Sex was represented equally within each age group. Criteria

---

[3] Alternate rather than consecutive years between ages five and ten were selected due to the frequent discrepancy between chronological age and maturity age. Some children at five, for example, may possess the maturity of six-year-olds. Selecting alternate ages tended to eliminate this problem and show a more realistic view of age differences and attitudes.

for selection of each group included educational attainment and willingness to verbalize. All the children were selected from one public elementary school and one nursery, both of which were known to consist almost completely of children from the middle socioeconomic class. In addition, the father's occupation was solicited as a serviceable index of social class."[4] No attempt was made to ascertain the intelligence level of each student, but it is believed that the majority of the children were of average or high intelligence.

There is no assumption that this group of children is typical of middle-class American children in the United States, but it is believed that many such children would give responses similar to those obtained in this study. It is also believed that responses would have differed somewhat from those obtained if social classes had been equally represented.

Analysis and Interpretation

The information elicited from each respondent was recorded on a separate *Guide to Interviewer*. The data were taken from the 60 *Guides* and categorized according to age and sex. Then these records were analyzed carefully, question by question, situation by situation, for each age group and each sex. For example, the responses to the question, "Do you ever go shopping by yourself?" were totaled for each age group and also separated and totaled according to sex. It therefore was possible, for instance, to ascertain the number of five-year-olds who shopped independently as well as the number of five-year-old girls and boys who shopped independently. As a result of this type of analysis, it was possible to get a profile of the attitudes and knowledge regarding the consumer role for each age group and the influence of gender on each profile.

The content of the profile for each age group was ascertained by noting the frequency of like answers by the group members to each question and frequency of like reported behaviors in the behavioral situations. These numerical representations were often modified by additional comments elicited from the children before a final description was drawn. Further, and probably more significant, various profile elements were determined by combining and/or comparing a number of answers and behavioral descriptions.

Comparison of profiles of the age groups was performed by analyzing differences in conclusive descriptions of each group. This often necessitated transforming some of the numerical representations into percentage frequencies. Since neither the numerical nor the percentage frequencies

---

[4] By the Warner social class system, most of the children were members of either the upper-lower or lower-middle class which together constitute what Warner terms the "common man level," the largest social group in the United States. See, W. Lloyd Warner, *American Life Dream and Reality* (Chicago: The University of Chicago Press, 1953), pp. 52-66.

were the sole basis for the final conclusions, they were not reported except where they lent clarity to the descriptions.

II. FINDINGS

Age and the Consumer Behavior Patterns of Children

One of the purposes of this study was to examine the differences in consumer behavior patterns of children that result from changes in chronological age. In view of findings by noted child psychologists and sociologists that illustrate that behavioral patterns of children do change with age, it may be expected that the consumer behavior profiles developed in this study will differ also.

Consumer Potentialities of Children

A potential consumer is typically an individual who possesses purchasing power and a desire for some good or service. An additional prerequisite necessary for considering a young child consumer potential is an understanding of the relationship between these two factors.

Purchasing power, or money, is commonly possessed by the five-year-old, being received either from a very small allowance or gifts, but is scarcely meaningful to him. If he has material wants, he generally seeks satisfaction of them from parents rather than the market process. The seven-year-old, on the other hand, views money as a necessity for acquiring goods and usually has a regular allowance, a small part of which he saves to accommodate future planned purchases. By age nine the youngster is a practicing consumer who possesses a regular allowance that often is supplemented by income from odd-jobs. He, in fact, is so accustomed to the use of money that possessing or spending it no longer excites him to the extent that it did when he was seven or eight.

From seven on, then, the child may be considered as a potential consumer. Although most of the children possess purchasing power, it is not until around age seven that there is a clear understanding of what it can do. The fact that five-year-olds usually have an allowance is not due to a need for it but to a modern-day social custom.[5]

Degree of Independence in Purchasing

Much less than half of the five-year-olds interviewed shop independently, but by age seven practically all the children do. While independent shop-

[5] Sidonie M. Gruenberg and Hilda S. Krech, "Your Financier: The Child with an Allowance," *National Parent-Teacher*, 53 (October, 1958), p. 7.

ping is a characteristic behavior of the child after age six, the extent of it
varies considerably between ages seven and nine. Very few of the seven-
year-olds shop independently in more than two different types of outlets,
while over half of the nine-year-olds patronize at least three. Also, the
independent purchases of the nine-year-old are often more complex than
those of the seven-year-old; that is, the nine-year-old's purchases are
usually greater in number and more costly.

The majority of children in all three age groups make independent
selections when they accompany their parents on shopping trips. The
selections of the seven- and nine-year-olds, however, are more oriented
toward family needs than those of the five-year-olds. Also, practically all
of the children make purchase-suggestions to parents on shopping trips,
and the number that make purchase-suggestions about goods for the family increase with age.

There is a marked increase in the desire for emancipation in the
buying process with an increase in age. Only a few of the five-year-olds
want to assume the buying of their personal needs, while nearly 50 percent of the seven-year-olds and over 50 percent of the nine-year-olds
would like to take over this function.

Four general conclusions can be drawn about the independent shopping of children.

1. Independent purchasing becomes significant near age seven. This is a
time when the child begins seeking independence in a number of his activities
while starting a gradual revolt against adult domination.[6]

2. With increase in age there is increasing parental permissiveness in children's independent consumer behavior. For example, the child is permitted to
make more independent selections on shopping trips with parents as he gets older.

3. With increase in age there is an increasing desire among children to
assume independent purchasing activities. They not only try to assume more of
the buying for their personal needs but also that for family needs.

4. With increase in age there is increasing complexity in the independent
purchases of children. From simple purchases of candy bars and soft drinks the
children progressively assume the responsibility for purchasing such items as toys,
school supplies, and family staples.

In sum, the combination of parental permissiveness and independ-
ence-seeking by the child fosters a rapid growth in independent consumer
behavior during the years five through nine. While it would be naive to
state that by age nine children are as capable in their independent shopping as the average adult, it would be just as naive to describe their independent buying behavior as child-like.

6 James H. S. Bossard, *The Sociology of Child Development*, Revised Edition (New
York: Harper & Brothers, 1954), p. 441.

Degree of Consumer Training

Training in the consumer role at a very early age, whether self-initiated or other-initiated, is a unique characteristic of our modern society.[7] Bandura notes that in our culture one significant means of training our children in adult role behavior is supplying them with play materials with which they can simulate grown-up activities.[8] The success of this technique is evidenced by the fact that "children frequently reproduce the entire parental role behavior including the appropriate mannerisms, voice inflections, and attitudes which the parents have never directly attempted to teach."[9] Casual observation of merchants' toy displays will show a variety of play materials with which children may play "store" and imitate their parents' shopping behavior, for example, a selection of miniature cake mixes, household cleaning materials, and cash registers. Many elementary schools also encourage consumer training of our children. The writer participated in a third-grade class in which the teacher and students were discussing the functions and relative profits of middlemen.

As shown by the present study, training of children by parents in the actual elements of the consumer role is prevalent at age five and becomes much more intense by age nine. Independent shopping, for example, is encouraged at age five, and by age seven almost all the children report that they shop independently. Starting at age five the child may be sent to a nearby store for one or two staple items while being permitted to make a small purchase for himself. By age seven he frequently is asked to make shopping trips for family items, and by the time he is nine he often makes purchase-errands for as many as a half-dozen items for his household and additional items for himself.

Every child in the study, regardless of age, reported that he accompanies his mother on shopping excursions from which he receives consumer training by observing her shopping behavior and by making selections and purchase-suggestions. Where the mothers seek the opinions of the youngsters about tentative household purchases, consumer experience is further obtained. The opinions of the five-year-olds are rarely sought, but 50 percent of the seven- and nine-year-olds report that their mothers ask them questions about household purchases.

Giving the children explanations for refusing to purchase items that they suggest is also effective experience in that it acquaints them with

[7] David Riesman, Nathan Glazer, Reuel Denny, *The Lonely Crowd* (New York: Doubleday & Co., Inc., 1953), p. 120.

[8] Albert Bandura, "Social Learning Through Imitation," in Marshall R. Jones (ed.), *Nebraska Symposium on Motivation 1962* (Lincoln: The University of Nebraska Press, 1962), p. 214.

[9] *Ibid.,* p. 215.

factors that the parents consider in purchasing various products. Only about half of the five-year-olds report that their parents offer explanations for refusals, while 75 percent of the seven- and nine-year-olds say that their parents give reasons for not purchasing suggested items. It might be expected and is usually true that the explanations are more detailed for the older children.

Degree of Involvement with the Consumption Process

Information generated from the present study shows that there is significant involvement with the consumption process as early as age five, and by age nine the child has generally assimilated the consumption process into his characteristic behavior and has become a fairly sophisticated consumer. The high degree of concern of children with the consumer role is due, according to Heckscher, to a leisure society with the emphasis on activity rather than passivity.[10] The word *leisure* has been associated with a passive mood in past generations, being used to describe those fortunate few who had achieved a reduction in working hours and thus had some time for relaxation. Today, leisure also means time for relaxation, but relaxation is described in terms of activities such as boating, water skiing, golfing, vacationing, and other expensive pastimes. The emphasis, then, is on *buying* leisure activities, and this "social ethic of consumerism" filters down to our children.[11]

The present investigation uncovered the following behaviors of children that evidence their involvement in the consumption process:

1. Preferences and dislikes for certain retail outlets. Starting as early as age five some children show likes and dislikes for certain stores as well as specific types of stores. For example, five-year-olds usually prefer to shop in a food store more than other types of retail outlets and show least desire to shop in a department store. Seven-year-olds practically always possess preferences for certain types of outlets, supermarkets and discount houses being most prevalent, and show a good deal of dislike for certain stores because of such factors as uncleanliness and inadequate stock of certain goods. By age nine preferences become more varied while antipathy toward stores declines. The diminution of dislikes probably implies that by age nine the child has reached a high degree of independence in his shopping and patronizes only those stores that he especially likes.

2. Knowledge of retail functions. The fact that children's knowledge of retail functions increases with age implies an increasing concern with sellers. At age five only 20 percent of the children have familiarity with three or more functions performed in a retail store. At age seven the percentage has risen to 35 percent, and by age nine it is over 80 percent. At age nine, also, 25 percent of

[10] August Heckscher, "The New Leisure," in Eli Ginzberg (ed.), *The Nation's Children*, Volume 1 (New York: Columbia University Press, 1960), pp. 227-247.
[11] *Ibid.*, p. 237.

the youngsters have knowledge of four or more retail functions, while none of the five- or seven-year-olds are aware of this many.

3. *Interaction with store personnel.*   From age five on, practically all of the youngsters hold conversations with store personnel. While the five-year-old's conversation is usually small talk about his personal interests, with advancement in age the conversations increasingly consist of the child asking for information or services, for example, the price or location of an item. As the child continues to interact with the store personnel he develops feelings about them. These feelings increase in variety with age.

Other behaviors described in a prior section to this chapter, such as increasing independence in shopping and the desire for more independence in buying personal needs, are also significant indicators of children's involvement with the consumption process.

Marketing Knowledge

It has already been pointed out above that the child's knowledge of retail functions grows very rapidly from age five through age nine. Knowledge about store ownership also develops well during this period. At all ages the children generally believe that stores are owned by individuals and as the youngsters advance in age they become progressively more capable of stating the owner's names. Even by age nine, however, there is almost no awareness of corporation-owned stores.

Knowledge about sources of goods also becomes more sophisticated with age. All of the children, regardless of age, believe that farm crops and animals are the most significant sources of products. As the child gets older he becomes aware of other sources. For example, while the five-year-old views the farm as about the only source of goods, many seven-year-olds are aware of manufacturers as an additional source. Nine-year-olds are strongly cognizant of processors and can also name a number of geographic origins of goods. During childhood there is apparently no knowledge of the role of wholesalers in the distribution of goods. Neither is the role of transportation considered significant by the youngsters.

In general, by nine years of age, knowledge about the process of making goods available for sale is reasonably sophisticated. Credit for much of this knowledge is due to the elementary schools in which there is increasing consideration of the marketing process.

Peer Influence on Consumption

Biber notes that in the process of the child seeking freedom from the control of parents he places himself in the control of peers, permitting them to dictate, in great part, his preferences and mannerisms.[12] This transference of dependence, according to Biber, can be expected to become significant simetime during the first and second years of school, that is, between the ages of 6 and 8 years.[13]

The influence of peers on children's consumption habits, according to the present investigation, is noticeable at age five but it is of no major consequence until age seven. About 20 percent of the five-year-olds interviewed realized any influence of peers on their consumption behavior. This low percentage might be expected since only a few five-year-olds buy independently, and their associations with friends their age normally are not close as compared with associations of a few years later. Around half of the seven- and nine-year-olds report considerable peer influence on their consumer behavior. They say that friends recommend flavors of soft drinks and ice cream novelties and kinds of candy bars. This is direct influence that the children themselves recognize. Throughout the interviews, however, a large number of seven- and nine-year-olds made various comments that implied that they desired to own items like those in possession of their peers. This type of peer influence might be termed indirect but probably modifies many of the purchases of personal items for the seven- and nine-year-olds.

The Significance and Social Value of Material Goods

The children in the present investigation displayed a good deal of "material envy"; that is, practically all of them voiced desires to own material goods owned by other children. The types of goods envied did vary with the ages of the respondents. Generalizing their comments, it was found that at age five the significant goods are sweets, such as giant sizes of candy, and toys, the former being most important. At age seven, the desires are just reversed, with toys more significant than sweets. By age nine, the desire for sweets has declined considerably and the significant goods have become toys, clothing, and various adult goods.

Children apparently begin assigning social value to goods around age seven, particularly to elaborate toys. Seven- and nine-year-olds assign prominence to those children who acquire certain relatively expensive toys, and they, themselves, apparently feel some degree of status when they are in possession of certain toys. Nine-year-olds also are slightly fashion conscious in the sense that they may express a desire for certain articles of clothing being worn by other children, for example, tennis shoes and skirts.

[12] Barbara Biber, "The School Years: Growing Independence," in Sidonie M. Gruenberg (ed.), *The Encyclopedia of Child Care and Guidance* (New York: Doubleday & Co., Inc., 1954), pp. 811-812.

[13] *Ibid.*, p. 811.

Children involve themselves considerably with some durable goods. In discussing automobiles with them, it was found that practically all of them have preferences for certain autos, over 60 percent of all three age groups are brand conscious, and most of them possess familiarity with numerous features such as speed, gas mileage, maneuverability, and size. Station wagons are more popular with the five- and seven-year-olds while prestige autos, such as Cadillacs and Thunderbirds, are more popular among the nine-year-olds. Prestige cars are desired for their beauty and speed and because they are owned by the parents of peers.

Attitudes Toward the Shopping Process

By age five children possess attitudes toward the shopping process and these attitudes grow in sophistication; that is, they get more adult-like with increasing age. At around age five the child begins viewing the shopping process as an additional source of immediate personal satisfaction. Up to this point in life his parents essentially have been his only source of such items as candy and gum. As he advances in years, the market place progressively replaces his parents as a source of satisfaction-giving items and his parents become a source of funds. By age seven the youngster thinks of the shopping process as a source of both personal and family items and functions as a purchaser of both. Before the child reaches age ten he realizes that the shopping process is the source of practically all material goods.

Children of all ages view the shopping process as exciting. Their comments imply that it contains many pleasure-giving things to be discovered. For the five-year-olds, particularly, going shopping usually will take precedence over any other activity. By age nine, however, the glow of the shopping process is wearing off, and, if he is permitted, the child may show discrimination in making shopping trips. This reduction of interest in the shopping process, or in any activity, can be expected as the task begins to lose its problem character and the child develops a feeling of competence in it.

At age five the food store is generally the hub of the shopping process in that it contains the majority of the items necessary to meet the child's demands. At age seven, to some degree, and particularly by age nine, the child expects to obtain his needs in a large variety of stores. He therefore is developing preferences for certain stores relative to specific wants.

Preferences among children for certain stores are present at all ages and depend on such factors as the cleanliness of the store (they like a clean store), the number of patrons in the store (they dislike a crowded store, and the length of time to get served (they do not like to wait once the buying decision has been made).

The behavior of the store personnel also may influence children's preferences for specific retail outlets. At age five the store personnel are not too important to the child except that he expects them to be cordial. Beginning at around age seven the child expects the store people to be considerate of children by helping them locate and retrieve items and furnishing necessary information that will speed up the shopping process. The seven-and nine-year-olds often label those store personnel who are not cordial and helpful as "unfair to children."

The majority of children feel that shopping is a feminine function. This feeling, however, extends to grown-ups only. Some of the children think that both husband and wife should do the shopping and a very small number believe it is the husband's job. Those that see shopping as a dual or masculine function are probably victims of what Barclay terms "confusion of sex roles" which often results in those homes where both parents work and everybody shares in household jobs.[14]

Attitude Toward Advertising

Most children are avid television viewers. A recent study showed that children, on the average, watch television "almost as many hours per week as they spend in school."[15] Children in the present study were no exception for all of them reported viewing television, and, except for two five-year-olds, all indicated a keen awareness of television advertisements.

Starting at age five there is increasing dislike and mistrust of television advertisements as the child advances in age. Half of the five- and seven-year-olds and over 75 percent of the nine-year-olds in the present study reported negative feelings toward television advertisements. They believe that the commercials are, in general, untruthful, annoying, and time-consuming in relation to the programs with which they are associated. Their feelings might be compared with those of an adult toward a carnival barker.

Those children expressing positive feelings toward television advertisements, which constituted around 50 percent of the five- and seven-year-olds and nearly 25 percent of the nine-year-olds, said the commercials were entertaining and informative. Those considered entertaining were usually animated cartoon commercials. Informative commercials were generally those of a public service nature, such as announcements of forthcoming programs.

14 Dorothy Barclay, *Understanding the City Child* (New York: Franklin Watts, Inc., 1959), p. 46.

15 Glenn W. Thompson, "The Effectiveness of Television Advertising on Children and the Relation of Televiewing to School Achievement" (Mead, Pennsylvania: Allegheny College, Department of Psychology), p. 3 (Mimeographed).

In spite of the dislike for television commercials, over half of each age group buy or ask their parents to buy many of the goods they see advertised. Some of the purchases result from curiosity created by the advertisements, but most of these children feel that the products are of acceptable or good quality. With increasing age, however, there is an increasing tendency among the children to not want to purchase those goods that they see advertised on television. By age nine this tendency is prevalent among 35 percent of the children. This finding is in general agreement with that of Thompson[16] as well as that reported by Brumbaugh.[17] Essentially, their reason for not desiring many of the goods advertised is that they feel the qualities of the products are exaggerated.

Sex Differences in the Consumer Behavior of the Child

During the past two or three decades there has been increasing fluidity in our sex roles. What was a masculine activity yesterday may be considered suitable for women today, for example, politics. This flexibility in sex roles may be due, at least in part, to the changes that have occurred in child-rearing practices. "Looking back only twenty or thirty years we realize that child care then tried much more to *shape* the child . . . ," whereas, "in modern child care our foremost goal is to interfere as little as possible with developmental trends."[18] Today's girls, for example, as Brown notes, usually have as much or greater latitude in sex-role development than boys.[19] Girls may dress like boys, play boys' games, and play with toys typically associated with boys without being censured. Boys, on the other hand, risk being ridiculed by parents and peers if they perform what typically are defined as feminine activities.

In our society the shopping function is typically sex-graded and thought of as being feminine in nature. Actually, this social attitude is a holdover of the past, for, as Britt[20] notes, men today are buying on a scale never dreamed of twenty years ago. Further, as findings from the present study have indicated earlier, differentiation according to sex is not expected in the consumption behavior of our children. There were some

[16] *Ibid.*

[17] Florence Brumbaugh, "What Effect Does Advertising Have on Children?", in Constance Carr (ed.), *Children and TV* (Washington, D.C.: Association for Childhood Education International, 1954), p. 40.

[18] Lili E. Peller, "Incentives to Development and Means of Early Education," in Judy F. Rosenblith and Wesley Allinsmith (eds.), *The Causes of Behavior: Readings in Child Development and Educational Psychology* (Boston: Allyn and Bacon, Inc., 1962), p. 144.

[19] Daniel G. Brown, "Sex-role Development in a Changing Culture," *Psychological Bulletin,* 55 (May, 1958), p. 235.

[20] Stewart H. Britt, *The Spenders* (New York: McGraw-Hill Book Company, Inc., 1960), p. 251.

sex differences found, however, between children's attitudes, knowledge, and activities relative to the consumer role. These are reported here.

Degree of Independence in Purchasing

Independence in the shopping function apparently is granted to the male earlier than to the female. Twice as many five-year-old boys as girls report doing independent shopping, and the male independent shoppers demonstrate a wider familiarity with types of retail stores than do the girls who shop independently. From age seven on, though, the amount of independent shopping performed is about the same for both boys and girls, and by age nine, girls show a broader knowledge of types of stores than boys.

About one-third again as many boys as girls at age five get to make independent selections when they shop with a parent, but by age seven this difference disappears. Practically all boys and girls in all three age groups report that they make suggestions while on shopping trips with parents, but with increasing age the suggestions of the girls become more oriented toward family needs while those of the boys remain mostly personal in nature.

The desire for emancipation in the purchase of personal items differs also for the sexes. At age five practically all of the boys and almost none of the girls wish to assume the purchase of their personal needs. Beginning at age seven, though, the number of boys wishing to assume the purchasing of personal items declines while that for girls increases. For the boys the most significant reason for wanting to take over this task is that they feel they could get more of those items that they want but that parents will not purchase for them. Girls, on the other hand, state as their important reason that the task would be fun.

On examining these findings regarding sex differences in independent consumer behavior one fact is obvious; namely, that by age nine the female is emerging with more interest and more experience in the shopping function. This probably reflects the children's growing realization that shopping generally is viewed as a feminine behavior in our society.

Degree of Consumer Training.

As we noted above, boys and girls receive a good deal of self-imposed training in the consumer role via independent shopping. In addition, children receive a large amount of consumer training directly from their parents.

One means by which children obtain consumer training from parents is through the process of expressing their opinions that are sought by their parents when making family purchases. This practice permits the child to gain experience in making decisions about family purchases and introduces him to the complexities involved in buying for the household. There are sex differences involved in this orientation. The opinions of very few of the five-year-olds are solicited regardless of sex. Starting at age seven and continuing through age nine the opinions of the children about household purchases are requested frequently, and the opinions of significantly more girls than boys are sought during this age span (over 60 percent of the girls as compared with 45 percent of the boys).

Another situation in which children receive consumer training from the parents is that where the child asks the parent to make a purchase and the parent refuses but offers an explanation. These explanations give the child knowledge of some of the factors that parents consider when making purchases, for example, comparative cost and usefulness of a product. Twenty-five percent of the girls and 15 percent of the boys among the five-year-olds report being given explanations for refusals, and as was noted in an earlier chapter, these refusals are rarely involved. As for the seven- and nine-year-olds, the majority receive fairly sophisticated explanations from the parents without any notable sex differences.

It can be concluded, therefore, that while parents deal about equally with children in regard to explanations for refusing to make purchases, they favor female children with more consumer training by soliciting their opinions about purchases more than those of boys. This differential, which is parental-caused, is probably due to the fact that most shopping is done with the mother; and mothers, by social custom, tend to teach the female child more than the male child about the elements of their role.

Degree of Involvement in the Consumption Process

It was concluded in an earlier part of this paper that by age nine girls show more of a desire for independence in shopping than boys. This attitude indicates a growing concern with the consumption function by both sexes, but a somewhat greater one for the female. Another sign of involvement, which is discussed at greater length in the following section, is the child's increasing awareness of retail functions. The number of functions known is approximately the same for both boys and girls at ages seven and nine, but at age five, girls show a slightly greater knowledge of retail functions than boys.

The fact that children may possess preferences or dislikes for certain retail outlets implies interest in the consumption function. About 20 percent more five-year-old girls than five-year-old boys have store preferences at age five, but this number equalizes by age seven. At ages five and seven the preferences of boys and girls are almost identical in nature, but at age nine boys are showing a stronger preference for specialty stores. Throughout the three age groups around 20 percent of the girls express dislikes for certain outlets, whereas 20 percent of the seven-year-old boys but almost none of the five- and nine-year-old boys show dislikes.

Interaction with store personnel is another indicator of involvement. About half of the boys and girls in all three age groups hold light conversations with the store personnel. By age seven, however, the conversations take on a more serious note in that the child starts asking for services and information. These purposeful conversations are held about equally by boys and girls at age seven, but at age nine twice as many girls as boys are making purposeful conversations with the store people. Accompanying this sex differential in purposeful interaction is the interesting fact that by age nine most girls describe store personnel as "helpful" while most boys simply describe them as "kind" or "good."

From the foregoing analysis two conclusions can be inferred: (1) the degree of involvement is about the same for boys and girls through age seven, but (2) by age nine girls demonstrate more concern for the consumption function than boys. These conclusions might be expected in view of earlier ones that noted that by age nine girls possess more experience and receive more training in the shopping function than boys.

Marketing Knowledge

It was noted above that knowledge of retail functions is about the same for both boys and girls in all three age groups. In investigating the children's knowledge of retail ownership it was found that in every age group girls show much less understanding of it than boys. At age five very few girls can state a reason for a person's owning a store whereas around 40 percent of the boys can. By age seven and through age nine the number stating ownership motives is about equal among the sexes. The motives stated, which are basically profit and service, also are stated in about equal proportions by both boys and girls after age seven.

Knowledge of sources of goods found in grocery stores is also nearly equal for both boys and girls in the three age groups. So, in general, it can be concluded that the marketing knowledge of boys and girls differs little in the age span of five through nine years. This finding appears to be somewhat inconsistent with previous conclusions that show the female child more involved and more experienced in the shopping process. One point that might be made, however, in defense of the present conclusion is that most knowledge of distribution is not obtained by children through the shopping process but is passed on from parents and teachers. It, therefore, might be expected to show about equally in both sexes.

Peer Influence on Consumption

Of those five-year-olds who shop independently very few report that they shop with friends. Direct influence by peers, therefore, cannot be expected to be significant at this age level. Upon reaching age seven, shopping with friends is reported by 80 to 90 percent of the boys and girls. About 40 percent of the seven- and nine-year-old boys and 60 percent of the seven- and nine-year-old girls who report shopping with friends state that their purchases are influenced by their companions. Also, around 40 percent of the boys and 50 percent of the girls in the seven- and nine-year-old age groups feel that they influence many of the purchases that their friends make.

There are implications of indirect peer influence on purchases evident in the children's discussions of their desires for certain material goods. In expressing these wishes, 30 percent of the boys and 20 percent of the girls in the seven- and nine-year-old age groups stated that their reason for wanting certain items was that their friends owned similar goods.

Based on these findings, it appears that girls are more susceptible than boys to the direct influence of peers. In view of the higher interest in shopping that girls have, this outcome might be expected. The fact that a slightly greater percentage of boys than girls report indirect peer influence on their material desires probably is not significant since it is quite possible that many children are not consciously aware of this influence and therefore would not report it.

The Significance and Social Value of Material Goods

There are certain items that are significant to children in that these items are at the top of their "want-lists" and manifest themselves repeatedly in "I wish I had" statements made by the children. These items are also those that are desired most frequently in the possession of others. The present study showed that there are notable sex differences in the assignment of significance to material goods. At age five the products most significant to boys are toys such as games and mechanical devices; for girls, foods such as candies and frozen desserts are most important. By age seven boys show about equal concern for toys and adult items such as fishing and hunting goods while girls divide their interest between foods and toys. Upon reaching age nine there are additional changes in material wants. Although boys are still concerned with toys and adult items, their interest in the adult items is greater. Girls, on the other hand, practically give up their interest in foods, reduce their interest in toys, and show a good deal of concern with clothing.

As noted earlier, children in the study showed a great deal of involvement with automobiles. Each child was given a behavioral situation in which he could influence his parents' purchase of a new auto. The results show that five-year-old boys and girls both want their parents to own medium- or low-priced station wagons more than any other style of automobile. Preferences between sexes differ at age seven. The boys primarily want a reasonably priced station wagon but show a growing interest in prestige cars such as Cadillac. Girls at this age divide their preferences mostly between station wagons and sedans. At age nine boys show greater interest in prestige cars and a slight concern for small foreign cars and station wagons. The preferences of the nine-year-old girls are divided equally among prestige cars, station wagons, and convertibles.

There are minor sex differences in the children's reasons for wanting their parents to own the various types of automobiles. Boys and girls both want station wagons because of their utility. Boys like prestige cars for their speed and beauty and because the parents of peers own them. Girls give the same reasons for desiring prestige automobiles except that they do not mention speed. Those boys and girls (mostly boys) wanting small foreign cars desire them for their economy. The reason for girls wanting convertibles is that "they let the wind blow through your hair while you ride in them."

These findings regarding the significance of various products certainly support the conclusion by the Gordons[21] that our children have become very materialistic. In four years, from five to nine, their wants grow from candy to outboard motors. The basic sex difference is not in the degree of materialism but in the type of goods desired. The development of the specific materialistic desires of boys and girls that were noted in this discussion is in keeping with societal expectations. As preschoolers, both boys and girls have an interest in toys and sweets, but as they advance in age, the interests of boys lean toward those items typically defined as masculine (fishing and hunting goods) while the interests of girls lean toward those items typically defined as feminine (clothing).

Attitudes toward the Shopping Process

From the time that boys and girls begin participating in the shopping process they find it exciting. Girls, however, show more enthusiasm about it than boys. At all ages, for example, more girls than boys prefer to go shopping with their mother rather than remain at home, and this preference decreases with age for boys while increasing for girls. To the question, "Do you enjoy going shopping?" almost one-third more girls than boys answer affirmatively.

Children's preferences for stores in which to shop vary somewhat with sex. Over one-third of the boys in each age group indicate that they enjoyed shopping in supermarkets; but, while around one-third of the five- and seven-year-old girls concur, practically none of the nine-year-old girls show this preference. Also, with increasing age, boys show increas-

[21] Richard E. Gordon, Katherine K. Gordon, and Max Gunther, *The Split-Level Trap* (New York: Bernard Geis Associates, 1961), p. 142.

ing preference for drug stores and constant preference for variety stores, while girls indicate increasing preference for specialty stores and a constant preference for discount houses.

The present study also uncovered slight sex differences in attitudes toward store personnel. Throughout the three age groups girls are more definitive than boys in their attitudes toward store people. While boys tend to describe them as "good" or "kind," girls are inclined to speak of them in terms of the aid they give and the degree to which they perform their jobs well. In view of the comments made by both boys and girls about store personnel, it is concluded that boys, in contrast to girls, do not regard store personnel as significant elements of the shopping process.

The major portion of boys and girls five through nine view shopping as a feminine role among grown-ups but do not sex-type the function among children. An equal number of boys and girls (about 20 percent of each) see shopping as a function for both sexes, and about 12 percent of the boys feel that shopping should be done by the male member of the household. The significant deviations from the traditional viewpoint that women should perform the shopping function is probably due, as pointed out earlier, to the current practice of both parents working and sharing the household tasks.

Attitudes toward Advertising.

Sex differences in attitudes toward television advertising are minor, but there is one significant sex difference in the development of these attitudes. Girls develop a disbelief of television advertising at an earlier age than boys. Although there is a good deal of dislike for television advertising at age five, there is little mistrust expressed at this age. At age seven, however, 40 percent of the girls and only 10 percent of the boys state that they do not believe most of the commercials. By age nine the number of boys and girls regarding television advertising with suspicion is about equal.

There seems to be no simple explanation for this earlier development of disbelief for television advertising among girls, but it may be contributed to the following reasoning: (1) boys and girls tend to do most of their television viewing in the daytime during which time the father is usually away; (2) children (when they are not in school) often join their mothers in viewing their (the mothers') favorite adult programs, and it may be that girls participate in this joint activity more than boys; (3) if so, then girls would be subjected more than boys to their mothers' attitudes toward television and advertising. Thus, there may be a greater opportunity for the mothers to caution girls about the dishonesty of many television advertisements.

III. CONCLUDING COMMENTS

When a study of human behavior is exploratory in nature there are always shortcomings. The most common is that the study could have embraced more variables. This is true of this study. Feelings of children about branding and pricing, for example, might have been expected to result from a study of this nature. Likewise, it would have been interesting to elicit children's attitudes toward new trends in distribution, such as discount houses, and shopping by telephone. The study, however, was not intended to ascertain all attitudes about all aspects of the consumer role, but was designed to explore the changing mind-world of the child relative to the consumer role. It was necessary, due to time and monetary limitations, to deal with a selected group of variables that would bear most heavily on the central aspects of this consumer orientation.

It is practically certain, as was indicated, that the results would have been different if social class had been employed as a criterion. The study, however, did concern itself with children of the social classes most prominent in this country. Similar information about children of the upper and lower-lower social classes would be much less useful to marketers and probably less typical of average development in consumer maturation.

In order to achieve functional consistency most questions related to shopping were oriented to shopping in supermarkets since the pilot study indicated that all the children interviewed had some experience with them. It is recognized that this procedure created a significant limitation; namely, that elicitation of the children's knowledge and attitudes toward full-service stores and downtown shopping was restricted.

The importance of the investigation is that it did produce some interesting hypotheses related to the beginning of consumer behavior patterns. Testing of these hypotheses with proper samples of children should result in a number of fundamental contributions to a body of knowledge about consumer behavior. An additional significance of the study is that the hypotheses that it generated should also be useful to the behaviorist or businessman who wishes to study further the consumer behavior of children. Work in this area is very meager.

Lastly, it should be mentioned that studying child behavior is a refreshing pleasure when compared with investigating adult behavior. With the exception of some introversion, children are willing respondents who possess very few defenses. Their natural honesty actually simplifies the design of interviewing tools as well as the interviewing procedure.

24

DO AD MEN UNDERSTAND TEEN-AGERS?

PRINTERS' INK

Soon after receiving their first driver's licenses, teen-age motorists start getting a bimonthly magazine published by General Motors for young drivers. It's free, designed to serve the interests of young motorists. It's one of the ways GM practices what many companies are beginning to learn: that to build a future in the consumer field, a company does well to build a present in the teen-age market.

Many companies have, during recent years, recognized the growing buying power of nearly 20-million U. S. teen-agers who will spend about $10-billion this year (and usually much more freely than their parents). Many companies have successfully won a share of the market. But in so doing, they have frequently tended to view the teen-ager only as an immediate customer.

I. MANY-SIDED BUYER

More companies, like General Motors, are recognizing that the main importance of the teen-age market is not immediately apparent. For apart from their obvious and growing power as purchasers, teen-agers play increasingly important roles as:

Indirect Buying Influence

The amount of family spending directly attributable to teen-age influence is immeasurable. As an indication, 55 per cent of the teen-age girls in a

Reprinted from *Printers' Ink,* Volume 272 (July 29, 1960), pp. 21-23, and 26, with permission of *Printers' Ink.*

survey made by *Seventeen* magazine said they thought they had exercised at least some influence on the family's most recent automobile purchase.

Innovator

Teens are quick to try anything new; many products that now have wide acceptance were first established among young people, particularly those in high school and college. The youth influence on clothing styles is widely recognized. Perhaps not as widely known is the fact that many other products—canned beer, frozen TV dinners and filter cigarettes, among them—established beachheads in the youth market before going on to wider gains.

Future Family Builder

The habits, attitudes and buying of teen-agers can be expected to help shape their consumer activity as parents. And, since youngsters are marrying earlier, teen-agers aren't far from parenthood. The median age of boys at marriage is 22, the peak marrying age for girls is 18—a fact of profitable significance in the long-range plans of many industries, including silverware, linen, furniture and housing.

Nor does this exhaust the inventory of teen-age influence. There is at least one other major area of significance for the marketing man in the teen-age market: the matter of corporate image building.

Like their elders, young people are much given to brand-switching, as they grow older and their interests change and—at every age level—as they are attracted to new product concepts. Also like their elders, youngsters appear to develop loyalty to a company more strongly than a brand image. And they seem to have firm opinions about different companies which would seem certain to have some influence on their purchase decisions regarding the products of these companies.

In this connection, a recent poll of 5,000 high school boys and girls by *Scholastic Magazine* revealed that General Electric has built a particularly favorable image among the students. By substantial margins over other major companies, the boys and girls listed GE first as the company they would choose to work for, as the company they consider the leader in scientific research, and as the company they consider the leader in engineering.

It is more than a coincidence that GE consistently has done an outstanding job in schools, selling nothing but scientific education—and a strong corporate image. The future value to GE of current gains is impossible to forecast. But it seems safe to say that the school activity is helping to create a favorable marketing atmosphere for the sale of GE products to those exposed to the GE programs for teen-agers.

II. AN INFLUENTIAL

The heavy emphasis placed on the teen-ager as an immediate customer is understandable, since teen-age preferences can make a product, a company or an industry. Their prejudice can seriously hurt.

The teen-agers have saved the movie industry (the teen-age 11 per cent of the total population accounts for perhaps half or more of the movie audience). They are mainstays of the record industry (one major company has reported that teen-agers buy 90 per cent of its single records and half of its albums). They are also major factors in a variety of other industries, from apparel (the teen-ager spends far more on clothes than the average for the total population) to bowling (which ranks with movies as a favorite pastime on dates) to cosmetics (the teen-age girls spend $300-million a year on cosmetics).

These conditions, not surprisingly, have been the making of many companies. In 1940, when Bobbie Brooks, Inc., was organized to make sweaters and sportswear for young women, the fashion industry operated on the tradition that designing for young women, "juniors," was a matter of size—physical proportion—rather than age (with its implication of needs, different taste preferences and desires). Bobbie Brooks was a pioneer in reversing the tradition and establishing the dynamic concept of junior as an age rather than a size. Carefully researching the attitudes of its market (actually, two markets: 15-18, 19-24) the company designed the kind of clothing that juniors wanted, and helped persuade stores to emphasize the difference of the new junior approach. Bobbie Brooks sold 20,000 garments in 1940, 6-million last year.

In another area, Esterbrook—unable to match marketing dollars in the general market with such pen-making giants as Sheaffer, Parker and Paper-Mate—has redirected its efforts toward the teen-agers. Since the first of the year, Esterbrook has been concentrating on the high school and college areas, becoming a dominant pen advertiser in the media serving those markets. While it is too soon to judge results, Esterbrook appears to be convinced that its future lies in those markets.

Many companies have long recognized the potential of the teen market. When American Tobacco Co. began a campus marketing program about ten years ago, American was third among college students, behind Liggett & Myers and Philip Morris. Today, American is the leading company in this area. Breck Shampoo has made and maintained itself as the number-one shampoo among teen girls through a consistently heavy advertising campaign carried in the specialized media that serve the market. Thom McAn shoes, popular with high school students, reinforces its popularity with a campaign that includes a program of bronzing the shoes of athletic stars. A teaching-aids program in schools is an important part of Bristol-Myers marketing program.

The roster of companies that have recognized the opportunity and benefited from it is long. It includes such varied organizations as du Pont, Simplicity Patterns and Eastman Kodak.

And the new opportunities are inexhaustible. It should, for example, be of more than passing interest to the egg industry that, according to one survey, on a typical morning only 13.5 per cent of teen-age girls surveyed had eggs for breakfast (64 per cent had milk, 59.3 per cent ate toast, rolls or buns, and 48.4 per cent drank juice).

Numbers, dollars and changing mores have combined to create a teen-age market of consumers with power going far beyond their numbers. Never have there been so many teen-agers, with so much money to spend and so much freedom to spend as they like.

III. TEEN INDEPENDENCE

This post-war phenomenon probably has its origins in World War II, when the absence of fathers in the service and mothers in defense industries thrust upon youngsters a degree of independence and maturity new in the American culture. The process has been accelerated since the war as many mothers continued to work, some fathers moonlighted on second jobs, and families moved to the suburbs, forcing fathers to spend less time at home with the children because of commuting. There are other factors that give teen-agers more freedom, including the increasing mobility of American families, about 20 per cent of whom change their residences each year; the increasing amount of business travel by fathers; and the increasing complexities and pressures in daily living which take more of parents' time, leave less for close supervision of children.

As one result, teen-agers feel much closer to other teen-agers. By overwhelming margins, they turn to friends rather than father or mother for guidance, solace and discussion of things that matter to them. Along with their increasing independence and maturity, has gone increased income. In 1944, the teen-ager was estimated to have an average income of about $2.50 a week. Today, it is four times that much.

Teen-agers form one segment of the larger youth market, and are themselves further divided into smaller (sex and age) segments. The youth market embraces youngsters from birth through the age of 24. The major segments are formed by preschoolers (0-5 years); grade school children (6-12-; the teen-ager (13-19), more than 80 per cent of whom are in high school or college; and the older collegian and young adult (20-24). Each segment has its own manners, mores and marketing significance.

Because they are coming into their first significant money and because they are the blooming, developing consumer, teen-agers are for marketing men the key youth segment. The teen years are major change years, the years of puberty, adolescence and early maturity, with the physical and psychological awakening and upheaval that these mean. There are new needs, new interests, new knowledge—all of which have a bearing on the teen-ager as a person and on his requirements as a consumer. Marketing men who best understand the teen-agers' condition are in the best position to win their loyalty.

This week, shedding additional light on the teen-age market, *Seventeen* magazine has released "The Teen-age Girl: 1960." It is the report of a survey among 4,532 unmarried, in-school, teen-age girls conducted by the Eugene Gilbert Co. under the direction of Seventeen's research director, Aaron Cohen.

The picture that emerges is, as described by Mrs. Enid A. Haupt, editor and publisher of *Seventeen,* the picture of "a well-groomed, hard-working, serious young adult who exerts influence on family purchases, is avid for new merchandise, commands a sizable amount of disposable income, and whose manners and mores are copied by young people around the world."

Teen-age girls do command a sizable amount of disposable income, an average of $9.53 a week—a total of about $4.8-billion per year. About two-thirds of it comes from allowances, the other third from part-time or full-time work.

The teen-age girl is well-groomed and spends heavily to stay that way: about $3.2-billion for apparel and footwear (20 per cent of all women's apparel and footwear expenditures) and about $300-million for cosmetics.

Her other major expenditures are for entertainment (including records, which 71 per cent of the girls buy); jewelry; food and soft drinks; hope chest items (silver, china, glass, linen); sporting goods (eight of ten girls participate in sports); and small appliances (including record players, which 72.9 per cent own).

Those 6-million families with a teen daughter are influenced by her in their purchases. More than half of the daughters, for example, play an active part in the decisions their families make to buy furniture.

One of three teen-age girls is employed this summer (as baby sitter, camp counselor, clerk, saleslady). Year-round, 39 per cent work part-time or full-time. Eighty per cent plan after-school careers, while also planning marriage (800,000 are engaged annually).

At home, four out of five cook and/or bake. On the day before the girls were interviewed, 46 per cent reportedly made breakfast, 38 per cent helped prepare dinner, and 68 per cent helped clean up. Fourteen per cent had shopped after school (mostly for family food).

She talks a lot to her girl friends and boys by telephone (on the average, probably more than an hour a day). When she isn't thus engaged, and often even when she is, she likes to listen to the radio (a median of two hours and 13 minutes a day) or records (79.8 per cent own record collections, of which 19 per cent include classical records). On the other hand, TV viewing—possibly because it is less easy to do something else while watching—isn't as popular (the peak viewing period is Sunday night, when 29.5 per cent of the girls watch TV).

A prime social focus remains the boy. Slightly more than half of all the girls reported that they date; one-third said they are "going steady."

IV. BOYS SPEND MOST

As for boys, there are slightly more of them—9,800,000—as the result of a slightly higher rate of male births (it isn't until the later years that males begin to die off faster and are outnumbered by women). The boys also are richer than the girls, with an average of about $10.25 a week ($4.16 at the age of 13; $16.65 at 18) because of somewhat higher allowances and earning power.

Boys are more taciturn (they spend an average of only about 42 minutes per day on the telephone) but just as addicted to disk jockey shows (they tune in their radios about two hours a day).

The boy, like the girl, is interested in personal appearance, but spends less for it (an average of $163 a year for his wardrobe, against the girl's $300).

His biggest expenditures are for food (32 per cent), sports (11 per cent) and dates (ten per cent). One of his major interests—cars—is supported by his direct expenditure of more than $200-million annually for autos and gas. It is subsidized to an even greater extent by his use of the family car and gas paid for by his parents.

Like his girl friend, the boy is very much group-oriented, sharing experiences with his friends, and learning from them. And, both the boy and the girl want and respond to sincere attention and respect from the adults they associate with.

In studying this data, the marketing planner does well to keep uppermost in his mind that these statistics represent *averages*. Variations in attitude and consumer behavior can vary widely by sex and age group, and what works with one segment may not with another.

Fortunately, the segmentation presents no serious problem. The market itself is concentrated: four of five teens are in school. And any segment or the market as a whole is easily reached through the broad array of efficient specialized advertising media that serve youth (advertising can be critical: the market leaders tend to be heavy advertisers).

V. "BE HONEST"

The problem, indeed, is not how to reach any part of the market or the teen group as a whole, but on what terms to reach them. Researchers, media people and marketing executives with experience in the market agree that the most surely fatal error is to make a false approach. As *Scholastic Magazine* points out in a brochure, "How to advertise to teen-agers," the "first rule for gaining the good will and confidence of teen-agers is always to be completely honest." They are, the advice continues, "quick to detect a spurious quality in people as well as in advertising." Once the word gets around (as it can quickly) that a product or service doesn't live up to its claims, that product has lost its market. In that connection, an item should never be advertised as "free" unless it is in fact free without any strings attached.

There are several other rules that guide successful advertising. They arise from the costly experience of many advertisers and may be stated as do's and don'ts:

Do understand precisely which segment of the total teen market you want to reach (and should reach). There are media to reach even the most specialized segments.

Do show an awareness of the special needs and interests of the market at which you aim, and approach the teen-ager in a friendly and adult manner. As the Scholastic brochure points out, such an approach, based on sympathetic understanding, can win the teen-ager's "enthusiastic friendship—and his business."

Don't write down to this market. A most common error is the attempt to use a jargon that can most quickly reveal the spurious. There is less teen jargon than adults imagine, and most of it is strictly local and incomprehensible in other areas.

VI. SOME TESTED TOOLS

There are other cautions that apply to different teen groups in various situations. The surest way to know what is right and what is most likely to succeed is to find out. The teen market is, for its size, perhaps the most thoroughly researched market of all. But it is a constantly changing market, and to keep abreast, constant research is necessary. Research provides a general background for understanding and solving the specific problems of individual companies (a bubble gum maker is researching the reason why young people like his product even when they don't blow bubbles; a distiller is exploring the drinking habits of college students whose per-capita consumption of spirits appears to be rising).

Having researched his problem, the marketing man is sure to find that as in other markets, advertising to teen-agers works best in conjunction with other marketing tools. There are many promotional techniques that have been proved and tested in the teen market:

Contests

These can be extremely useful, but aren't always. The successful ones are tied in directly to teen-age activities. And the prizes are realistic, offering immediate rewards (cash, goods), rather than futures (since most youngsters don't go on to college, a college scholarship as a prize in a high school contest is certain to arouse less interest than a contest with a free trip as the prize).

Sampling

With brand-switching prevalent, exposure is extremely important to a product. The Student Marketing Institute has distributed 100-million samples as part of its campus marketing activities. President Robert Stelzer of SMI points out that deals and special offers are popular because teens "are avid bargain hunters." Sampling may be accomplished through delivery to fraternity and sorority houses and dormitories, or through coupons in advertisements or at the point of purchase.

Merchandising

Teen-agers do a lot of shopping and are attracted by point-of-purchase displays, demonstrations and literature. The rules for advertising apply to p-o-p material, and the material carries its heaviest impact when integrated with advertising themes teen-agers are familiar with.

Publicity

The many media serving the market—daily newspapers with teen sections, the specialized teen magazines, teen radio shows and others, including school newspapers and radio stations—are interested in company news of value to their audiences. As with every other aspect of the marketing program, publicity is most effective when releases are shaped to the self-interest of the teen-ager.

In-School Programs

Essentially, these consist of teaching aids, primarily designed to help teachers teach specific subjects. When properly designed, such programs create good will and a favorable marketing climate. How important these programs are is indicated by estimates that American business spends more money on high school teaching-aid programs than all schools spend on textbooks. However, much of it is wasted, unused—largely because some companies show more interest in telling their own product story than in providing a meaningful teaching aid. Content is far more important than brand name. The most successful teaching-aid programs are those based on material that fits into the school curricula.

VII. LOOK TWO WAYS

What pioneer companies have learned in the teen-age market, particularly during the '50s, when the teen population increased from 15-million to 20-million, can be of great value to the increasing number of companies moving into this growing market. By 1970 the teen market is expected to increase another 35 per cent, to more than 27-million—with probable spending power of more than $14-billion, reckoned in today's dollars.

This is a market rich enough to turn any marketing man's head. But the more discerning marketing man will try to look two ways. He will keep one planning eye on the opportunities for serving the needs of the growing number of teen-agers during the '60s. And, looking beyond that to the development of future family consumers, he will realize, too, that many of the most acquisitive family-builders of 1970 are teen-agers today.

25

A MARKETING PROFILE of the SENIOR CITIZEN GROUP

DAVID E. WALLIN

Today the creed of the gerontologists is no longer John Donne's imaginative challenge—"Death, thou shalt die"—but rather, I think, "Death, thou shalt wait." Certainly, advances in control of infectious diseases, public-health measures, daring surgery and painstaking rehabilitation, have combined to lengthen the over-all U. S. life expectancy (at birth) from 47 years in 1900 to 69 today. Since life expectancy mounts as the hazards of successive age ranges are passed, an American woman of 65 at present still has an average of 15 years to live. Similarly, in this country, a man of 65 can look forward, on the average, to 13 years more of life. This then is, indeed, the Age of Age.

Now, in order to focus more sharply on the segment of the population which is central to this discussion, the terms "senior citizens" and "aged," used hereinafter, shall refer exclusively to persons who have attained at least the sixty-fifth anniversary of their birth. Defining the subject age group in these terms permits a cordial working relationship with the statistical data developed by government and private reporting agencies.

In the broadcast sense, this paper attempts to develop a profile of the important marketing characteristics of the Senior Citizen Group. Specifically, research has been aimed at answering some of the following questions of marketing interest relative to this aged segment of our population: How large is the market? Where do they live? How do they make a living? How much do they have to spend? And, what specific marketing opportunities exist?

Reprinted from Robert L. Clewett (ed.), *Marketing's Role in Scientific Management* (Chicago: American Marketing Association, 1957), pp. 250-261.

RESEARCH BARRIERS

Now, let me say first, before entering these questions directly, that one is confronted with a formidable problem in attempting to research this segment of the population. For while there is a great deal of talk and thought about Senior Citizens, there is very little marketing action relating to them—except perhaps in housing and drugs.

In most lines of marketing endeavor, the thinking is chaotic. Nobody seems to know what value to place upon the aging customer. Retailers, especially, tend to cast the over-65 market a worried glance—and go on selling to *other* markets. One might even be led to observe that: "The only businessmen who have their eyes on the Senior Citizen market are the undertakers."

Well, how can this be? Why should some 14 million consumers hold so little lure? The answer is that several factors work strongly against pinpointing this market. First, except for some special health and comfort items, it's a group that wants the same things other age groups want. In this respect, it differs from the children's and teen-age markets.

Next, it has less economic identity than most age categories. There seems to be no middle-income group here. The diamond-shaped income pattern of the whole population—with its broadest segment in the middle income group—changes to a triangle-shape, with by far the greatest number of oldsters at the base of the triangle. Yet, there's also a larger than average percentage at the very top—that is to say, there are more millionaires aged 65 than there are aged 30.

Finally, this is a group that indignantly resists identification. Partly, this seems to reflect the stigma that a youth-infatuated society tends to put on old age. And partly, it is because age itself is losing its meaning. The improved status of the Senior Citizen both physical and economic makes him act like, and want to be treated like, everyone else.

Despite the fact that you can't tell a Senior Citizen from any other citizen without a St. Petersburg program, it is still possible to suggest some answers to the questions posed earlier.

HOW LARGE IS THE MARKET?

The trend toward an increasingly larger proportion of Senior Citizens in our society has existed for well over a century, and has recently been greatly accelerated. Several factors combined to increase the number and proportion to the present high level: The post-Civil War rise in the birth rate; a small but significant increase in the expectation of life at age 65; the precipitous decline in the birth rate which took place between 1900 and 1936; and, the gradual aging of millions of immigrants.

Since 1900, our total population has doubled while the number of men and women 65 years and over has quadrupled. Furthermore, since 1930 alone, the number in this age bracket has risen 100 per cent, while the total population has risen only 30 per cent. Today, there are 14,127,-000 Americans who meet Senior Citizen requirements, of which about 6½ million (47 per cent) are men and 7½ million are women. The old age group accounts for about 8.5 per cent of the entire population.

Currently, the Senior Citizens are showing a net gain of 300 thousand a year. There is every reason to expect a continued sharp rise in their number. The factors which have produced the recent changes have not yet spent their effects. If no new and catastrophic influences enter, it is estimated that there should be just about 21 million aged 65 and over by 1975.

The proportion of the aged in the population also seems certain to increase during the next two decades—probably to about 10.0 per cent in 1975.

WHERE DO THEY LIVE?

Fully as important as the number of Senior Citizens, in developing a marketing profile, is their distribution through the several parts of the United States. Where, in fact, do they live? In 1950, aged families were distributed throughout the country, with one-third in the Northeast, one-third in the North Central states, and the remainder in the South and West. The larger local concentrations were in the more recently developed regions, particularly the Far West.

In New England, the aged constitute a larger proportion of the total population than elsewhere. In Maine, New Hampshire, Vermont and Massachusetts, the proportion is more than one-third greater than in the nation as a whole. In addition, four states in the farm belt—Iowa, Kansas, Missouri, and Nebraska—and one Mountain State, Montana, have relatively high proportions of aged persons as a result of emigration of the younger generations.

At the other end of the scale, low proportions of the aged in the population are most pronounced in the Southeast (with the notable exception of Florida) and in the Southwest, with less than pro rata shares being evident in South and North Carolina, Georgia, Arizona, Utah, and New Mexico.

Rural-Urban Distribution

Now, one of the more significant marketing aspects of the movement among the elderly population of the United States is the increased extent to which they are concentrating in the nation's towns and cities.

From a situation in which the urban districts had only 93 per cent of their proportionate share of the aged population in 1920, the percentage has risen consistently with each passing decade as follows: 95 per cent in 1930; 100 per cent in 1940; and 103 per cent in 1950.

To carry the analysis a bit further, we may briefly call upon the tabulation of population characteristics, according to size of place, which was introduced in the 1950 census. This tabulation affords some insight into the extent to which cities and towns of various sizes have more or less than their pro rata share of the nation's Senior Citizens. Calculations completed to date show, for example, that the central cities of urbanized areas having more than one million inhabitants had just 99 per cent of their pro rata share of the aged in the United States; those in urbanized areas of some 250 thousand to one million inhabitants had 102 per cent and those in urbanized areas of less than 250 thousand had 105 per cent.

The pro rata share of Senior Citizens continues to increase as the size of the population center is reduced in number. In brief, these data show clearly that the village or small town is still to a very considerable extent "America's old folks home."

Variations from City to City

The extent to which Senior Citizens are concentrated in certain cities, and their conspicuous relative scarcity in others, also deserves attention. According to the latest census returns, cities of 100 thousand or more where aged people are most concentrated include:

St. Petersburg	Portland, Me.
Pasadena	Lawrence, Mass.
Atlantic City	Portland, Ore.

At the opposite end of the continuum, the following cities are marked by a relative paucity of old people in the population:

Corpus Christi	Jackson, S. C.
Charleston, S. C.	Savannah
Columbus, Ga.	

Migration

Now as a final attempt to answer the query "Where Do They Live?" let's briefly consider the topic of "migration." Other than the fact that a considerable number of senior citizens have settled in Florida and California, little is known about the migration of the aged. What little is known may be summarized in three points:

Relatively few larger cities attract significant numbers of elderly men and women.

State capitols and university towns seem to attract old people and to afford the type of life sought by those who migrate.

Proportionately, elderly migrants figure most largely in the aged populations of Florida, Arizona, California, Louisiana and Texas. In fact in those five states the number of elderly migrants involved between 1940 and 1950 was about double that involved in the movement to those states in the previous decade.

WHAT DO THEY DO FOR A LIVING?

At this point, we now have some idea of how many Senior Citizens there are and where to find them. To further develop the marketing profile of this group and to possibly uncover some preliminary clues to their financial capacity, let's note briefly their employment situation.

In March, 1954, nearly one person in each four aged 65 and over was employed or actively seeking work (about 3,225,000). Now, specifically what do these people do for a living? About one-fourth of the aged men in the labor force are farmers or farm managers. About 10 per cent of the older men at work are "service workers," i.e., firemen, guards, policemen, barbers, janitors, etc. About 13 per cent work as managers, officials and proprietors other than farmers, and roughly a like number are employed as craftsmen, foremen, and kindred workers. Smaller numbers are operatives, clerical and sales workers. Most of the women workers aged 65 and over are employed as household servants. While operatives comprise only one-fifth of the total labor force, only one-tenth of the workers aged 65 or more fall in this category.

In general, then, the heaviest occupational concentrations of our Senior Citizens are in agriculture, manufacturing, and service industries. While such concentrations follow the specialization pattern of the nation's total working force, the concentration of men 65 and over in agriculture is inordinately large. That is, only one-twelfth of the total labor force is made up of farmers, while almost one-fourth of the working Senior Citizens make their living in this way.

HOW MUCH DO THEY SPEND?

Now, let's consider another dimension of central importance in the marketing view of any population group. Income and distribution according to income and particularly "How Much Do They Spend?"

Careful study has verified the intuitive judgment that families with an aged head have predominantly low incomes. If the family head is still employed, his earnings have shrunk; if retired, his retirement income tends to be low. Currently, half of the families with a head 65 years or over have an annual cash income below $2 thousand. Three out of 10 such families had less than $1 thousand in income.

However, the preponderance of low incomes for families with aged heads does not lessen the importance of analysis showing that there are about 2½ million Senior Citizen families with yearly incomes about $2 thousand. More important, it does not lessen the marketing importance of the nearly 700 thousand Senior Citizen families with annual incomes of $5 thousand and more.

What the income of the entire group adds up to is simply this: A disposable personal income in 1956 of $20 billion (or 7.4 per cent of total U. S. disposable personal income.) Now as stated here, disposable income is based only upon wages and salaries and does not include the effect of these additional buying power supplements: A Social Security pension of up to $162.80 a month for man and wife; a company pension, added in many instances to Social Security pay; a $1,200 personal exemption from federal income tax; no Social Security taxes to pay on the pension; priority in getting low cost housing; and liberal tax deductions for medical expenses.

Furthermore, Senior Citizens may be presumed to have more disposable income in the sense that they have fewer financial commitments as they get older. Their children are out on their own, and the mortgage is usually paid off. But this doesn't mean that they hoard the money thus freed. Instead, in their role as doting grandparents, they represent an important market for toys and children's clothes. Likewise, they buy a considerable share of refrigerators, washing machines, and TV sets as gifts for struggling young couples.

Taking everything together, what I'm saying is simply this: An important segment of the Senior Citizen market has money, and they spend it for goods and services. This spells marketing opportunity!

WHAT SPECIFIC MARKETING OPPORTUNITIES EXIST?

I trust that by this time the unique features of the Senior Citizen marketing profile are becoming more apparent. Here are several examples of how some businessmen have transformed a rather neglected segment of the population into an important marketing opportunity.

Retailing

Some retailers have made a definite play for the older customer. Apparel, for example, is one field where taste can be defined by age group. The elderly man is by no means the conservative one might think. He likes his argyle socks and seems addicted to gaudy shirts and sportswear. He has to be attired conservatively while he is working. When he retires, he cuts loose.

The elderly woman, as might be expected, is less predictable. She dresses conservatively, and appears to put comfort ahead of style. Dress specialty shops indicate that they sell 10 times as many size 16's as size 40's, which was not true 20 years ago. Why? Because the older woman presently is extremely conscious of her figure.

Lane Bryant in New York has specialized for some time in clothes for the larger figure (hence, in many cases, the older figure). About five years ago, it opened a Junior Plenty shop for chubby and out-sized young people. In a short time, female Senior Citizens invaded the youngsters' precincts.

The elderly women do, however, insist on long sleeves—because arms show age early. They are partial to "soft, full" lines and flattering lace. And, of course, they insist upon a certain propriety of style.

In general, observers in the apparel industry argue that the Senior Citizen market must be carefully courted. "It's the kiss of death to mention age," they say. That's one reason why many stores simply stock the size that elderly folk wear and then call the sales job done.

Lane Bryant's struggle to sell tactfully illustrates the problem. Its current slogan, "If You Are Not Slender," is perhaps an improvement over its old appeal to "Stylish Stouts." But its officials feel it still isn't perfect.

Housing

Turning to another field, undoubtedly housing is one of the primary needs of the Senior Citizen. In many cities, projects are either under discussion or in progress. Carroll City, Florida, is perhaps typical of the kind of real estate development that may soon make more appearances throughout the country. The city will develop ten thousand homes in the under $10 thousand bracket and which will be largely marketed to retired people. In this connection, the *Journal of Lifetime Living,* the magazine which caters to the "over 40 market" frequently carries advertisements like this one:

> "Improved Homesites in a Fashionable Florida Waterfront Subdivision— Lots only $7.50 down, $7.50 a month, no interest or taxes."

Of course, the market is not all on the low-income side. Some of the projects, especially in the Southwest, run to fairly high rents. At least one private operation, the Mayfair residential hotel in Houston, which opened a superswank set of units last October, indicates that more than 70 per cent of its units have been rented to people 65 and over—at $300 to $700 a month.

Curious about this fact, the management made a survey of its tenants to find out why the oldsters prefer the Mayfair. It found that Senior Citizens like the "extreme modern" decor better than the younger tenants. They appreciate the gimmicks and appliances in the dream-world kitchens. They appreciate the spaciousness—room in which to put their big, old furniture. Most of all, they like the privacy that the management insures them.

Mobile Homes

A certain segment of the Senior Citizen market, of course, appears not to be attracted by permanence and prefers to travel. This tendency is turning into a bonanza for the trailer and travel market. According to the Mobile Homes Manufacturers' Association, retired people accounted for only 5 per cent of the $321 million market in 1953, but represented about 10 per cent of the $324 million trailer market in 1954. Industry indications are that the percentage will increase in succeeding years.

Mobile Home Parks

In addition to providing impetus for the mobile home manufacturing industry, Senior Citizens' interest in mobile homes has led to the development of a rather new market for trailer parks (there are now twelve thousand in the United States). There are several currently under construction, the largest being the 540 acre Guernsey City development in Tampa, Florida. Advertised as "A Paradise for Retired People," the project will boast four and one-half miles of waterfront lots, 100 shuffleboard courts, three swimming pools, a 3,500-seat auditorium, a 300-berth yacht basin, an open-air amphitheater, and accommodations for three thousand trailers. Significantly, it will include a 22-store shopping center.

Travel

The Senior Citizens also seem inclined to undertake some travel. It is the almost universal illusion that no matter where you are, the best place to spend your Golden Years is somewhere else. In a Pan American-Grace Airways survey on its North-South American routes, the average age of passengers was nearly 55 years. "This," stated a Panagra spokesman, "made us realize that we were all wrong in keying our advertising to younger people who apparently have neither the time nor the money to go off on an extended tour to South America. Instead, we decided to aim for the 35 million Americans in the 47-70 age bracket who constitute a large group of people who can actually afford the luxury of a trip to South America."

Food

Other industries have also begun to examine the Senior Citizen market. For example, the food industry is well aware that eating habits change markedly after 40. As they advance in years, people require fewer calories, less salt and more protein and minerals. Early in 1955, H. J. Heinz Company launched a new line of Senior Foods specifically designed for old people and successfully test-marketed in Cincinnati and St. Petersburg. The first items in the geriatric line were beef stew, lamb stew and chicken stew in 8½ oz. cans. Heinz officials believe that the Senior Food line has excellent market potential, because unlike baby and junior foods the market does not turn over about every two years, but only after 15 years or more.

Geriatrics

A few companies have found the Senior Citizen market a really fertile field—especially those companies that deal directly in geriatric products. Generally speaking, there are at least seven types of products with geriatric appeal: A general tonic; dietary supplements (vitamins, minerals, and amino acids); digestive aids; cathartics (laxative); diuretics (exciting discharge or secretion of urine; a medicinal substance); oral and external analgesics and anti-rheumatics (absence of sensibility to pain); and products for denture wearers.

Basically, the success of a geriatric line, over and above the therapeutic efficiency of the products themselves, would seem to be the reflection of a keynote of hope and confidence; a central appeal that old age is a period to be enjoyed and not dreaded; an underlying theme which suggests that the last years of one's life should be the happiest, the most serene, and the most comfortable.

All things considered, in order to capitalize on the marketing opportunity afforded, remember what the experts say: Senior Citizens fear being put on the shelf. Therefore, I say, any merchandiser who can bring them off the shelf should find a welcome.

SOME CLUES TO SELLING

Finally, let's touch upon some noteworthy clues to selling this market—and then note the marketing responsibility inherent in servicing Senior Citizens.

First, some selling clues. The Senior Citizen often lives alone. He must make new friends after losing work and home relationships. Hobbies, which were once only peripheral when he was active, are often the center of his life.

But in marketing leisure-time products, care must be exercised. For instance, while retired men like hobby crafts, such older men are less inclined to use power-driven machinery. This suggests that power tool marketers may need to play up safety factors and speed control if they wish to sell to the retired.

Similarly, studies indicate that retired professional and businessmen prefer fly and plug fishing, while their working-man counterpart leans toward live-bait fishing. Another clue to marketing to the retired: Women and professional and businessmen are partial to exotic, decorative types of gardening, while wage-hour workers stick to regular gardens, and more prosaic floral arrangements. Furthermore, professional and businessmen prefer photography more than other retired workers.

Now, Senior Citizens often follow a kind of activity pattern which is of marketing interest. First, they go to rest and relax in St. Petersburg (eight thousand per year), or some other resort with a benign Southern climate. Then, they travel and acquire a few hobbies. Gradually, however, after a year or two, they settle into a single hobby or part-time occupation. As for hobbies, traveling, reading, gardening, sewing, and bridge are the most important interests. Hobbies, which as a group are of secondary interest include: Hunting, fishing, boating, music, photography, home workshops, and movies.

Finally, to conclude, I believe that the expanding Senior Citizen market offers at least two important possibilities to business and at least one challenging responsibility.

First, it is difficult to chart oldsters' needs. But needs do exist. Because elderly folk are somewhat bound by habit, the manufacturer who wants to sell them should start early and develop in the population a loyalty to his product that will be hard to break. If people are to drink milk after 65, they must be started drinking it long before they reach that age. If they are to be interested in a hobby using your materials, you'd better start interesting them now.

The second possibility is the development of products unique to the needs of older people. For example, "non-skid" paints that will keep the aged from slipping on wet floors, and special bathtubs that permit easy and safe entry and exit. In general, some work has been done along this line but not in any highly identifiable quantity.

The responsibility for business lies in conditioning the worker to retirement. This responsibility closely parallels the first possibility. If a person is to be active and happy in his retirement, he has to be taught how before the event occurs. In some businesses, personnel counselors are available to guide employees approaching retirement in plans to occupy leisure time—hobbies, social work, income-producing activities, etc. Although something is being done along these lines, it seems that more could and should be done if business is to fully tap America's most neglected market: The Senior Citizens group!

26

THE SIGNIFICANCE of ETHNIC GROUPS in MARKETING NEW-TYPE PACKAGED FOODS in GREATER NEW YORK

MILTON ALEXANDER

To manufacturers and distributors of new-type packaged foods, Greater New York ranks first as a market and as a marketing enigma. On the one hand, it is easily the largest spender for foods among the 168 standard metropolitan areas. On the other, it is most unyielding to product innovations.

Hence, the perennial question of food marketers: What is it that makes New York so different from other marketing areas? And what, if anything, can and should be done to adjust for the difference? According to a traditional hypothesis, the area's atypical pattern of consumer behavior stems from the heterogeneous nature of its population. New York is said to comprise a melting pot of several fairly distinct ethnic markets in one.

Based on a pilot study, this hypothesis oversimplified local food marketing problems. Furthermore, assumptions of ethnic difference were found to rest on long-established hunch rather than current fact. As such, they were largely unrelated to the present-day ethnic setting and to the new-type products which represent an ever-increasing share of consumer expenditures for food. In short, there was an evident need to modernize the traditional hypothesis and to establish guideposts for marketers in this and other heterogeneous areas. This study represents a beginning attempt to fill both needs. It brings up to date the food habits of four major ethnic groups—Italian, Jewish, Negro, and Puerto Rican. More pointedly, it explores the impact of inter- and intra-group differences on acceptance

Reprinted from Lynn H. Stockman (ed.), *Advancing Marketing Efficiency* (Chicago: American Marketing Association, 1959), pp. 557-561.

of six "model" new-type products—frozen food dinner, frozen red meat, frozen fruit pie, instant coffee, cake mixes, and dehydrated soups.

Despite all countervailing socio-economic pressures, ethnic food habits continue to prevail in Greater New York. The ethnic setting, therefore, remains a necessary basis for local food marketing strategy and practice. This is particularly so with regard to new products. Further, an awareness of ethnic differences and of dynamic internal changes (both socio-economic and dietetic) may lessen the marketer's acceptance of behavioral myths regarding ethnic groups.

From the marketer's point of view, the residual ethnic influence in food consumption is variously affected by demographic trends. In the case of Negroes and Puerto Ricans, by an accelerated rate of in-migration; a clustering in the inner city; and an apartness from the general population. In the case of Jews, by conflicting drives toward cultural assimilation and continued clustering even in the adjacent suburbs. And, finally, among Italians, by the increased incidence of inter-marriage with "outsiders."

Meanwhile, ethnic food habits have shown a remarkable resilience even under pressure for conformity. Consumption patterns are still evolving. The following is a sampling of significant ethnic attitudes toward foods new and old.

Beginning with typical second-generation Italian housewives, there appears to be a marked residual antagonism toward processed-packaged foods which, incidentally, fail to appear in 80 per cent of the group's lunches, 64 per cent of its suppers, and 95 per cent of its breakfasts. Also, freshness remains the dominant appeal in Italian usage of coffee, vegetables, and meat. At the same time, more housewives are being swayed toward product innovations by the convenience of new-type packaged foods.

The same is true of second-generation Jewish housewives. Thus, 90 per cent of Jewish families were found to prefer fresh to canned or frozen alternatives. And about one of three of their breakfasts and one of five of their suppers featured one or more traditional delicacies.

Many young Negro housewives also tend to adhere to their traditional diets. For example, the use of meat at breakfasts; the preference for starchy products; and the aversion for "raw foods." On the other hand, many ethnic traditions are weakening. By and large, young Negro housewives are found to rebel against the low-income meat-meal-molasses or rice-beans-plantain diets. And in growing numbers, they adopt processed-packaged foods as symbols of social status.

The Puerto Rican diet represents a unique blend of traditional and new-type food preferences. So strong is the ethnic effect, however, that the low-income tropical diet generally prevails. New-type foods, therefore, are supplements to, rather than substitutes for, traditional favorites.

Nevertheless, almost every type of packaged food innovation has breached the group's ethnic loyalties.

Now, specifically, how does this dynamic ethnic setting, for some 55 per cent of New York's population, affect the acceptance of new-type packaged foods? In partial answer, let us review the major findings for each of the six "model" foods featured in this study.

First, frozen food dinner. Italian acceptance is apparently hampered by deep-seated ethnic preferences for fresh meat and vegetables. Sales prospects are brightened only by two relatively minor offsets in the ethnic diet. First, by the continued simplicity of Italian meals. And second, by the group's traditional liking for processed-packaged fish. In any event, Italians place last in rate of consumption. In the Jewish group, a residual ethnic influence seems to militate against large-scale acceptance. The net upshot: Jews rank last in most indices of acceptance. Product convenience is recognized. But this "like" is outweighed by the "dislike" of product taste and expense. Negroes also tend to resist frozen food dinners—seemingly on traditional grounds. The net result is widespread use but in limited quantities. At the other end of the acceptance scale, Puerto Ricans are found to lead all other groups in rate of consumption, presumably due to the high incidence of working housewives within this group.

Italians rank at least second in ethnic acceptance of the second "model" product—frozen red meat. But consumption by Jews is obviously discouraged by the dietary laws—especially in the case of pork. Regardless of variety, however, Jewish consumers resist the product's taste and price. Frozen red meat is also opposed to the Negroes' traditional preference for fresh and fatty cuts. Their resistance is further hardened by the prevailing inadequacy of refrigeration in Negro homes. In the case of Puerto Rican housewives, ethnic distaste for the product is at least partly offset by the working housewives' need for convenience. Puerto Ricans lead in all indices of acceptance. This showing, however, is almost entirely confined to the more economical luncheon cuts.

Frozen fruit pie, the third "model" product, seems to hold but little interest for Italians. At any rate, they rank last in per-capita consumption—avowedly due to a marked dislike of flavor. Jewish consumers do relish sweet goods, but of a distinctive type—either baked at home or available in the many specialty bakeries throughout the area. Principally for this reason, they rank last in regular usage of the frozen product. Also, as per tradition, Negroes still do not "take to" fruit pies. Hence, their bottom score in rate of consumption. In contrast, the Puerto Ricans' craving for sweets is so intense that it seems to overcome the group's dislike of product taste and expense. Usage of the product is still spotty, however.

A strong residual preference for their special blend, sharpens Italian resistance to instant coffee—the fourth "model" food. As a result, Italians trail other ethnic groups (excepting Negroes) in rate of consumption. In contrast, instant meets with a favorable response from Jewish consumers. Due to the group's tea-drinking tradition, the rivalry of regular coffee is minimized. Instant, however, is found to be an addition to the group's cultural inventory rather than a replacement for an established item. While the Negroes' ethnic diet also favors acceptance of instant, countervailing socio-economic forces tip the balance against heavy consumption. Actually, Negroes are found to rank last in terms of actual purchases. As with Italians, the Puerto Ricans's traditional diet also features a distinctive type of coffee. Here, however, opposition to instant is tempered by light coffee-drinking habits. And according to the indices of acceptance, Puerto Ricans rank second in per-capita consumption.

Similar implications may be read into the acceptance ratings of cake mix. Here, for reasons already cited in connection with frozen fruit pie, both Italians and Negroes are found near the bottom of the acceptance index, but just a notch above the Jewish group, which is in last place. Puerto Ricans (for all their difficulty in deciphering package directions) seemingly lead the other ethnic groups.

The sixth "model" food—dehydrated soup—also fares rather badly in the Italian diet, at least in comparison with the sales potential of the generic product. Thus, while Italians rank first in usage (vs. non-usage), users in the group rank only fourth in per-capita consumption. In the Jewish group, non-usage still appears to be the rule. Typically, Negroes seem to use dehydrated soup in limited amounts; and they trail all other groups in the indices of acceptance. In rather familiar contrast, the elastic food habits of the young Puerto Rican group have also yielded to this new-type product in large measure.

Now, one may ask: How can manufacturers and retailers implement these varying manifestations of the ethnic effect? There is no simple answer because there is no pat formula for "segment selling"—one that would cover all products and all groups across the board and regardless of time period. An ethnic marketing approach, therefore, demands a separate and distinct adjustment for each combination of ethnic group and new-type packaged food.

For the manufacturer, this selective approach would find useful application in the formulation of marketing strategy and in estimating sales potentials—even if only as a qualitative guide. It would also help him capitalize on opportunities for sectional listing of new products in the large food chains, in in-store promotion, in couponing, and in the deployment of missionaries. At the very least, a fact-based approach to ethnic groups could reduce losses due to a misdirection of promotional efforts. Similar benefits would accrue to supermarket operators in developing new store locations and in making optimum adjustments, in their merchandising, for significant ethnic differences.

27

THE NEGRO as a CONSUMER — WHAT WE KNOW and WHAT WE NEED to KNOW

CHARLES E. VAN TASSEL

During the past few years, there has been a substantial increase in interest and in research effort on the part of marketing management regarding the Negro as a consumer. More and more companies are paying more and more attention to the Negro as they search for market expansion opportunities, and their action is prompted primarily by four factors.

First of all, there has been an increased economic awareness of the Negro in recent years. The sheer size of the Negro population and the magnitude of its purchasing power have certainly heightened the businessman's interest in what is commonly referred to as "the Negro market." Second, there is an ever-increasing social awareness of the Negro. Organized efforts ranging from local neighborhood demonstrations against various forms of discrimination to relatively large and powerful national groups such as the NAACP and CORE have been quite effective in increasing the awareness of the Negro by American industry. A third factor pertains to increased political involvement. The most obvious example of this, and one which has profound implications for the business community is the passage of the Civil Rights Bill. Government action, then, has been in part responsible for business being more attentive to the Negro. The fourth factor which has been instrumental in spurring business interest in the Negro relates to the increased availability of market information about Negroes.

While the economic, social, and political dimensions are certainly of profound importance, it is the fourth element, the nature and extent of

Reprinted from M. S. Moyer and R. E. Vosburgh (eds.), "Marketing for Tomorrow . . . Today," Chicago: American Marketing Association, 1967, pp. 166-169.

market information currently available about Negroes, which is of prime importance to the marketer.

NEGRO MARKET: DEMOGRAPHIC INFORMATION

Most of the data available now on the Negro market are of a demographic or descriptive nature. For example, it is known that:

(a) The Negro population rose from 13 million in 1940 to approximately 21 million today—an increase of over 60 per cent. By comparison the white population increased in size by about 45 per cent during the same period.

(b) Negro median family income is approximately one-half that of white median family income.

(c) Negroes have an aggregate annual purchasing power of between $25 billion and $30 billion—about 7 per cent of the U.S. total.

(d) Negro consumers represent a rather compact sales target. While about one-seventh of the white population lives in the 25 largest cities in the U.S., one-third of all Negroes are concentrated in these 25 cities.

(e) The Negro market is relatively young. Median age for whites is about 30. Median age for Negroes is around 23.

Additionally, there is a wide range of data available concerning such areas as geographic location, population mobility, job status and employment stability, educational levels, and family life, including such details as divorce, death, and illegitimacy rates.

This sort of factual knowledge is, of course, fundamental to an understanding of the basic dimensions of any market. It is not enough, however, to serve the purposes of management in setting policy relative to the Negro market.

NEGRO MARKET: PURCHASING PATTERNS

While most of the information about the Negro market is of a demographic nature, some data are being developed about Negro purchasing patterns.

In terms of relative purchase quantities, it is known, for example, that:

(a) Negro families tend to buy substantially more cooked cereals, corn meal, household insecticides, cream, rice, spaghetti, frozen vegetables, syrup, and vinegar, among others, than do their white counterparts.

(b) The average Negro male supposedly buys 77 per cent more pairs of shoes during his lifetime than the average white male and pays more for them.

(c) Reportedly, Negroes purchase as much as one-half of all Scotch whiskey consumed in the U.S.

(d) Negroes also apparently consume somewhat more flour, waxes, toilet and laundry soap, shortenings, salt, peanut butter, fruit juices, and canned chili than whites.

While Negro purchase habit information is not as readily available as descriptive market data on Negroes, a fund of knowledge is being developed in this area which should serve marketers well in the future. But the combination of information in these two areas is still not sufficient upon which to base a rational approach toward this market.

NEGRO MARKET: ATTITUDES AND MOTIVATIONS

One area remains to be explored: attitudinal and motivational dimensions of Negro consumer behavior. And it is here that the greatest void of knowledge exists.

Of course, some reliable information, some hypotheses, and some plausible suggested explanations are available regarding why Negroes act and react as they do in the market place. For example, many marketers have suggested that Negroes frequently attempt to emulate white society through purchases of products with high quality images. If this is true, it would at least partly explain the Negro's relatively higher expenditures on well known brands of Scotch, expensive clothing, quality furniture, appliances, and the like.

Another thesis is that Negroes as a group have accepted the values of white middle-class society, but, at the same time, experience difficulties in purchasing products which represent some of these values. A basic dilemma arises where the Negro must choose whether to strive, frequently in the face of formidable odds, to attain white middle-class values, and the products which are associated with these values, or simply give up and live without most of them.[1]

There are a variety of other explanations regarding why Negroes behave as they do in their roles as consumers. There is one major area, however, where relatively few explanations are available. This is also the

[1] Raymond A. Bauer, Scott M. Cunningham, and Lawrence H. Wortzel, "The Marketing Dilemma of Negroes," *Journal of Marketing*, Vol. 29, July, 1965, pp. 1-6, at p. 2.

area which probably provides the single greatest opportunity to influence the purchase behavior of Negroes—communications.

Communications Research

Probably the most frequently raised and most perplexing issue relates to the advisability of adopting an "integrated" approach toward advertising. Some questions frequently asked by companies regarding how to communicate most effectively with Negroes are:

(a) Should our advertisements be integrated or segregated; that is, should we use all white, all Negro, or white and Negro models?

(b) Should we attempt to reach the Negro consumer by placing our traditionally "white" advertisements in Negro media, or should we have specially designed advertisements for Negro media?

(c) If we produce integrated advertisements, should these advertisements be restricted to Negro media, or should they be exposed through general media?

(d) If Negro media are used, which media in particular are best?

(e) Does the Negro feel complimented or honored when he sees an advertisement specially designed to attract his attention and interest, or does he view this sort of thing as just one more reminder that he is different?

(f) How would our white customers react to integrated advertisements in general media?

A certain amount of research has, of course, been completed in this general area. Something is known, for example, about viewing, reading, and listening habits. It has been established that radio is the major medium for Negroes, followed by television, newspapers, and magazines. And this pattern is known to be different than that for whites. Studies have shown that radio stations employing rather tasteless music and advertising programming appeal to the Negro working class and frequently offend and alienate middle and upper class Negroes. Evidence is available to show that advertisements which are apparently designed to appeal to Negro buyers, but which show Negroes in a situation which the Negro viewer recognizes as unrealistic can do more harm than good.

Some work has also been done on Negro reactions to various advertising stimuli. It was found in one fairly recent study that when people were presented with a series of general concepts, such as integrated advertisements, segregated advertisements, and various media alternatives, there was a great similarity in responses by Negroes and whites. Whereas advertising strategies of many large companies would lead one to expect sizeable differences in reactions of Negroes and whites to these alternatives, they were surprisingly alike.[2]

Other research studies indicate that the use of Negro models can be quite favorable, as long as the advertisements are presented in a dignified, meaningful, and realistic way. And, importantly, it has been determined that Negroes frequently view companies which run integrated advertising campaigns as more progressive, more friendly, more desirous of the Negro's business, a fairer employer, and more anxious to work out today's social problems than companies which do not participate in integrated advertising.

Reactions of white respondents are also frequently more favorable than might be expected. They often view integrated advertisements which are tastefully presented as pleasant, appealing, meaningful and dignified. In addition, they too view a company which runs integrated advertising as generally more friendly, more progressive, and a fairer employer.

Research efforts of these types, however, are infrequent. Too little effort has been extended to date, in terms of uncovering Negro attitudes and motivations in the market place. The widely varying approaches taken by so many companies in an attempt to communicate with the Negro consumer strongly suggest that the answers to fundamental marketing questions simply are not available. It has been stated that, "Insufficient knowledge of the Negro consumer's motivations has led to sharp controversy over the direction advertisers should take to reach this market."[3]

While opportunities for the future lie partly in continuing to develop descriptive data and actual purchase behavior information on Negroes, significant gains will be primarily dependent upon ability of marketers to develop and properly interpret attitudinal data such that a sound basis can be established for understanding and communicating with the Negro as a consumer.

A LOOK AT THE FUTURE

In addition to reviewing past and present strengths and weaknesses regarding marketing to the Negro, it is useful to consider some expected future developments which will likely affect the approach taken by marketers in reacting to the ever-changing composition and requirements of the Negro market.

First, it is reasonable to expect a continued growth in the size and

2 Arnold Barban and Edward Cundiff, "Negro and White Responses to Advertising Stimuli," *Journal of Marketing Research,* November, 1964, pp. 53-56.

3 "Ad Men Straddle the Color Line," *News Front,* Vol. 10, No. 1, February, 1966, pp. 10-15 at p. 10.

importance of the Negro market. It is expected that by 1970 Negroes will number somewhere around 25 million, and personal income should rise to about $45 billion. The influence of Negroes as consumers will be increasingly felt.

Second, geographic shifts will continue as the Negro becomes increasingly more urban. During the 1970's there will likely be a trend away from the central city to the suburbs as social barriers fall and as income and educational levels rise for the Negro. These developments will certainly affect consumption patterns.

Third, there will be increased pressure applied by special interest groups and by the government for a speeding up of the aggregation of Negroes into the mainstream of American life, which will, in turn, influence purchase behavior.

Fourth, basic social and economic forces will serve to radically change Negro expenditure patterns. For as incomes increase, and as intellectual and social horizons are broadened for Negroes and whites alike, expenditures of Negroes will shift in favor of goods and services which will upgrade their levels of living. Many products which have long received a disproportionately large share of the Negro's income, such as food, clothing, liquor, and entertainment will probably realize much slower growth in the future. A higher percentage of the Negro's income will be channeled toward such items as education, housing, medical care, automobiles, furniture and appliances, travel, insurance, and banking and credit facilities—that is, forms of consumption which have heretofore been unattainable.

Finally, substantial changes will be required in corporate policies directed toward the Negro in the future. Companies which have avoided meeting this problem and this challenge will be forced to become actively involved. This, in turn, will place added emphasis upon the need for collecting, and properly interpreting data on the Negro as a consumer. Companies which have been actively involved in recruiting Negroes as customers will find a need to change their strategies and upgrade their abilities. For whereas the Negro may react favorably to an integrated advertisement now, no matter how ill conceived and how poorly represented, simply because it does finally represent a step forward, he will become more discriminating in his tastes over time and less tolerant of marketing programs borne out of inadequate knowledge on the part of management.

CONCLUSION

If one general obseration can be made from this brief analysis, it is that the Negro market is in a perpetual state of change, and that the change is of a more revolutionary than evolutionary nature.

The challenge of keeping pace with this change is based upon the recognition of two prerequisites which must be accepted in order to establish effective marketing policies directed toward the Negro. First, a complete understanding of the Negro as a part of American life is required. One must be aware of the deep-rooted social and economic forces which are changing the Negro's role in society. For these forces will, in turn, shape the Negro's role as a consumer. Second, marketers must develop more and better information regarding the true attitudes, experiences, and motivations which influence the Negro's behavior in the marketplace.

Until these two things are accomplished, companies will be placing themselves in the dangerous position of taking action based upon hunch and intuition. For only when a true understanding of the Negro is reached regarding his emerging role as a member of society, as well as the forces which specifically influence his purchase activities, will it be possible to develop intelligent programs designed to optimize the opportunities presented by this important segment of the ethnic market.

IV

RESEARCH TECHNIQUES IN CONSUMER BEHAVIOR

Masses of information have been gathered about consumers in our economy. We possess reams of data on such characteristics as how much money is earned, spent, and saved, how much of each product is consumed by various types of families, and how much supposedly will be spent on products in the future. Yet, we really know little about the causes behind consumer behavior. Far too much marketing research has concerned itself with *what* consumers are doing or will do rather than *why* they are doing it or will do it. In a medical sense, we have been concerned more with curing the disease than with determining its cause.

One only needs to note the excessive product mortality rate to know that there is something wrong somewhere. That "something," at least in great part, is our failure to understand why consumers behave as they do. It is folly to believe that we can deal millions of times daily with millions of customers spending billions of dollars without understanding clearly the causes of their spending patterns.

Recognition of this serious situation has brought a number of business practitioners and academicians to their feet—and they are doing something about it. First, they are changing their research approach from asking what and when to asking why. Second, they are realizing that their problems are behavioral in nature and are turning to the behavioral sciences for solutions.

In spite of a less than harmonious relationship with the behavioral scientist, business students have succeeded, to some extent, in borrowing a number of behavioral research tools and adapting them to the study of the consumer role. Numerous difficulties have been encountered in this undertaking and results have not always been desirable ones. Moreover, there have been a number of individuals, both businessmen and business teachers, who have discouraged the innovation with various denouncements. Nevertheless, this research procedure is paying off and shows great promise of becoming the basic methodology of future market research.

Most of the behavioral research techniques that have been adapted to consumer behavior research have been those of the psychologist and psychiatrist, that is, techniques for examining *individual* behavior. Recognizing that individuals make up groups, or markets, we have used these research procedures to examine the behavior of a few individuals and then tested the results on larger groups. This course of action has proven to be a productive one.

The series of readings in this section discusses some research techniques and concepts that have been borrowed from the behavioral sciences in an effort to advance our understanding of the causes of consumer behavior patterns. The reader is reminded that a few brief discussions of behavioral research techniques also appear in some articles in Parts II and III. Although these earlier comments are presented as incidental material, re-examination of them will broaden the value of the readings in this section.

The first of the articles in this group of readings, "How Psychiatric Methods Can Be Applied to Market Research" by James M. Vicary, provides a view of six behavioral research techniques that may be employed in researching consumer behavior. With his discussion of each technique, Vicary either presents actual applications of the technique to consumer behavior research or suggests how it might be used for this purpose.

The next presentation is one by Alfred E. Goldman, entitled "The Group Depth Interview." In this article the author describes a research tool, *the group interview,* that appears very useful in eliciting information that is often difficult to obtain with individual interviewing. Goldman notes that the technique already has a lengthy history of successful use and predicts more application of it to marketing problems.

Obtaining a quantitative measure of consumers' reactions to the image of a brand or product has always been a difficult task for marketers, but William A. Mindak, in his article "Fitting the Semantic Differential to the Marketing Problem," shows how to attack this problem with apparent success. He suggests that the *semantic differential,* a research technique originated by the psychologist, Charles Osgood, will obtain and allow quantification of the direction and intensity of consumers' attitudes toward any concept such as a brand or product. As evidence of the value of this research method, Mindak discusses a study in which the semantic differential was used to compare the personalities (images) of three local brands of beer with three national brands.

Montrose S. Sommers follows with the article, "Product Symbolism and the Perception of Social Strata," in which he demonstrates the *Q-technique,* a behavioral research technique developed by the psychologist William Stephenson. Sommers presents a research project in which he shows how the Q-technique may be used to compare the meanings of products to different social strata. His findings indicate that this research tool has great possibilities in improving market segmentation practices.

The next article, "Introduction to Attitude Research and Management Decisions" by Leslie A. Beldo, explains how studying and researching attitudes can be of significant value to management decision-making in marketing and advertising. Beldo sees attitudes as "predispositions to action or behavior." Thus, he feels that attitude research can provide a strong base on which to predict buying behavior. The author also proposes techniques and experimental designs for attitude research among consumers.

The two following papers exemplify the unusual possibilities available for researching the consumer. The first, by Krugman, suggests the use of eye pupil measurement; while the second, by McNeal, recommends consideration of handwriting analysis for consumer research.

The final article in this section, "The Use of Structured Techniques in Motivation Research," was written by three Northwestern University professors, Ralph L. Westfall, Harper W. Boyd, Jr., and Donald T.

Campbell. The article is more in the form of an argument that has enlightening results. The authors attack the use of clinical techniques in consumer behavior research. Their argument is that traditional structured techniques typically used by marketing research can produce the same results as those research tools borrowed from the clinical psychologist. To evidence their beliefs, the authors present the findings of a study using traditional structured methodology and show them to be the same as results obtained from an earlier study that employed a clinical technique. The writers conclude that there are many opportunities to make effective use of traditional marketing research techniques in searching the causes of consumer behavior patterns.

28

HOW PSYCHIATRIC METHODS CAN BE APPLIED to MARKET RESEARCH

JAMES M. VICARY

Good research, like journalism, answers the *who, what, when, where* and *why* of a problem. The standard survey method with its emphasis on nose-counting starts off strong on the *who* and *what,* weakens a bit on the *when* and *where* and frequently fizzles on the *why.*

People can usually be stimulated to tell what they *think* are the reasons for their behavior or preferences. All too often their rationalizations do not stand up. They may say they brush their teeth to prevent decay, but actually they brush their teeth most frequently before breakfast; they may favor anti-chain store legislation, but most of their shopping is at the local A&P; or as happened during the last war, they may favor strict rationing laws but actually engage in black-market buying.

There are ways to get behind these rationalizations. Rather than ask very precise and rigid questions, the approach is indirect. Responses from subjects are induced with purposely vague questions. The respondent is obliged to pour meaning into only partially defined situations, and this forces him back upon his own inner psychological resources. Here's how you can apply six approaches that were developed in the field of psychiatry to business research:

I. WORD ASSOCIATION

This is probably the best known of these methods. The respondent is asked to give the first word that comes to mind for each of a list of un-

Reprinted from *Printers' Ink,* Volume 235 (May 11, 1951), pp. 39-40, 44, 46, 48, with permission of *Printers' Ink.*

related words. Given the word *bread,* the first word that comes to his mind is *butter.* Despite its simple operation, it is a highly flexible method. It is a semantic test revealing the content of people's basic associations. Beside that, analysis of the time it takes for the respondent to give a response and his ability to give the same response quickly during a second test reveals his stability of association and the extent of his emotional reaction to each symbol.

By all odds the most obvious application of this method is screening a long list of names proposed for a new product or model. In the case of a new beer to be nationally distributed, it was found that people could not easily and readily associate beer with foreign sounding names. In some instances they confused this type of name with cheeses and other products.

Similarly new words to describe old products can be screened. Coined words for trade-mark names in particular are tricky. They are much sought after by advertisers because they can be legally protected, but their novelty of expression may create difficulties. Take a term like *Solium,* which has been heavily advertised. A totally new coined word for the same type of ingredient produced two and a half times as many appropriate associations as *Solium.* An important group of respondents confused *Solium* with drug or cosmetic products. Words like *complaint, cooperate* and *voluntary* have been shown to produce deep emotional disturbance with sizable groups of the general population and are dangerous to use in most contexts.

Controlled word association is a variation in which the respondent is asked to give only a certain class of word response. For example, a list of products is read to him one at a time, and for each he gives a brand name. Professor Houghton's *want-association* and Dr. Link's *triple associates method* are examples of the controlled approach.

Another example is the study made recently by Joe Belden & Associates, Austin, Texas, for an advertising agency. The objective was to explore the use of word association tests to measure the impact of advertising by the agency's clients.

A cross-section of 250 adults was asked to name the first business concern that came to mind when confronted with certain words: hotel, bread, bank, house paint, dairy, etc. The words were rearranged and the same questions asked again. And the same procedure was gone through with a list of the agency's clients in those businesses. As a result, Mr. Belden secured a statistical view of associations of products and services with certain advertisers and *vice versa.* The result was a view in depth of the relative impact of each of the advertisers involved.

Successive word association consists of asking not just for the first word that comes to mind, but for a long chain of associations. To the word *meat* a respondent might give, *potatoes, steak, food, bread, fish, red, eat, beef, pork,* etc. The method is useful in studying ways to change associations by substituting one symbol for another. It is also a means of quickly canvassing a person's associations on a particular subject. For example, before making up a questionnaire on soup or some other similar subject the researcher might do well to write a long succession of associations in order that he will be fully aware of all the allied subjects.

2. COMPLETION

The *sentence completion* method is the most familiar of this group of methods. In this type of questioning a word or phrase is given like "When I have a headache ——————" or, "Meat ——————." The respondent is asked to add any words that come to his mind to make a complete sentence. In the first item above a respondent might say, "I usually use Bayer Aspirin."

It can be seen that this method provides greater context and more information for the test item than the word association method.

In combination with the word association method the sentence completion approach is capable of very sophisticated use. In one instance where people would not openly admit their fear and annoyance about increased airport activities near their homes, a combination sentence-completion and word-association interview was successful in showing the character and extent of this hidden fear. The fear and annoyance was far more extensive than standard interviewing methods had indicated.

Wherever a respondent's answers might be embarrassing to him, as in drug or personal products or during times of crisis like strikes or failure of accepted practices, it is relatively easy to study these areas with such methods. As an added plus your respondents and even your interviewers need not know the purpose of the study since rather complete masking of test items is necessary for both methods. *Story completions* have also been used in much the same manner.

3. PICTURE AND VISUAL METHODS

Both the *Rorschach* and *thematic apperception* tests employ pictorial material. In the apperception test subjects are asked to tell a story about a picture. Most of the material revealed in this test is either directly or indirectly autobiographical, although respondents are not usually aware of the fact. These two methods in their orthodox use require technical training, and readers are referred to psychiatric manuals for an adequate discussion of their use.

Simple variations of the thematic apperception test have been employed in commercial research. Probably the most striking is the use of the *comic strip sequence* in which some of the balloons containing conversation of characters are left blank for the respondent to fill in.

4. ROLE-PLAYING AND SITUATIONAL METHODS

The forerunner of this type of test is the *psychodrama,* originated by Dr. J. L. Moreno. In personnel research in particular this method has been applied successfully. The respondent acts out a significant event in his life or plays the role of one of his superiors or subordinates. When an antagonistic employee, for example, acts out his impression of the boss's job, the reason why he is antagonistic may be revealed.

A *personification* method has been devised in which a respondent acts out the role of some non-living thing like a magazine, products or company with which he is very familiar. This method was used to find out whether the public understood the editorial policies currently in force by large circulation magazines.

In another approach respondents are asked to imagine in detail the kind of person who has bought a number of items at a store. One of the items in the list is under study; the others are used as a mask. The same list is used on a matched sample, except that the test item is changed to another product or brand for comparison with the best item.

Mason Haire of the University of California described such a test in an article in The Journal of Marketing for April 1950. He described how motivations for not buying Nescafé instant coffee were uncovered.

"Two shopping lists," Mr. Haire reports, "were prepared. They were identical in all respects, except that one list specified Nescafé and one Maxwell House coffee. They were administered to alternate subjects, no subject knowing of the existence of the other list. The instructions were: *Read the shopping list below. Try to project yourself into the situation as far as possible until you can more or less characterize the woman who bought the groceries. Then write a brief description of her personality and character. Wherever possible indicate what factors influenced your judgment.*

"Shopping List I—Pound and a half of hamburger, 2 loaves Wonder bread, bunch of carrots, 1 can Rumford's baking powder, Nescafé instant coffee, 2 cans Del Monte peaches, 5 lbs potatoes.

"Shopping List II—Pound and a half of hamburger, 2 loaves Wonder bread, bunch of carrots, 1 can Rumford's baking powder, 1 lb. Maxwell House coffee (drip grind), 2 cans Del Monte peaches, 5 lbs. potatoes.

"Fifty people responded to each of the two shopping lists given above. The responses to these shopping lists provided some very interesting material. The following main characteristics of their descriptions can be given:

"(1) 48% of the people described the woman who bought Nescafé as lazy; 4% described the woman who bought Maxwell House as lazy. (2) 48% of the people described the woman who bought Nescafé as failing to plan household purchases and schedules well; 12% described the woman who bought Maxwell this way. (3) 4% described the Nescafé woman as spendthrift; none described the Maxwell House woman this way. (4) 16% described the Nescafé woman as not a good wife; none described the Maxwell House woman this way. 4% described the Nescafé woman as a good wife; 16% described the Maxwell House woman as a good wife."

The woman who buys Nescafé, apparently, must feel guilty of laziness, poor planning and spending money carelessly. When people were asked directly why they didn't buy Nescafé, they blamed only the taste—none of the hidden connotations revealed through the personification technique.

5. CHAIN INTERVIEW METHODS

Since most people's information comes to them by word of mouth, it is important that we have a method of testing this natural *chain reaction of a message*. In this method we duplicate the children's game of telling a story around a circle in which each child whispers the tale to the next until a distorted version comes back to the first child.

The research method incorporates electronic recording of all the testimony in the chain so that each person's contributions in the chain can be studied. Each respondent is urged to repeat the test message as exactly as possible, adding any *bona fide* information to it which he considers important.

The experience of several different investigators shows that names of places, people and things normally drop out of the chain very rapidly. The possibility of a break in the chain of identification for a brand or company name is very important. The associational strength of the original name and the context in a message are both crucial in resisting this natural deterioration as people hand on your story. This test can show you how far word-of-mouth advertising will carry your slogan, brand-name, price, etc.

Perhaps more dramatic is the use of this method in picking up in advance of release any possible boomerangs in a message. In one case the announcement of a retirement fund for the elderly executives of a firm was found by this method to be capable of being twisted into a bad connotation by customers. It was said at the end of several chains that the graybeards were to be thrown out of the company pronto! The reader will no doubt recall actual examples where sudden or repeated ˙price reductions, entirely justified on an economic basis, have been very damaging to the product's reputation or that of the manufacturer. Something like this happened with the ball-point pen. A price reduction, announced without proper explanation, may start an idea rolling that you can not foresee unless you use a pre-test of this kind.

6. DEPTH AND CONVERSATIONAL INTERVIEW METHODS

The so-called depth interview method is probably the most popular way today of obtaining qualitative information. Interpretation of attitudes by this method is extremely difficult, primarily because it is not a systematic method. As a pre-test device before conducting the standard survey, it has been most valuable in obtaining more than an armchair view of a problem to be studied.

Most of the methods outlined above are not costly. They do not run to volume of nose-counting type of operation. Many of the problems uncovered by these studies, however, can be tested and given some validation by the survey method. Here the costly hit-and-miss method of speculative surveying is avoided, because the survey is limited to known problem areas.

There should be more use of these methods in market and public relations research. Too many researchers have been trapped in the assumption that mere statistical manipulation is a substitute for thinking. These methods force a more careful analysis of the reason behind consumer actions and reactions. They can be used to uncover the reason-why of success and failure in the field of marketing.

29

THE GROUP DEPTH INTERVIEW

ALFRED E. GOLDMAN

Consideration of each of the three elements of the name given to the group-interview technique suggests that, while the label may be as serviceable as any other, under certain conditions it is not wholly accurate. A comprehensive review of group methods is beyond the scope of this article; and the interested reader can refer to the voluminous literature on this technique and its application to marketing, education, and psychotherapy.[1]

Instead, the present article explains what is meant by *group, depth,* and *interview* in a group depth interview . . . the mechanics of moderating such interviews . . . and the five requirements of these interviews.

GROUP

A group is a number of *interacting individuals having a community of interests*. These two criteria of groups must be satisfied in order to derive the benefits of collecting information in a group setting.

Reprinted from the *Journal of Marketing*, national quarterly publication of the American Marketing Association, Volume 26 (July, 1962), pp. 61-68.

[1] Suggested sources: H. H. Lerner and H. C. Kelman, "Group Methods in Psychotherapy, Social Work, and Adult Education," *Journal of Social Issues*, Vol. 8, Whole issue No. 2, 1952, pp. 1-88; W. Mangold, *Gegenstand und Methode des Gruppendiskussions Verfahrens: Aus der Arbeit des Instituts für Sozialforschung (Frankfurt am Main: Europäische Verlagsanstalt)*, p. 176.

Interaction

In the group situation a person is asked an opinion about something—a product, a distribution system, an advertisement, a television program, or perhaps a candidate for office. In contrast to the individual interview in which the flow of information is unidirectional, from the respondent to the interviewer, the group setting causes the opinions of each person to be considered in group discussion. Each individual is exposed to the ideas of the others and submits his ideas for the consideration of the group.

This assumes, of course, that social interaction occurs at some overt level. If the group members do not interact with one another, but each member directs his remarks to the moderator, this is not a group. It might better be described as multiple or serial interviewing, since the advantages of the group setting are precluded. It is the interviewer's responsibility to stimulate the group members to interact with each other rather than with him.

Community of Interest

The establishment of group cohesiveness is dependent in large part on the second criterion of "groupness," namely, *sharing a common interest.*

This common interest should, of course, be relevant to the topic under discussion. A number of individuals may be very different in national origin, religious beliefs, political persuasion, and the like; but if they share a common identity relevant to the discussion (shoe buyers, drug manufacturers, purchasers of luxury items), a group can form. This involves some risks that can be minimized by thoughtful selection of group members. For example, in a discussion of a home-decorating product, the inclusion of one or two low-income people in a group of wealthy individuals may serve to inhibit the free expression of the attitudes of all.

How may these characteristics of a group be exploited in eliciting useful information, and in what way is this information different from that produced by individual interviewing?

1. First, the interaction among group members *stimulates new ideas* regarding the topic under discussion that may never be mentioned in individual interviewing. When a group member does bring up a new idea, however tangential, the group as a whole is given the opportunity to react to it in a variety of ways that indicate its interest to the group.

The idea can be readily and enthusiastically taken up by the group and ultimately accepted or rejected. The idea can be discussed without a decision being reached, with considerable confusion expressed in the process. The idea can be discussed briefly and then dropped not to be mentioned again. Sometimes, and most significant of all, it can be studiously ignored and avoided, despite the moderator's reiteration of the idea. This behavior, when accompanied by indications of anxiety, such as lighting cigarettes, shuffling uneasily in seats, clearing throats, and so on, suggests that a particular idea has provoked sufficient psychic discomfort and threat as to require its rigorous avoidance in open discussion.

2. These possible reactions to a new idea may also demonstrate a second value of group interviewing—*the opportunity to observe directly the group process*. In the individual interview, respondents *tell* how they would or did behave in a particular social situation. In the group interview, respondents react to each other, and their behavior is directly *observed*.

For example, a housewife who hesitantly and timidly describes how she cleans her floors suggests the tenuousness with which she herself regards these procedures. In one group, the timid admission by one housewife that she hated washing floors and did so only when forced to by fear of social rejection brought immediate and firm support from other group members. They then verbally "turned on" the two group members who washed floors more frequently and meticulously. Here the attitudes of women toward washing floors was reflected in the way they behaved toward each other *in the group*.

A purchasing decision is frequently a social act in that the items are considered in the context of what others think of the product, and what others will think of *them* for having purchased it. The group creates or recapitulates the marketing situation, depending upon the point at which the decision process is intercepted. Here the process of the decision is exposed in the sharing of experiences, rumors, and anecdotes that go on in a group discussion about a product, service, person, or event. Here we are concerned with the *process* of the purchasing decision, not just in the static end-result of that process. Effective marketing requires understanding of this decision process.

3. A third advantage of group interviewing is that it *provides some idea of the dynamics of attitudes and opinions*. The flexibility or rigidity with which an opinion is held is better exposed in a group setting than in an individual interview. Within the two hours of the typical group session, an opinion that is stated with finality and apparent deep convic-

tion can be modified a number of times by the social pressures or new information that may be provided by the group. As the discussion proceeds, some group members modify their initial reaction, some defend their positions even more rigorously, some admit confusion. In this way, the group setting offers some idea of the dynamics of opinion—its initiation and modification, and its intensity and resistance to change. This pattern of modification in opinion is often as rewarding with regard to understanding motives as the one initially stated.

4. Discussion in a peer group often *provokes considerably greater spontaneity and candor than can be expected in an individual interview.* This is its fourth advantage. The interviewer is frequently an "outsider," regardless of how skillful he or she may be. In the group setting it is not unusual for group members, after an initial period of orientation, to ignore completely the presence of the moderator. For example, in a group of small-business managers, several of them admitted blatant acts of petty dishonesty at the expense of their customers. It seems unlikely that this would have been admitted to an individual interviewer.

Because of the demands on their time, physicians are unusually difficult to interview at length. Yet in group discussions with other physicians, two hours does not seem to tax their interest or cooperation. Physicians who appear impatient, constrained, cautious, or curt when interviewed alone, seem considerably more garrulous, frank, and at times argumentative when in a group with other physicians.

Candor is permitted not only because the members of the group understand and feel comfortable with one another, but also because they drew social strength from each other. The group provides support to its members in the expression of anxiety-provoking or socially unpopular ideas.

An example may illustrate this. At the beginning of a 2½ hour session, a group of jobbers individually expressed loyalty to, and appreciation of, their suppliers. After an hour, most of these same group members joined in the expression of a pervasive and deeply felt antagonism toward their manufacturers—attitudes which they had not previously expressed for a variety of reasons, including fears of economic reprisal by the jobber.

In another instance, members of a minority group at first vehemently denied favoritism in buying from members of their own group. Later, following a profound and emotional discussion of racial and religious intolerance, *all* admitted that they preferred to buy from a salesman of their own ethnic group. By virtue of its community of interests, the group permitted exposure of feelings not ordinarily given casual or public expression.

5. A fifth advantage is that the group setting is *emotionally provocative in a way that an individual interview cannot be.* A group composed

of housewives ranging in age from 25 to 45 may serve to illustrate how the group can provoke reactions which elicit interesting and useful insights into the motives of its members. This discussion focused on how these women felt about their weight, and what effect this had on their diets. At one point in the discussion, the youngest and most slender woman in the group said, "Weight isn't a problem for me yet, but I imagine that for older women like yourselves it would be." Immediately, perceiving the unintended offense to the other group members, she explained, "Well, as you get older, you get fatter." This attempt at diplomacy fell somewhat short of soothing the injured self-concepts of some of the other women, but it did serve to provoke quite profound feelings toward "getting old" and how these feelings were expressed in their eating habits. Thus, a member of the group confronted the other group members with anxieties that the moderator could mention only at considerable risk to continued *rapport*.

Thus, by virtue of the interaction and common relevant interests of its members, the group offers more and qualitatively different information than can be obtained from the sum of its individual human parts.

DEPTH

The use of the word "depth," in the name given this technique, implies seeking information that is more profound than is usually accessible at the level of interpersonal relationships. While a respondent may be the best authority on *what* he did, he is often an unreliable source of information as to *why* he did it. His response reflects what he wants you to believe, and also what he himself wants to believe. Retroactive distortion helps him to maintain a self-concept of a wise, judicious buyer motivated by reason rather than feeling.

Much of our daily behavior is motivated by subliminal stimuli (sensory impressions of which the individual is only minimally aware). Depth interviewing seeks to bring these motives to light. Technically these motives are *preconscious,* and are distinguished from *unconscious* motives by the more profound depth of repression of the latter.

A study of the factors that determine which of several supermarkets were used by shoppers in a particular neighborhood illustrates the definitive and lasting reaction to subliminal stimuli. Some of the women in each of four group sessions were adamant in their intention not to shop in one of the markets, although they did not appear able to express their reasons in a clear or consistent manner. Some mentioned a vague feeling that the market in question was somehow messy or even dirty. Yet, upon further exploration, these same women agreed that the shelves were neatly stacked, the personnel clean, the floors swept, the counters well dusted. They could not point out anything to support their charges of uncleanliness. Further, they readily agreed that the store they did shop in was more messy than the one in which they refused to shop. A casual reference by one of the women to a peculiar odor evoked immediate recognition from the others. This occurred spontaneously in several of the groups and led to the consensus that it was a "bloody" or "meaty" odor. This process of "consensual validation" suggested that this vague impression of untidiness stemmed not from anything that could be seen, but rather from this faint yet pervasive and offensive odor. Later this information served to bring to the attention of the management an ineffective exhaust-and-drainage system in the supermarket's meat room.

In seeking "depth" material we do not make the assumption that we can in some way get the respondent to express unconscious motives *directly*. A thing is repressed, that is, remanded to the care of the unconscious, if it is too threatening to the self-concept to allow into consciousness. Generally there is little that a moderator can do, or ethically should do, to provoke the overt expression of such threatening material. What is usually done is to infer the nature of these impulses from who says what, in what sequence, to whom he says it, and how he says it.

However, there are certain conditions under which the moderator may wish to explore some facets on an unconscious motive. By focusing on the motives of one group member, the others are frequently provoked to react to the repressed motive, even if that motive is never made quite explicit. For example, in a discussion of an easy-to-prepare "instant" food, one woman made the following slip-of-the-tongue: "Especially when I'm in a hurry, I like foods that are time-*consuming*." The context of the preceding discussion, which centered upon the role that food preparation plays in the housewife's concept of herself, made it quite clear that the eagerness with which this woman embraced "instant" foods was not without psychic conflict. In this case, the moderator inquired into the error without interpreting to her the feeling of guilt that this slip may have revealed. It did serve, however, to stimulate other women to discuss this problem more openly.

Probing for unconscious material should be undertaken with extreme caution. The danger, in most cases, is not that any appreciable damage will be done to a reasonably stable personality; the normal protective mechanisms will adequately protect the ego from ill-advised assaults by the moderator. Rather, the danger of unskilled probing is represented by the risk of completely alienating the offended group member, and thereby limiting the cooperation and spontaneity of the whole group. In these situations, the professional psychologist with clinical experience is more likely to avoid such pitfalls.

INTERVIEW

The word "interview" has the least precise meaning of the three elements of the term, group depth interview. An interview implies an interviewer, rather than a moderator. The role of moderator requires using the group as the device for eliciting information. The moderator guides the discussion, keeping it within fruitful bounds, but rarely participates in it himself. When he can lead a group member to ask a question of the group, the moderator will not question them himself.

An interviewer, especially with a structured questionnaire, is frequently restricted to a direct question-and-answer approach, while the moderator has the greatest possible flexibility and freedom in pursuing motivational "pay dirt" and may seek to exploit unique characteristics of a particular group in the most effective way by whatever devices at his disposal.

THE MECHANICS OF MODERATING

The best way to describe group depth interviewing is in terms of the specific mechanics of moderating the group. Many of the techniques considered here have been suggested by those used in group psychotherapy. Although psychotherapy has a radically different primary goal, it shares with group interviewing the goal of eliciting information which the group member himself finds difficult, or impossible, to produce.

All sessions are tape recorded, with the recorder placed in full view. For training purposes and client observation a one-way vision mirror is used. All group members are paid, to compensate them for the expense of traveling to where the session is conducted, and to attract people other than the merely curious.

Rapport

The most important factor in producing usable information from the group depth interview is the relationship between the moderator and the panel members, and that among the panel members themselves.

The first job of the moderator is to structure the roles of all of the participants. The purpose of the session, how long it will last, and the manner in which it will be conducted are all explained in as comfortable and friendly a way as possible. Good *rapport* is crucial in establishing the candidness needed; and this is facilitated when the language of the moderator is not too discrepant from that of the majority of the group. For example, when the group is composed of young, poorly educated subjects of marginal socio-economic level, "they won't dig you if you bug 'em with a lot of high-falutin' jazz."

Verbal Activity

The verbal activity or passivity of the moderator is determined by the nature of the group and its goals. With alert and articulate people the moderator can assume a more passive role—passive, not inert. In an especially talkative group, or at the other extreme, with a very quiet group, a more active role will be required of the moderator, either to inhibit or provoke more discussion.

Relevancy

One of the most important things that the moderator does is to keep the discussion within relevant limits. Here he must be very careful not to rule out that which is apparently unrelated, but may reveal relevant unconscious motives. A general discussion of grandma and grandpa and the "good old days" may have extensive significance in marketing such things as upholstery fabric or canned foods. Sensitivity to unconscious processes is, of course, important here and a clinical background is helpful, although not essential.

Projective Questions

The researcher who pursues these motives of the buying decision of which the consumer is unaware must give particular thought to developing various "projective" techniques which expose these motives. The answer to a projective question enables the respondent to express needs which he cannot or does not wish to admit. These, of course, must be individually designed to fit the particular marketing problem. For example, in the selection of kinds of housing materials, material design, or fabric pattern, the following question was found to be very effective: "What kind of family would find this pattern appealing, and why?"

Different reactions to various designs may also be provoked by asking the group what well-known person each pattern suggests to them. In this way, a design that suggests Jayne Mansfield may be qualitatively differentiated from those which suggest Liberace, Eleanor Roosevelt, or Marshal Matt Dillon. Similar material may be provoked by *stereotype photographs and the illustrative case method.*

Illustrative Case Method

To explore personal habits, the illustrative case method is valuable. Several people are described who differ from each other according to the intensity or consistency of some behavior. Then the group members are asked to describe the other characteristics of the person. For example, Miss A uses underarm deodorant four times a day; Miss B uses one only in the morning—what kind of people are they? Or. Mr. A traded his Chevrolet in for a Pontiac; Mr. B traded his Cadillac in for a small foreign car—what kind of people are they? Intensive probing follows their responses in order to clarify what motivates Miss A or B, or Mr. A or B.

Stereotype Photographs

A related type of stimulus is represented by *stereotype photographs.* These are pictures of men and women who typify a particular age, income, or vocational group. Each of these variables, of course, can be independently varied to suit the objectives of the study. The appropriately selected photographs are exposed singly or all together, and a question might be asked, such as: "Which of these women would be most likely to use instant tea?"

The response is followed up with: "What is there about the woman you picked that makes you think that?" Such answers as "She looks as though she's always in a hurry and can't be bothered with brewing tea," or "Not that one! She looks rich enough to afford the best; she would have her maid brew tea," are quite revealing of attitudes toward a particular product.

Serial Association

In evaluating the effectiveness of advertising copy, controlled serial association may be used. Prior to exposure of the first ad, the group members are trained in the difficult job of saying words freely one after the other. In this way, they learn to respond to the test ads with some spontaneity.

For example, to evaluate the impression of the product conveyed to women by a pictorial advertisement in a magazine, group members were shown the advertisement and requested to associate ideas with it. It became readily apparent that this ad suggested licentious intrigue and adventure. While the symbolic meaning of the ad served to attract and hold the attention of the reader admirably well, the dynamic meaning it attached to this particular product apparently was not the most advantageous.

Deprivation Questions

Deprivation questions inquire into the relative value of various products or services. A question such as, "Which of the following canned foods would you miss most if it were no longer available to you?" is somehow more provocative than, "Which canned food is most important to you?"

Deception

A calculated "deception" is often effective in testing the limits of the respondent's convictions. A rich source of information and attitudes is tapped by the group's responses to the blatantly incorrect statement that all of ten very different fabrics are made of the same synthetic fiber.

There are times when none of these methods appears to stimulate any but the most mundane and obvious generalities. This, of course, may be significant in itself if it is not a facade behind which reside motives that are not being expressed. Some other procedures that may be useful in these difficult cases are *false termination* and *playing the devil's advocate.*

It is a rule of thumb in group psychotherapy that the most important material may be produced in the last few minutes of the session. In this way the person who would like to contribute something that may be embarrassing or threatening to him has only a few minutes during which he must endure the discomfort. Also, he may delibately inhibit ideas that he feels are irrelevant to the discussion proper.

Following this lead, especially in group interviews in which emotionally loaded material is involved, the session is "terminated" early by thanking the group members for being there and inquiring as to whether there are any other comments. Intensive probing into these "final" comments has been rewarding on a number of occasions.

For example, a group interview devoted to the motives involved in drinking in taverns as opposed to drinking at home uncovered very little more than mundane and superficial generalities. Following the *false termination,* a group member casually commented laughingly to his neighbor that he is hesitant to drink in a tavern because he holds his liquor poorly and is afraid of making a fool of himself in public. Further probing of this theme with the man who initiated it, as well as others in the group, revealed the specific moral prohibition against drinking at a bar made by the group member's father. More important, this "casual" comment led to a quite meaningful discussion about the variety and intensity of impulses and emotions that may be expressed in a tavern but are socially unacceptable elsewhere. Anxiety, provoked by the threat of such emotional expressions, may be sufficient to limit drinking to the relative "safety" of the home.

Playing the devil's advocate requires that the moderator take a very opinionated role. With the goal of provoking a reaction, the moderator may himself express an extreme viewpoint on the topic under discussion. This is usually sufficient to move the discussion into more productive channels. The same effect can be achieved without involving the moderator, through the use of an accomplice who takes a pre-established and adamantly stated point of view.

Sophisticated Naïveté

In most cases, however, the most effective pose is that of sophisticated naïveté. The group members are assigned the role of educating the unknowledgeable moderator. He thus forces the group members to explain even the obvious—those unverbalized habits of thought and action that are rarely subject to scrutiny.

Here the moderator may make frequent use of such probes as, "What do you mean?" "I'm afraid I didn't understand that" . . . or, "Remember now, I'm not a buyer; so, would you explain that to me?" Such probing elicited the realization on the part of one dress buyer that in making selections for her extensive clientele she had primarily four of her regular customers in mind.

Parrying Direct Questions

There are occasions in which a *direct question* may put the moderator "on the spot." Often these questions cannot only be diplomatically dodged, but at the same time they may be used to gain additional information. When group members ask, as they frequently do, about identity of the client, this may be used to open a discussion concerning the relative activity in consumer and scientific research of various companies and the interest of these companies in the needs of the consumer. An effective gambit here in response to, "What company is paying for this anyway?"

is something like, "I'm curious about why you ask," or "What's your hunch about who is sponsoring this research?"

Gesture

The use of gestures should not be ignored in conducting the group interview. A raised eyebrow can be an effective probe; leaning forward on the table may encourage more comment by a reluctant or shy person; a shrug of the shoulder can parry many direct questions.

Attention to the gestures of the group members frequently tells more than what is said. Reserve, disgust, disdain, irritation, enthusiasm, and myriad other emotional subtleties are conveyed by gesture. Here is an example. In a discussion of a building material, one woman, while describing her impression of it, continually rubbed her thumb and forefinger together. Her words expressed a mildly favorable opinion, but the gesture revealed a fear of which she was only slightly aware herself. Despite the fact that the material itself was very rigid and hard, probing as to the meaning of her gesture revealed a fear that it would be "crumbly" and soft.

Non-Directive Comments

Non-directive comments often help to focus attention on the emotion implicit in a discussion. A non-directive comment such as, "You seem angry about that," or, "That memory seems to give you pleasure," recognizes and accepts emotion, and at the same time encourages the group member to reflect further on his feelings in relation to the topic under discussion. Most people need such encouragement to express strong feelings in a group setting, particularly feelings of tenderness and sentimentality.

FIVE REQUIREMENTS
OF THE GROUP DEPTH INTERVIEW

Five factors are required of the group depth interview in order to serve its research objectives: *objectivity, reliability, validity, intensive analysis,* and *marketing applicability*. While the first four are required of any scientific research, the last is more relevant to marketing studies. Any endeavor that presumes to be marketing research cannot ignore these guideposts of sound inquiry.

1. Objectivity

Avoidance of the bias of the interviewer and client indicates *objectivity*. Respondents are usually sensitive to the attitudes and opinions of the group moderator; and if these are allowed to manifest themselves without the moderator's awareness, it can grossly affect the nature of the data. To further objectivity, it is usually necessary to disguise the identity of the client, and for the moderator to observe rigorous neutrality (except when being the devil's advocate). Objective summary of attitudes sometimes requires the use of some quantitative technique, such as a scaling device, within the context of the group interview.

2. Reliability

The degree to which the information produced is representative of the population to which it is generalized is called *reliability*. The question of reliability of the sample, or generalization of the results, directs attention to the purpose of the group depth interview. Its basic function is to indicate "why" rather than "how many." That is ,it focuses on understanding the motives of behavior rather than cataloging the number of individuals who behave in a particular way.

The group interview is particularly useful in the developmental phases of a research program. It establishes the range of attitudes without, however, asserting the representativeness of these attitudes. Perhaps the major function of the group depth interview is to generate creative and fruitful hpotheses. It does not generally permit broad generalization and thus, in most cases, it should be followed by a probability survey to substantiate these hypotheses.

In certain cases, small-sample group interviews can produce generalizable results. For example, a group panel has represented in its members jobbers who controlled 50% of all automotive parts distributed in a particular city. The opinions they expressed represented a considerable portion of the automotive parts jobber universe in that city.

In special circumstances which limit a study to a small sample for security reasons, the problem of sample representativeness may be academic. A manufacturer may need to limit a study to a small sample, in order to present too many people from knowing about a new product prior to its introduction to the market.

Group interviewing does not preclude quantitatively adequate sampling; but in most cases it makes it very expensive.

Another kind of reliability problem is the representativeness of the time sample. Purchasing decisions for higher-priced items begin as vague, general ideas of the product and become progressively more specific as decision-making proceeds. Intersecting this process at any one point in time may not adequately reflect its dynamic nature. The purchasing decision can be viewed as a learning process that may be altered many times from the initiation of the need to the actual purchase of a product.

One way in which this process may be investigated may be illustrated by a problem involving the assessment of consumer reaction to a radical styling innovation of a major appliance. Six groups of eight members each were shown scale models of the appliances at three different sessions held at weekly intervals. At each session, attitudes were intensively probed. A gradual shift in acceptance of the radical change was observed over the three week period. However, when those who had been exposed to the product three times were combined in the same group with people who had never seen the product, the effect was immediate and dramatic: the quality and intensity of their attitudes reverted to what they had been at the very first exposure. Since this kind of interaction duplicates what happens in the market place, it produced a valuable insight into this social-learning process and permitted a more effective marketing decision to be made.

This study suggested that while there may be increasing acceptance of the styling innovation with more exposure to it, this preference was not a stable one and could be reversed by contact with someone who was seeing the radically styled appliance for the first time. Here, it was decided that the style was too radical, and a more moderate style was elected.

3. Validity

A source of continual concern to researchers is the *validity* problem, the assumption that a measure really measures what it purports to measure. The group situation attempts to get as close to the actual purchasing decision as possible.

For example, the task given the group member in a problem which concerned purchase of pre-packaged bacon was actual selection from among a number of samples the very bacon that she would serve her family, and not merely enumerating the criteria according to which she usually buys bacon.

Similarly, in a discussion of wine preference, the group members ordered and drank the wine of their choice.

When the topic was that of selecting a garment for themselves, women were asked to act out in detail, using a number of blouse samples, the act of buying one for themselves. Here the moderator took the role of salesman.

A problem involving the factors which are important in home decorating was approached by having groups of married couples go through the actual task of decorating a small-scale model home, using reduced-sized flooring materials, wallpaper prints, drapery fabrics, upholstery fabrics, and a wide variety of miniature furniture of various styles. Each couple decorated in the presence of other couples, and each did so with a conscientiousness that left little doubt that this task had considerable ego-involvement. These various devices tend to decrease the discrepancy between attitude expression and actual purchasing behavior.

4. Intensive Analysis

A fourth requirement of the group depth interview is that the often voluminous data be *intensively analyzed*. Discussion material of this kind defies routine analysis. The method of analyses employed here is similar to that by which group psychotherapy sessions are analyzed.

Qualitative analysis of group-interview material focuses on several kinds of data. At the most superficial level are the opinions easily verbalized. They may at times give only some indication of the attitudes that group members are willing to express to others. Subconscious buying motives may be reflected in such data as: what topics are discussed, what kinds of people bring them up and with what degree of intensity, to whom they are said, and, perhaps most important, the temporal sequence in which they are said.

For example, a product that had enjoyed the highest market share in a particular city for fifteen years began to decrease in sales to members of a minority group. The drop in sales did not appear to be attributable to changes in product, package design, or sales policy. In several group sessions, the following sequence of themes was discussed: minority and national groups are becoming more alert and militant all over the world; domination by the more powerful majority must stop; sometimes members of minorities are dealt with unfairly by the police; the company in question makes a good product and is the biggest manufacturer of that product; other companies that also produce a good product are entering the field. These themes, in the context of the total group session, suggested an identification of the minority group member with the smaller producer in opposition to the large "powerful" company. To this extent that their buying behavior was consistent with this psychological identity, the "big" company was being hurt.

5. Marketing Applicability

The group depth interview is designed to *solve marketing problems*. Even if a study satisfies the other four requirements, it is just an "academic exercise" if its findings cannot be put to use in the market place.

A variety of marketing problems in which the group depth interview is applicable have already been indicated. As noted above, the group depth interview is most frequently useful and appropriate in the developmental and exploratory phases of research. Here it is used to make it more likely that the correct questions are asked in large sample surveys to follow.

The group depth interview is also helpful in cases where broad sampling is prohibited by security requirements. For example, when used as a complement to new-product development, group sessions are conducted at several points in the process, to aid management in decisions which are not best left for a point later in the process. In this way, management has available consumer reactions *before* large investments of time and money are committed.

For example, development of a new food product may begin with an exploration of several food concepts in order to expose which of several alternative directions would serve the consumers' needs best. Or, perhaps a manufacturer might wish to know which of several kinds of materials are best suited for a home building item before one of them is committed to intensive laboratory development. When one of these materials is selected by the groups and is developed further, the graphic design of the product also is explored by the group method. In a final research phase the progressively refined and elaborated product may be discussed by various kinds of groups in order to help to guide advertising themes, promotional campaigns, and perhaps distribution systems.

The group depth interview has been used to explore attitudes about corporate images, public relations, personnel-turnover rate, recruiting appeals, health problems, container design, political issues, and many other marketing and social problems. The full potential of the method has yet to be realized.

30

FITTING the SEMANTIC DIFFERENTIAL to the MARKETING PROBLEM

WILLIAM A. MINDAK

Advertising and marketing men frequently are faced with the problem of qualifying highly subjective data, representing difficult-to-verbalize reactions of people to the "image" of a brand, product, or company.

Consistent with this attempt to define an "image" is the technique originated by Charles E. Osgood and his associates, called the semantic differential.[1] This technique attempts to measure what meaning a concept might have for people in terms of dimensions which have been empirically defined and factor-analyzed. Since this concept can indeed be something as abstract or nebulous as a company image, the semantic differential has seen increasing use in various ways.[2]

Osgood's semantic differential involved repeated judgments of a concept against a series of descriptive polar-adjectival scales on a 7-point equal-interval ordinal scale. These scales were usually selected from 50 pairs of polar adjectives, with heavy factor loadings labeled "evaluative" (on which are based the attitudinal measures), "activity," and "potency."

An example would be:

good—:—:—:—:—:—:—:bad

Progressing from left to right on the scale, the positions are described to the subjects participating in the experiment as representing "extremely

Reprinted from the *Journal of Marketing*, national quarterly publication of the American Marketing Association, Volume 25 (April, 1961), pp. 28-33.

[1] Charles E. Osgood, George J. Suci, and Percy H. Tannenbaum, *The Measurement of Meaning* (Urbana, Illinois: University of Illinois Free Press, 1957).

[2] William A. Mindak, "A New Technique for Measuring Advertising Effectiveness," *Journal of Marketing*, Vol. 20 (April,, 1956), pp. 367-378. Mogul, Lewin, Williams & Saylor, Inc., "Product Semantic Indices," (private publication) (New York, 1958). John F. Bolger, Jr., "How to Evaluate Your Company Image," *Journal of Marketing*, Vol. 24 (October, 1959), pp. 7-10.

good," "very good," "slightly good," "being both good and bad," "slightly bad," "very bad," and "extremely bad." Subjects are encouraged to use the scales as quickly and as honestly as possible and not to puzzle over any particular concept.

In scoring the differential, weights can be assigned to each position; and these in turn can be converted to individual or group mean scores and presented in "profile" form. Reliability of the differential is reasonably high, and the measure has a high degree of face validity.

SEMANTIC DIFFERENTIAL IN MEASURING "IMAGES"

The semantic differential has a number of specific advantages for marketing researchers interested in measuring brand, product, or company images:

1. It is a quick, efficient means of getting in readily quantifiable form and for large samples not only the *direction* but *intensity* of opinions and attitudes toward a concept . . . be it brand, product, or company. If desired, these "profiles" can be used as a guide to indicate areas for more intensive research or interviewing.

2. It provides a comprehensive picture of the "image" or meaning of a product or personality. Duncan Hines and Betty Crocker as corporate personalities might both be looked upon favorably, but reacted to differently in terms of "activity," "strength," "warmth," "helpfulness," etc.

3. It represents a standardized technique for getting at the multitude of factors which go to make up a brand or product "image." Comparison of one brand with another must take into consideration *specific brand attributes* (size, shape, price, ingredients, etc.) as well as *general product class characteristics* (including competition); the *sources* of the impressions (merchandising, packaging, advertising, media, etc.); the *company* that makes the product; and *types of consumers* associated with the product.

4. It is easily repeatable and quite reliable. Therefore, it can be used as a continuing measure sensitive enough to note changes in consumer reactions from year to year.

5. It avoids stereotyped responses and allows for individual frames of reference. The sheer number of scales and concepts and the speed of administration (both with groups and individuals), encourage quick "top-

of-mind" responses. For this reason it has sometimes been called a "semantic projection" test.

6. It eliminates some of the problems of question phrasing, such as ambiguity and overlapping of statements. In addition, it facilitates the interviewing of respondents who may not be too articulate in describing their reactions to such abstruse factors as a brand, product, or company image.

MODIFICATIONS FOR ADVERTISING RESEARCH

To make the differential even more sensitive in evoking subtle distinctions in the images of physically similar products, researchers have suggested many modifications. The most important of these are:

1. *Descriptive nouns and phrases.* These are in addition to (and sometimes as a substitute for) simple one-word adjectives. The original differential dealt primarly with single-word adjectives such as "good-bad," "weak-strong," "pleasant-unpleasant," etc. The "evaluation," "activity," and "potency" factors are still retained, but with increased shades of meaning provided by these longer, more involved scales.

Here is an example for a beer:

> Happy-go-lucky—kind of serious
> Something special—just another drink
> Little after-taste—lots of after-taste
> Really refreshing—not really refreshing
> American flavor—foreign flavor

Here is an example for people who drink beer:

> Live in average homes—live in expensive homes
> Take life easy—always on the go
> Drink just to be sociable—really enjoy it
> Really know beer—can't tell one from another
> Snobs—regular guys
> Housewife—career girl

Edmund W. J. Faison, President of Visual Research Inc., in an attempt to match personality types with package designs, labels, colors, etc., has used these phrases as one end of a scale:

> Stands out in a crowd
> Self-made man
> Likes to hunt and fish
> Factory worker making $400 a month
> Belongs to a higher social class than his parents

2. *Tailor-made scales.* In attempting to set up standardized scales, certain researchers have concentrated on the classic list of 50 word-pairs, factor-analyzed by Osgood. This direction offers comparative possibilities and a hope of generalized attitude scales. In rating TV commercials, Burleigh Gardner of Social Research, Inc., consistently uses 30 word-pairs, with heavy factor loadings on evaluation, activity, strength, etc.

But for many researchers such a standardized list lacks flexibility and appropriateness to the specific problems at hand. They find it necessary to construct tailor-made word and phrase lists. Sources for these lists are content analyses of their own and competitive advertising, word association tests with consumers, individual or group interviews, and factor analyses.

In such exploratory or pretests, simple opposites are used, often without the 7-point scale. Once it is agreed that these adjectives and phrases cover the factors best delimiting the image, they are then scaled to permit profile comparisons.

3. *"Connotative" and "non-polar" opposites.* Although in theory every adjective or phrase should have a denotative opposite (true-untrue, good-bad, bright-dull), researchers have found that in practice respondents often refuse to "play the game," as it were. In an advertising context or in rating large well-known companies, subjects often balk at using negative sides of scales or to gradate a concept negatively.

Respondents can, and do, make sharp distinctions as to the level of believability of a company's advertising or of a particular claim. But they either hesitate to rate a concept as unbelievable (feeling that "if it is advertised, it must be true") or they are unable to gradate their feelings of unbelievability.

This failure frequently results in indiscriminate clustering about the middle of the scales, thus making it difficult to differentiate among concept profiles. Some researchers have attempted to circumvent this tendency either by "heightening" the level of the dimensions or by using phrases which, although not necessarily *denotatively* opposite, still seem to fit more logically and naturally into people's frame of reference. Scales such as these are used:

> Really modern—sort of old-fashioned
> High-quality product—so-so quality product
> Heavy beer drinker—a "sometimes" beer drinker
> Really peps you up—somehow doesn't pep you up

4. *Built-in control concepts.* As a realistic control, it is helpful to get ratings on such concepts as, "the ideal company," or "my favorite brand," or "brand I would never use." These control profiles can be compared with test concepts or competitive concepts. Although one might ex-

pect respondents simply to use the extremes on all scales to represent their "ideal" or their "least-liked," such is not really the case.

5. *Personal interviews and mail questionnaires.* Early experiments with the differential usually were conducted with "captive" audiences, often students in class. In the main, though, the advertising researcher prefers to do field studies and depends on individual personal interviews. The differential has been used in these situations, and respondents show little reluctance in performing the task of checking several concepts on a variety of scales. The need for tailor-made scales is often quite apparent, however, in that certain age groups and certain socio-economic groups find it relatively difficult to think in terms of various continua and to deal with such abstractions as "concepts."

Other researchers have even experimented with the differential in mail questionnaires, although this means of delivery obviates most of the projective qualities of this test. Respondents have too much time to deliberate over their judgments and have too much control over their ratings. Personal supervision is necessary to assure speed and "top-of-mind" responses.

A BRAND-IMAGE STUDY

The following case study demonstrates the use of the differential, as well as some of the modifications discussed. This particular study's purpose was to determine beer drinkers' reactions to the personalities of three local brands of beer (and specifically Brand Y), compared with three competitive national brands in a large midwest city. Various facets of this image were to be explored, such as specific characteristics of each brand, the attitudes toward advertising, the image of the company, and feelings about various consumers who might be associated or not associated with each brand of beer.

Respondents were asked to rate these six beers on several dimensions. Scales were selected from content analyses of depth-interview responses, as well as from advertisements for the various brands. The mean ratings were converted into profiles for comparison purposes. Figures 1 through 4 illustrate certain critical scales for three local brands of beer.

Results

1. Looking at the profiles of products, company, and advertising image, (Figures 1, 2, and 3) it is apparent that Brands X and Y enjoy many more

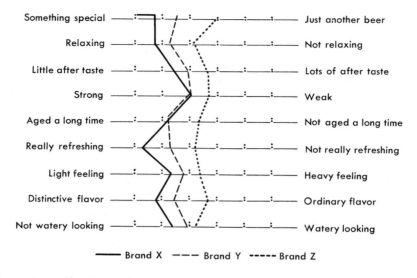

Figure 1.   Specific product image.

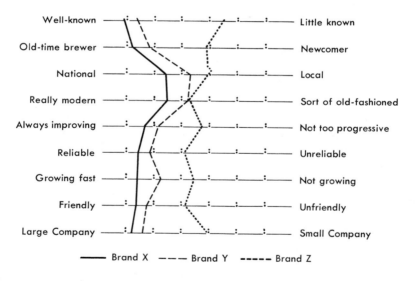

Figure 2.   Company image.

positive or favorable ratings than Brand Z. This reflects X and Y's domination of sales and their large market share. None of X's or Y's mean
ratings fall on the negative side; and very few are in the neutral or indifferent area (3.5 to 4.5).

Brand X received essentially positive ratings in regard to specific

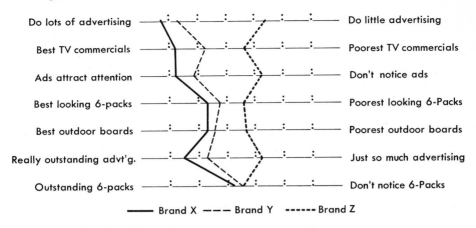

Figure 3.   Advertising image.

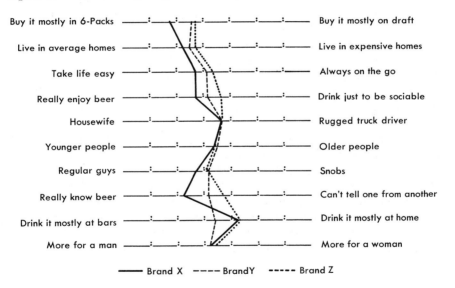

Figure 4.   Consumer profile.

product (it was quite refreshing, something special, relaxing, and had a distinctive flavor); advertising (it was outstanding, it was attention getting, and there was lots of it); and company (it was friendly, large, well-known, and an old-time brewer who still manages to grow fast and always improve).

Although Brand Y's ratings usually were favorable, they were not as extreme as Brand X. The only two exceptions occurred in ratings of the specific products. Beer drinkers rated Y about the same as X on the "weak-strong" scale and the "aged-a-long-time" dimension. *Brand Z, a* relatively newcomer to the city, was reacted to quite neutrally—in this case, an indication of little consumer experience with, or knowledge of, the beer. In addition to its "militant indifference," Brand Z was thought to be less well-known than the other two brands, to do less advertising, and to be more of a local beer.

2. In products such as beer, advertising researchers are interested in determining the "types" of consumer most often associated with a particular brand. Social Research, Inc., the Psychological Corporation, the Institute for Motivational Research, Inc., and other organizations increasingly emphasize psychological typologies rather than conventional demographic characteristics.

In this case, Figure 4 shows that the consumer profile ratings, that is, the types of people considered likely to buy each of these beers, tend to cluster much more than for the other three factors. It might be advantageous for a beer *not* to be inordinately connected or identified with a particular type of consumer.

Beer drinkers thought Brands X and Y more "universal" than Z. They were "all things to all beer drinkers." Brand X was thought of as being consumed more at home and by average people who really enjoy and know beer. Brand Y was considered to be drunk more in bars. Brand Z's image tended toward home drinking and use by less discriminating beer drinkers.

The results of this study were interpreted by the management of Y company to be quite favorable, particularly when the advertising budgets of X and Y were compared. Management was pleased with reactions to the company which a few years back had not enjoyed the best of reputations. Possible weak areas which might need strengthening were Brand Y's dealer displays (6-packs); the feeling that the company was not as modern as it could be; and the need of upgrading the image of the beer among "higher-class," sophisticated, home beer drinkers.

Implications

A great deal of controversy (some genuine, some "strawman") exists between the "quantifier" and the "qualifier" in attempting to delineate the image of a product, brand, or company. The semantic differential and techniques similar to it help to quantify what too often has been considered abstract, mysterious, and qualitative material regarding consumers' opinions, feeling tones, and emotional reactions. In addition, the modifications suggested by advertising researchers (phrases and nouns in addition to single adjectives, connotative as well as denotative opposites, tailor-made scales) add more scope and direction to what may be superficial quantitative information.

The differential serves as a two-edged tool: (1) It is a simple, large sample, nose-counting device which can be repeated from time to time to detect trends in consumer reactions, and to measure interaction between advertising and consumer attitudes. (2) In addition, the differential "profiles" serve as useful directional indicators for further and more intensive probing, using many of the qualitative projective techniques.

In either case, this knowledge can be quite useful in deciding on a possible advertising or marketing plan, in spotting weak areas which might need to be strengthened or strong areas which might need to be emphasized.

31

PRODUCT SYMBOLISM and the
PERCEPTION of SOCIAL STRATA

MONTROSE S. SOMMERS

The question: "Why do people buy?" is constantly being answered in innumerable ways. One approach to answering it is to focus on what people buy and their perceptions of products. Newman views a product as

"a symbol by virtue of its form, size, color, and functions. Its significance as a symbol varies according to how much it is associated with individual needs and social interaction. A product, then, is the sum of the meanings it communicates, often unconsciously, to others when they look at it or use it."[1]

If such a concept of a product has merit, if products do have symbolic values and these are perceived differently by individuals and groups, it should be possible to relate differential product perception to those who hold these perceptions. As far as a marketer is concerned, if a product is the sum of the meanings it communicates, and these meanings may be many, a basic problem he faces would be ascertaining the different perceptions of his products which are taken by actual and potential consumers. Insofar as he can do this, he is better able to develop effective marketing strategy and achieve a more efficient allocation of his resources.

In order for marketers to make use of this concept of perception of product symbolism, a suitable research technique and instrument that can be handled with ease must be available. It was the basic objective of my research *to design a research instrument for studying perceived product symbolism* so that this concept could be more easily applied to practical marketing problems.

Reprinted from Stephen A. Greyser (ed.), *Toward Scientific Marketing* (Chicago: American Marketing Association, 1964), pp. 200-216.

[1] Joseph W. Newman, "New Insights, New Progress, for Marketing," *Harvard Business Review* (November-December, 1957), p. 100.

Design of the Research

The project was undertaken on an exploratory basis and designed so that products became the vehicle for expression for housewives. Product symbolism was investigated within two frames of reference, the Self (S) and the described Other (O). Basically, housewives were asked to describe themselves in terms of a set of products and then to describe a particular other housewife using the same products as descriptive symbols.

When a subject adopts the frame of reference of the Self, she is saying: "What kind of a person am I? How do I see myself? What is my image of myself?" The answers elicited are in very specialized terms, in terms of products as they embody and stand for role components.

When the housewife adopts the frame of reference of the described Other, she is role playing and acting as if she were this person. From this position she is saying: "If I were she, how would I answer the same questions; what kind of a person am I? How do I see myself? What is my image of myself?"

By having subjects describe themselves and another person, it is possible to get 'an indication of the different descriptive symbolic values of the products used. The Self description provides an indication of perceived product symbolism and the nature of the Self perception; that is, through the relationship of product and role, which of the feminine role components are most important and their order of importance. The description of the Other provides an indication of how a subject perceives the descriptive product symbolism of another person. This description illustrates something of the perceived nature and importance of product symbols and related roles which are attributed, possibly inaccurately, to Others.

Operational Hypotheses Tested

The operational hypotheses which were tested were designed to determine whether or not a product test of the type designed could actually differentiate between members of two different social strata; the nature of the perceptions of Other and the solidarity of perception of Self and Other that exists within strata. The statement of the major hypothesis is: *members of a high stratum (H) describe Self and Other significantly differently from members of a low stratum (L)*.

The theoretical basis of this hypothesis is the sociological theory of symbolic interaction. The expectation that social strata will demonstrate unique stereotypes is based on the communication process used to transmit symbolic meaning and value. "The basis of symbolic interaction is the communication process, for society exists in and through it. Shared perspectives are the products of common communication channels."[2] The variations which arise in the modes of life of different social groups and the group perspectives which develop result "not because of anything inherent in economic position but because similarity of occupations and limitations set by income level dispose them to certain restricted communication channels."[3] Each social world is a culture area with its boundaries set neither by territory nor formal group membership, but by the limits of effective communication.

Our view of a social stratum is that while individuals within one certainly do not form a reference group in terms of formal associations, as long as there are mutual understandings and common presuppositions which are shared, as a result of a basic similarity in communication channels, there can be a common pattern of behavior. The concept of the reference group is maximized when it signifies "that group when presumed perspective is used by an actor as the frame of reference in the organization of his perceptual field."[4] The broad category used here is not an organized group or a voluntary association but an unorganized informal group which offers a common frame of reference.

The research which is pertinent to this hypothesis is that which focuses basically on the solidarity of meaning and value within a social stratum. The early work of Chapin in 1933 in developing a Social Status Scale commonly called the "livingroom scale" was a pioneering effort in this area.[5] A similar type of scale was constructed by Sewell for use in measuring the status of farmers.[6] While both of these scales were criticized, their basic contributions stand as the first systematic attempts at making use of products as indicators of social strata.

The well-known community studies of Warner, Hollingshead, and Kaufman, while they also raised methodological problems, still result in the conclusions that a rank order or hierarchy of social strata exists and that the criteria which people use in perceiving of the hierarchy is expressed in the vague term "the way they live." The most conspicuous aspect of the "way they live" is, of course, consumption behavior. Warner summarizes his view on this by saying "it is certain that the use and meaning of most objects sold on the American market shift from class to class."[7]

2 Tamotsu Shibutani, "Reference Groups and Social Control," in Rose (ed.), *Human Behavior and Social Processes* (Boston: Houghton Mifflin Co., 1960), p. 134.

3 *Ibid.*

4 *Ibid.*, p. 132.

5 F. Stuart Chapin, *Contemporary American Institutions* (New York: Harper and Bros., 1935), pp. 373-397.

6 William H. Sewell, "A Short Form of the Farm Family Socio-Economic Status Scale," *Rural Sociology*, Vol. 8 (June, 1943), pp. 161-170.

7 W. Lloyd Warner, Marchia Meeker and Kenneth Eells, *Social Class in America* (New York: Harper and Bros., 1960), p. 31.

The work of Centers exemplified the objective approach to this type of research in that, rather than using placement in a stratum based on objective factors or community judges, he relied on self-awareness and self-placement.[8] This subjective approach of Centers' comes closer to our theoretical position that a stratum can be viewed as a reference group in that there is a basic degree of subjective solidarity within the stratum. Support for this approach also comes from the work of Bott which was concerned with class ideology and which illustrates that strata or classes are constructed reference groups which are psychologically real even if they do not appear to be objectively real.[9] The Bott research aids in explaining some of the inconsistencies which are found when the data from objectively and subjectively oriented research projects on social class are compared.

The above research findings not only suggest the major hypothesis but also the supporting ones below.

The second hypothesis, that *members of H are more accurate in perceiving members of L than are members of L in perceiving those of H* is suggested by the tradition of upward mobility in American society and the idea that people in higher social strata not only have had experience in reference groups in lower strata but also are more articulate regarding prestige differences and make more divisions into groups than those in lower strata.

The third hypothesis, that *members of L demonstrate greater agreement in describing Self than members of H* is based on the idea that individuals within a stratum generally have access to similar communication channels but that members of a lower stratum have fewer alternatives in terms of roles and communication channels than those of a higher stratum. Because of the smaller numbers of alternatives available to those in the lower stratum, it is expected that there will be a greater degree of homogeneity of Self descriptions in the lower stratum than in the higher one.

Hypothesis four, that *members of H demonstrate greater agreement in describing an Other than members of L* relies on the same basic position as those that preceded. Members of a higher stratum can be expected to demonstrate greater agreement in Other description than those of a lower one for the same reasons that they are expected to be more accurate in their perceptions. The better the persons and occupations are known, the more agreement concerning them.

Members of the lower stratum can be expected to have diverse concepts of Other because of their lack of actual reference group knowledge and relationships with members of groups like those in the higher stra-

[8] Richard Centers, *The Psychology of Social Classes* (Princeton: Princeton University Press, 1949).

[9] Elizabeth Bott, "The Concept of Class as a Reference Group," *Human Relations*, Vol. 7 (August, 1954), No. 2, pp. 259-283.

tum. In addition, the multiplicity of reference points presented by radio, television, newspapers, magazines, and other media is also expected to result in a diversity of descriptions of Other. The fifth hypothesis, that *members of H demonstrate greater agreement in describing an Other than in describing Self* develops naturally from the previous hypotheses dealing with accuracy of perception and agreement on Self descriptions for a higher stratum.

The sixth hypothesis is based on the same type of logic. Because *members of a lower stratum (L) have fewer role alternatives, they demonstrate greater agreement in Self description than members of H*. Because they have not had actual reference group contact with members of a higher stratum and receive much conflicting information through the mass media, their perceptions of Other are diverse and relatively inaccurate.

MEASURING PERCEPTIONS OF SELF AND OTHER

The basis for measuring the perceptions of products and their use lies in Q-methodology as propounded by William Stephenson.[10] Stephenson's intent was to deal with the total personality in action, with "wholes" and "descriptions" rather than traits or characteristics. The evidence of the total personality in action would be represented in the recorded reactions a person had with reference to a large number of test items. What is important in the approach is the form in which recorded reactions appear. It is the distribution of reactions, a forced normal distribution, which allows for the use of correlation and factor analysis techniques.

The test that an individual takes, under Q-methodology, is composed of items drawn from some type of population, in this case, a population of products. The methodology does not concern itself with the populations as such but with the statistical universes which are derived from them. In the product test designed for this project, the concern is not with the representativeness of the products selected, but with the manner in which an individual, when she is asked to grade products on a scale, from those which best describe her to those which least describe her, arrays these products. The procedure for evaluating each item and placing it in some kind of an array is called Q-sort. The method of evaluating such arrays and the position of items within them requires the establishment of a number of classes, each with a different score, and with each class containing an appropriate number of test items so that the array takes the shape of a quasi-normal frequency distribution. The quasi-normal frequency distribution for a sample of 50 products is shown in Table 1.

[10] William Stephenson, *The Study of Behavior* (Chicago: University of Chicago Press, 1953).

TABLE 1

FREQUENCY DISTRIBUTION AND SCORES FOR PRODUCTS (N = 50)

	Best describes					Least describes			
Score	9	8	7	6	5	4	3	2	1
Frequency	2	3	6	9	10	9	6	3	2

Those two items which a subject places in the class on the extreme left receive a score of 9 for each. These would be the two products in the group available which best describe Self or Other. The second class contains the next three items which best describe Self or Other and each receives a score of 7. The score for items in each subsequent class is reduced to the point where the last two items, those which least describe Self or Other, receive a score of 1. From the frequency distribution it can be seen that those classes at the extremes of the distribution can be considered to be highly discriminating and have few items falling within them while those classes in the central positions could be less discriminating and have a greater number of items falling within them. The scores which the different items receive, under the two conditions of sorting, Self and Other, become the basis for analysis and comparisons.

Comparisons and analysis of arrays resulting from Q-sorting operations can be made using product moment correlation (Pearson r). The array which results from the Q-sort technique can also be scored on a rank order basis with the first item placed (that one being most descriptive) scored 1 and all the other items placed (in succeeding order to least descriptive) so numbered that the last items receives lowest ranking or 50. The technique is therefore flexible from the point of view of analysis.

In determining what kinds of items are to be used for Q-sorting operations, two basic considerations are to be heeded. Care must be taken to see that none of the items included are so apparently similar as to make distinctions between them extremely difficult. In addition, a basic type of homogeneity of class of items is important so that a subject can make decisions about how the items are related and what their relative values might be. For the Q-sorting operations of this project, the items included in the test are products which can be and are used in the fulfillment of feminine role components either in the home environment, with members of the family or as a representative of the family.

Five classes of products were selected for inclusion in the product test: (1) clothing; (2) toiletries and cosmetics; (3) food; (4) household appliances; and (5) leisure products. Each class was divided into 5 products defined as standard and 5 defined as specialty; in the case of leisure products the dichotomy was made for items which have a non-participative individual or participative group orientation in use. The complete listing of products which comprised the test is shown in Table 2.

TABLE 2

TEST ITEMS BY CATEGORIES AND SUB-GROUPS

CATEGORY	STANDARD SUB-GROUP	SPECIALTY SUB-GROUP
1. Clothing	shoes	hat
	skirts	gloves
	dresses	lingerie
	blouses	hosiery
	suits	slacks
2. Toiletries and cosmetics	toothpaste	hair spray
	hand soap	permanent waves
	deodorant	eye shadow
	facial tissue	lipstick
	hair shampoo	nail polish
3. Food	catsup	frozen orange juice
	flour	instant coffee
	shortening	frozen sea food
	potatoes	cake mix
	bread	refrigerator biscuits
4. Household appliances	refrigerator	electric can opener
	iron	automatic dish washer
	toaster	rotisserie
	stove	food blender
	washing machine	automatic clothes dryer
5. Leisure products	NON-PARTICIPATIVE— INDIVIDUAL	PARTICIPATIVE— GROUP
	television	sports equipment
	books	playing cards
	magazines	camping equipment
	records	boating equipment
	Hi-Fi set	cocktail set

Implementation of the Instrument

The instrument, the product test, was used to test the product perceptions of housewives who represented two social strata. Fifty subjects were selected from each of two census tracts using a sampling design termed area sample with quota controls. One census tract (designated Low or L) was generally equivalent to a combination of the Warner classifications upper lower-lower middle. The second tract (designated High or H) was generally equivalent to the Warner classification upper-middle.

Each subject, using the product test which was presented as a deck of 50 cards with a product name on each card, sorted the cards to describe

TABLE 3

RESULTS OF TESTS OF THE HYPOTHESES

HYPOTHESIS	OPERATIONAL STATEMENT	MEASUREMENT	FINDING
H I	$r_1(LS:HS) = 1.0$ and $r_2(LO:HO) = 1.0$	$r_1 = .669$ $r_2 = .185$	Accept
H II	$r_1(LS:HO) > r_2(LO:HS)$	$r_1 = .919$ $r_2 = .601$	Accept
H III	$W(LS > W(HS)$	$W(LS) = .481$ $W(HS) = .303$	Accept
H IV	$W(LO) < W(HO)$	$W(LO) = .181$ $W(HO) = .541$	Accept
H V	$W(HS < W(HO)$	$W(HS) = .303$ $W(HO) = .541$	Accept
H VI	$W(LS) > W(LO)$	$W(LS) = .481$ $W(LO) = .181$	Accept

TABLE 4

PRODUCT ARRAYS FOR LS, HS, LO, AND HO WITH ITEMS FROM MOST DESCRIPTIVE TO LEAST DESCRIPTIVE

Scores	LS	HS	LO	HO
9 (n=2)	washing machine stove	washing machine dresses	dresses automatic clothes dryer	refrigerator stove
8 (n=3)	refrigerator electric iron hand soap	refrigerator books shoes	shoes hosiery automatic dishwasher	electric iron bread washing machine
7 (n=6)	toothpaste hair shampoo potatoes bread toaster television	skirts blouses lingerie lipstick stove automatic dishwasher	television refrigerator lingerie hats washing machine skirt	blouses television dresses flour electric toaster potatoes
6 (n=9)	dresses blouses lingerie shoes deodorant facial tissues	hand soap toothpaste deodorant hair shampoo toaster electric iron	suits blouses deodorant gloves electric toaster lipstick	frozen orange juice shoes deodorant toothpaste shortening

TABLE 4   (Cont'd)

books	clothes dryer	electric rotisserie	hair shampoo
flour	records	hi-fi	hand soap
shortening	television	stove	lipstick
			skirts
5 (n=10) skirts	slacks	hair spray	suits
slacks	hosiery	slacks	slacks
hosiery	suits	toothpaste	catsup
lipstick	gloves	hair shampoo	hosiery
hair spray	facial tissues	electric can opener	permanent waves
catsup	bread	hand soap	books
magazines	potatoes	electric iron	lingerie
cake mix	playing cards	facial tissues	facial tissues
frozen orange juice	hi-fi	nail polish	cake mix
refrigerated biscuits	frozen orange juice	records	magazines
4 (n=9) frozen seafood	hats	frozen orange juice	instant coffee
suits	hair spray	sports equipment	hair spray
gloves	nail polish	playing cards	playing cards
permanent waves	catsup	permanent waves	gloves
nail polish	flour	books	frozen seafood
camping equipment	shortening	eye shadow	hats
records	magazines	cocktail set	nail polish
clothes dryer	cake mix	bread	refrigerated biscuits
sports equipment	sports equipment	blender	records
3 (n=6) instant coffee	instant coffee	instant coffee	sports equipment
playing cards	camping equipment	shortening	camping equipment
electric can opener	frozen seafood	boating equipment	automatic dishwasher
blender	eye shadow	frozen seafood	eye shadow
hi-fi	blender	magazines	automatic clothes dryer
hats	refrigerated biscuits	refrigerated biscuits	hi-fi
2 (n=3) automatic dishwasher	permanent waves	flour	cocktail set
eye shadow	electric can opener	potatoes	blender
electric rotisserie	cocktail set	cake mix	electric rotisserie
1 (n=2) boating equipment	boating equipment	catsup	electric can opener
cocktail set	electric rotisserie	camping equipment	boating equipment

Self. The Self sorts for both strata (LS and HS) were recorded and then subjects assumed the role of a member of the opposite stratum. This was done by presenting subjects with a "cue" card which characterized a typical member of H for members of L and a typical member of L for members of H. Assuming the appropriate roles and again making the descriptions of Self and Other ("as if I were this person") resulted in Other sorts for both strata; the Low stratum descriptions of H (LO) and the High stratum descriptions of L (HO).

The implementation of the test resulted in the four basic sorts; LS, LO, HS, and HO which provided the measurements necessary for hypothesis testing. The four basic sorts were obtained by developing a mean array for Self and Other for each stratum.

Test Results

The hypotheses were tested with the results shown in Table 3. Two statistics were used in demonstrating the relationships between the sorts: (1) Pearsonian r; (2) the coefficient of concordance W. Product movement correlation was used to correlate the basic product arrays, and the coefficient of concordance was used as a measure of the level of agreement to be found in each of the basic arrays.

Being able to accept the first research hypothesis, that members of different strata have different Self and Other perceptions, was a major objective of the study. This is not because the finding is significant, *per se*, but because of the method used. The support of this operational position demonstrates the ability of the Q-sort procedure, given a selection of items to be arrayed, to yield results which distinguish between members of two social strata.

An analysis of the four basic arrays LS, HS, LO, and HO (shown in Table 4), resulted in information demonstrating which products were most and least descriptive and how members of both strata viewed each other.

1. The basic product categories of Clothing, Toiletries and Cosmetics, Food, Appliances, and Leisure Products were too broad and too mixed in order to demonstrate the descriptive properties of products in terms of their item scores. By breaking the basic categories into Standard and Specialty Sub-groups, much more accurate and descriptive information was obtained on which types of groups of products best describe Self and Other. Virtually all the Standard Sub-group items were found to best describe with higher descriptive scores than the Specialty Sub-group items.

2. The product categories were also found to be not accurate enough in demonstrating which types of items were responsible for differences between pairs of basic arrays. The Standard and Specialty Group sub-group breakdown showed

that the largest differences between LS and HS were accounted for by the different scores given to Specialty Appliances and Standard Clothing items. The largest differences between LS and HO were accounted for by H's inaccurate perception of how members of L would score Specialty Appliances and Standard Toiletries and Cosmetics. The largest differences between HS and LO were accounted for by L's inaccuracy in perceiving how members of H would score Specialty Appliances.

3. In the analysis of descriptive ability of Sub-groups related to accuracy of description, it was found that members of L were generally accurate in best describing members of H but they were inaccurate in being able to select items which were least descriptive of members of H. On the other hand, members of H were generally accurate in being able to select those items which both best and least describe members of L.

4. The analysis of the scores which individual items received for the descriptions of Other (LO and HO) compared to the descriptions of Self demonstrated that members of L generally focused on the differences which actually existed between LS and HS and tended to magnify them or overestimate scores. Members of H, on the other hand, tended to minimize differences between LS and HS by tending to project their own descriptions to members of L.

MARKETING IMPLICATIONS

The marketing implications of this exploratory study flow from two bases: the characteristics of a Q-array of products and the implications of an item's position in an array, and the differential perception of products and the accuracy of perception demonstrated by L and H.

This discussion of the marketing applications is based, in part, on two assumptions.

1. That product appeals and presentations are most effective when they are meaningful to consumers in terms of portraying roles and symbols which are perceived as being accurate and realistic in their own terms.

2. That product presentations may also be effective when a product or idea is presented to consumers without any role relationship. The absence of a structured role allows a consumer to structure the role which she feels is properly related to the product.

Significance of Item Scores

The position of individual items in a Q-array has marketing implications insofar as the placement aids marketers in determining how their products are viewed. The scores which each of the 50 products in the test received, both in the Self and Other sorts, are indicative of the potential sensitivity of the item in a product appeal. The items which appear in the tails of the Q-array are those most easily discriminated. Items with high scores (9, 8, 7 . . .) best describe while those with low scores (1, 2, 3 . . .) least describe. A marketer who deals in products which appear in the tails of a product array must be aware that he is dealing with highly descriptive and easily discriminated items. Items which appear in the central scoring classes of an array are not as easily discriminated nor are they highly descriptive. The items appearing in the tails would be most sensitive in product presentations in terms of obviously attracting attention. Inaccuracies and errors in the presentation of easily discriminated items would be more easily discerned than in the presentation of less easily discriminated items. The amount or degree of error which would be accepted in a presentation before it would be rejected as unrealistic or too inaccurate is something upon which we have no information.

Products which receive high scores in LS and HS are, in general, most appropriate in presentations to members of L and H. These are items which are not only highly descriptive but are perceived of accurately by members of L and H when they view each Other. If a marketer feels that perceived reality is most effective in product appeals, the inclusion of items with high scores should increase the probability of acceptance. On the other hand, products with low scores may be scored as least descriptive because they are related to "improper" roles or because they are unobtainable although related to desirable role components. High scoring products, because they are so descriptive, can stand on their own in a presentation and may be acceptable to large audiences. Low scoring products, because they are not descriptive in a positive sense when presented by themselves, may be acceptable to only a small audience. One way for a marketer to deal with low scoring items would be to avoid role presentations and allow the consumer to relate the item to roles as she sees fit. Another approach may be to relate a low scoring item to a high scoring one and thus attempt to identify it with a highly descriptive role component.

Implications of the Hypotheses

The implications of differential and accurate product perception concern the marketing strategies of product differentiation and market segmentation. The fact that a Q-sort of products successfully distinguishes between strata (Hypothesis I) aid in the determination of strategies for items which are viewed as common to both strata and which distinguish them.

When members of the two strata agree on the Self descriptive ability of an item, the marketer knows that the item and its related role is viewed with the same amount of importance when it comes to describing members of these strata. On this basis, he faces a potentially broad unsegmented market composed of both L and H insofar as he can make one product presentation to both. His appeals to this broad market should be based on symbols and roles which are common on both strata. He always has the alternative of product differentiation or segmentation if he so chooses.

When the members of two strata disagree on the Self descripitive ability of an item, the marketer is faced with a different set of alternatives. He can always make product presentations which do not rely on role portrayals and allow members of each stratum to construct their own frame of reference. Using this approach, he need make but one presentation. If he feels that role portrayals are more effective, he can attempt differentiation or segmentation or both. The fact that members of each stratum view the same product with a different amount of descriptive importance indicates the differential value it has. This is particularly true with items which are easily discriminated (with scores of 9, 8, 7 . . . 3, 2, 1) but it also applies to items which are more difficult to discriminate (with scores of 6, 5, and 4). As long as members of L and H disagree on the descriptive ability of an item, different product presentations should be made to each stratum, for if a common one is made, it may be rejected by either or both strata because of its perceived inaccuracy.

The support of the second hypothesis, that members of a high stratum have a better perception of members of a low stratum than those in the low have of the high, helps clarify when differentiation and segmentation strategies are suitable. Consumers who are very adept at discerning the differential meaning and value of symbols are likely to view and react to their presentation in a much clearer manner than those who are not as adept. Thus, when roles are portrayed, members of H should be presented with appropriate (in this case, quite accurate) symbols in product appeals. If this is not done, the appeals may be rejected because they do not coincide with the perceived evaluation of product symbols. The fact that members of H are more adept at perceiving symbols which both best and least describe does not allow too much room for error in terms of presenting products with mixed symbolic meanings and values. If a specific "class" or group market segment is important, and this segment is accurate in perception, accuracy in presentation is important. The accuracy of perception demonstrated by members of H shows that differentiation of product appeals is important. Segmentation strategy would perhaps be an even more effective approach because variations of a product, supported by different appeals, could be presented to each stratum instead of just differentiated appeals.

When a marketer deals with a stratum, like L, which does not have accurate perceptions of higher strata or groups, he faces a different problem. He must concern himself with the possible rejection of symbols which are in fact accurately descriptive of a higher stratum. This means he must be aware of any discrepancy in scores between symbols which are Self descriptive and the perception which Others have of them. If he is not aware of such discrepancies, his appeals may be rejected because, while they are accurate, they are perceived as being inaccurate.

Because of lesser accuracy of perception, as well as the possiblity of emulation, the problems a marketer faces in dealing with L are more complex than those which exist in dealing with H. In dealing with H, a marketer must, if he relies on role presentations, be able to present accurate symbols in product appeals. The problem of H emulating L is not considered to be present. In dealing with L, the marketer must, if he relies on role presentations, generally be able to present symbols which are both perceived as being accurate (although they may not be) and those which are accurate (for L is not always inaccurate). In addition, the predisposition of L to emulate H further complicates presentation problems. Either the strategy of differentiation or the use of presentations without role portrayals would both be appropriate where members of L inaccurately perceive differences between themselves and H and are not prepared to emulate H. Where they inaccurately perceive similarities, differentiation of presentations or presentations without role portrayals would also be necessary as accurate presentations may be rejected. Where they inaccurately or accurately perceive differences and are prepared to emulate H as well as when they accurately perceive similarities, differentiated product presentations without role portrayals are not necessary.

The testing of the four hypotheses (III, IV, V, and VI) dealing with the solidarity of perception of Self and Other within the strata have further implications for marketers. The level of solidarity of perception exhibited by a stratum will influence the need for differentiated appeals, the presentation of appeals do not rely on role portrayals and the usefulness of segmentation strategy.

The fact that members of L demonstrate greater agreement in making Self descriptions than members of H (Hypothesis III) indicates that a marketer may make product presentations, using roles, to L as if it were a single market segment. The need for further differentiation is not as pressing as it would be if there were a great deal of variation in Self descriptions. It can be expected, of course, that a single presentation will be rejected by some. Segmentation may prove to be a worthwhile strategy but it is not necessary because of the homogeneity of perceptions.

On the other hand, the lack of agreement or solidarity of Self description exhibited by members of H points out the need for presentations which either do not rely on roles or differentiated presentations, using roles, in dealing with this stratum. If a marketer wishes to deal with all members of the stratum, then either presentations without role portrayals or differentiation of products appeals are essential. The diversity of Self descriptions indicates that segmentation strategy may be feasible.

Hypothesis IV, that members of H demonstrate greater agreement in describing an Other than members of L is a reinforcement of Hypothesis II which finds H more perceptive of the Other than L. This finding also reflects on the problems of using emulative appeals directed at members of L. The low level of agreement demonstrated by L in describing H implies a great diversity of perceived Others. If members of L perceive a number of Others, product presentations which rely upon emulation must present the correct Other. If the marketer can define those groups within L which emulate a particular Other, it may be possible to both differentiate and segment the stratum.

The marketing implications of Hypotheses V and VI, that members of H demonstrate greater agreement in describing an Other than in describing Self and that members of L demonstrate greater agreement in describing Self than in describing an Other, have already been amplified above.

While it has been demonstrated in general terms what the implications of Q-sort can be for marketing much more intensive investigation of different types of sorts for different purposes is required in order to apply the approach to specific marketing problems. Further exploration is warranted in the areas of the structuring of product tests, product perception amongst other strata and groups, stability and change through time in item arrays as well as the implications of the positions of items in arrays.

32

INTRODUCTION to ATTITUDE RESEARCH and MANAGEMENT DECISIONS

LESLIE A. BELDO

John Maloney remarked, "The techniques of attitude scaling are thoroughly and competently described in scale manuals and a vast body of excellent professional literature. It's there for the reading." Thus, the panel came to the accord that a researcher can develop, adapt or borrow an attitude scaling technique for his problem at hand. But the problem of the day in attitude research that grounds our cause of aiding decisions, we believe, is the misuse of well-developed scaling techniques by faulty definition and attitudes and misinterpretation of attitude measurements.

Our objective is to talk about what few certainties there are in attitude research, to explore the great unknown masses of meaning and, on occasion, to indulge in a few polemics, as we discuss: a definition of attitudes, their meaning and interpretation, their measurements, their predictiveness with respect to behavior, and their potential contribution to advertising and marketing decisions.

It is the belief of the panel that:

1. There may be very little authentic attitude measurement in advertising and marketing, but a great deal of quasi-attitude measurement.

2. Most advertising and marketing decisions are made from survey information, from historical data, sales particularly, and from product and marketing tests, preferences, and opinions, but not attitudes.

3. Many management meetings are wasted on quasi-attitude research. No decisions but only frustration and fulmination and maybe the question, "Who wanted this consumer image study anyhow?" results.

Reprinted from George L. Baker (ed.), *Effective Marketing Coordination* (Chicago: American Marketing Association, 1961), pp. 583-594.

4. On a more positive note, consumer attitudes are potentially one of the most exciting, most valuable and most overlooked subjects for market research:

They are cause, not effect.

They look to the future; they aren't history.
They are dynamic, not dead and gone.

The limited universe of true attitude research has two causes. The first is a research predilection for numbers, methods, systems, operations and ornate formulas rather than abstract variables, complex meanings and probabilistic interpretations. The second is a management predilection for the ostensive—sales, consumer preference tests, data concretely translatable into actions and decisions.

The refrain of Management-Research conflict has been well fiddled before, often with a throbbing of research intrapunitiveness (It's my fault, chief), or among the more confident researchers, a bipunitiveness (It's both our faults).

I'd like to add a couple of notes to this old obbligato, since we're concerning ourselves here with attitude research and management decisions to the extent of equal billing.

Research and management are inevitably at other poles:

Management demands:	*Research offers:*
Simplicity (Can't you just ask "yes" or "no"?)	Complexity (The variability of response indicates . . .)
Certainty (It is or it isn't)	Probability (Maybe)
Immediacy (Now)	Futurity (It appears that by the end of the year . . .)
Concreteness (Aren't we Number 1 yet?)	Abstraction (Our exponential gain indeed appears favorable)

The problem of Management and Research is further aggravated by the daily conversations of other gentlemen in the corporation who precede research in the front office parade.

A production man walks in to present his case to the president: "Sir, the new applejack bottling automator costs have just come in. The unit will come to $400,000 installed, and that includes tearing down your new office for installation room and moving you and your staff to the east wing. However, sir, we can save one-fifth of a cent on the cost of each bottle of applejack.

"With 100 million unit sales per year, that's $200,000 cost saving the first year. Marketing research tells us that the automated process somehow imparts a noticeable flavor improvement to our applejack. The Sales Manager expects another million sale units at our normal net profit, so that's another $50,000. At annual savings and profits of $250,000 the first year, the machine will pay for itself in less than two years." And so on.

The real estate man walks in next. "Buy an extra section of apple orchards in California. Save on costs. High quality apples. Higher juice yield. More sales. More profits." Then the finance man. "Stock split. New tax loophole. Apple tree depletion. Costs. Sales. Profits."

After this sweet overture, guess who comes in next? Our researcher, just as the president is about to decide to spend $2,000,000 in the next two years to make $3,000,000 in the next two years. He's almost over the irritation of moving his office.

I don't think we have to pursue this hypothetical dialogue any further. It's safe to assume that a researcher would not say anything like this: "Sir, the cost of creating 1000 units of net consumer predisposition to buy our applejack in the newly opened Eastern region will be $500. That's using Theme X with the agency's recommended media schedule.

"With complete distribution and the competitive advantage of our price discount for the first five months . . . costs will be _____. Sales will be _____. Profits will be _____. We recommend creating this consumer attitude toward our product."

Attitude researchers may have to make a choice if they want to march in the Cost/Sales/Profits procession and speak the language of Management.

1. Reduce attitude measurement to simple consumer choices and preferences. Translate them into sales, with all the perils of fallible forecasting and inevitable sawing of that old recrimination: Research can't tell what people will do, only what they've done.

2. Improve our definition of attitudes and attitude measurement, isolate and measure relevant attitudes. Validate measurements against market occurrence and consumer behavior. Develop interpretations and recommendations that may never be precise to dollar decimals, but can offer a *direction,* if not a *degree,* for decision.

I don't think much of the first choice and would prefer to call the second an imperative, starting here with a definition of attitudes that will be amplified and illustrated by this panel.

Definition of Attitudes

The classical words from the excellent professional literature, from books like Krech and Crutchfield's,[1] define attitudes with a combination of traditionalism and dynamics. The abundance of great professional litera-

[1] Krech and Crutchfield, *Theory and Problems of Social Psychology* (New York: McGraw-Hill Book Co., Inc., 1948).

ture on attitudes and its meager transfer to marketing research, suggest a little paradox when you consider the popularity of certain applied mythologies in some motivation research, which have little of relevant substance in the professional literature. (Relevant, here, is supposed to exclude psychoanalytic literature.)

In a way, Attitude Research is a mistake in commercial appellation. A title like *Modern Behavioral Dynamics,* some esoteric language and a lore of pansexuality might have made it a sure addition to the old bag of standard nostrums and abracadabra.

Classically, attitudes are abstractions, inferences from observable behavior, verbal expressions and other symptoms of behavior in readiness. An attitude is a predisposition to behave positively, negatively or almost indifferently toward a given object, event, situation, person or group of persons.

The attitude bearer may have an aggressive attitude toward you, expressed obliquely by innuendos, directly by caustic remarks, or physically by a punch in the nose or completely repressed if you are stronger, his superior, and so on, when attitudes of deference or survival transcend an attitude of aggression.

The important words in the definition of attitudes are: predisposition, behavior, and object. Without a predisposition there can be no continuity or consistency of behavior toward a specific object, as Krech and Crutchfield so succinctly put it. Clearly, attitudes are not numbers or scale scores, a set of operations and calculations, a polynomial equation, a residual of meaning (What's left over after the visible, the touchable, the concrete have been screened out), or a timorous euphemism for motivation.

The classic crystalline definition of attitudes will shatter at high frequency criticism. It's too general, almost pat, to include all the exceptions, the circularity, the interactions, the effects of qualities of attitudes, qualities of behavior and qualities of objects, the specificity and generality of attitudes, their continual evolution and hierarchical structure.

But for all the qualifications, predispositions are vastly more helpful to attitude measurement and prediction of behavior than the barren operationism of "Attitudes are what attitude scales measure," or the a priori, "This is the attitude and I'm going to measure it." A definition of attitudes must be multiplied by its psychic components, the cognitive and the affective. If that leaves you in psychological limbo, attitudes are a summation of:

1. Knowledge and understanding of the object (the cognitive). He knows and understands this object

> Very much
> Partially
> Not at all

2. Motivations (the affective)
   He wants this object
   > At any price
   > Possibly at this price
   > Not at all
3. Perception
   He sees this object
   > Clearly, as it really is
   > Distortedly, as he thinks it is

We could go on forever describing motivation by its psychic elements; perception by its elements and each sub-element by its components. A component of motivation, by the way, is attitude, here an independent variable in its endless role-playing. Psychological definition of interacting variables can be the beginning of seeming chaos.

Attitudes must be defined in quantities as well as qualities. The quantification of attitudes should never depart from the two great statistical axioms of contemporary psychology, the continuity and variability of psychological phenomena.

Market research tends to adapt attitude data to categories of "it's there," "it's not there," "it's important," "it's not important," "it's strong," "it's weak." Variation and continuity disappear into unnatural dichotomies. For measurement, understanding and prediction, attitudes should be rendered in degrees, by a frequency distribution, rather than discrete counts in a four-fold table. Attitudes should be measured, not enumerated. As the definition of attitudes gets more involved, we add the notion that attitudes are not measured as entities in themselves, just as we don't measure people, only their heights, weights, intelligence or other specific traits.

Attitudes are measured by specific characteristics or combinations of characteristics, with measurements appropriate to variation and continuity:

1. Intensity is one of the most important characteristics, or sub-variables of attitudes. An attitude may vary from an intensity beyond the threshold of behavior, almost waiting for the specific object or any object to come along.

An aggressive attitude at the height of intensity may emerge in a variety of behaviors toward a variety of objects. Swearing at the neighbor's kids, watching cathartic TV shows of hostility and aggression, and so on.

2. Direction of an attitude is a major dimension. An attitude may emerge into behavior toward or against an object. An attitude denotes "pro-ness" or "con-ness." For it or against it. In consumer research, pro-ness is far more common in product and advertising research than con-ness. Consumers don't fling products off supermarket shelves or organize product investigating committees. No products are noxious and some are at least mediocre, and no one is much

against that. Or, a class of brands may all be exceptionally good to the point of non-differential attitudes. All brands are good and none is much better than another.

The commonly observed degrees of pro-ness in consumer research suggest measuring intensity of attitudes toward products by elimination of the negative side of an attitude scale and extending the positive side to include the most extreme statements, like "wildly enthusiastic," or "superlatively good."

3. Modifiability is one of the rarer attitude dimensions in consumer research, yet potentially one of the most significant for marketing and advertising direction.

If an atitude is intense, can it be abated, or re-directed? Can incipient attitudes be accelerated and intensified? Can indifference be converted to pro-ness? Can an attitude toward an established brand be weakened by a competitor?

Other sub-dimensions of an attitude are saliency (an attitude at the apex of a hierarchy of attitudes, so foremost that it asserts itself to open-end questions).

Attitudes may vary from simple specificity to great complexity. An attitude toward symphony attendance seems rather simple. You go or you stay home. You like symphony or you don't. But the predisposition to attend a concert is an almost enigmatic mixture of:

> Attitude toward the orchestra
> Attitude toward the conductor
> Attitude toward the programming
> Attitude toward the audience
> Attitude toward culture
> Attitude toward self concept, etc.
> Attitude toward social position
> Attitude toward family

And one of these sub-attitudes can determine symphony attendance, in varied combinations with other attitudes. A man may barely tolerate classical music, doubt the conductor's heterosexuality, yet attend symphony out of deference to, or at the intimidation of, his wife.

Attitude Measurement

If attitudes haven't been defined away by now, there should be something left for measurement and scaling. It's not our purpose to discuss the techniques of attitude measurement in detail. In fact, a well defined attitude should be amenable to reliable measurement by any one of the many techniques available. It may be that different attitude scales will vary in results when you're measuring nothing, an attitude that isn't there until it's put there by the scale. The scales may be consistent, however, when an attitude really exists.

Product attitudes can be measured by the semantic differential: You can measure a predisposition to buy a brand of bourbon with seven point scales. But, you could adapt the simpler Bogardus technique and get the same results (admit to country . . . marry a member of my family). Here's how it would go:

> *Brand of Bourbon:*
> 1. ——Never touch the stuff
> 2. —Buy it if nothing else is available
> 3. —
> 4. —
> 5. —
> 6. +Insist on it
> 7. ++Serve it to my boss

Experimental Design in Attitude Research

After the choice of attitude scales, attitude measurement grows complex at an accelerating rate as we depart from the notion of "other things being equal."

1. The hierarchy of attitude has already been mentioned. Day by day, attitudes can shift position. One attitude may be dictator in the morning, only to be deposed in the afternoon by a subordinate. Pure attitudes are the subject of measurement, but behavior is determined by net predispositions, the final resolutions of vectorial attitudes. We measure one attitude, but behavior may be influenced or resolved by a half dozen others.

He has an aggressive attitude, but he also has a deferential attitude, an attitude to survival, a conforming attitude. What do we measure? How do we determine the net attitude?

2. Attitudes are not only confounded by conflicting and allied attributes, but measurement itself adds the confusion of living-room attitudes, the desire to be compliant, to appear rational and intelligent ("Yes, I know Laos. Lovely dancing girls. Wonderful place to vacation.") general levels of suggestibility, optimism and obstinacy.

Modern multivariate experimental designs that assume suggestibility and respondentmanship in all its inevitable and fatuous forms are as important as attitude measures for some of these problems. Attitude research should proceed, not with an hour of unrelated questions, whose answers are desperately related by cross-tabulation, but with experimental controls and self-containment that add meaning and interpretation to otherwise confusing numbers. Probably the most common design, or sometimes a study without design, is product or concept testing with a sample of presumed prospects and solicitation of preference ratings and purchase intent.

Previous tests of similar products or known market failures and successes add an implicit element or experimental design and control. But without historical standards, studies can be distorted and lead to misinterpretation by: over-exposure of product concepts, including "training" in product usage, taste, adaptation, etc.; respondent confusion, indifference or indiscrimination; interviewer bias; and limited sample of product executions.

An ideal new product experimental design might look something like this, a design with an obvious disregard for costs:

	Use of Product X		Use of known test market failure in product category		Use of known test market successes	
	Prospects A_1 B_1 C_1	Non-prospects A_2 B_2 C_2	Prospects A_1 B_1 C_1	Non-prospects A_2 B_2 C_2	Prospects A_1 B_1 C_1	Non-prospects A_2 B_2 C_2
1 week usage	X X X Att. meas.					
2 weeks	X X		←	Replicated		
3 weeks	X X Att. meas.		(Group A_1 uses Product X for one week, followed by attitude measurement. Group B_1			
N weeks	X Att. meas.		uses Product X for three weeks followed by attitude measurement, etc.)			

Designs like this can be replicated with varied product qualities (different form, different ingredients, etc.) to sample and measure the great hidden variables of product execution or with consumer needs "varied" by experimental consumer "training," information or education.

An ideal experimental design should introduce controlled variation of significant variables and self-containment, for definitive answers. The significant variables of a new product study that affect attitude formation may be: time, or quantity of exposure, sample groups (independently defined prospects, non-prospects, etc.), product quality, salient product attributes, product execution, and present consumer needs.

Usage tests of completely new products without ready markets or established consumer needs are in some degree measurements of product attitudes or predispositions to buy. Test product usage and exposure to verbal concepts is essentially a market simulation to measure product attitudes and likelihood of direction and intensity under actual marketing conditions.

Overlooking some of the logical inconsistencies and practical problems of product variation, we believe the advantages of wide-ranging experimental design are mainly in the measurement of modifiability, direction and intensity of product attitudes, with controlled variation of the product, the market, the consumer and exposure time.

To reduce what may seem sheer academicism to a practicality for today, we might say that experimental design in attitude research can increase the chances of developing a product with the most likelihood of market success, or reduce the odds of forecasting success for a product failure by accommodating the multiple variables that produce consumer attitudes.

Although the professional literature defines the problems of scaling attitudes, surprisingly little space is given to what should be just as important to measurement and prediction—scaling behavior. We tend to be overly categorical about behavior. It happened or it didn't happen. She bought the product or she didn't buy it. For sensitive measurements with continuity and variation, behavior should be scaled as precisely as attitudes, by intensity, complexity and direction. Behavior, by definition, is an attitude turned inside out. Analogy alone seems to be a sufficient reason for scaling behavior, but the definitive argument comes from the need for prediction of degrees and probability of behavior. Predicting all or nothing for a continuous phenomenon is inaccurate and irrelevant.

Buying behavior is categorical, it might be argued. The customer buys or doesn't buy. But behavior of the moment is too susceptible to other causes to consider prediction of a discrete purchase sensible. Cumulative buying behavior should be scaled over time, within the universe of happenstance and peculiarity.

A predisposition should be allowed time to emerge. A single purchase is discrete, but cumulative buying behavior can be gradated:

> A brand is purchased ten times out of ten purchases in the product category (intense buying behavior)
>
> A brand is purchased five times out of ten opportunities
>
> A brand is purchased once
>
> A brand is purchased zero times

The gradation can be continued:

Pre-buying behavior

> The brand is noticed on the shelf.
> It is priced and compared.
>
> It is consumed outside of the home.
> Its advertising is read.

Verbal behavior

The brand is talked about, criticized, praised, etc.

Indifference

Awareness but no comment, no prepurchase behavior.

For each class of gradation the frequency of consumers could be counted and a frequency distribution described with continuity and variation.

The object of an attitude should be scaled as well as attitudes and behavior, particularly for intensity and complexity. A product may be scaled for price or quality or complexity and, as with attitudes and behavior, described in some kind of frequency distribution.

Prediction from Attitude Research

Prediction of behavior from attitude measurement should be the goal of everyone in research and is a purpose expressed in every psychological text. Yet the dominance of scaling and technique in the literature suggests that prediction is more a verbal desire than a practical reality.

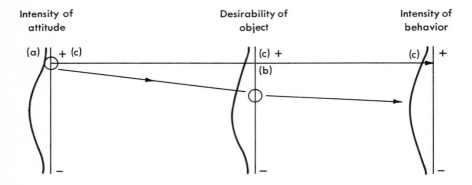

The prediction of consumer purchasing behavior from attitudes should take into account these considerations, among others:

1. Measurement of net attitude or net predisposition. Attitudes come in complexes that may be modified, inhibited or intensified by each other and by conditions of the moment. A housewife may scale 90/100 on favorable predisposition toward one product, but 100/100 toward a competitive product. A woman may scale 100/100 on predisposition to buy a mink stole, 200/100 on an attitude of conformity in a neighborhood where wearing a mink stole is deviant class behavior, or the other way around, if you like.

2. Scaling attitudes, scaling objects and scaling behavior for description in frequency distributions help set up certain axioms and models for prediction. Assuming continuity and normality of distribution, we propose these axioms of prediction:

- a. The more intense the attitude, the more likely the behavior.
- b. The more desirable the object, the more likely the behavior.
- c. The more intense the attitude (male amorousness) and the more desirable the object (beautiful blonde), the more intense the behavior.
- d. Converse axioms.

Summary

Attitudes and predispositions to action or behavior, a psychic summation of knowledge and understanding, emotions, motivations and intentions. Attitude scaling or measurement should be applied in the context of the meanings of an attitude. The concept is more important than technique.

Prediction of buying behavior from attitudes has been rather neglected despite the principles of continuity and variation and the theory and techniques of experimental design.

Attitudes, because they are latent behavior, are potentially significant measures and predictors for aiding management decisions in marketing and advertising.

33

SOME APPLICATIONS of PUPIL MEASUREMENT

HERBERT E. KRUGMAN*

In 1960, Hess and Polt[1] reported finding a relationship between pupil dilation and the interest value of visual stimuli. Since then, over seventy studies utilizing measurement of changes in pupil diameter have been conducted by Marplan personnel on problems involving the evaluation of advertising materials, packages and products. These studies have led to a growing conviction that in many areas of human behavior one might make better predictions of behavior from pupil responses than from verbal or opinion data. The purpose of this report is to provide a brief review of the concepts involved, method of measurement, measurement goals, problems of data collection, two recently completed validation studies, and some objectives for the future.

CONCEPT

Hess and Polt reported the "Increases in the size of the pupil of the eye have been found to accompany the viewing of emotionally toned or interesting visual stimuli." A technique for recording such changes was

* Reprinted from the *Journal of Marketing Research,* national quarterly publication of the American Marketing Association, Volume 1 (November, 1964), pp. 15-19.

[1] The basic design for the equipment and data handling procedures were developed by Dr. Eckhard Hess and Mr. James Polt, both of the University of Chicago, under a grant from Marplan.

Grateful appreciation is extended to the management, and particularly to Mr. Just Lunning, President of Georg Jensen, Inc., for providing the opportunity to collect and report the sterling silver data presented in this article.

developed so that the factor of adjustment to light was eliminated as a measurement problem. While the pupil is capable of changes from about 2 to 8 mm. in response to light, or an areal increase of 16 fold, the variation in pupil diameters involved in studies of interest is usually well within ±10 percent and often within ±2 percent.

The "plus or minus" quality referred to here is an operational function of the method of measurement (to be described). However, it does raise the question of what kinds of stimuli create measurable dilations and what kinds create measurable contractions.

Apparently there are two broad categories of affect-arousing or interest-producing stimuli that create dilations. The first category involves pleasant stimuli; the second involves stimuli that evoke fear, anxiety or shock. Contractions, on the other hand, are associated with stimuli that lack the power to interest or arouse the viewer. While stimuli that evoke fear, anxiety or shock are usually absent in commercial objects and symbols, the meaning of stimuli must be considered before one can infer that a dilation indicates pleasurably toned interest.[1] Airline, insurance, and drug advertising, for example, might be ruled ineligible for measurement of pupil response because a dilation might represent anxiety rather than pleasurably toned interest. In the case of such questionable stimuli one might have to consider the circumstances, inquire of the respondents, and exercise a degree of judgment before deciding that dilation represented a favorable response. While such problems are in fact quite rare in the commercial environment, their possibility must be noted.

METHOD

To conduct pupil dilation studies in the manner developed by Hess and Polt, three work stages are required.[2] First, the material to be tested is prepared in 35 mm. slide form and each stimulus slide is matched for reflected illumination with a neutral control slide containing nothing but the numbers one through five. Each study usually accommodates ten stimuli, or a total of ten pairs of stimulus and control slides.

In preparing stimulus slides it may be necessary to reduce light/dark

---

[1] Presumably we are concerned here with the parasympathetic branch of the autonomic nervous system (vegetative functions) whereby the pupil may be dilated via inhibition (the lay term might be "relaxation") of that system and a weakening of control of the sphincter muscle in the iris; one would hope to eliminate the role of the sympathetic branch (fight, flight, *etc.*) whereby the pupil may be dilated via stimulation of the system and a contraction of the dilator muscle in the iris.

[2] For further details of the method see E. H. Hess and J. M. Polt, "Pupil Size in Relation to Mental Activity During Simple Problem Solving," 143, *Science* (1964), 1190-1192.

contrasts within a picture. Modification of the stimulus to reduce light/ dark contrasts may diminish somewhat the aesthetic value of pictures, but this has not yet seemed to present a problem.

The subject looks at each slide for ten seconds while his left eye is photographed at the rate of two photographs per second. While looking at each control slide, the pupil diameter is primarily a function of the light value of the slide.[3] As the matched (for light value) stimulus slide comes on, the pupil diameter may increase (as a function of greater interest) or it may decrease (as a function of lesser interest). It is this increase or decrease which is measured for each pair of control and stimulus slides.

The films are developed and each negative is projected onto a special scoring table large enough for the pupil to be measured with a ruler. The basic measure is the percent increase or decrease in the average pupil diameter for the twenty photographs taken while viewing a stimulus slide, in comparison with the average pupil diameter for the twenty photographs taken while viewing the control slide.

MEASUREMENT GOALS

Early studies were concerned primarily with measuring the pleasurably toned interest or "appeal" of individual ads, packages or product designs.[4] To this was added before-and-after measurement in which responses to a photo of the product were measured twice. Between exposures to the photo of the product, different respondents were exposed to different information (*i.e.,* different ads, paragraphs of copy, *etc.*) to see which information was more persuasive or which added more appeal to the product (which, along with awareness, is the goal of advertising).[5]

Television commercials have also been inserted as "in-between" stimuli for before-and-after studies. In this indirect manner, animate stimuli were evaluated for the first time. Equipment has since been developed to take direct measures of response to animate stimuli, so that pre-testing of television commercials, television programs and motion pictures can be considered as possible applications of pupil research.

[3] The control slide probably has some interest in its own right or as a signal to anticipate something of interest. Contraction may involve disappointment. Rotation of stimuli is, therefore, quite important.

[4] By-product data obtainable from pupil photographs include where subjects are looking during the period of exposure. Thus, dilation or contraction can be traced approximately to parts of a stimulus. In addition, a persistently ascending or descending response can be identified, if such occurs during the period of exposure.

[5] This may circumvent the problem of an anxious response to airline, insurance, or drug advertising, *i.e.,* instead of measuring response to the ad itself the emphasis is on shifts in the non-anxious product appeal.

DATA COLLECTION

Conventional measures usually require the subject, as he views stimuli, (1) to decide whether he likes or dislikes the stimuli, (2) to decide how he will tell this, and (3) to tell it. These three operations or units of response are absent in pupil measurement. Pupil measurement therefore circumvents language and translation problems in cross-cultural opinion and attitude surveys.

Subjects who participate in pupil measurement studies look at slides with the assumption that questions will be asked when the slides have all been shown. To fulfill this expectation, and also to interrelate pupil with verbal data, an interview is always conducted. The camera is quiet though visible and few subjects comment about it. Those who ask are answered frankly.

VALIDATION

A number of studies suggested the usefulness of pupil measurement as a predictor of behavior. In the case of products, pupil response was found to be related to sales data for watches, while in the case of ads, pupil response was found to be related to (split-run) coupons returns.[6] These studies, however, were confined to pairs of stimuli. To evaluate the extent of the relationship, or to determine whether pupil response was perhaps more predictive of sales than were other measures, it became desirable to compare an array of pupil responses and an array of verbal responses (*e.g.,* ratings) from the same subjects against a similar array of sales data. Two such studies were conducted and are reported here. They involved greeting cards and sterling silver patterns.

Greeting Cards

Ten humorous greeting cards (four friendship and six birthday) were chosen by a cooperating manufacturer to represent wide ranges in sales performance. Each card was photographed with the first and third slides of the four-sided (foldover) card showing on the slide. This eliminated the surprise element of "turning the page" and, in one card, of a mechani-

---

[6] Conducted and to be published by F. J. Van Bortel of the Chicago office of Marplan.

cal pop-out device. More recently developed equipment permits a film presentation of realistic card handling and card opening.

Camera equipment was installed in a rented store in the Roosevelt Field Shopping Center (Garden City, Long Island) during January 1964, and twenty-three male and twenty-six female subjects were recruited from among passing shoppers.[7] Immediately after pupil measurement, interview data were obtained on order of recall, and then with the actual cards shown, on "card liked best" and "card liked least." The data were given to the manufacturer who then provided rank order information on sales. Results are shown in Table 1.

Table 1

COMPARISON OF SALES, PUPIL RESPONSES, AND VERBAL
RATINGS FOR GREETING CARDS

Title of card		*Pupil response*		*Verbal rank*
	Sales Rank	*Rank*	*Percent change*	
(Friendship)[a]				
Hil	1	3	− .1	2
Awkward Age	2	1	+1.7	3
Dolce Vita	3	2	+1.0	1
You're Nice	4	4	− .2	4
(Birthday)[b]				
Old as Hills	1	1	+2.9	4
Elephant	2	6	− .1	2
Swiss Cheese	3	2	+2.7	5
Cane	4	4	+1.7	1
Witch	5	3	+1.8	6
Horn	6	5	+ .4	3

[a] Rank order coefficient: Sales rank with Pupil rank = +.4
                                   Sales rank with Verbal rank = +.4
                                   Neither value is significant.
[b] Rank order coefficiant: Sales rank with Pupil rank = +.37
                                   Sales rank with Verbal rank = +.09
                                   Neither value is significant.

Although the pupil response correlated approximately +.4 for both sets of cards, because of the small number of cases neither correlation is statistically significant. The correlation of pupil response with sales rank would possibly have been higher if the testing procedure had not required removal of the pop-out spring from "Hi!" before photographing.

[7] Actually, a total of 57 subjects was tested, but records for eight had to be discarded because of incomplete or blurred photographic plates.

It may also be worth noting that, in the case of the larger group (birthday cards), the correlation between pupil response and sales was numerically larger than that between verbal rank and sales, but also that pupil response was negatively correlated with verbal rank (R = —.60).[8]

Sterling Silver Patterns

A cooperating retailer (Georg Jensen, Inc.) selected ten sterling silver patterns to represent a wide range in sales performance. These patterns are an exclusive line identified with the retailer. Each pattern was represented by a single place setting consisting of knife, fork, and spoon, and was photographed on a blue velvet background.

Camera equipment was installed in an alcove at the rear of Jensen's Fifth Avenue store during February 1964, and thirty-nine female subjects were recruited from among those shoppers entering the silverware section to examine this category of merchandise. Immediately after pupil measurement, respondents were shown the ten actual place settings and were asked to rank them in order of liking, *i.e.*, 1 high to 10 low. As it happened, the thirty-nine subjects included thirteen who reported that they were actually shopping for sterling and twenty-six who were only browsing. The data were given to the retailer who then provided retail sales data for the completed year of 1962. It must be noted, however, that these 1962 data represent a combination of sales of flatware (primarily) and serving pieces and are not available on a separate basis. However, to supplement these data, Table 2 includes some retailer comments which appear relevant.

For both the shoppers and the browsers, the correlation between sales history and pupil response was numerically larger than the correlation between sales and verbal ratings (the difference was not statistically significant, however).[9]

It is interesting to note that the pupil response and verbal rating differed sharply for "Pyramid," with the pupil response in "agreement" with sales. "Pyramid" received the highest verbal rating from both

---

[8] The agreement between sales and pupil response is relatively independent of the influence of verbal rating, as determined by the Kendall partial rank correlation coefficient. With verbal rating partialled out, the Kendall coefficient increased +.04, a negligible change. (See S. Siegel, *Nonparametric Statistics*, New York: McGraw-Hill, 1956, 223-229, for details of this test.)

[9] A more precise test of interpretations of this order might be to compare the predictive power of pupil and verbal data against the later sales behavior of the same group, *i.e.*, even though it may be practical to use pupil data on small groups to predict something about larger groups, he interpretations underlying these predictions would in most cases require special testing.

shoppers and browsers, but ranked tenth and eighth, respectively, in pupil response. Apparently the public showed better taste than their verbal ratings would indicate.

Table 2

COMPARISON OF SALES, PUPIL RESPONSES AND VERBAL RATINGS FOR SILVERWARE

Pattern[c]	*Sales*[a] *rank*	*Shoppers*[b]			*Browsers*		
		Pupil rank	*Percent change*	*Verbal rank*	*Pupil rank*	*Percent change*	*Verbal rank*
Acorn	1	5	+ .5	8	1	+1.0	2
Acanthus	2	1	+2.3	6.5	3	+ .2	4.5
Cactus	3	7	− .9	3	6	− .1	3
Cypress	4	3	+1.7	4	5	0.0	7
Continental	5	2	+2.1	2	2	+ .6	4.5
Pyramid	6	10	−2.6	1	8	−1.4	1
Blossom	7	9	−2.2	10	10	−3.7	10
Caravel	8	4	+ .8	9	4	+ .1	9
Argo	9.5	6	− .1	6.5	7	− .9	8
Nordic	9.5	8	−1.4	5	9	−2.2	6

[a] The following rank-order correlations were obtained:
Sales rank with shoppers' pupil rank = +.43
Sales rank with shoppers' verbal rank = +.14
Sales rank with browsers' pupil rank = +.60 (p = .05)
Sales rank with browsers' verbal rank = +.60 (p = .05)

[b] The shoppers' percent change in pupil dilation was more favorable than the browsers', *i.e.*, larger +% or smaller −%, for seven of the ten patterns, suggesting greater interest in silverware in general on the part of the shoppers. A one-tail test of this hypothesis shows that t = 1.84, df = 9, p = .05.

[c] Retailer's comments:
Acorn   "This gets the bulk of our advertising by far"
Acanthus
Cactus
Cypress   "Sells better out of town"
Continental "Only pattern that doubled its volume in recent years—will be advertised next year"
Pyramid   "What the public thinks is tasteful but isn't"
Blossom
Caravel   "A 'designer's design'—not expected to sell in the USA"
Argo   "Introduced in 1963 and not doing well"
Nordic   "Discontinued years ago—didn't sell"

Logically, we would expect that shoppers (who are actually planning to purchase silver) would be more "interested" in sterling than browsers. The results of the pupil response, *i.e.,* shoppers having larger percent increases and smaller percent decreases in pupil size, support this expectation. This finding, which was statistically significant, adds suggestive, though not definitive, indication of validity.

RELIABILITY

The results of the studies reported in this paper, as well as the accumulating results from a variety of similar studies, encourage the belief that pupil response is a promising new tool for study of consumer behavior.

However, because the magnitude of changes in pupil diameter are relatively small, the question of reliability of measurement becomes important. For example, in view of the relatively small range of pupil response (from approximately -2 percent to $+3$ percent in the studies reported in this paper), are the responses to these stimuli really significantly different, or are they simply within the range of random fluctuation? Furthermore, is there any real agreement from subject to subject? We shall present what data are available bearing on these two questions.

SIGNIFICANCE OF STIMULUS EFFECTS

An analysis of variance was performed at the time the pupil response data were collected for the greeting cards. This analysis was designed to evaluate the effects attributable to sex stimuli (the greeting cards), and interaction of sex and stimuli. The results are presented in Table 3.

The results presented in Table 3 may be interpreted as follows:

1. On the whole, male and female subjects do not differ significantly in their pupil responses to greeting cards.

2. The various greeting cards do evoke significantly different pupil responses.

3. Male and female subjects *do* differ significantly in their pupil responses to certain greeting cards.

In other words, the differences in pupil response, though numerically small, are real.

Table 3

ANALYSIS OF VARIANCE SUMMARY

Source of variation	Sum of squares	d.f.	Mean square	F
Sex	17,987.72	1	17,987.72	2.78
Error I	304,064.39	47	6,469.46	
Greeting cards	57,157.72	9	6,350.86	5.29[a]
Sex x cards	46,848.62	9	5,205.40	4.33[a]
Error II	508,264.86	423	1,201.57	

[a] p = .01

INTERSUBJECT CONSISTENCY

In Tables 1 and 2, pupil responses were averaged for all subjects, then ranked for comparison with sales rank data. The question remains, to what extent do pupil response rankings agree from subject to subject? To answer this question, Kendall's coefficient of concordance (W) was computed with the results shown in Table 4.

Table 4

INTERSUBJECT CONSISTENCY

Stimulus	Shoppers	W	P
Greeting cards	Total (49)	.11	<.001
Sterling silver	Shoppers (13)	.19	<.01
Sterling silver	Browsers (26)	.11	<.005

For each of the groups, the odds are better than a thousand to one that the consistency of pupil response ranking was not due simply to chance. In short, the answer to the question is that pupil response rankings do agree significantly from subject to subject. Furthermore, in the case of the greeting card study, the average pupil response rank of cards for male subjects correlated +.77 (p = .01) with the average pupil response rank of cards for female subjects. For shoppers and browsers in the sterling silver study, the correlation was +.81 (p = .01).

THE FUTURE

In general, the results of our experience with measurement of pupil response indicate that this is a sensitive and reliable technique with considerable promise for study of the interest-arousing characteristics of visual stimuli. The impact of the environment is often difficult to determine from conscious impressions verbally reported. For a variety of reasons, people may not be practiced or competent to accurately verbalize their feeling in certain areas of living. Pupil measurement seems to provide a powerful new tool for the study of these areas.

REFERENCE

1. E. H. Hess and J. M. Polt, "Pupil Size as Related to Interest Value of Visual Stimuli," 132, *Science* (1960), 349-350.

34

GRAPHOLOGY: a NEW MARKETING RESEARCH TECHNIQUE

JAMES U. McNEAL

Graphology is the study of handwriting. Its goal is usually to determine personality characteristics of a writer. Handwriting is an expressive behavior or one's style of response. Thus it possesses individuality, an expression of the person creating the writing.[1]

Marketers are increasingly turning their attention to personality to obtain a better understanding of consumer behavior [5, 14]. Consequently, graphology, which can examine personality, may be of value in marketing research. Of course, there are already a number of fine techniques available for the investigation of personality, but graphology has some significant advantages over many of these methods.

Graphology has been used by educators, law enforcement agencies, physicians, psychologists, and psychiatrists [2]. Recently, its application was extended to business [10, 12, 13]. Despite its wide usage, suspicion surrounds it. And mistrust is mainly caused by misuse.

About 20 years ago, Bell [I, p. 291] summed up the state of graphology:

Graphology, a stepsister of American psychology for so many years, has finally found a rationale for its existence in this country. Within the field of personality diagnosis it is now recognized and accepted as a projective technique. This does not suggest that graphology has managed to overcome the widespread suspicion that has surrounded it, or has reached a state of development that merits uncritical acceptance of its findings. It has, however, begun to emerge as a highly legitimate field of psychological experimentation and research.

Reprinted from *Journal of Marketing Research,* national quarterly publication of the American Marketing Association, Volume 4 (November, 1967), pp. 363-367.

[1] Although the principal uses of graphology are psychodiagnostic, its application is varied. For example, it has been used to study body build, influence of alcohol, drugs, medical treatment (see [2]).

During the past few years, the status of graphology has improved considerably. Today it might be compared with motivation research in the 1950's. One group of proponents in the various professional fields mentioned above praise and use it; another group suggests it should be used with caution, and still another group feels that it has no usefulness [2].

THEORETICAL FOUNDATIONS OF GRAPHOLOGY

The graphologist is supported by several theoretical assumptions. After much perusal of the literature, Bell [1, pp 292-3] summarized them as follows, noting that many have considerable support from experimentation and others are definitely open to criticism until they receive scientific confirmation or denial.

1. Handwriting is not simply peripheral manual movement. It is the activity of the Gestalt that is called the personality.

2. Handwriting, though bearing traces of training in penmanship, is an individual movement, resulting in graphic products with unmistakable individuality.

3. Individuality in handwriting is an expression of the personality that creates the writing.

4. Variations in personality are accompanied by variations in script.

5. Graphology is not concerned with the written symbol, itself, but with the symbol's expressive value. That is, it does not matter in what context the symbol is used or whether it is neat or untidy but rather what the symbol suggests about the writer.

6. A script is a dynamic whole that does not consist of a summation of isolated signs but of a group of different graphic criteria forming a dynamic relationship. In other words, to the graphologist a piece of correspondence, for example, is not a list of words ordered into rows, but a set of symbols related to the writer's personality.

7. The traits of handwriting when seen as a part of a Gestalt are capable of interpretation and give clues to the personality that has produced them.

8. Handwriting varies in expressiveness from one person to another and according to the writer's age and penmanship training.

9. Any handwriting trait varies in its intensity and frequency, not only in the same specimen, but in the same line. Therefore, single-trait analysis, while amenable to statistical treatment, is bound to discredit graphology. . . .

10. There is a natural limit to the variability of every single trait in a person's handwriting, except in rare, mostly psychopathic, cases.

In essence, then, handwriting traits manifest personal traits and, under the careful scrutiny of an experienced graphologist, offer information about the writer. This concept also underlies other well-known projective techniques such as finger-painting [9] and figure drawing [6].

HOW DOES THE GRAPHOLOGIST OPERATE?

A graphologist's methods differ according to his goals. Let us assume that the goal is to ascertain the writer's personality traits, since it is this ability that should most interest marketers. His activities would include the following:

1. Obtain a handwriting specimen. Ideally, this specimen should contain variety, that is, most of the letters of the alphabet, capitals, etc., and should be 50-100 words long. If possible, it should be written with pen on unlined paper. It is believed that more can be discovered about the writer if two or three specimens are obtained over a month or two, although the actual additional value of other specimens is not certain. Also, knowing the age, sex, and race of the writer will improve the quality of the findings.

2. Analyze the handwriting specimen according to a set of criteria. The actual criteria vary somewhat by the school to which the graphologist belongs. Generally, most graphologists use the criteria of Ludwig Klages with various modifications [7].

Measurement consists of two types: measuring with common tools such as a ruler or protractor those criteria objective enough to yield measurable items, e.g., slant, height, width; and determining the presence or absence of various factors, e.g., regularity, harmony, degree of connectedness.

3. Interpret the results of the handwriting analysis through comparison and summation of the measures obtained. Bases for interpretation are derived from empirical evidence of earlier investigators as they are for other projective techniques.

VALIDITY AND RELIABILITY OF GRAPHOLOGY

"There seems to be as much justification for believing that handwriting is a valid expression of personality as finger-painting, copying a Bender-Gestalt design or drawing a person would be, although more of the personality is likely to be projected into some of these techniques than others" [3, p. 212]. In a review of graphology by Fluckiger, Tripp, and Weinberg the following support for its validity as a personality diagnostic tool was indicated [2]:

1. Ratings of handwritings by a graphologist for aesthetic interest agreed ($r = .40$) with the Allport-Vernon scores for the same item. There was also some agreement for economic ($r = .29$) and theoretical interest ($r = .25$). There was not, however, agreement for political ($r = .07$) and religious interests ($r = .06$).

2. Findings from graphology on the personality variables of ascendance and psychoneurosis were statistically correlated (.60 and .80) to findings using the Allport-Ascendance-Submission Scale and the Thurston Personality Schedule, Clark Revision.

3. A graphologist's ratings for neuroticism correlated significantly (.70) with an objective measure of neuroticism derived from 17 tests, but his ratings did not agree better than chance with those of a group of psychiatrists.

4. Positive correlations (typically around .70) between handwriting characteristics and intelligence were found using a variety of subjects and intelligence criteria. Many studies have been done to test this relationship.

In a classical study by Ruth Munroe in which she analyzed the personality of one college student, substantial agreement was obtained between graphology and two other projective techniques, the Rorschach test and spontaneous drawings [8].

Though there are many other positive assessments of the validity of graphology as a psychodiagnostic tool, there are also studies that did not support its validity [2]. These contrary findings together with often low validity ratings should cause the new user of graphology to approach it carefully. Wolfson summed up her investigation of graphology and its validity: "Altogether, research findings appear to favor as psychologically most tenable and fruitful the hypothesis that handwriting expression and personality functioning are intricately related, but the problem of handwriting as a testing device persistently raises obstacles to quantification and interpretation" [15, p. 427].

Studies of reliability of graphology are scant. Between 1933 and 1960 Fluckiger, Tripp, and Weinberg [2] found only two studies of intra-judge reliability. Both studies produced low reliability coefficients. The reviewers found four studies of inter-judge reliability, but because of differing conditions under which the judgments were made, assessment was difficult. They concluded that "judges agree when the scoring categories are crude and simple or when they are defined clearly in quantitative terms" [2, p. 73].

Recently, Galbraith and Wilson [4] conducted an investigation of inter-judge reliability. They had three trained judges to examine for five personality traits handwriting samples of 100 subjects. Reliability coefficients ranged from .61 to .87 (the greater agreements being significant at the .05 level).

GRAPHOLOGY IN BUSINESS

Banking has always relied on handwriting analysis for identifying signatures as genuine or forged. Some banks in Cleveland, Denver, and San Francisco are experimenting with it as a check for credit risks [13]. George Rast [12, p. 78], a bank vice president, states:

> A credit manager has an added 'ace in the hole' if he can discern from handwriting that a credit applicant has pride, an ethical approach to problems and is orderly and well balanced. If, on the other hand, a specimen of writing showed vanity, excessive generosity or extravagance, ostentation and impulsiveness, the credit manager would do well to think twice before granting an unsecured loan.

Personnel administrators also are considering graphology. A large manufacturer, for example, has been conducting a systematic study of graphology in personnel selection for attempting to identify creative marketing talent [13]. It is quite pleased with its efforts which showed graphological evaluations to be related to actual performance and job success.

In another instance the handwritings of employees of 18 companies were examined for dishonesty [1]. Fourteen employees were labeled by the graphologist as dishonest; this figure was confirmed by the employers. Moreover, an honest person was never classified as dishonest.

Frederick reports that graphology is used by European personnel management [3]. Here the graphologists are trying to identify effective leaders and potential supervisors. Finally, through analysis of handwriting specimens, as well as the writing paper and word usage, Plog developed an index of literacy for letters received by the editors of the *Boston Herald* [10.]

Graphology for Marketers

It was shown earlier that graphology is a projective technique for revealing personality elements. It also may be a valuable research tool to those marketers who view personality as a variable of consumer behavior. In some cases the marketer may find graphology more useful than another projective technique; in many cases it will be used as a supplement to exploratory research.

The application of handwriting analysis to marketing research, like most projective tools, is limited only by the marketer's imagination and skill. The suggestions made are only to create an awareness of the possibilities.

Graphology is useful for personality description whenever an adequate handwriting specimen is available. Thus, a marketer may discover personality characteristics, for example, for the following groups.

Users and applicants for credit.   For retail businesses such as department stores and service stations that rely on credit for much of their business, graphoanalysis of credit application forms should be valuable. It might be most productive to first graphoanalyze the applications of people who already have favorable credit ratings as well as those who have been rejected. The study should produce some personality-based guidelines for accepting or rejecting credit applications. These guidelines would then form the structure for an ongoing graphoanalytical credit acceptance program. By looking for personality characteristics believed to be associated with credit risk, losses may be reduced.

Purchasers of durable and semi-durable goods.   Most durable goods manufacturers require the purchaser to complete and return a warranty card. Typically, the information on these cards is used for marketing research purposes. Assuming they contain an adequate amount of handwriting, which can be required, graphoanalysis of the cards may reveal additional valuable data about the people buying a given product. The data may reveal a typical personality type attracted to the product or the stores from which the item is purchased.[2]

Durable goods are often produced with a personality type in mind. Graphoanalysis of the warranty cards can provide a check on such product strategy. The resulting data also may aid in the refinement of advertising strategy since advertisements are often developed for specific personality types.

Respondents to contests.   Each year millions of consumers complete contest entry blanks "in 25 words or less." Examination of the resulting handwriting specimens might indicate personality characteristics of people who (a) consume the sponsors' products, (b) like contests, or (c) respond to the particular advertising medium in which the contest appeared. Additional research probably would be necessary to find the degree of overlap among these three kinds of people.

Writers of letters with complaints, compliments or requests for information.   Marketers frequently receive letters from irate as well as satisfied consumers. Graphoanalysis of these letters might show the type

[2] Store-related information can be returned to the various retailers so they may use it in sharpening their marketing strategies.

of personality that is satisfied or dissatisfied with the product. Too, it may give an indication of the kind of person that generally writes complaint letters.

Requests for information are also a useful source of market data. The handwriting in these requests should give some clues to the personality types showing an interest in a marketer's product offering.

Respondents of any questionnaire. The typical marketing research questionnaire that asks the respondent to answer a series of questions (usually via mail) can offer much additional information if graphology is used. Not only does the marketer receive the answers he sought, but also much data about the person completing the questionnaire. For example, the diaries required of consumer panelists should contain much information about the panel if handwriting analysis is applied.

Writers of merchandise orders. Graphoanalysis of completed order blanks for merchandise may reveal valuable data about the personality of those using a catalog and those who prefer certain products offered in the catalog. A manufacturer or wholesaler could also get some idea of the personality make-up of retailers who do business with him by examining the written orders from them.

Though unrelated to consumer research, it seems appropriate to mention that a check on the personality of one's salesmen is possible by periodic graphoanalysis of order forms they complete or other written materials, such as itineraries. If a periodic examination is made of a salesman's handwriting, it may be possible to note serious changes in his personality that might hamper his effectiveness.

Miscellaneous written materials. Finally, it may be possible to obtain personality information about persons, for example, who sign in at motels and hotels and who buy insurance at air terminals. The applications usually required for life and casualty insurance purchases might furnish important additional insurance guidelines if graphoanalysis is applied.

WHY USE GRAPHOLOGY?

Graphology may be used instead of another projective technique to supplement other projective techniques or other standard marketing research methods. In any case, graphology offers a number of advantages.

Handwriting specimens are usually available or easily obtained. Consequently, when personality data are required about a group of consumers, the planning and execution of a long research project may be unnecessary. A simple graphoanalysis of existing handwriting (such as warranty cards) may provide the needed information. Obviously, much money and time are saved.

Handwriting specimens are often by-products of other market research instruments. Yet, much information about respondents can be found in these specimens, and additional valuable information is learned about consumers at minor costs. (The only costs would be for analysis and interpretation.) This advantage of graphoanalysis should encourage the marketing researcher to seek more written responses instead of oral responses.

Handwriting is almost impervious to fraud. Falsification is common among many personality inventories and projective techniques, but handwriting is difficult to distort.

A handwriting specimen can be obtained without respondent knowledge of its purpose. Thus it discourages faking and eliminates test jitters that often occur among respondents, and it minimizes respondent disinterest and impatience with abstract tests such as the Rorschach or Thematic Apperception Test.

Finally, handwriting specimens are available for reference. They can be reexamined for additional data or compared with later specimens.

Problems in Graphology

A major problem in using graphology for marketing research is obtaining acceptance. Even open-minded researchers may feel a sense of embarrassment about a technique equated with such unscientific practices as palmistry and astrology. A similar feeling, however, probably was experienced by the first marketing researchers who attempted to use TAT pictures. Even if researchers find graphology useful, they may have difficulty selling its results to management.

Another serious problem is the reliability and validity of graphology; there is little substantial evidence about these factors. Thus, the researcher intending to include graphology in his tool kit must do so cautiously and open-mindedly. He should not be frightened because the technique is not perfect. His application of it can enhance its quality. Had earlier market researchers ignored other projective techniques because of warnings of validity and reliability (see, for example, [11]), market research would not be so advanced.

There are some inherent technical problems in using graphology in market research. Obtaining adequate handwriting samples will require special attention. There is a tendency to make warranty cards and research questionnaires, for example, more simple (often to the point that they require only checkmarks). Here graphology would be useless. So, the market researcher must decide if the data generated by graphoanalysis merits written warranty cards and questionnaires.

Further, there is the question of who actually did the writing on, for example, the warranty cards. Was it the purchaser, another member of the family, or the salesman who sold the goods?

Also, people tend to print or type responses, particularly if such instructions are given. If graphology is to be used, the instructions must be changed to require a handwriting sample and perhaps, even a signature to validate the handwriting.

Assuming a firm does wish to use graphology as a market research technique, there is still the problem present when the use of any new projective technique is attempted, that is, finding personnel who can properly use it. Few marketing researchers will probably be skilled in graphoanalysis. Certified Graphoanalysts and Master Graphoanalysts can be found by contacting the International Graphoanalysis Society (Chicago). Also, many psychologists at universities are qualified to give assistance with graphoanalysis. Finally, there are graphoanalysts already in medicine, law enforcement, banking, etc., that might welcome the chance to practice with marketing problems.

REFERENCES

1. John E. Bell, *Projective Techniques,* New York: Longmans, Green & Company, Inc., 1948, Chapter 14.
2. Fritz A. Fluckiger, Clarence A. Tripp, and George H. Weinberg, "A Review of Experimental Research in Graphology, 1933-1960," *Perceptual and Motor Skills,* 12 (January 1961), 67-90.
3. Calvin J. Frederick, "Some Phenomena Affecting Handwriting Analysis," *Perceptual and Motor Skills,* 20 (February 1965), 211-8.
4. Dorothy Galbraith and Warner Wilson, "Reliability of the Graphoanalytic Approach to Handwriting Analysis," *Perceptual and Motor Skills,* 19 (September 1964), 615-8.
5. Morris J. Gottlieb, "Segmentation by Personality Types," in James U. McNeal ed., *Dimensions of Consumer Behavior,* New York: Appleton-Century-Crofts, 1965, 83-92.
6. Sidney Levy, "Figure Drawing as a Projective Test," in Lawrence E. Abt and Leopold Bellak eds., *Projective Techniques,* New York: Grove Press, Inc., 1950, 257-97.
7. T. Stein Lewinson, "An Introduction to the Graphology of Ludwig Klages," *Character and Personality,* 6 (June 1938), 163-76.
8. Ruth L. Monroe, "Three Diagnostic Methods Applied to Sally," *Journal of Abnormal and Social Psychology,* 40 (April 1945), 215-27.
9. Peter J. Napoli, "Finger-Painting and Personality Diagnosis," *Genetic Psychology Monographs,* 34 (July 1946), 133-230.
10. Stanley C. Plog, "A Literacy Index for the Mailbag," *Journal of Applied Psychology,* 50 (February 1966), 86-91.
11. Alfred Politz, "Motivation Research from a Research Viewpoint," *The Public Opinion Quarterly,* 20 (Winter 1956-1957), 663-73.

12. George H. Rast, "Value of Handwriting Analysis in Bank Work," *Burroughs Clearing House,* 50 (March 1966), 40-41 ff.

13. Ulrich Sonnemann and John P. Kernan, "Handwriting Analysis—A Valid Selection Tool?" *Personnel,* 39 (November-December 1962), 8-14.

14. W. T. Tucker and John J. Painter, "Personality and Product Use," in James U. McNeal ed., *Dimensions of Consumer Behavior,* New York: Appleton-Century-Crofts, 1965, 75-82.

15. Rose Wolfson, "Graphology," in Harold H. and Gladys L. Anderson eds., *An Introduction to Projective Techniques,* Englewood Cliffs, N. J.: Prentice-Hall, Inc., 1951, 416-56.

35

THE USE of STRUCTURED TECHNIQUES in MOTIVATION RESEARCH

RALPH L. WESTFALL, HARPER W. BOYD, JR., and DONALD T. CAMPBELL

THE PROBLEM

During the past several years individuals engaged in marketing research have borrowed heavily from the clinical psychologist's battery of "projective-test" and "depth interview" techniques to measure consumer motives.[1]

But some researchers have raised serious objections to use of these "new" techniques.[2] They point out that these techniques were developed to obtain intensive information from a single individual over a long period of time and that it is difficult and perhaps impossible to get such data from typical consumers on the basis of doorstep interviews.

The strain on respondent cooperation is great, biasing the sample toward the idle, articulate, and garrulous. The need for interviewers trained or even willing to conduct such research provides a bias toward large urban centers where such interviewers are available. These difficulties often lead to samples that are small (ten to fifty respondents) and also

Reprinted from the *Journal of Marketing,* national quarterly publication of the American Marketing Association, Volume 22 (October, 1957), pp. 134-139.

[1] For a classification of methods see Donald T. Campbell, "The Indirect Assessment of Social Attitudes," *Psychological Bulletin,* XLXII (January, 1950), pp. 15-38, and "A Typology of Tests, Projective and Otherwise," *Journal of Consulting Psychology,* XXI (June, 1957).

[2] See N. D. Rothwell, "Motivation Research Revised," *The Journal of Marketing,* XX (October, 1955), pp. 150-154. Also see "Politz Tags Motivation Research 'Fake,' 'Hah!,' Hahs Dichter Group," *Advertising Age* (September 19, 1955), p. 3.

incredibly informal. The interviews cannot easily be quantified because of small samples and because "answers" vary greatly from respondent to respondent. Advocates of the new techniques reply that their methods turn up ideas which can be obtained in no other way. Is this really true?

Borrowing from Psychology

In borrowing from the psychological clinic, an assemblage of features has been adopted *en toto,* without much regard for their appropriateness to the particular marketing research situation. These features include:

1. The aim of diagnosing consumer motives rather than past consumer actions.

2. The aim of diagnosing consumer motives of which the consumer himself is unaware.

3. The aim of diagnosing consumer motives, attitudes, intentions without the consumer being aware that this is being done.

4. The aim of assessing the respondent's "product image," "image of the typical user," "phenomenological field," "idiosyncratic perspective," etc.

5. The introduction of biological and socially unacceptable motivational considerations such as sex, toilet-training, and nursing as motivational residues affecting consumer choice. Greater attention to selfishness, greed, envy, prestige, sadism, love of violence, etc.

6. The employment of free-response, open-ended, unstructured interviews.

7. The shift of interviewing effort so that more time is spent on fewer respondents.

8. The shift of balance between preparation and analysis effort, so that more time is spent on analyzing responses and less on preparing questions.

9. The reduction of the proportion of interviewing and analysis effort which can be delegated to conscientious but uninsightful (uninspired, unindoctrinated) clerical workers.

10. The virtual abandonment of the effort to specify the frequency of given actions, motives, and attitudes in the consumer population, and the substitution of the more modest goal of learning about some of the motives that at least occasionally occur.

The authors believe that the first five innovations may be adopted without the second five: that the "what question" issue is separable from "how asked."

In the shift to "motivation research" the traditional structured survey methods were discarded without any serious attempt to modify them to ask the new questions. It is the purpose of this article to show that some of the insights on human beings turned up by the newer techniques might also be found through a more imaginative application of the older structured techniques which lend themselves better to controlled samples and to the type of interviewers and data analysts readily available. At the very least, the authors feel that the more traditional methods can be used to extend and better confirm the findings obtained by the newer techniques.

INSTANT-COFFEE STUDY

One of the classics in motivation research is the study of Mason Haire.[3] He reported that direct questions on why people did not use instant coffee indicated a dislike of the flavor. Haire then developed a Thematic-Apperception-Test type of approach to the problem. Two groups of fifty people each were shown shopping lists. One group was shown a shopping list which included instant coffee on it; the other group was shown the same list except that drip-ground coffee replaced instant coffee. Respondents were asked to describe the housewife who made up the shopping list. From a comparison of the answers, Haire drew conclusions about what people thought of housewives using instant coffee.

Although Haire does not describe the field work and sampling methods used, it would appear that the usual difficulties of motivation research were encountered. It would be difficult to get cooperation from a controlled sample; field work would have to be handled by a specially trained force, would be slow and costly; and tabulation and analysis would be laborious.

In the present study, data on what people think of housewives who use instant coffee were secured through a structured, more direct type of questioning. The comparison is not precise since Haire's study was made prior to April, 1950, apparently in the Bay Area of California, while the present study was made in Chicago in February, 1955. Nevertheless, the results are surprisingly similar and suggest that further efforts along the line of using more of the structured type of approach might be productive.

Study Design

The sample in the present study was made up of housewives (N = 199) selected by probability methods from selected Census tracts in Chicago. The questionnaire consisted essentially of three questions:

[3] Mason Haire, "Projective Techniques in Marketing Research," *The Journal of Marketing,* 14 (April, 1950), pp. 649-656.

(1) "Have you prepared coffee in the last week?" (If yes):

(2) "The last time you prepared coffee, which method did you use—percolator, drip method, vacuum method, instant coffee, or some other method?"

(3) "Now I would like to read off a list of different types of people. After each one, will you tell me whether you think that person prepares coffee by one of the regular methods or by using instant coffee?" (The interviewer then read off such types of individuals as the best cook you know, the poorest cook you know, a thrifty housewife, a housewife who is not thrifty, a lazy housewife, a housewife with lots of energy, an elderly single woman, a widow living on a small pension, the wife of a business executive, and a married woman who has a job outside the home. A total of nineteen "types" were read to respondents.)

These are questions that could be handled by the typical field interviewer under conditions permitting normal sampling procedures and routine tabulation.

Results

Haire's first study showed that housewives thought women who used instant coffee were lazy, poor planners of purchases, spendthrifts, and poor wives.[4] Data from the present study tend to support Haire's findings; that is, respondents associate instant coffee with the same types of persons to the degree indicated below:

Lazy housewife	86%
Housewife who dislikes to cook	75%
Woman who likes to sleep late	67%
Poor cook	51%

On one point findings from the present study do not agree with Haire. He found that women believed thrifty housewives would not be likely to use instant coffee. In the present study, thrifty housewives as instant coffee users received no more "votes" than did spendthrifts (30 per cent and 31 per cent). Respondents, however, were more in doubt about the housewife who was not thrifty—32 per cent reported "don't know" as compared to 10 per cent for the thrifty. In a further question, respondents were asked whether they thought instant coffee was cheaper than coffee made by the vacuum method. Forty-four per cent thought instant coffee was cheaper, and only 17 per cent thought vacuum-method

---

[4] Haire, same reference as footnote 3, p. 652.

coffee cheaper. Thirty-nine per cent thought there was no difference or didn't know. If this same opinion was held in Haire's universe, it would be hard to interpret his findings as supporting his "spend-thrift" conclusion.

In Haire's second study, he compared the opinions of women who buy instant coffee (as determined by a pantry check) with the opinions of those who do not buy instant coffee. His results were as shown in Table 1.

TABLE 1[5]

Opinions of Women Who Buy Nescafe Versus the Opinions
of Those Who Do Not Buy Nescafe

| | INSTANT COFFEE | |
	In house	*Not in house*
Woman who buys Nescafe is seen as:	(N = 32)	(N = 18)
Economical	78%	28%
Not economical	0	11
Cannot cook or does not like to	16	55
Plans balanced meals	29	11
Good housewife, plans well, cares about family	29	0
Poor housewife, does not plan well, does not care about family	16	39
Lazy	19	39

In the present study respondents were separated into users (N = 19) and non-users (N = 158) of instant coffee on the basis of whether or not they reported using instant coffee the last time they made coffee. The findings agree with those given by Haire so far as economy is concerned. Fifty-eight per cent of the housewives who use instant coffee thought a thrifty housewife would use this type of coffee; only 27 per cent of the non-users thought so. Haire's figures were 70 per cent and 28 per cent. The relative values are reversed in both studies for spendthrift housewives.

Haire found a large difference between users and non-users of instant coffee on the question of the poor cook. Only 16 per cent of the users associated instant coffee with a poor cook, but 55 per cent of the non-users did. In the present study, comparable percentages were 42 per cent and 52 per cent for the poor cook, and 95 per cent and 83 per cent for the woman who dislikes to cook. The latter data show less difference between the two groups than do Haire's.

Results relative to the housewife who is a good planner and who is

5 Haire, same reference as footnote 3, p. 655.

interested in her family are similar in the two studies. On the question of whether or not women thought instant coffee users are lazy, Haire found a difference of opinion between the two groups (19 per cent and 39 per cent); but in the present study practically no difference showed up (80 per cent to 86 per cent).

Hot-Cereal Study

The authors have used approaches similar to the one described above on several other occasions. Unfortunately data from "identical" studies using the newer motivation research techniques are not available and, thus, no comparison can be made as was done with Haire. It is thought, however, that a brief report of one such study will be of some value since it might suggest additional ways of using a structured approach to certain motivational research problems.

One part of a hot-cereal study was designed to obtain a stereotype of the person who eats hot cereal. The following question was asked of over 1,200 respondents:

"Now we'd like to find out what kind of people you think eat hot cereal the most. For each of the following groups indicate whether you think they eat a lot of hot cereal, a little hot cereal, or practically no hot cereal." (Interviewers then read off such types of persons as city people, farmers, 'teen-age girls, 'teen-age boys, men, women, children, doctors, lawyers, airplane pilots, and elderly people.)

Most respondents had a stereotype of the person who eats hot cereal. Definite patterns developed. Thus, about two-thirds of the respondents believed that children, farmers, athletes, poor people, and elderly people eat a lot of hot cereal. Over half thought that movie stars ate practically none, and one-third thought the same of rich people and 'teen-age girls. Doctors, lawyers, and airplane pilots are the ones for whom the most "don't knows" were given. Males are thought to eat more hot cereal than females. It is considered to be good for those doing physical work. Significant regional differences were found, with the South having the most favorable attitude (each type of person is thought to eat more) and the Northeast being the least favorable. There was little difference by city size, but income did appear to influence results.

Note that this question, although structured, tapped the respondent's "phenomenological field" or "view of the world." The respondent's product image and image of the typical user has been delineated. Note also the degree of indirection or disguise involved: the respondent has not been asked to report on his own attitudes and reasons for cereal buying—rather he has been asked to report on the nature of the external world as he sees it. These invaluable features of the typical projective technique are thus, in part at least, available in this structured format which is appropriate for use with large-scale opinion sampling.

Information and Misinformation Tests

The questions about hot-cereal usage in various groups were in a sense *factual;* that is, they asked the respondents about matters for which "right" answers potentially existed. If unconscious attitudes are of interest, they can be diagnosed by the direction of the wrong answers as well as by the selectivity of the right answers in a person's responses to a bona fide information test. The reasoning here is that these unconscious attitudes are very often "projected" into the biases in what a person regards as facts.[6] In the hot cereal study, several questions of this more explicitly informational nature were employed. The general order was as follows:

"How much do you think it costs for the hot cereal alone in an average bowl of cereal such as you'd serve for breakfast?"

¼¢ or less, ½¢, ¾¢, 1¢, 2¢, 3¢, 4¢, 5¢, 6¢ plus—Don't Know

"Which of the following cereals do you think costs more per serving than a hot cereal and which costs less?"

"Do Corn Flakes cost more or less than hot cereal?"

"Do Wheaties cost more or less than hot cereal?"

"Do Cheerios cost more or less than hot cereal?"

Questions similar to the last one above were asked on the vitamin quality, the protein content, and the fattening aspects of hot cereal versus selected brands of cold cereal. As a result of these questions, certain interesting and useful findings were obtained. For example, non-hot cereal users (younger age groups living in the larger cities) exaggerated the costs for an "average" bowl of hot cereal. With respect to perceived vitamin content, differences were found between users, regions, and city-size groups. Thus, the larger the city size, the better was the vitamin rating for dry cereals. These structured questions and others focused more directly on motives were judged in this case to have provided evidence on the consumer product and user image comparable to, but more precise than, what would have been provided by more "typical" research procedures.

[6] See Donald T. Campbell, "The Indirect Assessment of Social Attitudes," same reference as footnote 1. Also see Kenneth R. Hammond, "Measuring Attitudes by Error-Choice," *Jounral of Abnormal and Social Psychology,* XLIII (January, 1948), pp. 38-47.

CONCLUSIONS

In recent years some individuals engaged in marketing research have borrowed heavily from the clinical psychologist in an effort to find techniques to measure consumer motives. Other researchers have viewed this "borrowing" with much concern and have been quick to point out the limitations of the new techniques. In the shift to motivation research, the traditional structured type of questionnaire was quickly discarded without any real attempt made to determine whether it was worthy of modification. It is our belief that the more traditional structured methods still can be of considerable value in attempting to gain data on consumer motives.

At this point the reader may well point out that it is one thing to build a tightly structured approach when findings are already available (as in the Haire study), and quite another literally to start from scratch and get the same results. Others might contend that the results reported in this article only prove what they have long argued—namely, that it is *not* necessary to employ large samples to obtain correct results with the newer techniques.

Both criticisms are valid, but the authors would contend that it is possible to obtain useful motivational data using nondisguised-structured techniques, which have certain operational advantages over disguised-nonstructured techniques. It is not always necessary to have "findings" from a Haire type study available on which to construct a more structured approach. For example, in the hot-cereal study, a structured-question approach revealed that most respondents had a stereotype of the person who eats such a product. Definite patterns were in evidence. Thus, the respondent's classification of the world of hot-cereal eaters was to some extent revealed. Further, the respondent's image of the product and its typical user was brought into focus. In addition, information and misinformation tests were used to get at certain unconscious attitudes such as those pertaining to vitamin quality and protein content in hot versus cold cereals.

Any study, regardless of the techniques employed, reflects the use of the researcher's hypotheses and imagination. One could even argue that the more traditional methods frequently offer an easier way to testing hypotheses. In any event, it is not our intent to present these findings on an "either-or" basis. Certainly, there are times (perhaps even a majority of times) when the research can be accomplished only through a use of the newer techniques. What the authors *do* contend is that there are opportunities to make effective use of the traditional techniques in motivation research. At the very least, such techniques frequently offer an opportunity to validate the small study results by using a larger and better controlled sample.

V

CONCLUSIONS

36

BUYING BEHAVIOR: SOME RESEARCH FINDINGS

FREDERICK E. MAY

This article reviews, collates, and summarizes results of empirical research on buying behavior of household consumers. Some related information of the buying behavior of farmers and doctors is also included. The research objectives are to discover specific buying activities which have been investigated in a competent, professional manner and adequately described; to discover explanations of buying behavior which have been hypothesized and empirically tested; and to establish more general empirical propositions supported by a variety of pieces of evidence from a number of studies. The review should also lead to a definition of problem areas in the study of buying behavior where additional research would be desirable both from the standpoint of the marketer and other social scientists.

METHODS AND CRITERIA

The basic data of this research are abstracts of investigations containing their objectives, methodology, findings, and relationship to other work in

Reprinted from *The Journal of Business,* Volume 38 (October, 1965), pp. 379-396, by permission of the University of Chicago Press. Copyright 1965 by the University of Chicago.

This study was initially discussed during the 1963 Faculty Research Workshop in Marketing, sponsored by the Ford Foundation and held at the University of Chicago. Particularly helpful was discussion with Professors John E. Jeuck, Irving Schweiger, and Gary Steiner of the University of Chicago, and with Professors William Wells, Rutgers University, and Kurt Kihlstedt, University of Lund, Sweden. The University of Missouri financed several assistants who helped in the search for the relevant literature.

the same area. A reasonably systematic search of the apparently relevant literature was undertaken. Sources that we searched included selected professional journals in marketing, business, and the social sciences, and abstracts of articles and books in marketing, psychology, sociology, and economics.

To be included a study had to be a report of an empirical investigation. The selected reports generally meet certain criteria as acceptable evidence of research quality. Most are investigations by professional researchers and were published in professional journals. They have been subjected to critical review by qualified specialists. Reports of doctoral dissertations are also assumed to have had some critical review. To be selected, reports of investigations generally had to include a detailed description of their methodology and research design, and the findings of the study had to be supported by a presentation and analysis of the data collected. Thus, limitations of the results are either implicitly or explicitly stated by the researcher.

RESULTS

Some general observations are in order about the degree of documentation behind the propositions and their generality. At the lowest level of generality are hypotheses about some specific aspects of buying behavior which are supported by one or two pieces of evidence. The statements of these propositions are generally qualified, although by no means all the qualifications surrounding them are given. They are preceded or followed by reference to the investigators, and the appropriate publications are cited in the bibliography. Unfortunately, very few investigations replicate tests of hypotheses about specific aspects of buying behavior, so that at best two or three references can be cited for any one proposition. In general, the degree of confidence with which these individual hypotheses can be accepted is quite low and depends to some extent on the research design employed to test them.

At a middle level of generality between specific propositions and the general conclusion that some people make buying decisions are inferences drawn from a variety of studies on a fairly general aspect of buying behavior. The general conclusion that people make buying decisions is in some degree supported by all of the reviewed studies and can, therefore, be held with a high degree of confidence.

The research method employed most often in past investigations has been the questionnaire, either single-survey or panel studies. The method of observation, and particularly the experimental research design, has been employed only too rarely. Recent research on the validity of consumer reports reveals important inaccuracies in surveys and panel diaries which may be a more serious problem than sampling errors. Sudman [*39*] summarizes the literature on over- and underreporting in surveys as follows:

Neter and Waksberg measured response errors in a survey of homeowners' expenditures for alterations and repairs and found that respondents overstated expensive repairs while forgetting minor ones. Lansing, Ginsburg and Braaten in a study of consumer saving behavior observed substantial understatements of amounts in respondents' savings accounts. In earlier studies, Metz measured the accuracy of response in a study of milk consumption, while Drayton compared a survey on cheese consumption to a wholesale audit. In both cases, substantial recall overstatements of consumption were observed. A U.S. Department of Agriculture study compared the results of four different recall methods to purchase results obtained from a consumer panel. Four products were studied—butter, oleomargarine, fresh oranges, and frozen orange concentrate. Again for all four recall methods on all four products, serious overstatements of consumption appeared.

In consumer panels, too, recording errors are very important. Previous literature is sparse. Soon after World War II, researchers [24, 36] found that a weekly diary gave more complete results than a monthly one for most grocery products [39, p. 14].

Sudman [*39*] finds that diary records of consumer panels are "less accurate for products in the rear and in the middle of the diary" [*39*, p. 18]. Accuracy declines as the complexity of the entry increases. Complexity of entry is related by Sudman to the possibility of deliberate omission. He further finds that "infrequently purchased products and those not purchased by the housewife are less accurately recorded. The more prominently mentioned products are more accurately recorded as are products at the top of a page" (p. 18).

Since the validity of studies involving verbal rather than observed activities is sometimes questionable, it is important to note that most of the research studies examined in this review are based on reports by the buyer or potential buyer, rather than on observation. Some of the findings may conflict with what marketing managers believe to be the effects of their activities on buyers. Where findings are based on verbally reported behavior rather than on observed behavior, I take the precaution of prefacing it with "respondents' report" or "buyers' say." Nevertheless, it is a report from the view point of the customer, as he perceives his own actions and preferences and influences upon him. If he underreports the influence of marketing activities or overreports his purchases of certain products, it is also of some interest to marketers.

I. PRODUCT

A. Brand Choice

A phenomenon that a number of investigators designate as brand loyalty —and each defines it differently—can be inferred from several studies of buying behavior.

1. Proportion of Purchases in a Single Brand

One early investigator analyzed family diaries of a consumer panel for purchases in seven food and household-product classes—toilet soap, canned peas, frozen orange juice concentrate, scouring cleanser, regular coffee, margarine, and headache tablets [10]. He found that higher numbers of families reported percentages of total purchases in a single brand than he had expected on the basis of his assumptions about buyer opportunity to make random brand choices among apparently available brands in the average store. Taking coffee as an example he apparently computed the probability of randomly selecting the same brand of coffee at least five times out of ten from eight available brands. Cunningham then concludes for his sample size of 244 families, that "the random data would predict that only about 3 per cent of the families would be above 50 per cent brand loyal, but the observed data show that about half of the families purchased their favorite brand more than 50 per cent of the time" [10, p. 123].

    Retail availability.   Evidence that Cunningham's brand-loyalty measure is likely to be confounded with retail availability is presented by Farley [14]. He analyzes panel diary data for seventeen product classes of food and household items and finds high and significant simple correlations between two measures of brand loyalty and the number of brands available in the market, the market share of the leading brand, and the dispersion of brands in the market.

    Since Farley's measures—the average number of brands bought during a year and the percentage of families switching favorite brands during the period—are strongly correlated with indexes of retail availability, such brand-loyalty measures cannot be used alone to indicate the existence of the phenomenon or the degree of brand loyalty.

2. Sequences of Brand Choices

Several investigators analyze sequences or runs of individual brand choices and compare them to models of random buying behavior. Tucker [41] reports a controlled experiment in which forty-two housewives were ob-

served. The participants made twelve successive choices among four identical bread loaves presented on a tray. The bread was distinguished only
by a neutral letter designation, and the loaf positions on the tray were
controlled. The loaves were taken from a single oven on the morning of
delivery to the participants' homes. Throughout the experiment a significantly larger number of women selected the same brand in three consecutive trials than can be expected by chance at the .05 level of significance.

Strength of loyalty.   After a participant had selected the same
brand three times in succession Tucker introduced a second experimental
variable by adding a new penny to the bread most seldom selected in all
previous trials. If the subject did not switch to the brand with the penny
premium on the next trial, an additional penny was added until a switch
to the brand with the money premium occurred. "Six of the brand-loyal
women switched to the premium brand for premiums varying from 2-7
cents. The average value of these accepted premiums was $3\frac{1}{2}$ cents. Eight
women were still selecting their favorite brand when the experiment
ended. Premiums that they refused on the last opportunity varied from
1 to 7 cents. Their average was $3\frac{1}{2}$ cents" [*41*, p. 35].

The experiment is so far the best single piece of evidence from which
one can infer some deliberate buyer behavior with respect to brand, since
brand designation was the major experimental variable, and other factors
that might influence choice were apparently reasonably well controlled.

The results of the experiment suggest the following tentative generalizations to Tucker: "1. Some consumers will become brand loyal even
when there is no discriminable difference between brands other than the
brand itself. 2. The brand loyalty established under such conditions is not
trivial although it may be based on what are apparently trivial and superficial differences" [*41*, p. 35].

3. Loyalty as a Dimension

Tucker [*41*] and Cunningham [*10*] do not resolve the problem of establishing a criterion value for what they call brand loyalty. For example,
Tucker arbitrarily defines brand loyalty as three successive choices of the
same brand in his experiment. Cunningham never clearly specifies what
percentage of purchases going to a single brand indicates brand loyalty.
In order to avoid the problem of deciding on a criterion value one can
define it as a dimension. Two reviewed investigations operationally define
the phenomenon as the family's repeat-purchase probability of a particular brand which takes on values between zero and 1 [*15, 20*].

4. Repeat-Purchase Probabilities

Analysis of family diary data of five sequential purchases of frozen orange-
juice brands show that the proportion of families reporting purchase of a

particular brand on the fifth trial varies with the number and time sequence of previous purchases of the brand [20]. That is, on the fifth trial, the greater the number of previous purchases of the particular brand in the four previous trials, the greater the repurchase probability, and the more recent the previous purchase prior to the fifth trial, the greater the repurchase probability.

Run length.   The last finding is challenged by Frank [15], who analyzed coffee purchases in diary data. He too finds that the proportion of families purchasing a particular brand of coffee at first appears to increase as the number of previous consecutive purchases of the brand increases. If family purchase reports are observed over a longer period, however, then the repurchase probability seems to become constant.

The somewhat contradictory results obtained by Kuehn and Frank may be due to confounding of run length during a given time period with the repeat-purchase measure of brand loyalty.

5. Brand Preferences

In further support of the existence of the brand-loyalty phenomenon are studies that report expressed brand preferences. Interviewed in consumer surveys, most new car buyers and a substantial proportion of major household-appliance buyers say they made their choice of brand before shopping [1, 28]. In addition, many new car buyers report that they confined their shopping only to the dealers of the make originally preferred [1].

6. Brand Loyalty as a Phenomenon

It may be concluded that there is some evidence that a general phenomenon called brand loyalty in buying behavior exists for some buyers some of the time. How strongly brand loyalty influences buying behavior is much more difficult to say.

B. Factors in Brand Choice

Some investigators have also examined the relationship of brand loyalty to other variables, such as the frequency of purchase over time in a product class and within and among different product classes, special deals and price activity, and the seller.

1. Frequency of Purchase

Both Kuehn [20] and Farley [14] find that the frequency of purchase during a period is strongly associated with their measures of brand loyalty. Farley finds a significant simple correlation between the percentage of families switching favorite brands from the first half of the year to the second half and the average number of purchases reported in a product class. In a multiple regression analysis of seven variables on the percentage switching favorite brands, the probability that the regression coefficient for the average number of purchases in a product class is significantly different from zero is found to be .99. Among the seven regression coefficients tested it is the only coefficient significant at the .01 level. Family brand loyalty over time appears to be greater the larger the average number of purchases made in the product class, given similar levels of median expenditure, degree of retail availability, price activity, and multiple product use within the product class.

Kuehn shows that the range between upper and lower limits of brand-repurchase probability varies positively with the frequency of purchase. He infers that high frequency purchasers of frozen orange juice learned to reject or accept a particular brand, whereas very infrequent purchasers of the product appeared to follow a random pattern of brand choice.

2. Variation Within and Among Product Classes

What appear to be preferences or loyalties to secondary brands are reported by food and household item buyers and by major appliance buyers within product classes in studies by Cunningham [10] and Mueller [29]. The evidence for secondary brand loyalties is, of course, considerably weaker than that for single brand loyalties.

There appear to be differences in degree of brand loyalty among product classes, but the evidence is largely confounded with other factors. Farley [14, p. 14] concludes that "much of the apparent difference over products in some important aspects of brand choice can apparently be explained on the basis of structural variables describing the markets in which the products are sold, and does not depend on specific characteristics of the products or on attitudes of consumers toward products." A difference in brand awareness among product classes is also reported by Mueller [29], who found that almost all buyers of major household appliances told the interviewer the name of the brand they purchased, whereas the majority did not name the brand of the sport shirt they reported purchasing.

3. Special Deals and Price Activity

Some reduction in brand loyalty appears to be the result of special deals and relatively high price activity in a product class [10, 14]. Cunningham found that the percentages of purchases going to the most often reported brand were higher after special-deal purchases were subtracted. Farley finds a significant simple correlation between an index of price activity in a product class and the percentage of families switching favorite brands. In two multiple regression analyses the price-activity-index regression coefficients are not found to be significantly different from zero, however. This would indicate that when other variables, such as retail availability, frequency of purchase, and multiple use of products, are held constant within a product class the relative amount of price activity in the product class is not associated with the level of brand loyalty.

4. Source or Origin of Product

There is some evidence that brand or product preferences are associated with the source or origin of the product, that is, producer, retail seller, and country of manufacture. An experiment involved semantic differential product ratings of a canned juice and a textile sample by two hundred Guatemalan participants [35]. The product samples were identical and distinguished only by the designation of the country of manufacture on the label—three Central American republics and Mexico.

Each of four randomly selected groups of fifty participants rated the two products from the same manufacturing country. Significant differences are found in the group rating scores between countries of origin but not between the two products within each country. Although the experiment involved two products said to have been manufactured in four different countries rather than brands associated with specific producers, it does suggest that products from the same source were rated similarly, but that sources were rated differently.

In another investigation involving a survey of doctors attending professional meetings, those who reported a preference for a pharmaceutical house also frequently expressed an associated preference for specific drug brands marketed by the preferred manufacturer [3].

A study involving panel-diary analysis of families who reported a high proportion of food and household purchases in a single store shows that these families also report somewhat higher proportions of purchases in a particularly private brand of the seller than families who do not report heavy concentrations of purchases in a single store [11].

Discoveries of various factors that appear to be related to brand choice suggest several explanatory hypotheses to a number of investigators.

C. Explanations for Buying Decisions

Buying decisions are explained as a learning process, with differing amounts of exploratory-search effort depending on various conditions, that takes place when there is uncertainty about product quality.

1. Learning Process

In his study of frozen orange juice purchase sequences Kuehn [20] finds the following behavior which appears to be similar to that observed in the process of habit formation and memory decay.

a. "The probability of a consumer's buying the same brand on two consecutive purchases of frozen orange juice decreases exponentially with an increase in time between those purchases" [20, p. 397].

b. "Consumers buying frozen orange juice with greatest frequency have the highest probability of continuing to buy the same brand" [20, p. 397].

c. The probability of a consumer's buying a particular brand on the fifth trial in a purchase sequence decreases exponentially with the recency of the last purchase of "the" brand. That is, if the most recent purchase of "the" brand occurred on the fourth trial the probability of repurchase on the fifth trial is significantly higher than if the most recent purchase occurred on the third trial and so forth.

d. "A model equivalent to a generalized form of the Estes and Bush-Mostellar stochastic learning models appears to describe consumer brand shifting quite well. . . . Using Bush and Mostellar's terminology, this would be referred to as an incomplete learning, incomplete extinction model. . . . This is equivalent to saying that consumers will generally not develop such strong brand loyalties (or buying habits) as to insure either the complete rejection or acceptance of a given brand" [20, pp. 390–91, 392].

Some evidence that experience plays a role in choice among major appliance brands is presented by Mueller [29]. She finds that regular users of an appliance say they looked at and considered only one preferred brand more frequently than those who reported no experience with the product. She also finds that those expressing satisfaction with a major-appliance brand report considering only the preferred brand and repurchasing the brand more frequently than those expressing dissatisfaction with the brand. In Mueller's single-survey attempt to reconstruct purchase decisions she finds that consumers report varying amounts of effort before their purchases.

2. Amount of Effort

Indications of careful evaluation or deliberation, such as reports of consideration of alternatives, discussion with family members, and information-seeking activities, as well as choosing with respect to price, brand and other attributes are reported: (a) more frequently before the purchase of major appliances than sport shirts; (b) by about a quarter of buyers of major appliances and not at all by another quarter of buyers; the rest say they deliberated for short periods of time in a casual manner and concentrated on one or two product features, neglecting others. Indications of careful evaluation and deliberation are *not* reported when: (i) the income of the buyer was relatively high; (ii) the price paid was relatively low; (iii) the years of education were few; (iv) a special opportunity to purchase was perceived; (v) need for the product was urgent; (vi) a similar article previously used was satisfactory. It should be noted that these findings may be confounded with "yea- and nay-saying" response sets which were not investigated.

Farley [13] assumes that search effort for food and small household items should be related to the quantity purchased and measured by prices paid. He finds that families reporting heavy buying in a product class also tend to pay less for a given container size than those reporting light purchases in their diaries. He infers support for the hypothesis that the amount of search for lower prices is a function of the expected gain relative to the cost. Tucker, in the previously mentioned experiment involving bread selections among four "unknown" brands [41], finds what appears to be exploratory-search behavior in the first four choices made by participants.

3. Uncertainty About Quality

Several investigators attempt to explain how buyers evaluate products under conditions of uncertainty. Donald F. Cox [8] assumes that consumers assign value to information about a product on two independent dimensions—predictive value and confidence value.

Specific product attributes that in the evaluator's judgment are likely to give the over-all product good quality have high predictive value, that is, are highly predictive value cues. For example, knowledge that a stereo amplifier contains high-quality internal components is a highly predictive value cue that the amplifier is of good quality, whereas the knobs on the front of the amplifier are a low predictive value cue to the set's overall quality.

Confidence value is a measure of the consumer's degree of certainty about the existence of the specific attribute in the product. Thus, to someone unable to evaluate the quality of the highly predictive value cues (internal components), they would have low confidence value. An experiment was performed which confirmed the following hypotheses:

a) When confidence value was held constant, the higher the predictive value of a cue, the higher the probability that it would be utilized as the primary basis for evaluating a product or product attribute.

b) When predictive value was held constant, the cue highest in confidence value was most likely to be utilized.

c) Consumers faced with a choice between a cue high in predictive value but low in confidence value, and a cue low in predictive value, but high in confidence value favored the latter. In other words, consumers base their evaluations on low predictive value information when they are quite uncertain (have low confidence) about their ability to evaluate the highly predictive product attributes.

The hypotheses help to explain quality discriminations of identical hosiery on the basis of scent [21], richness of flavor in ice cream on the basis of color, cleaning power of a detergent on the basis of suds level and smell, mildness of a detergent on the basis of color, power of an electric hand mixer on the basis of noise made by the motor, and acceleration of a car on the basis of the ease with which the accelerator pedal can be depressed (tension of the spring).

Price cues. The hypotheses also help to explain trading up to higher priced brands when price is the only cue to product quality and consumers perceive quality differences. In two separate experiments subjects say they would often choose the higher priced of two alternative brands when their only information differentiating the brands was price. Particularly, if quality differences between brands (floor wax and razor blades) were first seen as large, subjects were more likely to choose the higher priced brand [23, 42].

Producer and risk reduction. Bauer [3] hypothesizes that when doctors have to deal with risky drug situations they rely on their preference for a pharmaceutical house in their choice among drug brands. He finds evidence in the previously mentioned survey among doctors at a professional meeting [3] that expressed brand preferences for risky drugs are associated with state preferences for a company, rather than for an individual salesman. He finds no association of preferences for relatively safe drugs with either company or salesman. Bauer also finds that reported use of drug brands in the first year of market development is associated with preferences expressed for specific producers and that there is a marked decrease in such associations in later stages of market development.

II. PROMOTIONAL AND OTHER SOURCES OF INFORMATION

All of the following studies investigate the use of information sources as reported by individuals in personal interviews. One group of studies also investigates their function in the buying–decision-making process, and several studies make an attempt to have the buyer assess the influence of the source in the buying decision. The reviewed studies involve situations in which many buyers are likely to report the use of new information, as in choosing to buy new products or brands, large expenditure items, or items involving fashion changes. It should be noted that these studies deal with products in both early and advanced stages of market development. Information use by stage of market development is reviewed at the end of this section.

A. Use of Information Sources

1. Personal contacts with friends, relatives, or neighbors, or professional contacts with medical journals, specialized farm papers, or colleagues are very frequently mentioned sources of information in all studies reviewed.

2. Use of advertising, publicity, sales promotion, and personal selling appears to vary among product classes.

a) In choosing new food and household products or brands buyers mention use of radio advertising (1945), newspaper advertising, magazine advertising, and salespersons in that order of frequency [*19*].

b) In choosing new fashion items, such as clothing and hairdo styles, make-up techniques and cosmetics, buyers mention exposure to magazines more frequently than salespersons. Radio and newspapers are mentioned rarely [*19*].

c) In the selection of movies, buyers mention newspapers more frequently than magazines; radio and salespersons are mentioned rarely [*19*].

d) Buyers of major established appliances most frequently mention shopping among stores, advertisements and circulars, magazines or newspaper articles in that order. Reports of testing agencies and mail-order catalogues were mentioned rarely. These sources were specifically mentioned in the questionnaire. Radio and television were not specifically mentioned [*29*].

e) Buyers of new major appliances mention shopping among stores infrequently. Those who do consult reading material frequently mention buying guides [*5*].

f) Doctors choosing among new drugs usually cite detail men (missionary salesmen), journal advertising, and direct mail in that order as dominant commercial sources. The two most frequently cited professional sources are journal articles and colleagues [*3, 6, 26*].

B. The Function of Information Sources

Use of sources appears to vary by their reported function in the buying process of individuals.

1. First Knowledge or Awareness

a) Man-made fabrics (nylon, orlon, dacron) were first seen or heard about by farm housewives in a rural community in the following order of frequency of mention of commercial sources: magazines and papers, store displays or salespeople, television and radio. Friends, neighbors, and relatives were the most important informal personal sources of first knowledge but ranked second to magazines and papers [*4*].

b) In the process of adopting hybrid-seed corn, about half the farmers cite personal contact with salesmen, and an additional tenth cite radio sales talks as their earliest commercial sources of knowledge. Among professional contacts, neighbors and farm journals—a weak second—are cited most frequently [*34*].

c) Several studies of farmers in the process of adopting new products and practices for farm use find printed mass media to be most frequently cited of all sources of first knowledge. Unfortunately, specific media are not tabulated. Radio, television, and other personal commercial sources (dealers and salesmen) are found to run a very weak second to the printed mass media. Among professional sources, various agricultural agencies, such as county agents, college-extension services, and soil-conservation specialists, are usually more important than other farmers [*7, 25, 32, 45*].

d) Doctors describing the histories of use of pharmaceutical products first mention the following commercial sources: detail men about a third of the time, direct mail about half as often, and journal advertising quite infrequently. Among professional sources journal articles are mentioned somewhat more frequently than colleagues [*6*]. These findings are substantially replicated for the order of frequency with which they are mentioned, and for some sources even the magnitudes of the frequencies agree closely, that is, detail men, direct mail, and colleagues. Journal advertising was not separately tabulated in this study [*26*].

2. Interest or Information-gathering

a) Additional, more detailed information about man-made fabrics was obtained from the following commercial sources in their order of mention: magazines, salespeople or displays, television, newspapers, and radio. Informal personal sources are now as frequently mentioned as mass media [*4*].

b) In securing additional information about 2, 4-D weed spray, which required the purchase of a power sprayer, regarded as a major piece of equipment, mass media are more often mentioned than dealers and salesmen, but the latter are now mentioned more frequently than they were as a source of first knowledge and are mentioned more frequently than agricultural agencies. Among professional sources, informal personal are mentioned more frequently than agricultural agencies, and the former are the most frequent of all sources cited [32].

c) When dairy farmers felt that three practices—spittle-bug control, grass sillage, and artificial hay-drying—were a workable solution to a farm problem, they cite most frequently farm magazines, radio, and personal commercial sources, in that order. Professional sources, particularly contacts with extension teachers and agents and colleagues, are cited more frequently than in the awareness stage [7].

3. Evaluation, Application, or Acceptance

a) Commercial information that helped decide whether or not farm housewives would really try man-made fabrics for themselves was most frequently obtained from salespeople and displays. All mass media taken together are mentioned less frequently. Informal personal sources are cited more than any one commercial source at this stage in the buying process [4].

b) In the adoption of 2, 4-D weed spray for field weed control, farmers cite personal commercial sources much more frequently than mass media when considering the relative advantage of the new product over other alternatives and making a decision whether to try the new product. Among professional sources, informal personal sources are again more often cited than farm agencies [32].

c) Findings cited immediately above (b) are replicated for the order of selection of sources in a study that asked farmers to cite sources of new farming ideas at this stage in their buying process [45]. Farm magazines are mentioned more frequently than personal commercial sources or radio in the adoption of three practices in a third study [7]. However, a more thoroughly conceived analysis by Mason [25] shows the following:

In two of the three studies (Wilkening, Rogers and Beal) items representing sources of information used have been incorporated as part of the stage of the adoption process question. Hence, in order to answer what is basically an item about the use of information sources, the respondent must tacitly agree that he has passed through the adoption stage mentioned. Items used in these studies appear to have forced the respondent to structure the process of adoption as derived by the researchers. . . . The rural sociologists cited had confounded the use of various information sources with identification of stages in the adoption process [pp. 42, 51].

Mason finds that independent evaluation of sources at each stage shows that "the use of mass media increases at successive stages for soil testing and joining a community drainage project. Use of mass media increases, then decreases for tile drainage [p. *51*]. Mason's analysis confirms that:

> The use of mass media sources is higher at the awareness stage, than for any other information source, except for peer source use by influentials. This is true for all practices [he investigated]. Use of mass media sources also is lower than all other sources in the final adoption stage. This is also true for all three practices. The findings for use of authoritative, peer and personal commercial sources are consistent with those reported in previous research. Use of all three sources increases as farmers pass through the stages of the adoption process [p. 51].

d) Doctors cite journal advertising about twice as frequently as detail men and direct mail as their second sources in their chronological accounts of drug adoptions. Journal advertising was cited infrequently as a first source of information in II B2(*a*). Druggists now receive some mentions. Among professional sources journal articles, colleagues, and meetings are cited in that order of frequency [*6*].

4. Trial or First Use

a) After the decision to try out the new man-made fabrics, housewives say that among commercial sources they most frequently obtained help or information on where to get the fabrics, what kind of care they require, and how to use them from clothing tags and information with the garment, next from salespeople, and least often from mass media, with magazines leading. Among other sources informal personal are mentioned most frequently, and some mention is made of self experimentation and existing information [*4*].

b) In the adoption process of 2, 4-D spray personal commercial sources receive their most frequent mention when the farmer is trying out the spray, usually on a small scale. Printed media, including printed directions on sacks or containers as well as other mass media, are mentioned less frequently than verbal commercial sources. Unfortunately, individual categories are not tabulated for the printed media. Discussion with neighbors and friends is still most often mentioned, and contact with farm agencies is mentioned least of all sources [*32*].

c) The more frequent use of personal commercial sources relative to mass media as discussed above (*b*) is confirmed in two studies of products for farming use [*7, 45*].

d) In the chronological accounts of drug adoptions, third mentions of journal advertising rise is frequently relative to second mentions. Direct mail and detail men are now mentioned in that order of source use. The study as reported does not specifically tabulate mention of druggists or indicate at what stage the first prescriptions were written [*6*].

C. Effectiveness or Influence of Sources in the Buying Decision

The degree of influence of personal selling appears to differ from its frequency of use. In the three studies that follow, the influencing effect of a source is self-evaluated by the interviewed respondent.

1. Katz and Lazarsfeld [19] establish a fairly elaborate effectiveness-of-exposure index as follows: People who mentioned a given source, claimed that it played a specific role (such as having taught them something or directed them toward something), and stated further that this source was the most important factor in their decision, were assessed by the researchers to be *effectively exposed*. The source was considered to have a *contributory effect* if both exposure and specific role was mentioned but it was *not* said to be the most important one. People who do not acknowledge a specific role to a source in their decision but mentioned only exposure were assessed as *ineffectively exposed*. Still, these cases are obviously different from those in which the respondent does not mention contact with the source.

a) In decisions to buy new products or brands of small household items and food, commercial sources in order of their frequency of mention as both effective and contributory exposures were as follows: radio advertising (1945), salespeople, newspaper advertising, and magazine advertising. It should be noted that in IIA2(*a*) use of salespeople is mentioned least often. Personal contacts were judged most effective of all sources mentioned.

b) In decisions to make fashion changes, the only important commercial sources were salespersons and magazines in that order of frequency, for both effective and contributory exposures. Again in IIA2(*a*) "ineffective" exposure is more frequent to magazines than to salespeople. Both verbal personal and visual personal contacts were judged to be more effective than the commercial sources by respondents.

c) In choosing to attend movies, newspapers contributed more effective and contributory exposures than magazines, but again personal contacts were most effective of all three. "Ineffective" exposure is in the same order.

2. When farmers were asked to evaluate their various sources of information as to relative influence in leading them to use hybrid-seed corn, neighbors were cited more frequently than any other source, and among commercial sources salesmen were cited most frequently by about a third of the respondents. All other sources were mentioned rarely [34].

3. In choosing drugs for prescriptions doctors appear to judge sales-

men as "most important" sources of influence—at least under certain circumstances, such as relative isolation from colleagues [18, 26]—and again in the adoption of relatively safe drugs rather than "risky" drugs. In the case of risky drugs confidence or trust in the company producing a brand seems to be more influential than compliance to a preferred salesman's attempt to introduce the drug [3].

D. Stage of Market Development

Use, function, and influence of sources appear to vary by stage of market development.

1. Farmers who say they first heard of hybrid-seed corn in the early stages of market development cite salesmen and radio much more frequently as sources of information than those who first heard in later stages of market development. Neighbors replace salesmen as first informants with increasing relative frequency over the product cycle. Two-thirds of the earliest adopters credited salesmen with the most influence in their decision, whereas in later stages of market development the proportion of self-assessed influence of salesmen declines to about 30 per cent [34].

2. Two investigations appear to show that the function of information sources differs by stage of market development. As market development proceeds commercial sources appear to be consulted earlier in the buying process of individuals. In the last stages of market development personal informal sources are most frequently cited in all phases of the buying decision [7, 32].

3. Doctors who choose new drug brands in the first stages of market development read more medical journals but recall the same information sources as those adopting in later stages of development [18].

4. Buyers of consumer durables in the first stage of market development, such as color television, stereo equipment, dishwashers, and air-conditioners report as follows:

a) Over one-third of the innovators responded that friends were the original source of information regarding the products studied. Less than 15 per cent mention any type of mass media. They do have substantial exposure to media, however. Almost half of the innovators report an average figure of at least three hours of television exposure daily. The average number of magazines in each innovational home is six.

b) Three-quarters of the innovators indicate that they consult no persons outside the home when making a decision to purchase a new product. Over half indicate that they do some type of consulting, however.

Again, three-quarters of those who do consult utilize buying guides such as *Consumer Reports*. Although the innovators do not consult others concerning prospective purchases, they do evaluate the products themselves, usually on the basis of literature.

c) There is evidence that innovators do not shop in many stores before buying innovations. For example, when asked how many stores they visited before purchasing, over three-quarters asserted they visited none or one. Over half went to one store and bought the product there [5].

III. DISTRIBUTION

A. Number of Outlets Shopped

1. Respondents reporting on individual purchases in surveys very frequently say they visit only one seller both for "shopping goods" and "convenience goods." On major purchases such as new cars, television sets, refrigerators, washing machines, stoves, etc., about half the buyers say they visited only one store, where they made their purchase [1, 2, 29]. A majority of farm equipment buyers say they visited only one dealer [33]. On purchases of less expensive items shoppers say they infrequently investigate more than one retailer [2, 29].

2. Families reporting food and household purchases in diaries over the period of one year indicate that a large proportion of their purchases is concentrated in a few stores [11, 40]. Tate [40] finds in a national panel study that about half the families report shopping four stores or fewer; one-quarter shop one or two stores, and less than 10 per cent shop seven or more stores. He also finds that families who shop only one or two stores live in areas where there is a limited choice of outlets (South, Southwest, and mountain states) and tend to be low-income families with low educational achievement. Families shopping a large number of outlets tend to live in the Northeast and Pacific regions, in metropolitan areas, and tend to be in middle and upper socioeconomic groups. The amount a household reports spending in a store is closely related to the reported number of visits to the store.

B. Proximity of Location

1. A shopper's second-choice store after visiting the first choice tends to be in the same neighborhood as the first-choice store if there are nearby stores similar in character to the first choice store [2].

2. People traveling to a regional shopping center over a short distance say they planned to buy both "convenience" as well as "shopping" goods, whereas those traveling longer distances say they planned to buy "shopping" goods primarily [37].

C. Retail Assortment

Stores offering either a deep assortment or a wide variety of product lines are preferred over stores with medium depth or breadth of assortment, both in a laboratory experiment and in survey interviews [2].

D. Retail Prices and Price Lines

1. Price in the form of "receiving best deal or trade-in price" is the factor most frequently mentioned by new car buyers as outstanding in the choice of dealer. Those who actively shopped among dealers mention it twice as often as those who did not shop [1].

2. Price is infrequently mentioned by buyers of sport shirts and major household appliances [29].

3. A wide range of price lines offered by an individual store is preferred to a medium or narrow range of lines, both in a laboratory experiment and a survey [2].

4. A majority of major-appliance buyers say they considered models in only one price line [29]. (a) Only 9 per cent say they considered less expensive models than the one purchased (traded up). (b) One in six say they considered more expensive models than the one purchased (traded down) [29].

5. Trading up (purchase of higher-priced brand) is more likely to occur when quality differences among brands are perceived to be large than when they are small or no difference is perceived [23].

6. Among brands that are seen as all alike the purchaser is more likely to choose the lower-priced brand [23].

E. Service

1. Expectation of good service is among the least frequently mentioned outstanding factors which new car-buyers say caused them to select the dealer from whom they bought the car [1]. Service is among the least frequently mentioned dealer characteristics looked for by buyers of major

appliances [29]. Purchasers of farm equipment say they based their choice of dealer most frequently on their expectation of adequate and prompt service [33].

2. Customers of department and discount stores in New York and Cleveland say they value delivery service for its convenience and not only for help with heavy packages. Customers of department stores rank delivery as an important service and are aware of variations in delivery policies as well as differences in the efficiency of delivery service among stores [31].

F. Special Deals

1. In a study of panel diaries [10], special-deal purchases appear to be concentrated among families with low brand loyalties.

2. Panel-diary reports of vegetable-oil-product purchases (margarine, shortening, salad oil) and butter indicated that (a) a small proportion of households accounts for a large number of purchases; (b) almost no one bought deals in more than two product classes studied; (c) frequent users of special deals had above-average incomes and were larger, younger, and better educated white families [38].

3. When end-of-gondola displays in supermarkets contained intensively promoted sale-priced items, traffic around these displays was observed to increase, but an equal and opposite change in traffic flow was observed in the aisles of the grocery department. Location of special deals within the gondolas made for a more desirable distribution of traffic [17].

G. Personal Selling

1. Nearly half of new car buyers say they had met the salesman before they visited the selling dealership [1]. About a third say they previously bought a car from the same salesman [1]. One in six say they were contacted by the selling dealer [1].

H. Telephone Orders

1. Telephone sales in department stores tend to be additional sales rather than substitutes for floor sales, a survey of New York and Cleveland shows [31].

2. Executives believe that low- and middle-income women do most of the telephone ordering. A shopping survey found that high-income

women most frequently say they order by telephone, measured both by the total phone purchases reported and the relative importance of phone orders as compared with in-store shopping [*31*].

3. Newspaper advertising appears to be an important determinant of phone orders. Some orders are also based on the customers' familiarity with an item [*31*].

J. Traffic in Supermarkets

An observational survey of traffic in supermarkets by Havas and Smith [*17*] revealed evidence in support of the following patterns of behavior:

1. There was considerable variation among shoppers in over-all store coverage, and purchases were generally related to the degree of store coverage.

2. Customer traffic flow was concentrated along the perimeter of the store, including grocery gondola ends, and in the cross aisles of grocery gondolas.

3. Stores with continuous gondolas generally experienced greater coverage and a more evenly distributed customer traffic flow than those that had the gondolas divided into unequal length forming a cross aisle in the grocery department. There are strong indications that customers tend to shop the short aisles visually from the ends instead of walking through the aisles.

4. End displays accounted for less than 3 per cent of store purchases; the same amount of space on regular shelves accounted for about 6 per cent of purchases.

5. Among foods the most frequently purchased were cookies and crackers, coffee, and canned vegetables. Among non-foods the most frequently purchased were paper products, soaps, and health and beauty aids.

6. The relative position of produce, bakery, and meat departments in the line of customer flow had no apparent effect on the pattern of customer traffic flow in that department. Customers rarely by-pass a department to return to it later. The ratio of produce to meat sales remained about the same regardless of the departments' locations relative to store entrance and customer traffic flow. Nearly 70 per cent of the customers shopped in the bakery and dairy departments regardless of the location of these departments. These two departments were often found to be located adjacent to each other, resulting in overcrowding during peak shopping periods.

7. Customers averaged more time in the store and bought more items, at the same rate of expenditures per minute, Thursday through Saturday than Monday through Wednesday.

8. Special island-display sales averaged fewer sales per square foot than regular or permanent displays.

9. The placement of commodities within departments affected traffic flows and sales. (*a*) When bread was shifted from the head of the bakery department to last position in the department in terms of normal traffic, sales of cakes increased while bread sales remained unchanged. (*b*) When tea and cocoa were placed opposite the coffee display, traffic in that aisle increased.

K. Shelf Space and Sales

Two experiments test the effects of variations in shelf-space allocation on sales of packaged food-product categories in supermarkets. The first reported by investigators for the U.S. Department of Agriculture [*43*] in 1952 measured sales response to variation in displays of from two to six rows of seventeen canned vegetable and fruit product classes. The second experiment performed by Keith Cox [*9*] involved four product classes, baking soda, hominy, powdered orange drink, and powdered coffee cream. Both experimenters employed latin-square designs and apparently controlled displays, prices, shelf locations, and promotions during the term of the experiments.

It should be noted that the experiments involved product categories such as peas, fruit cocktail, applesauce, and the items mentioned above, rather than individual brands within these categories. The USDA [*43*] test distinguished between can sizes. Cox [*9*] does not make any distinctions within product categories, either by size or brand.

Using analysis of variance, he finds no significant difference in sales response to variations in shelf space for baking soda, powdered orange drink, and instant coffee cream at the .05 level. Only the sales of hominy varied significantly with the number of shelf spaces at the .01 level.

Linear regressions of the number of shelf spaces on average weekly sales indicate that there was some increase in sales in all four product classes as the number of shelf spaces was increased, but only one of the products, hominy, responded with consistent and large changes in sales.

In the USDA study, average weekly sales for all seventeen items tested varied consistently with the number of rows displayed. Total sales for six shelf-row displays were only 41 per cent higher than for two row displays, however, and the effect of doubling the space allocation from two to four rows was to produce an increase of only 13 per cent in sales. Unfortunately, analysis of variance was not used to test for differences between shelf-space treatment means in the earlier study.

REFERENCES

1. ALDERSON ASSOCIATES, INC. *A Basic Study of Automobile Retailing.* Dearborn, Mich.: Ford Motor Co., 1958.
2. ALDERSON AND SESSIONS. "Basic Research on Consumer Behavior: Report on a Study of Shopping Behavior and Methods for Its Investigation," in R. E. FRANK *et al.* (eds.) [16], pp. 129-45.
3. BAUER, R. A. "Risk Handling in Drug Adoption: The Role of Company Preference," *Public Opinion Quarterly,* XXV, No. 4 (Winter, 1961), 546-59.
4. BEAL, G. M., and ROGERS, E. M. "Informational Sources in the Adoption Process of New Fabrics," *Journal of Home Economics,* XLIX (October, 1957), 630-34.
5. BELL, W. E. "Consumer Innovators: A Unique Market for Newness," in S. A. GREYSER (ed.). *Toward Scientific Marketing.* Boston: 1963, pp. 85-95. Proceedings of the Winter Conference of the American Marketing Association, 1963, pp. 85-95.
6. CAPLOW, T., and RAYMOND, J. J. "Factors Influencing the Selection of Pharmaceutical Products," *Journal of Marketing,* XIX, No. 1 (July, 1954), 18-23.
7. COPP, J. H. SILD, M. L., and BROWN, E. J. "The Function of Information Sources in the Farm Practice Adoption Process," *Rural Sociology,* XXIII (June, 1958), 145-57.
8. COX, D. F. "The Measure of Information Value: A Study in Consumer Decision-making," in W. S. DECKER (ed.). *Emerging Concepts in Marketing.* Chicago: American Marketing Association, 1962, pp. 413-21.
9. COX, K. "The Responsiveness of Food Sales to Supermarket Shelf Space Changes," *Journal of Marketing Research* I, No. 2 (May, 1964), 63-67.
10. CUNNINGHAM, R. M. "Brand Loyalty—What, Where, How Much?" *Harvard Business Review,* XXXIV (January-February, 1965), 116-28.
11. ———. "Customer Loyalty to Store and Brand," *Harvard Business Review,* XXXIX (November-December, 1961), 127-37.
12. DRAYTON, L. "Bias Arising in Wording Consumer Questionnaires," *Journal of Marketing,* XIX (1954), 140-45.
13. FARLEY, J. U. " 'Brand Loyalty' and the Economics of Information," *Journal of Business,* XXXVII, No. 4 (October, 1964), 370-81.
14. ———. "Why Does Brand Loyalty Vary over Products?" *Journal of Marketing Research,* I, No. 4 (November, 1964), 9-14.
15. FRANK, R. E. "Brand Choice as a Probability Process," *Journal of Business,* XXXV, No. 1 (January, 1962), 43-56.
16. FRANK, R. E., KUEHN, A. A., and MASSY, W. F. (eds.). *Quantitative Techniques in Marketing Analysis.* Homewood, Ill.: Richard D. Irwin, Inc., 1962.
17. HAVAS, N., and SMITH, H. M. *Customer's Shopping Patterns in Retail Food Stores* (AMS 400). Washington: U.S. Department of Agriculture, Agricultural Marketing Service, Marketing Development Research Division, August, 1960.

18. KATZ, E. "The Social Itinerary of Technical Change—Two Studies on the Diffusion of Innovation," *Human Organization* (Summer, 1961), pp. 70-82.

19. KATZ, E., and LAZARSFELD, P. F. *Personal Influence.* Glencoe, Ill.: Free Press, 1955.

20. KUEHN, A. A. "Consumer Brand Choice—a Learning Process," in R. E. FRANK *et al.* (eds.) [16].

21. LAIRD, D. A. "How the Consumer Estimates Quality by Subconscious Sensory Impressions," *Journal of Applied Psychology* (June, 1932), p. 241.

22. LANSING, J., GINSBURG, G., and BRAATEN, K. *An Investigation of Response Error.* Urbana: Bureau of Economics and Business Research, University of Illinois, 1961.

23. LEAVITT, H. J. "A Note on Some Experimental Findings about the Meaning of Price," *Journal of Business,* XXVII, No. 3 (July, 1954), 205-10.

24. LEWIS, H. "A Comparison of Consumer Responses to Weekly and Monthly Purchase Panels," *Journal of Marketing,* XII (1948), 449-54.

25. MASON, R. G. "The Use of Information Sources in the Process of Adoption," *Rural Sociology,* XXIX, No. 1 (March, 1964), 40-52.

26. MENZEL, H., and KATZ, E. "Social Relations and Innovation in the Medical Profession: The Epidemiology of a New Drug," *Public Opinion Quarterly,* XIX, No. 4 (Winter, 1955-56), 337-52.

27. METZ, J. *Accuracy of Response Obtained in a Milk Consumption Study.* (Marketing Paper 5.) Ithaca, N.Y.: New York (Cornell) Agricultural Experiment Station Methods Research, July, 1956.

28. MUELLER, E. "The Desire for Innovations in Household Goods," in L. H. CLARK (ed.). *Consumer Behavior: Research on Consumer Reactions.* New York: Harper & Bros., 1958, pp. 13-38.

29. MUELLER, E. and KATONA, G. "A Study of Purchase Decisions," in L. H. Clark (ed.). *Consumer Behavior: The Dynamics of Consumer Reaction.* New York: New York University Press, 1955, pp. 36-87.

30. NETER, J., and WAKSBERG, J. "Measurement of Non-Sampling Errors in a Survey of Home Owners Expenditures for Alterations and Repairs," *Proceedings of the 121st Annual Meeting, American Statistical Association, Social Statistics Section* (1961), pp. 201-10.

31. RICH, S. U. *Shopping Behavior of Department Store Customers.* Boston: Harvard Graduate School of Business Administration, 1963.

32. ROGERS, E. M., and BEAL, G. M. "The Importance of Personal Influence in the Adoption of Technological Changes," *Social Forces,* XXXVI (May, 1958), 329-35.

33. ROGERS, E. M., MITCHELL, G. H., and KENDRICK, J. G. "The Farmer Buys a Machine," *Implement and Tractor,* September 3, 1961.

34. RYAN, B., and GROSS, N. C. "The Diffusion of Hybrid Seed Corn in Two Iowa Communities," *Rural Sociology,* VIII (1943), 15-24.

35. SCHOOLER, R. D. "An Inquiry into Product Bias and Predilection within the Central American Common Market." Unpublished Ph.D. thesis, University of Texas, 1964.

36. SHAFFER, J. "The Reporting Period for a Consumer Purchase Panel," *Journal of Marketing,* XIX (1955), 252-57.

37. SILVER, J., and HANSEN, G. "Characteristics of Travel to a Regional Shopping Center," *Public Roads,* XXXI, No. 5 (December, 1960), 101-8.

38. STOCKMAN, L. H. "The Influence of Consumer Deals on Urban Household Purchases of Butter, Margerine, Vegetable Shortening, and Salad and Cooking Oils in Metropolitan Chicago," in F. M. BASS (ed.). *The Frontiers of Marketing Thought and Science.* Chicago: American Marketing Association, 1957, pp. 241-46.

39. SUDMAN, S. "On the Accuracy of Recording of Consumer Panels: I," *Journal of Marketing Research,* I, No. 2 (May, 1964), 14-20.

40. TATE, R. S. "The Supermarket Battle for Store Loyalty," *Journal of Marketing,* XXV, No. 6 (October, 1961), 8-13.

41. TUCKER, W. T. "The Development of Brand Loyalty," *Journal of Marketing Research,* I, No. 3 (August, 1964), 32-35.

42. TULL, D. S., BORING, R. A., and GONSIOR, M. H. "A Note on the Relationship of Price and Imputed Quality," *Journal of Business,* XXXVII, No. 2 (April, 1964), 186-91.

43. U.S. DEPARTMENT OF AGRICULTURE. *Better Utilization of Selling Space in Food Stores.* ("Marketing Research Report," No. 30.) Washington, 1952.

44. ———. *Response Variations Encountered with Different Questionnaire Forms.* ("Market Research Report," No. 163.) Washington, 1957.

45. WILKENING, E. A. "Roles of Communicating Agents in Technological Change in Agriculture," *Social Forces,* XXXIV (1956), 361-67.

37

CONCLUSIONS: CONSUMER BEHAVIOR as a DISCIPLINE

A Discipline?

Consumer behavior as a field of study is in its growth stage. In spite of the great need for understanding, explaining, and predicting consumer behavior, only a small amount of concrete work has been done in this area. Businessmen generally are still more willing to risk their financial lives on their intuitive skills than on research about their customers. And they usually prefer to spend much more money on advertising and public relations than on consumer behavior research. Yet, they know well that their profits are directly related to the extent to which they understand the desires of their customers. The mortality rate of new products is shocking proof of this.

Presently, it would be an exaggeration to refer to consumer behavior as a discipline. But it will become one. The works in this book and others are evidence of it. A number of colleges and universities are teaching courses in consumer behavior and others are planning to do so soon. An increasing number of articles about consumer behavior are appearing in business journals as well as behavioral journals. And workshops in consumer behavior are appearing more frequently.

The new discipline of consumer behavior likely will come to rest in the domain of marketing. Eventually, it probably will flow over into the various behavioral sciences just as the field of personnel management has done. This should not only be expected but hoped for. As evidenced by the material in this book, much reliance is being placed on the behavioral scientist for useful data about consumer behavior. He therefore has as much claim on this new discipline as anyone. Because consumer behavior data will be employed mainly by the marketer, though, the realm of marketing logically will be expected to house the consumer behavior discipline.

Some would argue that it is ridiculous to view consumer behavior as a discipline, now or ever. Those who possess this viewpoint generally advance one or more of the following reasons:

1. Consumer behavior is simply one of the important matters to be dealt with by marketing research.

2. Consumer behavior is important only to the extent that it has relevance to such functions as advertising and packaging, in which case the persons responsible for these functions should also be responsible for the necessary related information about consumer behavior.

3. Consumer behavior is impossible to predict to any useful extent. Therefore, the efforts of businesses and business teachers would be better spent on the functions of business—not with the fickle consumer.

The first two arguments are very narrow views. They maintain that consumer behavior is something to be researched when the necessity arises. The third reason is merely a product of the defeatist—and a very naive one at that. All three views have served only to hamper the inevitable development of a discipline of consumer behavior.

We should bear in mind that a discipline built around the consumer role is no less important and no more unusual than disciplines established about other human roles. Just note the fruitfulness of other role disciplines such as child psychology and personnel management. This "rifle" approach to ascertaining facts about behavior not only produces directly applicable data but actually enhances the "shotgun" disciplines such as sociology and psychology. Moreover, we can no longer wait for the generalists to refine their thinking to the point that it would explain consumer behavior. The thing for us to do, though seemingly selfish, is to take what the generalists (psychology, sociology, economics, and so on) have to offer and get busy integrating it with available material from the business student. This is being done now, to some extent, and eventually should produce a nucleus on which to build a unified body of knowledge about consumer behavior.

Present Status of Knowledge about Consumer Behavior

It was indicated earlier that a body of knowledge about consumer behavior is in its growth stage. In space-age terms this means that we have it off the ground, but it has a long way to go before it achieves orbit. Let us review some accomplishments in the area.

Interest of the Behavioral Scientist

Probably the major breakthrough in consumer behavior knowledge is the greatly increased concern of the behavioral scientist in the subject. As indicated in Chapter I, it is the behavioral scientist, above all, who is most capable of making significant advances in this new area of study. In the past, however, he generally has refused to work seriously with marketing problems. To quote Lazarsfeld[1]: "Aiding the doctor, promoting justice, or supporting the agencies of the law—all of these are in accord with accepted norms; helping the businessman make money is not." This attitude generally still prevails but shows signs of breaking down.

Just recently there has been a noticeable increase in the behaviorist's interest in consumer behavior. There is no simple explanation for this "change of heart." One behaviorist who now uses his talents to help explain consumer behavior summed it up this way: "If one wants to test his [behavioral] ideas, what more important behavioral patterns could he work with than those of consumers?" Apparently, then, there is a growing recognition among behavioral scientists that consumer behavior is virtually an untapped source of problems that often lend themselves to being solved with presently established behavioral concepts.

Some welcomed indications of the behaviorist's concern with consumer behavior are his willingness to

a. teach courses in consumer behavior in marketing departments.

b. conduct extensive research aimed at the understanding of consumer behavior. The very fine research conducted by Dr. Rainwater, a psychologist with Social Research, Inc., in which he compared the behavioral patterns of middle class and "working class" wives, was directed, in part, toward consumer behavior.[2]

c. theorize about consumer behavior. There is a great deal more effort by behaviorists to discuss the applications of behavior theories to explaining consumer behavior. Dr. Bayton, Professor of Psychology, is an example of an excellent contributor in this respect.[3]

d. to participate in seminars and workshops devoted to advancing the understanding of consumer behavior. Such activities are becoming numerous and provide a means by which marketers, interested in consumer behavior can share the views and knowledge of the behavioral scientist.

[1] Paul F. Lazarsfeld, "Reflections on Business," *The American Journal of Sociology,* LXV (July, 1959), p. 1.
[2] Lee Rainwater, Richard P. Coleman, and Gerald Handel, *Workingman's Wife* (New York: Oceana Publications, Inc., 1959).
[3] See his article in Section II.

Consumer Segmentation

A significant area of accomplishment using consumer behavior data has been the increased practice of consumer segmentation. Consumer, or market, segmentation involves the development and marketing of products for a specific, homogeneous group of potential consumers. The thinking behind consumer segmentation is that people with like characteristics may possess similar needs. Manufacturers can, therefore, at least theoretically, identify groups of people with like characteristics and develop products specifically to satisfy their needs. Such thinking is in marked contrast to the practice of developing a product to satisfy as many people as possible and is in keeping with the marketing concept that was discussed in Chapter I. Consumer segmentation also insures better acceptance of new products and reduces product failures that are caused by attempting to sell products to uninterested markets.

A great deal of success has been experienced in consumer segmentation employing visible characteristics. Some evidence of this success has been noted in various articles throughout this book. Markets have been identified according to sex (p. 237), age (p. 277), and race (p. 303). Further, markets have been described according to other visible characteristics such as income, geographic location, and occupation.

Less visible characteristics[4] have also been employed, with varying amounts of success, to divide consumers into homogeneous markets. Many favorable results have been obtained using social class as a base (p. 223). A great amount of effort presently is being made to segment groups of consumers according to a variety of personality elements (p. 125 and p. 135). Some might term the latter psychological segmentation.

The apparent success in consumer segmentation reflects the increasing understanding of the consumer role and the factors that determine behavior within it. In reverse, as we increase our understanding of consumer behavior, we can categorize consumers with greater exactness. The results should be greater consumer satisfaction with less marketing costs (resulting from fewer product failures).

Behavioral Research Techniques

Next to the behavioral scientist's thinking, his research techniques have been most important in advancing knowledge of consumer behavior. Many of the behavioral science techniques have been applied to the study of consumer activity with generally good success. Some of these applications are discussed and illustrated in Section IV. Such borrowing is a logi-

---

[4] It probably would be more useful to view these characteristics on a continuum that ranges from visible to nonvisible.

cal action. As emphasized in Chapter I, the study of consumer behavior is also a study of human behavior; thus, the techniques used to study human behavior should also be applicable to examining consumer behavior. It is true, of course, that it may be necessary to modify the techniques in order that they fit the particular role being studied (in this case, the consumer role.)

Both approaches, direct application and modified application, are being used in consumer behavior research with increasing success. The article by Tucker and Painter (p. 125) is a good example of the direct application of a behavioral research technique to the examination of the consumer role. In this case, the authors used a personality inventory, the Gordon Personal Profile, to determine the influence of certain personality traits on given consumer activities. No changes were made in the research tool. On the other hand, Mindak (p. 337) showed that the Semantic Differential, a behavioral research tool developed by the noted psychologist, Charles Osgood, could be very useful to the study of consumer behavior when the polar adjectives used in the instrument were modified to concur with the particular consumer behavior under study.

There is still the problem of teaching consumer behavior researchers who do not have a behavioral background how to use these research techniques and interpret the results they produce. Where the technique is to be modified, thorough knowledge of it must be possessed by the researcher. Presently, the dissemination of such knowledge is limited mainly to college courses in the behavioral sciences and, to a lesser extent, to training under behavioral scientists who are devoting their efforts to consumer behavior research in private businesses and research firms.

A need also exists for examination of many other behavioral research techniques to determine their usefulness to consumer behavior research. Further, new behavioral techniques appear frequently and it behooves the consumer behavior researcher to keep abreast of these. Apparently, there is no institution or group of individuals that has formally assumed the responsibility for these two tasks.

Computerized Research

Practically all fields of research have been enhanced by the advent of the electronic computer. Certainly, the study of consumer behavior has gained tremendously from its development. Simply speaking, the computer has allowed consumer behavior to be approached more scientifically. Because of its capacity to work with an almost unbelievable amount of data in a very short time, the computer has permitted consumer behavior research to deal with larger numbers of people and a wider range of variables.

Often, in the process of developing a research project, a researcher will limit such items as sample size and number of questions asked because he has looked ahead and realized that the data that will be produced will require far too much time and man-hours to analyze. Such procedure, however, may reduce the quality of the research and thus limit its usefulness in making decisions about such matters as introducing a new product or starting a new promotional campaign. While the researcher should always keep efficiency (cost and time relative to data needed) in mind, there is a tendency to conduct a more detailed search when a computer is available to aid in the calculations.

Even in those universities and business organizations where electronic computers are available, they too often are not being used in consumer behavior research because the researchers lack knowledge in their operation. For instance, it is often necessary for the researcher to develop the program (instructions) for the machine which is a fairly complex process that many researchers do not know how to perform. Therefore, it is necessary that consumer behaviorists, now and in the future, avail themselves of courses and instructions in the use of electronic computers. As the computer becomes an integral part of consumer behavior research, the quality and sophistication of research results will increase and thus hasten the maturity of a consumer behavior discipline.

What's Ahead in Consumer Behavior

Since the discipline of consumer behavior is relatively new, many changes and many new developments can be anticipated. Some of the significant changes that seem forthcoming are the following.

Increased Interests

It seems logical that most businessmen should be interested in learning what is known about consumer behavior. Such information would help them to understand their own customers and make their marketing efforts more effective. Ironically though, many businessmen have shied away from "motivation research junk," as some of them call it. Perhaps, many of those had a right to condemn it. All too often consumer behavior research was "sold" without proof of its value.

Today, there is ample proof of the value of such research, and much of the proof is becoming public.[5] Consequently, we can anticipate an accelerated interest among businessmen in consumer behavior research. Relatively more research dollars will be spent on the analysis of the behavior of present markets. More emphasis will be placed on learning the research techniques of the behavioral scientist. Businessmen will increase their

[5] Unfortunately, a great deal of consumer behavior research results are not made public for competitive reasons.

attendance at seminars and meetings that explore consumer behavior. And as these activities begin to pay off via more efficient marketing, interests in consumer behavior will accelerate at an even greater pace.

If we can assume that the behavioral scientists are as devoted to solving major human problems as they say they are, we can expect great numbers of them to begin directing their efforts to the understanding of the consumer role. What other role behavior could they work with that embraces so many people? Surely, their realization of this fact is coming soon. And the great challenge that it will offer should overcome any qualms that they have about working with business problems.

A marketing teacher at a small Southwestern university recently commented that "as soon as there is enough there to teach" his department would begin offering a course in consumer behavior. The point is that he was thoroughly convinced of the necessity of a course in consumer behavior in his marketing curriculum, but that he was waiting until enough information was available that would provide a practical course on the subject. This position probably prevails in a number of our universities and indicates that it is only a matter of time until there will be a great deal of attention in universities to the teaching of consumer behavior material.

A Break With Tradition

Since the discipline of consumer behavior is new, it can, and no doubt will, avoid many of the less fruitful research approaches employed in traditional human behavior disciplines. As noted earlier, we have the opportunity to benefit from the multitude of human behavior research that has already been conducted by behavioral scientists. And we should do so! Much of future consumer behavior research will be conducted by businessmen, and they have little room for error. At least, their errors are usually very expensive ones. Therefore, it is logical to avoid those human behavior research practices that, in the past, have produced questionable results. Some of those practices are the following:

1. Inadequate sample size. A significant amount of human behavior research has been conducted with groups of 10 to 50 individuals and often it has been implied that the results were representative of such large groups as teenagers, social classes, and religions. Assuming that these samples were probability samples, and many were not, their results often contained so much sampling error as to render them useless for making predictions about the behavior of the groups with which the students were concerned. Such research provides a very weak base on which to make, say, a ten million dollar decision.

Small samples, such as those referred to here probably are not useful to support business decisions regarding consumer behavior. They are useful, however, for generating ideas, but these ideas should be tested with larger samples that will produce more reliable results.

The increasing use of electronic computers should reduce the practice of employing inadequate sample size, particularly in those cases where the small sample was used to avoid massive calculations.

2. Using convenience samples. In their haste to test their ideas, behaviorists frequently have selected a group of respondents from any body of individuals that happened to be convenient. College teachers, for example, often select college students for their samples. The students are conveniently available, they usually cost nothing, and they typically make good research subjects. The danger in this procedure is that the reports of the research often imply that the results are applicable to groups of individuals other than college students. More often than not, the results are not even representative of college students. It is easy to see that testing college students' attitudes toward deodorants, for example, and then assuming that the results are representative of almost everyone, is a pretty risky business practice. A major reason for using convenient samples is to save money or operate within a given financial budget. As the value of good consumer behavior research becomes apparent, more research money will become available and the practice will be minimized.

3. Using hypotheses based on specific motives. During the past 30-40 years behavioral scientists have developed lists of motives to help explain why people behave as they do. For instance, upon observing behavior pattern A, the researcher hypothesizes that motive X is operating and causing the individual to behave in that manner. The researcher then tests to see if motive X was operating. His research report, then, essentially will state that motive X is or is not a cause of behavior A.

This research procedure often bears fruit but it has limitations, mainly because of the assumptions underlying it. The idea that we can classify causes of behavior into four, ten, thirty, or any number of categories is a convenient but very weak kind of thinking. It naturally produces narrow research results. Also, this approach assumes that we must account for man being active rather than inert. This assumption was refused in the early part of this book as being needless. We may need to account for why man moves in one direction rather than another but not for why he moves at all.

There are more powerful approaches to explaining human behavior, and thus consumer behavior, than a list of motives.[6] The fact that this is known should make consumer behavior a more advanced discipline in a shorter length of time than earlier role behavior disciplines.

All three of the above questionable procedures unfortunately can be

[6] Four of the more common approaches to studying human behavior that show much promise are the following: (1) Self Actualization Theory. See, Carl Rogers, "The Actualizing Tendency in Relation to Motives," in Marshall R. Jones (ed.), *Nebraska Symposium on Motivation, 1963* (Lincoln: University of Nebraska Press, 1963), pp. 1-24. (2) Cognitive Dissonance Theory. See, Leon Festinger, *A Theory of Cognitive Dissonance* (Evanston, Ill.: Row-Peterson, 1957). (3) Personal Construct Theory. See, George Kelly, *The Psychology of Personal Constructs,* two volumes (New York: W. W. Norton & Company, 1955). (4) Adaptation Level Theory. See, Harry Helson, "Adaptation Level Theory," in Sigmund Koch (ed.), *Psychology: A Study of Science,* Vol. I (New York: McGraw-Hill Book Co., Inc., 1959).

found in early consumer behavior research. However, it would be naive to expect perfection in the exploratory stage of a discipline as complex as consumer behavior. The point to be made, though, is that future consumer behavior research should and no doubt will recognize the serious limitations of these procedures and avoid them.

Yes, a Discipline

In the title of this part of the book, consumer behavior has been referred to as a discipline. Also, in the beginning of this discussion, the state of consumer behavior was discussed as well as its chances of becoming a discipline. As sort of a summary, let us take a firm stand. *Yes, consumer behavior will become a discipline.* Now that the statement is record, what do we mean by it and why do we make it?

What we mean by it is this. Understanding consumer behavior deserves supreme priority among the business world's problems. Our whole economic system revolves around the consumer—yet, we do not understand his behavior. Therefore, consumer behavior demands separate treatment and will receive it. It finally will be considered as a distinct field of thought rather than something with which marketing research concerns itself when the necessity arises.

We make the statement that consumer behavior will become a discipline because so many significant factors point in that direction. The four-to-five-billion-dollar bill that product failures cost each year is an excellent reason for enhancing our knowledge of consumer behavior. In fact, if just one percent of this waste was spent on advancing a discipline of consumer behavior, the businessman would be rewarded many times over. Further, we know that the relatively high costs of marketing are due, in part, to our lack of understanding of the consumer. This is particularly significant in view of the profit squeeze that flows throughout most businesses today. Both of these costs beg to be reduced, and an extensive understanding of consumer behavior can do just that.

Last, the marketing concept as a business philosophy is increasingly embracing the business world today. This notion essentially implies that a business is consumer oriented. If businesses do subscribe to this concept, and surely they must for long-term survival, then they must also recognize the serious need for a body of knowledge that will permit them to understand the people whom they are dedicated to serve.

BIBLIOGRAPHY

The following list of writings are included in this book in order to permit the reader to broaden or intensify his knowledge of the elements of consumer behavior. Like the articles in this volume, this enumeration attempts to list only those materials that are directly concerned with the consumer role. The writings are grouped according to the divisions of the book. Naturally, there are some selections that do not fit into any one of the categories well. In such cases the basis of the classification was the editor's judgment. Last, it should be mentioned that this list does not represent an attempt to bring together all materials regarding consumer behavior. Of the writings with which the editor is familiar, he has selected those which seem to make an additional contribution to the book.

I. CONSUMER BEHAVIOR—GENERAL

BOOKS AND MONOGRAPHS

Bliss, Perry (ed.), *Marketing and the Behavioral Sciences,* 2nd edition (Boston: Allyn and Bacon, Inc., 1967).

Britt, Steuart H. (ed.), *Consumer Behavior and the Behavioral Sciences: Theories and Applications* (New York: John Wiley & Sons, Inc., 1966).

———, *The Spenders* (New York: McGraw-Hill, 1960).

Clark, Lincoln, *Consumer Behavior* (New York: Harper, 1958).

Dichter, Ernest, *Handbook of Consumer Motivations* (New York: McGraw-Hill Book Company, 1964).

———, *The Strategy of Desire* (New York: Doubleday, 1960).

Douglas, John, George A. Field, Lawrence X. Tarpey, *Human Behavior in Marketing* (Columbus, Ohio: Charles E. Merrill Books, Inc., 1967).

Engel, James F., David T. Kollat, Roger D. Blackwell, *Consumer Behavior* (New York: Holt, Rinehart, & Winston, Inc., 1968).

Katona, George, *The Powerful Consumer* (New York: McGraw-Hill, 1960).

Martineau, Pierre, *Motivation in Advertising* (New York: McGraw-Hill, 1957).

Myers, James H. and William H. Reynolds, *Consumer Behavior and Marketing Management* (Boston: Houghton Mifflin Company, 1967).

Newman, Joseph W. (ed.), *On Knowing the Consumer* (New York: John Wiley & Sons, Inc., 1965).

Nicosia, Francesco M., *Consumer Decision Processes* (Englewood Cliffs, New Jersey: Prentice-Hall, Inc., 1966).

Packard, Vance, *Hidden Persuaders* (New York: McKay, 1957).

Tucker, W. T., *Foundations for a Theory of Consumer Behavior* (New York: Holt, Rinehart and Winston, 1967).

————, *The Social Context of Economic Behavior* (New York: Holt, 1964).

Wasson, Chester R., Frederick D. Sturdivant, and David H. McConaughy, *Competition and Human Behavior* (New York: Appleton-Century-Crofts, 1968).

ARTICLES

Bell, Gerald D., "Developments in Behavioral Study of Consumer Action," in L. George Smith (ed.), *Reflections on Progress in Marketing* (Chicago: American Marketing Association, 1965).

Britt, Steuart Henderson, "The Strategy of Consumer Motivation," *Journal of Marketing*, 14 (April, 1950).

Drucker, Peter F., "Meet Thomorrow's Customer," *Nation's Business* (June, 1963).

Herzog, Herta, "Behavioral Science Concepts for Analyzing the Consumer," in Delbert J. Duncan (ed.), *Proceedings: Conference of Marketing Teachers from Far Western States* (Berkeley: University of California, 1958).

Howard, John A. and J. N. Sheth, "Theory of Buyer Behavior," in Reed Moyer (ed.), *Changing Marketing Systems* (Chicago: American Marketing Association, 1968).

Lazarsfeld, Paul F., "Reflections on Business," *The American Journal of Sociology*, 65 (July, 1959).

Lazer, William and Eugene J. Kelley, "Interdisciplinary Horizons in Marketing," *Journal of Marketing*, 25 (July, 1960).

Martin, Harold H., "Why She Really Goes to Market," *Saturday Evening Post* (September 28, 1963).

Newman, Joseph W., "New Insights, New Progress, for Marketing," *Harvard Business Review*, 35 (November-December, 1957).

"The New Consumer," *Chain Store Age* (January, 1964).

Wagner, Louis C., "What Responding Behavioral Scientists Feel Their Disciplines Could Contribute to Certain Specialized Areas of Advertising," in William M. Stevens (ed.), *The Social Responsibilities of Marketing* (Chicago: American Marketing Association, 1961).

II. PSYYCHOLOGICAL ASPECTS OF CONSUMER BEHAVIOR

ARTICLES

Auld, Frank, Jr., "Tight and Loose Thinking About Unconscious Processes," in Charles H. Hindersman (ed.), *Marketing Precision and Executive Action* (Chicago: American Marketing Association, 1962).

Bauer, Raymond A., "Limits of Persuasion," *Harvard Business Review*, 36 (September-October, 1958).

Bilkey, Warren J., "Psychic Tensions and Purchasing Behavior," *Journal of Social Psychology*, 41 (1955).

Blake, James A., "How Much Thinking Before Buying?" *Dun's Review and Modern Industry*, 66 (August, 1955).

Bursk, Edward C., "Opportunities for Persuasion," *Harvard Business Review*, 36 (September-October, 1958).

Grubb, Edward L. and Gregg Hupp, "Perception of Self, Generalized Stereotypes, and Brand Selection," *Journal of Marketing Research*, 5 (February, 1968).

Hamm, Curtiss B., "A Study of the Differences Between Self-Actualization Scores and Product Perceptions Among Female Consumers," in Reed Moyer (ed.), *Changing Marketing Systems* (Chicago: American Marketing Association, 1968).

Kangun, Norman, "How Advertising Can Use Learning Theory," *Business Horizons*, 11 (April, 1968).

Katona, George, "Rational Behavior and Economic Behavior," *Psychological Review*, 60 (September, 1953).

Laird, Donald A., "How the Consumer Estimates Quality by Subconscious Sensory Impressions," *Journal of Applied Psychology*, 16 (June, 1932).

Leavitt, Clark, "The Application of Perception Psychology to Marketing," in Charles H. Hindersman (ed.), *Marketing Precision and Executive Action* (Chicago: American Marketing Association, 1962).

McConnell, James V., Richard L. Cutler, and Elton B. McNeil, "Subliminal Perception: An Overview," *American Psychologist*, 13 (May, 1958).

McNeal, James U., "The Disappearing Motive in Motivation Research," *Business Topics*, 12 (Autumn, 1964).

Miller, Robert L., "Dr. Weber and the Consumer," *The Journal of Marketing*, 26 (January, 1962).

Richins, Dwaine W., "Human Motivation—A Basic Factor in the Marketing Process," *Oregon Business Review*, 17 (December, 1958).

III. SOCIOLOGICAL ASPECTS OF CONSUMER BEHAVIOR

BOOKS AND MONOGRAPHS

A Profile of the "Upper-upper" (Princeton, New Jersey: Public Opinion Surveys, Inc., 1967). Prepared for and distributed by *Réalités Magazine*.

Cateora, Philip R., *An Analysis of the Teen-Age Market* (Austin: The University of Texas Bureau of Business Research, 1963).

Katz, Elihu and Paul F. Lazarsfeld, *Personal Influence* (Glencoe, Illinois: The Free Press, 1957).

Opatow Associates, Inc., *Room at the Top* (New York: Sandgren and Murtha, Inc., 1963).

Rainwater, Lee, Richard P. Coleman, and Gerald Handel, *Workingman's Wife* (New York: Oceana, 1959).

Riesman, David, *The Lonely Crowd* (New Haven: Yale University Press, 1954).

Roberts, Edwin A., Jr., (ed.), *The Busy Rich* (Silver Spring, Maryland: The National Observer, 1967).

Wolff, Janet, *What Makes Women Buy* (New York: McGraw-Hill, 1958).

ARTICLES

Andreasen, Alan R., "Leisure/Mobility and Life Style Patterns," in Reed Moyer (ed.), *Changing Marketing Systems* (Chicago: American Marketing Association, 1968).

Bartels, Robert, "Sociologists and Marketologists," *Journal of Marketing*, 24 (October, 1959).

Bauer, Raymond A., Scott M. Cunningham, and Lawrence H. Wortzell, "The Marketing Dilemma of Negroes," *Journal of Marketing*, 29 (July, 1965).

Berey, Lewis A., and Richard W. Pollay, "The Influencing Role of the Child in Family Decision Making," *Journal of Marketing Research*, 5 (February, 1968).

Coleman, Richard P., "The Significance of Social Stratification in Selling," in Martin L. Bell (ed.), *Marketing: A Maturing Discipline* (Chicago: American Marketing Association, 1960).

Cunningham, Scott M., "Perceived Risk as a Factor in the Diffusion of New Product Information," in Raymond M. Hass (ed.), *Science, Technology, and Marketing* (Chicago: American Marketing Association, 1966).

Fallers, Lloyd A., "A Note on the 'Trickle Effect'," *Public Opinion Quarterly*, 18 (Fall, 1964).

Glock, Charles Y. and Francesco M. Nicosia, "Uses of Sociology in Studying 'Consumption' Behavior," *Journal of Marketing*, 28 (July, 1964).

Hughes, Emmet J., "The Negro's New Economic Life," *Fortune*, 44 (September, 1956).

Jacobi, John E. and S. George Walters, "Dress-Buying Behavior of Consumers," *The Journal of Marketing*, 23 (October, 1958).

Katz, Elihu, "The Two-Step Flow of Communications: An Up-to-Date Report on an Hypothesis," *Public Opinion Quarterly*, 21 (Spring, 1957).

King, Robert L., "Life-Style Research and Consumer Behavior," in L. George Smith (ed.), *Reflections on Progress in Marketing* (Chicago: American Marketing Association, 1965).

Lapham, Lewis H., "Old Money, New Money," *Saturday Evening Post* (December 30, 1967).

Nicosia, Francesco M., "Opinion Leadership and the Flow of Communications: Some Problems and Prospects," in L. George Smith (ed.), *Reflections on Progress in Marketing* (Chicago: American Marketing Association, 1965).

Orth, Penelope, "Teenager: What Kind of Consumer?" *Printers' Ink* (September 20, 1963).

Peterson, R. D., "Contributions of Rural Sociology to Marketing," *The Southwestern Social Science Quarterly*, 48 (March, 1967).

Pirie, Margaret C., "Marketing and Social Classes: An Anthropologist's View," *The Management Review*, 49 (September, 1960).

Reinecke, John A., "The 'Older' Market—Fact or Fiction," *Journal of Marketing*, 28 (January, 1964).

Reynolds, William H., "The Wide C-Post and the Fashion Process," *Journal of Marketing*, 28 (July, 1964).

Rich, Stuart U. and Subhash C. Jain, "Social Class and Life Cycle as Predictors of Shopping Behavior," *Journal of Marketing Research,* 5 (February, 1968).

Roseborough, Howard, "Some Sociological Dimensions of Consumer Spending," *Canadian Journal of Economics and Political Science,* 26 (August, 1960).

Seligman, Daniel, "The New Masses," *Fortune,* 49 (May, 1959).

Wadia, Maneck S., "The Concept of Culture in the Analysis of Consumers," in Reed Moyer (ed.), *Changing Marketing Systems* (Chicago: American Marketing Association, 1968).

Wells, William D. and George Gubar, "Life Cycle Concept in Marketing Research," *Journal of Marketing Research,* 3 (November, 1966).

Winick, Charles, "Anthropology's Contributions to Marketing," *Journal of Marketing,* 26 (July, 1961).

IV. RESEARCH TECHNIQUES IN CONSUMER BEHAVIOR

BOOKS AND MONOGRAPHS

Cheskin, Louis, *How to Predict What People Will Buy* (New York: Liveright, 1957).

——, *Why People Buy* (New York: Liveright, 1959).

Ferber, Robert and Hugh G. Wales, (eds.), *Motivation and Market Behavior* (Homewood, Illinois: Richard D. Irwin, Inc., 1958).

Henry, Harry, *Motivation Research* (New York: Frederick Ungar, 1958).

Newman, Joseph W., *Motivation Research and Marketing Management* (Boston: Harvard University Garduate School of Business Administration, 1957).

Smith, George H., *Motivation Research in Advertising and Marketing* (New York: McGraw-Hill, 1954).

ARTICLES

Bilkey, Warren J., "A Psychological Approach to Consumer Behavior Analysis," *Journal of Marketing,* 18 (July, 1953).

Black, Percy, "Two 'Why's?' in the Market Place," *Journal of Marketing,* 21 (October, 1956).

Blankertz, Donald F., "Motivation and Rationalization in Retail Buying," *Public Opinion Quarterly,* 13 (Winter, 1949-50).

Britt, Steuart Henderson, "Advertising," in *American Management Association Management Report No. 15* (New York: American Management Association, 1958).

Brown, George H., "Measuring Consumer Attitudes Toward Products," *Journal of Marketing,* 14 (April, 1950).

Cohen, Joel B., "An Interpersonal Orientation to the Study of Consumer Behavior," *Journal of Marketing Research,* 4 (August, 1967).

Fisk, George, "A Conceptual Model for Studying Customer Image," *Journal of Retailing,* 37 (Winter, 1961-62).

Gustafson, Philip, "You Can Gauge Customers' Wants," *Nation's Business,* 46 (April, 1958).

Haire, Mason, "Projective Techniques in Marketing Research," *Journal of Marketing,* 14 (April, 1950).

Kirkpatrick, F. R., "New Methods of Measuring Consumer Preferences and Motivations," *Journal of Farm Economics,* 39 (December, 1957).

Paradise, L. M. and A. B. Blankenship, "Depth Questioning," *Journal of Marketing,* 15 (January, 1951).

Pessemier, Edgar A., "A New Way to Determine Buying Decisions," *Journal of Marketing,* 24 (October, 1959).

"Probing Consumers' Minds—A Way to Build Better Advertising, More Sales," *Printers' Ink,* 270 (January 29, 1960).

Richards, Elizabeth A., "A Commercial Application of Guttman Attitude Scaling Techniques," *Journal of Marketing,* 22 (October, 1957).

Stryker, Perrin, "Motivation Research," *Fortune,* 43 (June, 1956).

"The Role of Behavioral Laboratories in Marketing Research," Section A, Part 4, of Raymond M. Hass (eds.), *Science, Technology, and Marketing* (Chicago: American Marketing Association, 1966).

Tucker, W. T., "Consumer Research: Status and Prospects," in Reed Moyer (ed.), *Changing Marketing Systems* (Chicago: American Marketing Association, 1968).

Udell, Jon G., "Can Attitude Measurement Predict Consumer Behavior?" *Journal of Marketing,* 29 (October, 1965).

Westfall, Ralph L., "Psychological Factors in Predicting Product Choice," *Journal of Marketing* 26 (April, 1962).

Wilson, Clark L., "The Depth Interview as a Research Tool," in Richard M. Hill (ed.), *Marketing Concepts in Changing Times* (Chicago: American Marketing Association, 1959).

Zober, Martin, "Some Projective Techniques in Marketing Research," *Journal of Marketing,* 20 (January, 1956).